Financial Management and Accounting in the [illegible] *successful text for non-financial majors. In the book Gary Bandy manages to explain the essentials of the financial world in a profound and clear way. It is the standard work for our finance classes.*

Dr. Tom Overmans, Utrecht University School of Governance

The latest edition of this excellent text by Gary Bandy has been updated post-pandemic, with the crisis illustrating just how important it is to have national and local government agencies that have appropriate public financial management systems for financial stewardship, value for money and equity. The book is particularly useful for students of public management/public administration, but is also written with non-financial public managers in mind, to help them understand the financial aspects of their jobs.

Laurence Ferry, Head of Department and Professor in Accounting at Durham University (UK) and Senior Distinguished Visiting Fellow at Rutgers University (USA)

This is a must read for any public management student. Gary Bandy brings the subject to life through an engaging combination of academic theory and practical application.

Dr Ian C Elliott, Associate Professor of Public Leadership and Management, Northumbria

Your book is the best resource on this topic and my version of the second edition has been a great reference for many years now.

Andrew Kendall, Chief Commercial Officer, Alternative Futures Group

Financial Management and Accounting in the Public Sector

The importance of public financial management for the health and wellbeing of citizens became dramatically apparent as governments sought to respond to the coronavirus pandemic in 2020. Now, governments and other public sector organizations face the challenge of recovering from the pandemic whilst also seeking to achieve Sustainable Development Goals, with squeezed budgets and ever-increasing demands for public services.

Public sector managers are confronted daily with targets and demands that are often set in confusing accounting and financial language. In *Financial Management and Accounting in the Public Sector*, Gary Bandy employs a clear and concise narrative to introduce the core concepts of public financial management to help those managers to deliver programmes, projects and services that are value for money. As the author puts it, managing public money is an art, not a science.

This third edition has been revised and updated throughout, offering:

- a structure that is more clearly linked to the stages of the public financial management cycle;
- greater coverage of transparency and accountability issues;
- a broader view of public procurement to include goods, works and services and effective contract management; and
- an increased focus on public spending in the context of a post-COVID environment.

With a glossary of terms to help managers understand and be understood by accountants, as well as learning objectives, discussion questions and exercises, this practical textbook will help students of public management and administration to understand the financial and accounting aspects of managing public services.

Gary Bandy has been an independent public financial management consultant since 2005. He has advised organizations in the charity sector, education, policing, local government and the private sector. Gary has an MPA from Warwick Business School and has taught public financial management at several universities in the United Kingdom as well as sharing his expertise with civil servants in many places, including Rwanda, South Sudan, Sri Lanka and Kazakhstan.

MASTERS IN PUBLIC MANAGEMENT

Series Editor: Stephen P. Osborne

Providing students and practitioners a series of concise and coordinated learning resources, this series offers an integrated and up-to-date collection of applied textbooks across public management and administration.

Books in the series go beyond the "toolkit" or "recipe" format, instead encouraging readers to develop the core managerial skills and critical thinking required to excel in the field.

Contracting for Public Services
Carsten Greve

Managing Change and Innovation in Public Service Organizations
Stephen P. Osborne and Kerry Brown

Ethics and Management in the Public Sector
Alan Lawton, Karin Lasthuizen and Julie Rayner

Managing Local Governments
Designing Management Control Systems that Deliver Value
Emanuele Padovani and David W. Young

Making and Managing Public Policy
Karen Johnston Miller and Duncan McTavish

Financial Management and Accounting in the Public Sector
Gary Bandy

Risk and Crisis Management in the Public Sector
Lynn T. Drennan, Allan McConnell and Alistair Stark

Strategic Management in the Public Sector
Paul Joyce

Performance Management in the Public Sector
Wouter van Dooren, Geert Bouckaert and John Halligan

Strategic Leadership in the Public Sector
Paul Joyce

Marketing Management and Communications in the Public Sector
Martial Pasquier and Jean-Patrick

Digital Government
Managing Public Sector Reform in the Digital Era
Miriam Lips

Research Methods in Public Administration and Public Management
An Introduction
Sandra van Thiel

For more information about this series, please visit: www.routledge.com/Routledge-Masters-in-Public-Management/book-series/PUBMAN

Financial Management and Accounting in the Public Sector

Third Edition

Gary Bandy

LONDON AND NEW YORK

Designed cover image: © Vadim Sazhniev / Getty Images

Third edition published 2023
by Routledge
4 Park Square, Milton Park, Abingdon, Oxon, OX14 4RN

and by Routledge
605 Third Avenue, New York, NY 10158

Routledge is an imprint of the Taylor & Francis Group, an informa business

© 2023 Gary Bandy

The right of Gary Bandy to be identified as author of this work has been asserted in accordance with sections 77 and 78 of the Copyright, Designs and Patents Act 1988.

All rights reserved. No part of this book may be reprinted or reproduced or utilised in any form or by any electronic, mechanical, or other means, now known or hereafter invented, including photocopying and recording, or in any information storage or retrieval system, without permission in writing from the publishers.

Trademark notice: Product or corporate names may be trademarks or registered trademarks and are used only for identification and explanation without intent to infringe.

First edition published by Routledge 2011

Second edition published by Routledge 2014

British Library Cataloguing-in-Publication Data
A catalogue record for this book is available from the British Library

ISBN: 978-1-032-16891-3 (hbk)
ISBN: 978-1-032-15730-6 (pbk)
ISBN: 978-1-003-25083-8 (ebk)

DOI: 10.4324/9781003250838

Typeset in Perpetua and Bell Gothic
by Deanta Global Publishing Services, Chennai, India

To Charlie, the latest generation.

Contents

Illustrations

FIGURES

TABLES

BOXES

Foreword

I am very pleased to recommend the third edition of this tried and tested textbook on financial management in the public sector. The public sector is very big business, with major impacts on local, regional and national economies. It therefore needs as robust management of its budgets and finances as any private sector business. However, public sector business is much more complex because it is set in a democratic context, and it is accountable not only to shareholders and stakeholders, but also to elected politicians, users of services, the wider public as citizens and communities, voters and taxpayers—and to future generations yet unborn.

Gary Bandy's book occupies a crucial, distinctive place in this field. He has written a book which we've all secretly hoped for but were too embarrassed to admit we needed! He unlocks the secrets of budgeting and reveals the mysteries of financial management and accounting, in plain intelligible language which even non-financial managers can understand. Never again will treasurers be able to mystify us with their jargon! Gary's primer provides clear explanations of complex concepts and procedures. It is a key resource for all public leaders and managers.

I am proud to have been one of the midwives to the birth of this important book. Gary was one of our mature students on the Warwick MPA (Masters in Public Administration) part-time modular programme, which I taught from the 1990s onwards. He also came on one of the MPA elective modules we ran in South Africa in partnership with Witwatersrand and Stellenbosch Universities. As we visited and stayed in the black townships to study first-hand the causes and consequences of apartheid, Gary impressed me with his openness to challenging ideas and experiences, and his calm and creative thinking,

So, when in 2008 Warwick Business School staff were invited to teach some short courses for the newly appointed ministers and managers in the interim government of South Sudan, I asked Gary to come and teach the basics of financial management in the public sector. On the journey home, during a long layover at the Nairobi airport, I told Gary how impressed I was by his ability to explain the concepts, principles and procedures of financial management in clear and intelligible terms and suggested he might write a book, for non-financial specialists. So here it is, now in its third edition.

Gary has substantial experience himself as a Treasurer/Finance Director in local government and later as a consultant and teacher. He draws on this to show how finance can be a crucial part of both strategic thinking and operational management, helping corporate leadership teams to grapple with difficult decisions.

This magnificent handbook is essential not only for financial managers, but also for anyone trying to improve their organization's performance in these volatile and uncertain times. Gary writes clearly, coherently and concisely—and the fact that he practises what he teaches (in several countries including South Sudan) gives this book real practical clout.

John Benington CBE
Emeritus Professor of Public Policy and Management,
Warwick University
Vice-President, Friends of Ibba Girls School, South Sudan.

Preface to the third edition

This book is aimed at public managers and students of public administration and it concerns itself with helping them:

- to understand the principles of how public bodies (from small charities to national governments) manage their finances;
- to pick up skills and knowledge to manage public money; and
- to develop their thinking about public financial management in the future.

This third edition is still different, I believe, from other financial textbooks in two ways. Firstly, it is focused on the public sector, with examples that are specific to the sector. Secondly, it aims to help the reader to learn about financial management in a way that helps them do their job better, whatever their job is. A public manager cannot escape the reality that to achieve their job's objectives they will have to spend money on staff, supplies, premises, transport and so on, and, in many cases, they will have to collect income from their users/customers, too. Ultimately, I want this book to help those managers to use the resources at their disposal as well as they can to create public value.

I know that many public managers are not comfortable working with numbers. Some might be anxious not to display their ignorance to their accountant whilst others are suspicious that accountants are proponents of a dark art. This is not helped by the images we see of accountants in popular culture. One only has to think of the dull, grey stereotype featured in *Monty Python's Flying Circus* or the accounting trolls in Scott Adams's *Dilbert* cartoon strip for evidence of this.

Public sector accountants do not feature often in popular culture, but there is a recent example worth mentioning. In Seasons 4 and 5 of HBO's *The Wire* television show, there are scenes where Baltimore's mayor is facing a financial crisis caused by a $50 million deficit in the schools budget. These scenes feature the city's budget director giving advice to the mayor. Whilst I have never worked in American local government, the nature of the meetings and the advice sought and given rings true to my experience in the United Kingdom. In Season 4 Episode 11, there is a scene that captures, I think, the perennial tension between politicians and public managers and their financial advisors. The budget director's explanation of the financial consequences of each possible solution is met by the mayor's increasing frustration. He wants advice on how to solve the budget problem but what he gets is advice about what he can't do ('A New Day,' 2006).

This book is aimed at public managers in general rather than public sector accountants in particular. It is based on the premise that a public body's accountants will prepare accounts and provide advice on the organization's financial affairs and therefore the public manager does not need to know how to do those things (although there is a glossary of terms at the back of this book to help public managers understand what their accountants say). Reading this book will not convert you into a para-accountant, but I hope that it will help you to understand financial management principles and the role of accountants so that you may better explain to your accountants and financial advisors what you want to do. I have found that being able to ask a question of an accountant in the right way improves the chances of being advised how to achieve one's objectives rather than being hindered.

I believe a public manager is charged with creating public value (Moore, 1995), and, however that is achieved, the public manager must also ensure that the outputs and outcomes are value for money. Creating public value is not achieved by creating and studying spreadsheets, nor by luck; it requires the application of skills and knowledge by public managers. This book shows how complicated and difficult it is to manage public money in order to create public value for money. I very much think it is an art, not a science. First you have to understand the principles, then figure out how to apply them to the situation in front of you.

A public manager's job requires decision-making skills. Often the decisions are complex and it is possible two managers might make different decisions from the same information. Whilst there may not be a single right answer, there are definitely some wrong ones: where a manager fails to consider or deliberately ignores relevant factors or is influenced by irrelevant factors or their personal interest.

The public have high expectations of public servants, possible higher than they have for themselves. It goes without saying that a public manager should not steal, commit fraud, lie or cheat. But there is more to it than that. Being accountable goes hand in hand with having the responsibility for spending public money. In recent years public expectations have been growing beyond accountability to demand more transparency from their public organizations. This means, essentially, that if a manager does not want to be open and transparent about what they do and have done, they should not work in the public sector.

I believe that this means public managers should always do the right thing. That means being selfless, objective, and always complying with the spirit, as well as the letter, of the seven principles of public life mentioned in Chapter 8. It may mean, at times, standing firm against pressure from politicians or other stakeholders. I know from personal experience that this can be uncomfortable, but I also know that it is easier to live with doing the right thing than the wrong thing.

Public services are expected to be efficient and effective, to improve continuously, to achieve more and more each year from fewer resources. To achieve such improvements in value for money requires the public manager to be creative in terms of challenging how things are done, innovating, operating systems that are as lean and efficient as possible, finding and engaging with effective and efficient partners and co-producers, reducing waste and eliminating fraud. A public manager who can find better and better ways to do those things will create public value for money, which is, ultimately, the outcome everyone wants.

Gary Bandy
Derbyshire
July 2022

REFERENCES

'A New Day'. (2006). *The Wire,* Season 4 Episode 11. Directed by Brad Anderson. Written by David Simon, Ed Burns and Chris Collins. First broadcast 26 November 2006 [DVD] London: Warner Home Video.

Moore, M. H. (1995). *Creating Public Value: Strategic Management in Government.* Boston: Harvard University Press.

About the author

Gary Bandy has been a chartered public finance accountant since 1990. His career until 2005 was mostly in local government and included three years as the chief finance officer of a metropolitan council.

Since becoming an independent public financial management consultant in 2005, he has advised organizations in the charity sector, education, policing, local government and the private sector. He has particular expertise in outsourcing and partnerships.

Gary has an MPA from Warwick Business School and has taught public financial management at several universities in the United Kingdom as well as sharing his expertise with public servants in many places, including Kazakhstan, Kenya, Myanmar, Pakistan, Rwanda, South Sudan, Sri Lanka and Uganda.

He is the author of two textbooks about public financial management. He has also authored a MOOC (massive open online course) about managing public money for the Open University and written a major online course for the Association of Chartered Certified Accountants (ACCA).

Gary can be followed on LinkedIn, and you can read more of his writing at www.managingpublicmoney.co.uk.

Acknowledgements

First, I am grateful to Routledge for inviting me to update this book to a third edition. I am flattered that it has been so successful.

Since the second edition was published, I have had many opportunities to teach public financial management topics, either in person or, since 2020, online. I have also had the chance to write training materials, a book and some reports. I am grateful to the various people who have hired me to do such work. My thanks, therefore, go to Ananda Amarawansa, Vikas Bhatia, Hilary Collins, Istemi Demirag, Alan Edwards, Salema Hafiz, Jean Hartley, David Henderson, Pauline Jas, Zukhra Karamalayeva, Simeon Khakata, Stewart MacLeod, Alex Metcalfe, Tara Monkman, Liz Moody, Joseph Mugo, Ahmed Munawar, Terry O'Sullivan, Tom Overmans, Rhiannon Price, Peter Redfern and Khalisa Sunday.

One might expect updating a book to be easier than writing one from scratch. I have not found that to be the case over the last few months. My thanks go to my friends Sarah Farmer and Paul Hart for their encouragement, John Benington for writing the foreword and to Chathurani Rathnayaka for writing a case study just for this book.

Bigger than all of these, though, is my gratitude to my wife, Carolyn, for her constant support and encouragement to get the book finished.

Abbreviations

ABC	activity-based costing
ABM	activity-based management
ARR	accounting rate of return
BBC	British Broadcasting Corporation
BCCI	Bank of Commerce and Credit International
BCE	Before Common Era
BCR	benefit–cost ratio
BOO	build-own-operate
BOOT	build-own-operate transfer
CBA	cost–benefit analysis
CIPFA	Chartered Institute of Public Finance and Accountancy
COSO	Committee of Sponsoring Organizations of the Treadway Commission
CPI	Corruption Perceptions Index
DBFO	design-build-finance-operate
DWP	Department of Work and Pensions
ERM	enterprise risk management
EU	European Union
FMIS	financial management information system
GAAP	generally accepted accounting principles
GAO	General Accounting Office (USA)
GDP	gross domestic product
GPFR	general purpose financial report
IAASB	International Auditing and Assurance Standards Board
IASB	International Accounting Standards Board
ICT	information and communications technology
IFAC	International Federation of Accountants
IFRS	International Financial Reporting Standard

IIA	Institute of Internal Auditors
INTOSAI	International Organization of Supreme Audit Institutions
IPSAS	International Public Sector Accounting Standard
IPSASB	International Public Sector Accounting Standards Board
IRR	internal rate of return
ISA	International Standard on Auditing
MTEF	medium-term expenditure framework
NAO	National Audit Office
NDPB	non-departmental public body
NFA	National Fraud Authority
NPM	new public management
NPV	net present value
OBR	Office of Budget Responsibility
OECD	Organization for Economic Co-operation and Development
OMB	Office of Management and Budget (USA)
ONS	Office of National Statistics
OTS	Office of Tax Simplification
PBE	public benefit entity
PDIA	problem-driven iterative adaption
PEFA	Public Expenditure Framework Assessment
PFI	private finance initiative
PFM	public financial management
PI	performance indicator
PON	Program on Negotiation
PPP	public–private partnership
PV	present value
QALY	quality-adjusted life year
SAI	supreme audit institution
SDG	Sustainable Development Goal(s)
SEC	Securities and Exchange Commission
SMART	specific, measurable, assignable, realistic, time-related
SORP	statement of recommended practice
SPFR	special purpose financial report
SROI	social return on investment
TED	Technology, Entertainment, Design
TSA	treasury single account
VAT	value-added tax
VPF	value of a prevented fatality
VSL	value of a statistical life
WGA	whole of government accounts
ZBB	zero-based budgeting

Chapter 1

The context of public financial management

LEARNING OBJECTIVES

By the end of this chapter you should:

- be able to explain the differences between the private and public sectors;
- understand the objectives of public financial management;
- recognize the stages of the public financial management cycle; and
- be aware of some of the challenges relating to financial management in the public sector.

KEY POINTS OF THIS CHAPTER

- The achievement of the Sustainable Development Goals (SDGs) as well as the delivery of vital public services, such as security, clean water, safe food, education, health care and transport, all depend on governments (national, regional and local) being effective at public financial management.
- The public sector is a large proportion of national economies (although it varies from less than 10 per cent in some countries to more than 40 per cent in others).
- The management of public money is different from financial management in the private sector for many reasons, including the accountability that comes with democracy.
- Public expectations about the proper use of public money are very high.
- Financial management is a critical skill for public managers and it is as much an art as a science.

DOI: 10.4324/9781003250838-1

KEY TERMS

Market failure—the situation where a free market fails to produce the best allocation of resources for society

Merit goods—commodities (goods and services) that are valued by the public but excludable (such as education) and which governments decide to provide because the market would under-provide them

Public financial management—the art of managing public money to deliver and improve vital services to the public. It involves budgeting, accounting, controlling, auditing, reporting on spending and performance, policymaking and good governance

Public goods—commodities (goods and services) that markets would fail to provide and which are non-rivalrous (the use by one person does not restrict the use by others) and non-excludable

Public money—the money used by government to provide or pay for public services

Public sector—the part of the economy made up by the government and public services

Public value theory—the theory put forward by Mark Moore (1995) that public managers seek to create public value for stakeholders just as managers in the private sector seek to create shareholder value.

This opening chapter is in three parts. First, it looks at why there are public services provided by government (the public sector), and therefore a need for public financial management (PFM). Second, as this book is about managing public money, it considers what public money is and the public's expectations about managing public money. The third part is concerned with the features of financial management in the public sector. It includes an explanation of public value theory and describes some of the challenges facing public managers that make PFM different from financial management in the private sector.

This chapter, and the rest of the book, uses the term 'public manager' to refer to those who are involved in the executive management of government and other public sector organizations. As well as line managers, the term includes the members of the governing body whether they are elected politicians, appointees or volunteers. The term is not used quite as broadly as Moore (1995: 2–3) uses it: 'supervising agents, judges, lobbyists and interest group leaders' (Rhodes and Wanna, 2007: 408) are excluded here because they are not in a position to manage a public benefit entity's (PBE's) finances although they may have influence on the public managers who do.

The book also uses the term PBE (public benefit entity) when referring to the organizations that public managers work in or with. Laughlin (2008: 251) cites Simpkins's summary of the features of PBEs:

- Their objective is to provide goods and services to various recipients or to develop or implement policy on behalf of governments and not to make a profit.
- They are always characterized by the absence of defined ownership interests that can be sold, transferred or redeemed.
- They typically have a wide group of stakeholders to consider (including the public at large).
- Their revenues are generally derived from taxes or other similar contributions obtained through the exercise of coercive powers.
- Their capital assets are typically acquired and held to deliver services without the intention of earning a return to them.

Therefore, the term includes organizations, such as state-owned industries, that are managed on a commercial basis but are owned by a government, and voluntary and charitable organizations, as well as the government ministries, hospitals, schools, police forces, local governments, courts, armed forces and so on that are commonly thought of as comprising the public sector.

WHAT IS PUBLIC FINANCIAL MANAGEMENT?

The quotation at the beginning of this chapter makes the point that government matters. As we will see later, governments provide many important services that either would not exist or would be available only to the people rich enough to pay for them, if it were not for governments. And the coronavirus (COVID-19) pandemic in 2020 and 2021 reminded people, should they have forgotten, that they rely on governments as their ultimate insurance policy. As Micklethwait and Wooldridge (2020) put it:

> It matters enormously whether your country has a good health service, competent bureaucrats and sound finances. Good government is the difference between living and dying.

Governments responded to the coronavirus pandemic in different ways. There were direct increases in spending on extra health care and vaccine programmes. There were other spending programmes aimed at shoring up the economy during the periods of lockdown. There were also less obvious financial policies such as deferring the due dates for people and businesses to pay their taxes, and granting of loans, perhaps in the knowledge that the borrowers may never be able to repay them.

This activity involved all the main elements of PFM: budgeting, employing staff of all kinds, procurement of goods and service, collecting income, borrowing funds, making payments, accounting, reporting and auditing.

Even in normal times, what governments do is enormously challenging. They provide universal services where the demand will almost always exceed the capacity to deliver. Behn (2013) makes this point by citing Joseph Bower: 'Strategy in business is "the application of massive resources to limited objectives". In contrast, strategy in government is "the application of limited resources to massive objectives".'

All of this makes PFM extremely important. Governments cannot be effective if they cannot manage their finances. It does not matter how great your education policy is if you cannot get money into a village school to pay the teachers.

The objectives of PFM for a government or any other public benefit entity (PBE) are:

- to maintain a sustainable financial position;
- to allocate resources effectively to sectors, ministries, departments, projects and programmes; and
- to provide public goods and services efficiently.

The above objectives can be seen in respect of the responses to the coronavirus pandemic. Governments were implementing policies to support the economy such as welfare benefit payments to people who could not work. They were also having to review and amend their spending plans at a time when tax receipts were likely falling. The need to increase the allocation to health programmes had to be balanced by reductions in other programmes and/or additional income or borrowing. The achievement of the third objective perhaps suffered as a result of the urgency of action with, for example, competitive tendering of supplies contracts not being used and the subsequent contracts not delivering value for money.

PFM has stages that are often referred to as the public financial management cycle or budget cycle. The stages are:

- **budget formulation**, which includes strategic financial planning and details preparation of budgets;
- **budget approval**, which includes debate and legislative approval of the budget;
- **budget execution**, where the actual collecting and spending of money happens, and includes accounting and budget monitoring; and
- **budget oversight**, which includes reporting and auditing.

These phases or stages of public financial management do flow one from another, with evaluation feeding into budget formulation, but the oversight must happen after the period of the budget has elapsed so it feeds into the budget formulation of the subsequent period. In practice, at any moment in time public managers are executing the current budget whilst thinking about or preparing the budget for the next period and evaluating the performance of the period that most recently ended.

The budget period, by the way, might most often be a full year (whether the calendar year or some other continuous 12 months) but it could be a month, quarterly or even biennial. The latter is used by, for example, global organizations like the World Health Organization.

PFM is most often written about in terms of governments but it is needed at all levels of government and public service. In many countries, the PFM system is codified in a public financial management act or organic budget law. In other countries—the United Kingdom is one—the PFM arrangements are scattered in different laws and regulations, codes of practice and so on.

Clearly it is important that national governments have good and effective PFM arrangements because citizens want their governments to provide services and PFM enables this to happen in an efficient, effective and fair way. In practice, though, national government ministries deliver very few services directly to citizens. Instead, public money passes through one or more PBEs before it reaches the schools, hospitals, police stations, construction sites, etc. where public services are actually delivered to citizens. It is important, then, that all of the PBEs involved in these chains have effective PFM arrangements in place.

Why do we have public services?

There are many goods and services that are desirable but which a free market economy cannot supply effectively. Governments can, and do, address this market failure by providing the goods and services using government resources. Some of this provision is direct, using government employees and other resources; and some of it is commissioned by government to be delivered by other actors, such as private businesses or non-governmental organizations (NGOs).

The public sector provides two types of goods: public goods and merit goods.

Public goods

Public goods (and services) are commodities that are non-rivalrous and non-excludable. Non-rivalrous means that the consumption of the commodity does not reduce its availability to others and non-excludable means that no one can be effectively excluded from enjoying the benefits of the commodity. If the market were to provide such goods and services the providers would have the potential problem of free-riders, people consuming the goods without purchasing them, because of the non-excludability (i.e., the free-riders could not be excluded). The provision of such goods by the government is feasible because of the enforcement of taxes. Examples of public goods include street lighting, national defence and lighthouses.

Merit goods

Merit goods (and services), in contrast to public goods, are commodities that are excludable but:

- they produce positive externalities, meaning that there are benefits to society that are not taken into account by the individual who consumes them; and
- individuals seeking to maximize their short-term benefits fail to take into account the longer-term benefits that often accrue from the goods.

An externality is a cost or benefit arising from production or consumption of a commodity that falls upon someone who did not agree to be part of the transaction. This means that the cost or benefit is not taken into account in the market price of the transaction. Costs that spill over to third parties are called negative externalities and benefits that spill over are called positive externalities.

The problem is that negative externalities cause the market to over-provide the goods or services because all of the costs are not taken into account in the price of the goods; and positive externalities under-supply the goods or services because all the benefits are not taken into account.

A classic example of a negative externality is pollution emanating from a factory. If there were a completely free market the factory owners would not bear the cost of the damage done by the pollution nor would they have any incentive to spend money on technology to eliminate the pollution. In practice, governments implement systems of regulation that require factories to reduce their pollution, thus forcing factory owners to bear the cost of cleaning up their emissions to meet the regulations and/or they impose a direct tax or levy that makes the polluter suffer a cost relating to the pollution.

An example of the latter would be a tax on waste going to landfill sites. A business (or person) can then make a choice about whether to send their waste to landfill and pay the tax or take other actions (which would have their own costs) to reduce the amount of waste going to landfill. The actual level of tax set by the government (i.e., how expensive it is to dispose of a tonne of waste in a landfill site) will affect the incentive that the business has or does not have to reduce the waste produced.

Whilst governments can use regulations and taxes to address problems from negative externalities, they tend to address goods and services with positive externalities by providing them. Indeed, most government services are merit goods rather than public goods. The alternative to this (and the reverse of a tax or levy) would be government subsidising the goods and services so that more of them are provided than the free market would deliver.

Health care is an example of a merit good rather than a public good. A visit to a doctor is rivalrous because the individual has used an amount of the doctor's time, thereby reducing the amount of the doctor's time that others can use, and it is excludable because the doctor can decide not to see an individual at all. Health care also has positive externalities. If an individual is treated for a contagious disease, then other individuals benefit. All of this means that governments provide health care even though there may be an effective market for private health care running in parallel with the public provision (as there is, for example, in the United Kingdom).

There are other merit goods, such as education (where again there may be fee-charging schools operating alongside free, state-provided schools), public safety, environmental health, waste collection and public parks, which are provided because they have external benefits.

The fire and rescue service is another example. Fire and rescue services are not public goods as such because the service is excludable. The origin of the fire service is as a type of insurance where a property owner would pay a premium and if their property caught fire then they would be attended to by the company to which they had paid their premiums. However, putting out a fire has externalities because if the fire is put out the neighbouring properties are saved. Conversely, if a property owner had no insurance and their property caught fire the neighbours will suffer the externality of either seeing their property damaged or destroyed or calling out their own insurers, too. It makes sense, then, for a government to provide a universal fire service funded by taxpayers.

Given that governments provide directly (or commission and pay for) a wide range of public and merit goods because, in part at least, the market would fail, it would not be possible for the government to use a market mechanism (that is, charge fees to service users) to pay for the services. Instead, governments finance their services from taxes, except, perhaps, for minor aspects where fees are charged to service users. The cost of all these services therefore falls within the public sector.

Monopolies

Another way that governments intervene in the free market is for the management of monopolies, especially natural monopolies, such as utility services, where a very high capital investment in infrastructure is required. Previously such monopolies were owned and managed directly by the government, but under new public management (NPM) the preference is for such services to be provided by profit-seeking private sector organizations that are regulated by the government. The regulation protects consumers from unwarranted price rises and also sets terms for allowing competitors to access the private company's infrastructure. For these services public money is spent on the regulation and, in some cases, on subsidies to private sector operators.

WHAT IS PUBLIC MONEY?

The answer that first comes to mind is that public money is the money government collects as taxes and spends on the provision of public services. There are, however, many nuances to consider in the definition. Governments get money not only from taxes. In addition to taxes, they get some of their income from fees and charges, from properties and investments, from grants, donations and legacies, from state lotteries and from borrowing. And public services are not only provided by government, whether national or local. Services are provided by charities, voluntary organizations, faith-based groups and philanthropists as well as the wide range of services provided by private sector organizations either under direct contract with a public body or in some way regulated by the government.

One of the features of the modern public sector that a public manager has to contend with is its ambiguity. Public managers have to manage messy problems that do not have easy solutions, or even any solution at all. Sometimes these are referred to as wicked problems (Conklin, 2006), not because they are inherently evil but because their complexity makes them resistant to being solved. The chances are that 'solving' a wicked problem would result in a new problem or problems to deal with.

Also, no longer are the services wholly delivered by civil servants working in a classical hierarchical bureaucracy (Mintzberg, 1983). In the modern age a public manager might be directly employed by a central or regional or local government body but they also might be employed by a charity or private sector body. Regardless of the nature of their employer they will likely be operating in a network (Benington, 2009) where they may directly manage the delivery of a service, commission it from a partnership or third party or co-produce it with the service user. The public manager may be responsible for a range of services and each one may be produced in a different way. This book is concerned with the financial management arrangements that are required to sustain the public manager's network rather than trying to put a boundary around it.

In a sense public money is the money that might be referred to as 'our money' or 'taxpayers' money'. This is not legally the case. Once you have paid the debt you owe in tax to the government, the money is the government's and the government can choose when, where and how to spend it. This is just like any other debt a person or business pays. Taxpayers' money is also somewhat misleading because governments spend a lot more than just the money they collect in taxes (as explained further in Chapter 3).

Regardless of the legal niceties, citizens see money that they have paid over to government in a different way to money they have paid to a for-profit organization. When a company declares large profits or losses only the shareholders see the money as theirs, not every customer who has provided the turnover in the first place. So, public money might mean all the money received and managed by a government, but, if that were the case, how should we regard the money donated to charities and used to provide public services?

It is from this that we get to the essence of the difference between the private sector and the public sector. For the private sector the goal is to make money but for the public sector money is the means to the end. As Mark Moore put it:

> [PBEs] have to be able to sustain themselves financially and to do that they may have to compete to some degree with other non-profit firms. But their ultimate goal is not to capture and seize value for themselves, but to give away their capabilities to achieve the largest impact on social conditions that they can.
>
> (Moore, 2003)

In the report *Holding to Account* (2001), Lord Sharman of Redlynch proposed a definition of public money for the purpose of accountability that picks up all these separate actors and facets. He wrote that public money is:

> all money that comes into the possession of, or is distributed by, a public body, and money raised by a private body where it is doing so under statutory authority.
>
> (Lord Sharman of Redlynch, 2001: 15)

How much money are we talking about?

The public sector spends around 30 per cent of the world's gross domestic product (GDP). Data from the World Bank (2022) show globally that government expenses were 29.3 per cent of GDP in 2010 (just after the global financial crisis) and fell steadily towards 27.2 per cent in 2018 and 27.3 per cent in 2020. Post-2020 the level has increased dramatically.

There is a link between the wealth of a country and the size of its public sector. Prior to the Industrial Revolution the size of the public sector in what are now developed countries would have been around 10 per cent of GDP since at that time government did not provide public services other than defence. From the late nineteenth century and through the twentieth century the size of the public sector in these countries grew rapidly as the citizens expected their government to provide more, including sanitation, transport, education, health care and welfare benefits. By the end of the twentieth century the size of governments in developed countries equated to 30 to 40 per cent of their GDP.

As a rough guide, in high income countries the median level of tax as a percentage of GDP is about 30 per cent, in middle-income countries the median is about 20 to 25 per cent and in low-income countries it is about 10 to 15 per cent (Glenday and Hemming, 2013: 425). OECD (2021: 17) puts government expenditure at 40.8 per cent as the average in OECD countries in 2019.

Of course, in absolute terms, the amount of money spent per head is vastly different as 30 per cent of the GDP per head of a high-income country could be 40 or 50 times as much as 15 per cent of the GDP per head of a low-income country. In 2020 the Netherlands government expenses were 38.0 per cent of GDP and Indonesia spent 14.1 per cent of GDP. These translate into government expenditure per capita of around $20,000 in the Netherlands and $600 in Indonesia.

Public expectations feed into the picture, too. Opalo (2021) observed:

> The experiences of many African countries over the last two decades have strengthened [the] implied fiscal pact. For example, the region's successes with universal primary education under the millennium development goals have created enormous public demand for secondary and tertiary education.

Table 1.1 shows the size of the public sector in a range of countries in 2010 and 2020. The table is ranked by the size of government in 2010 and shows that some countries have increased whilst others have fallen. These changes will be a combination of changes in government spending programmes and changes in a country's GDP.

The size of the public sector is not static, rising and falling from year to year as a function of both the growth rate of the economy and changes in government policies. The COVID-19 pandemic happens to have had a dramatic effect on both a country's GDP and its government spending but government policy changes and other real-world activities means government spending as a proportion of GDP moves from year to year.

Table 1.2 shows the financial impact of COVID-19 policies for a sample of countries from the start of the pandemic to June 2021. It separates spending on the health sector from the other parts of government. The percentage of GDP is versus the 2020 GDP.

Table 1.2 also shows the impact of policies that do not directly count as spending, such as lending money, equity injections, asset purchases and giving loan guarantees.

Tables 1.1 and 1.2 should be used with caution. The public sector in different countries is not directly comparable because the calculations depend on definitions about what is and is not public expenditure. In some countries the large

Table 1.1 *Public sector expenses as per cent of GDP in 2010 and 2020*

Country	*2010 GDP%*	*2020 GDP%*
Bangladesh	9.3	9.3
Burkina Faso	10.6	18.4
Paraguay	11.8	17.3
Singapore	12.4	14.6
Guatemala	12.9	12.5
Sri Lanka	16.8	15.6
Thailand	17.4	18.8
Korea	17.6	27.4
Canada	19.1	17.3
Chile	20.1	23.1
Lebanon	25.8	26.3
United States	26.2	21.7
Australia	26.7	26.8
South Africa	28.6	35.2
World average	**29.3**	**27.3**
Trinidad and Tobago	30.7	35.7
Norway	34.9	40.2
Netherlands	41.6	38.0
United Kingdom	42.7	35.6
Afghanistan	50.9	38.1
Greece	51.0	48.2
Ireland	62.4	18.5

Source: World Bank (2022).

infrastructure-based services, such as energy distribution and railways (so-called natural monopolies), are owned and delivered by the government as public services. In others, such as the United Kingdom, utilities such as water, electricity and gas are provided by regulated private sector companies. This puts the services outside the definition of the public sector.

The other type of privatization, where government bodies award contracts to suppliers of services like cleaning, catering, refuse collection, payroll and information and communications technology (ICT) is within the definition of the public sector because the expenditure on the service contracts is incurred by the government body (not by the consumer as in the case of utilities). If one is undertaking comparative research about the public sector in two or more countries it is critical to understand what is included and excluded in each country's figures and make adjustments accordingly.

Table 1.2 *Analysis of COVID-19 policies*

Country	*Spending policies*				*Below the line*	
	Health sector		*Other gov sectors*			
	US$ bn	*GDP%*	*US$ bn*	*GDP%*	*US$ bn*	*GDP%*
Australia	250	18.4	236	17.4	38	2.8
Canada	261	15.9	279	17.0	126	7.7
China	711	4.8	921	6.2	251	1.7
Indonesia	48	4.5	29	2.7	16	1.5
Kenya	3	2.5	3	2.5	—	—
Korea	73	4.5	106	6.4	226	13.8
Netherlands	40	19.3	37	17.7	5	2.4
Pakistan	5	2.0	7	2.8	—	—
Peru	16	7.8	16	7.8	6	1.6
South Africa	19	2.7	27	3.7	112	15.8
Vietnam	6	1.7	5	1.5	14	4.2
United Kingdom	440	16.2	250	9.2	905	33.4
United States	5,328	25.4	4,659	22.3	964	4.6
Zimbabwe	—	—	1	3.4	2	6.2

Source: IMF (2021).

Comparing a country with itself over time is safer but there can still be issues. For example, the trend of the United Kingdom's public expenditure as a percentage of GDP has been affected since 2008 due to the government taking a stake in some banks and therefore bringing them within the definition of the public sector. The effect of COVID-19 in 2020 and 2021 (and perhaps beyond) will be evident in trend analysis of government spending that will have to be taken into account before drawing conclusions.

UK Government spending

The UK Government spending as a proportion of GDP between 1971 and 2021 is shown in Figure 1.1 using data from the Office of Budget Responsibility (2022).

You can see the size of the public sector in 1970/1, as measured by the government's Total Managed Expenditure (TME), was 39.5 per cent of GDP. It rose to 49.7 per cent of GDP by 1975/6, not falling below 40 per cent until 1988/9. It then stayed between 36 and 44 per cent until 2009/10 when it rose to 46.1 per cent (and the nominal level of expenditure was £665.4 billion). Over the next ten years it fell steadily to 39.0 per cent before the dramatic increase in 2020/21 to 51.9 per cent of GDP.

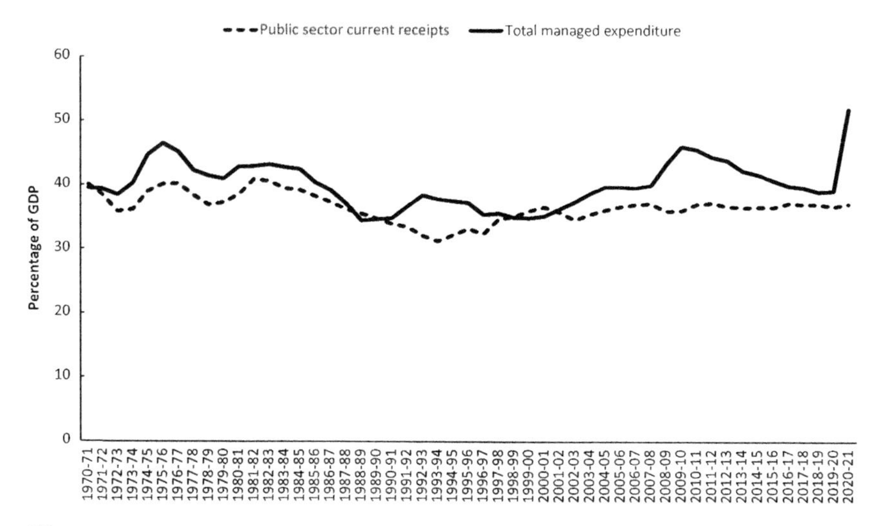

Figure 1.1 *UK Government spending and receipts as per cent of GDP from 1970/1 to 2020/1.*

Figure 1.1 also shows the government's net receipts from taxes and other sources over the same 50-year period. The difference between the two lines is the extent of government borrowing needed each year to finance the spending. You can see almost every year the UK Government borrows money and 2000/1 is the last time that receipts exceeded spending.

In 2021/2 public sector net spending in the United Kingdom was estimated to be £1,053 billion (HM Treasury, 2021). Table 1.3 shows the main Services Areas that comprise this amount.

The United Kingdom's 2022/3 budgeted spending was to be paid for by receipts from taxes and other sources of government income of £820 billion, leaving a gap of £233 billion to be financed by borrowing (see Table 1.4 for details).

You ought to be able to do a similar analysis of your national government's consolidated budgets. You may be able to obtain data directly from the ministry of finance's website or, failing that, from the websites of institutions like the World Bank, the International Monetary Fund (IMF) and development banks. It can be more difficult to find budget information about sub-national public bodies. Where local government organizations have tax-raising powers they will usually be obliged to publish budget information to accompany the tax bill, but for the many other organizations that comprise the public sector it may take some digging around to find a budget statement.

This is the case even in a country like the United Kingdom where policies and regulations about public transparency are in place. The UK national government's budget reports are easily found on HM Treasury's website (www.treasury.gov.uk)

Table 1.3 *Analysis of UK Government spending 2021/2*

Service area	*£ billion*	*%*
Social protection	302	28.7
Health	230	21.8
Education	124	11.8
Industry, agriculture and employment	70	6.6
Defence	60	5.7
Transport	51	4.8
Debt interest	45	4.3
Public order and safety	41	3.9
Personal social services	40	3.8
Housing and environment	33	3.1
Other	57	5.5
Total	1,053	100.0

Source: HM Treasury (2021: 5).

Table 1.4 *Analysis of UK Government receipts 2021/2*

Income type	*£ billion*	*%*
Income tax	198	24.1
Value-added tax	151	18.4
National insurance contributions	147	17.9
Other taxes (incl. capital taxes, stamp duty, vehicle excise duties and non-tax receipts)	84	10.2
Excise duties	48	5.9
Corporation tax	40	4.9
Council tax	40	4.9
Business rates	24	2.9
Other non-tax receipts	88	10.8
Total	820	100.0

Source: HM Treasury (2021: 5)

or the Office for Budget Responsibility (https://obr.uk/data/) These resources tend to identify global figures for expenditure on national programme areas and ministries (called departments in the United Kingdom). Following the thread to the budgets of various agencies and operational units can be more difficult.

Where does public money come from?

Predominantly public money comes from taxes but governments have other sources. There are services that are provided in return for a fee and there will be income from investments in the form of rents, dividends and interest. There can be income from the sale of assets, such as the sale of franchises to mobile phone operators or when nationally owned organizations are privatized. A government might also receive income in the form of grants and donations, possibly from overseas governments, aid agencies, charities or faith-based organizations. All of these sources of income are discussed in detail in Chapter 3.

Even with all these sources of income, governments often have spending plans for a given year that exceed the total amount of money they will receive from taxes and charges, sales and investments; thus, they have to borrow money to bridge the gap. To the extent that the borrowed money is used to pay for the investment in new capital projects, there is an argument that the repayments of the debt will be paid over the following 20, 30 and 50 years by the taxpayers who will benefit from the capital project.

Even so, just as a responsible private citizen maintains their indebtedness to a level they can afford to repay, so do governments. The affordability of debt repayments has come into focus for many governments since the global financial crisis in 2008. There are, however, two ways to look at government debt.

Classical economics describes the operation of government like a business or other entity. To be sustainable a business needs to manage its cash flow. If it does not have enough cash from sales then it needs to borrow from its owners and/or banks and eventually, if things go well, it will repay the borrowed money from profits. Translated to the government, this view says that governments need to collect taxes in order to pay for the services they provide. If they spend more than they receive then the difference (the 'deficit') is covered by borrowing in the short term. In the longer term the government will have to repay that borrowing, which will require a period of time where its spending is less than its tax receipts.

Modern monetary theory (MMT) turns this on its head. It notes that governments are not like businesses or households in one very important aspect: they can lawfully create money. Under MMT, governments do not need to collect taxes in order to spend money; they can simply create as much money as they need to spend. This money will be injected into the economy in the form of salaries for civil servants and payments to suppliers. Unchecked this injection of money would cause inflation so, under MMT, taxation is how the government manages inflation. It has to remove some money from circulating in the economy but, rather than using tax receipts to finance more spending, it will destroy the money. Under MMT the difference between government spending and tax receipts is not a deficit but instead is the net investment in the economy.

If you are resisting the MMT description of how money and economics works think back to the COVID-19 pandemic. In countries where the government controls the money used in the economy (including the United States, the United Kingdom, the countries of the EU, Korea, Japan, China) the governments did not wait to collect taxes before spending money on the pandemic response. Look again at the data in Table 1.2 and note the scale of spending increases in absolute terms and as a proportion of GDP.

What is public money spent on?

PBEs cover such a broad range of functions and responsibilities that almost anything might be purchased by a PBE.

As a generalization, the public sector provides services to or on behalf of citizens much more than it provides goods. Services are intangible, existing only at the point they are delivered. Historically such service-based organizations would spend the majority of their expenditure on staffing, perhaps 75 or 80 per cent of the total spending. The move towards commissioning and partnerships (discussed in Chapter 6) means that an increasing proportion of expenditure by public organizations will be on service contracts and/or grants to third parties rather than on direct employee costs (although the chances are that the contractors and third parties will use the majority of the money they receive to pay for their staff to deliver the services). The Open Contracting Partnership (no date) estimates one-third of global government spending is spent on purchasing goods and services (and getting value for money on all this purchasing is why fair, open and competitive public procurement matters).

FEATURES OF FINANCIAL MANAGEMENT IN THE PUBLIC SECTOR

The existence of PFM as a concept or discipline with its own language, accounting standards and specialist texts like this one demonstrates that financial management in government and other public sector organizations has some special features.

This section explores some of these features. First, the concept of public value is outlined, followed by a discussion of the new public management (NPM) paradigm. The section ends with a discussion of some ways in which PFM is different from private sector financial management.

Public value management

Moore (2003: 15) wrote that in the public sector 'Financial performance is [...] the means to an end rather than an end itself.' This goes to the heart of one of the key differences between PFM and financial management in the private sector. In the latter, the aim is to use money to make more money. The whole idea of return on investment is that money (or capital) is working to deliver a return, whether as interest payments or dividends or some other increase in value.

In the public sector, by contrast, generally money is spent rather than invested and there is no financial return. Instead of such a financial return there is, or should be, the value of the services created and delivered to the public. This 'public value' is the end that Moore was referring to.

This leads to a concept of public value management. There is still debate about exactly what this concept is (Bryson, Crosby and Bloomberg, 2014) but, its core principles are:

> (1) a broad perspective on the aims of government by focusing on creating collectively desired outcomes, (2) a strategy to achieve this by working together with the different stakeholders affected, and (3) a realization that what is valuable and how it is to be achieved will change over time and between contexts.
>
> (Douglas and Overmans, 2020)

Public managers have different specific goals and objectives from each other but they share the need to spend public money to achieve them. Managers of many (but not all) companies are spending other people's money and they are expected to do so in a way that creates more money for the owners. However, rather than simply maximizing profits in the short term, they are expected to do something that is strategically important in the longer term, namely, increase shareholder value. Public managers spending public money are expected to do something similar: to create what Mark Moore called 'public value'. Moore conceptualized the challenge facing public managers as a strategic triangle:

> the three key questions managers must answer in testing the adequacy of their vision of organizational purpose: whether the purpose is publicly valuable, whether it will be politically and legally supported and whether it is administratively and operationally feasible?
>
> (Moore, 1995: 22)

The answer to Moore's three key questions will inevitably feed into the budgeting process because, as you will see in Chapter 2, a budget links an organization's governance (whether the authority comes from political or other sources) with its operational capacity and values everything by expressing the plans in money terms. Moore's notion of creating public value extends beyond the boundaries of the organization to include co-producers, but to the extent that there is a financial relationship between the organization and the co-producers it should also be included within the budget (and the statement of accounts). This idea is picked up in Chapter 2 on budgeting.

Moore sees financial management and the achievement of financial performance targets as the means to the end of creating public value. A PBE needs to do this if it is to survive, but it needs to do more than that if it is to create public value (Moore, 2000: 195; 2003: 7). It follows that it is important for a public manager to exercise control over the financial resources at their disposal and to use financial performance measures to assess whether they are on course to achieve the organization's goals. Issues relating to this will be discussed in Chapter 7.

New public management

New public management (NPM) (Hood, 1991; Diefenbach, 2009) describes the broad policy approach adopted by governments and public organizations in many OECD countries since the mid-1970s. Similar policies have also been adopted elsewhere, often at the behest of aid donors who promote them as best practice (although they might ultimately prove to be disappointing to the governments [Lapsley, 2009]).

NPM is the context in which modern public managers are likely to find themselves these days. Broadly speaking, NPM is a movement away from bureaucratic administration of public services towards professional management using private sector techniques. This has implications for financial management skills and for the knowledge that public managers are expected to have.

There are numerous instances where professional management has been introduced to PBEs. Hood (1991) referred to this as 'named persons at the top, "free to manage"'. It is also the case that there is an increase in professional managers in non-profit organizations, replacing the volunteering basis and when this happens it can increase the rationalization of the organization (Hwang and Powell, 2009).

Financial management is affected by the increased professionalism in two ways. First, public managers in general need to have financial skills. This extends beyond the most senior managers because of the decentralization that is also a feature of NPM (see later in this chapter). Job descriptions for middle management grades of teachers, nurses, librarians, probation officers, etc. would typically include a requirement to manage the finances of their team/department/unit or whatever. Basic financial skills training, such as finance courses for non-financial managers, would be an element of the management training that a public manager can expect to undertake.

Second, professionally qualified accountants in senior roles in public organizations have grown in numbers. The most senior finance manager in a police force will now be a civilian accountant rather than a uniformed officer; the boards of National Health Service (NHS) trusts have to have a finance director as well as a chief executive and local authorities must have a chief finance officer who is a member of one of six prescribed accounting bodies.

CIPFA (the Chartered Institute of Public Finance and Accountancy) goes further than this in the foreword of its 2011 statement, stating that the chief financial officer in a public service organization:

- is a key member of the Leadership Team, helping it to develop and implement strategy and to resource and deliver the authority's strategic objectives sustainably and in the public interest;
- must be actively involved in and able to bring influence to bear on, all material business decisions to ensure immediate and longer-term implications, opportunities and risks are fully considered and alignment with the authority's financial strategy; and
- must lead the promotion and delivery by the whole authority of good financial management so that public money is safeguarded at all times and used appropriately, economically, efficiently and effectively (CIPFA, 2011: 2).

To fulfil the above responsibilities, CIPFA states that the chief financial officer, 'must lead and direct a finance function that is resourced to be fit for purpose; and must be professionally qualified and suitably experienced' (2011: 2). (CIPFA has produced a series of statements about the role of chief finance officers in a variety of PBEs, including local government.)

Under NPM there is a trend to devolve power to local units, for example, to regional government bodies, to individual hospitals, to schools or to operational teams. Responsibility for the financial management of these smaller units accompanies the devolution of power.

Prior to NPM an organization's financial management was likely to have been concentrated in the hands of the finance department and administrative teams at, say, a departmental level (or in the case of a central government in the hands of the ministry of finance). The result of such an arrangement was that senior managers who might have been responsible for significant public services would have little or no information about the cost of their services and would have to ask the administrative team whether they could spend money on a specific item or project. Effectively, relatively junior members of staff managed the budgets and arguably, therefore, controlled the development of the services.

Devolving financial responsibility has changed this: public managers know that they are expected to have financial skills as well as other management skills and professional knowledge. In the United Kingdom the devolution started with the concept of district general managers in the NHS, but it was perhaps more noticeable when the Education Reform Act, 1988 enacted the local management of schools regime. This gave responsibility to headteachers and school governors for the financial management of their school's share of the local education authority's total budget for schools. The process has developed over the last 30 years so that now each school has much greater freedom over how it spends its budget share and if it under-spends the budget share in any particular year it may save that money to spend in a later year.

In the United Kingdom there are similar decentralized financial arrangements operating across the rest of local government, in hospitals, in the police service and so on and the term 'budget-holder' would be widely understood. Finance departments have developed their financial systems to produce monitoring reports for each and every budget-holder on a monthly or quarterly basis.

The devolution of financial management is now being pushed beyond the front line of public organizations as they try to involve individuals and communities in service delivery. The personalization of social care is an example of this. It is a regime where individuals receiving a social care package from a local authority can instead opt for a budget allocation and then choose how best to use that amount of funding to meet their needs. They might choose to continue to receive exactly the same care package that the local authority had been providing but they might choose to spend the money in a completely different way. For example, instead of attending a social services drop-in centre for social contact a person might use the funding to pay for theatre visits because they get more benefit (i.e., value) from the cultural experience.

In a similar vein, encouraging community volunteers to take over the running of facilities like swimming pools and libraries is likely to require some public funding to be devolved to them. In such a situation a key issue for the relevant public manager is that they will remain accountable for the public money being spent by the volunteers but have less control than if the facility was managed directly by employees. The public manager needs to trust both the volunteers and the financial systems that are in place to account for and manage the public money.

NPM requires discipline in use of resources. As Hood (1991: 5) puts it, this boils down to the expectation to 'do more with less'. Arguably, since the financial crises in 2008 and subsequent pressure to reduce public expenditure in many countries this has become more urgent and explicit than in the preceding two decades.

NPM also puts a greater emphasis on demonstrating value for money. This can be clearly seen by the changes made to the public sector audit regime in 1983 to extend the remit of auditors to assess and report on value for money (Coombs and Edwards, 1990). That was when the Audit Commission and the National Audit Office (NAO) were formed, each with a mandate that included assessing and reporting on value for money. These remits were broader than the predecessor organizations, the District Audit Service and the Exchequer and Audit Department, respectively, which had been focused on the probity of accounts and controlling expenditure through accountability.

The NPM paradigm's promotion of private sector management techniques also embraces an increase in using outsourcing/privatization of public services. When a third party is used to deliver all or part of the service a public manager is responsible for it has an impact on the associated financial management. There is a need to manage the cost of the commissioning/procurement process in the first place and whenever the contracts are due for renewal. There are two broad scenarios: a commissioning regime where lots of small packages of services are purchased on a routine basis, such as in health care; and large-scale, intermittent procurement, such as contracting out a whole service for five or ten years. For the former the public manager needs a budget to cover the running costs of commissioners and their systems and processes whereas, for the latter, the public manager will require an occasional budget to cover the cost of the procurement process.

The public manager who uses contractors or partnerships to deliver services has to have regard for the following ongoing financial management issues:

- the committed expenditure;
- claims from the contractor;
- contract price increases;
- the flexibility of the contract; and
- risk management

These financial management and other issues relating to outsourcing are discussed in detail in Chapter 6.

By private sector styles of management Hood (1991) meant a 'move away from military-style' towards something more flexible. There are ramifications of this in terms of financial management. Perhaps the most significant of these has been the broadening of the role of the finance department. The traditional role of finance had been one of stewardship, of being able to produce accounting statements that showed every penny of money received and when, where and how it was spent. This role, which would be termed nowadays as financial accounting, has been joined by management accounting, the provision of advice and guidance to budget-holders and senior managers. The latter role has required changes to financial systems, to allow financial information to be recorded in a way that is relevant and meaningful to budget-holders. It has also required the accountants and finance staff to learn new skills (such as costing techniques, database interrogation and reporting and communication skills). Lapsley and Wright's (2004) survey indicated that 'accounting innovations have mainly originated in the private sector and adoption of these innovations by public sector organizations is largely attributable to government influence' (2004: 372).

There are other ways that private sector management has affected financial management in the public sector. There has been an initiative to harmonize the public sector's accounting practices with those that are used by the private sector. This is discussed in more detail later in this chapter and in Chapter 8, but an important aspect has been the move away from the (relatively simple) accounting on a receipts and payments basis to accounting for income and expenditure, including accounting for the use of fixed assets with depreciation. This latter change is crucial. Without it, public managers may perceive that their use of assets (such as operational buildings) is free. Depreciation accounting gives the manager a financial signal that they are using (i.e., wearing out) the assets.

PFM CHALLENGES

A public manager faces a number of challenges when it comes to financial management and some of them are outlined in this final segment of Chapter 1. Whether financial management in the public sector is more difficult than financial management in the private sector is hard to assess, but it is different.

The nature of public services

Boyne (2002) wrote: 'The public and private sectors are alike only in the unimportant ways.' They are alike in terms of hiring staff and buying goods and services from suppliers but no business can demand and collect taxes. There are many other ways that the two sectors are different in nature that has implications for the way organizations function and how finances are managed.

One of the most significant differences relates to objectives. In the private sector the prime objective is to increase shareholder, usually by making profits. Profits are what remains when expenses are deducted from revenues so a business aims to earn more in revenue than it spends on its expenses.

Aside from the case of state-owned enterprises, there is not a profit motive in government or other PBEs. In its place a PBE may have multiple objectives that are, or have potential to be, in conflict. It is very difficult, for example, to deliver services that embody equality, liberty, community, transparency and sustainability at all times. Often there will need to be compromises or trade-offs.

Even with just one objective a PBE may have an objective that is more complex than earning a profit. The quotation at the start of this chapter emphasized how critical governments are because they provide services that can literally be the difference between living and dying. They also provide a great many other services that contribute to the quality of life. These are all services that a free market would, at best, under-produce. As Keynes (2010) put it:

> The important thing for Government is not to do things which individuals are doing already, and to do them a little better or a little worse; but to do those things which at present are not being done at all.

PBEs are often faced with delivering services that address a 'wicked problem' (Conklin, 2006). A wicked problem is a problem that is difficult or impossible to solve because of incomplete, contradictory and changing requirements that are often difficult to recognize. Tackling a global pandemic is a very recent and real example of a wicked problem. Other examples are climate change and tackling the issues around illegal drug trafficking and usage.

Conklin (2006) wrote the solutions to wicked problems are not right or wrong and, even when found, there is no stopping rule, meaning the issue or problem will continue.

The nature of the objectives of PBEs and expectations about public money adds some extra complexity to making a decision to spend money. In simple terms, a private sector manager faced with an option to spend some money could ask themselves one question: if I spend this money will I get more back, either now or in the long term? If the answer is yes then they expect a positive return on the expenditure. If there are two or more options, they would choose the option with the greatest expected return.

A public sector manager, on the other hand, has three questions to ask themselves:

- Is this spending within the rules?
- Can we afford it?
- Is it value for money?

Three yeses are required before proceeding. And notice that these three questions are another parallel with the three points of Moore's strategic triangle (1995). The first is about authority, the second about capacity and the third about value.

Customers or service users?

Private sector businesses make products to sell to customers. To be successful they have to make products that customers want and sell them at a price that customers are willing to pay. Businesses can choose the customer types they want to target, whether by demographics or by geography or by income level or by whatever. The relationship also works the other way around: customers can choose which business they want to buy from and which businesses they do not want to patronize.

Public services, by contrast, tend to be universal in nature. That is, they are produced and available to everyone. This has implications for the cost of service because the public body has to deliver the service to the remote, hard-to-reach parts of the country. A business could simply decide that customers in such places are not profitable because the expenses would be too high, or they would sell the product at a premium price to compensate for the extra expenses.

Some universal public services are also delivered to people who do not want them. A criminal is not a customer of the prison service but the rest of society wish for the criminal to be detained in prison as a punishment for their crimes. Again, there are no parallels in business, where a company imposes its services on a non-paying service user.

Lastly, as mentioned earlier, governments sometimes decide to operate monopolies directly in order to protect the customers from the potential abuse of power that a commercial monopoly might have. By definition, the government monopoly would not have to compete for customers because the customers have no choice of an alternative supplier. The government may operate the monopoly in a way that protects the customers from unfair pricing but the lack of competition may result in the organization being inefficient.

Politics

Another way that the two sectors are different is the importance of politics. The private sector is driven by money, the aim being to use money to generate more money. To get things done in government does not just require money, it also requires political support.

Countries have different constitutions and differing degrees of democracy but still politics plays a part in government. This is perhaps most clearly seen in the budget formulation stage. The decisions that are made about taxation (what is taxed as well as the rate of tax) and public spending are political. They will reflect the policies that the decision-makers wish to implement. This is true at a national and a local level.

A public manager needs to have the knowledge and skills to work in a political environment. They may have some degree of influence as an advisor to the politicians who are the decision-makers and if they do they need to know how and when to use that influence.

Public managers also get their authority to act, and therefore spend public money, from politicians. This will come with a duty or obligation to be accountable to politicians for the delivery of the policy objectives that are desired.

The scale of public services

The government and public sector ranges from 5 to 55 per cent of the economy. The chances are that it will include some huge organizations, bigger than all but the biggest companies in the country. For example, the National Health Service (NHS) in England (there are separate NHS organizations in each country of the United Kingdom) has an operating budget in 2021/2 of about £139 billion and 1.37 million employees (NHS Digital, 2022).

This is also replicated at local level with, for example, a city government likely to be one of the biggest employers in the city.

Managing large public sector organizations has all the challenges of managing a private enterprise, such as coordinating very many people to deliver the objectives, as well as the accountability expectations that are peculiar to the public sector.

Measuring performance

NPM places a great emphasis on performance management. If a public manager's job is to create public value then it feels like we should be able to express the public value created in financial terms, or at least in numerical terms.

We can do this for the value created by a manager in a private sector organization in a number of ways. We can point to the profit earned in a period, the return on investment, the net worth of the business on its balance sheet, the share price and the market capitalization value. Furthermore, the revenue from sales is a measure of the value that customers place on the goods or services that they purchase (assuming that the customers are being rational) so it is possible to calculate a proxy measure for the aggregate value created for customers.

Things are not so clear-cut in the public sector. It is relatively easy to identify financial performance indicators relating to spending. These can be the cost per unit of service produced (such as the cost per library book loaned out) or the cost of the service per head of population served. The former is probably more useful in terms of making comparisons between organizations, or between units within an organization. This is because it is difficult to compare the cost per head of a service which covers a million people with one that covers a population that is a tenth of the size.

Without sales revenue, it can be difficult to measure the value of what is produced by the public sector. A public manager cannot claim that the value of what they create is equal to the amount spent on the delivery of the service. If that were the case it would mean that spending more money always creates more value. Sometimes it may be the case that extra spending improves the quality and/or quantity of services produced but it clearly is not the case if the extra spending is on waste and extravagance. Thinking about this as an economist would, if public money is expended on some goods or services that are valued (by the public) at something less than their cost then society is worse off than if the public money had not been spent at all. In that scenario, the citizens could have paid less tax and used the extra money in their pockets to buy something they valued more than the money. It is important, therefore, that the public value that is created is at least as great as the value of the resources that are expended in its creation.

Somewhere in this calculation, then, we have to take account of the efficiency (or productivity) of the organization in converting inputs (i.e., money and other resources) into outputs (i.e., services or goods). National statistics include a measure of public sector inputs and outputs (and thus productivity can be calculated) but the quality of service is not reflected in the figures. How the value created by a PBE might be measured is picked up in Chapter 7.

Accountability and public expectations

The general public have long expected governments to be accountable for the use made of taxes but public expectation is growing for improved transparency in the use of public money, enabled by modern technology. The IMF defines fiscal transparency as the clarity, reliability, frequency, timeliness and relevance of public fiscal reporting and the openness to the public of the government's fiscal policymaking process.

Many countries systematically publish data about public sector budgets and spending. The UK data are available at https://data.gov.uk/. Other countries and cities have similar portals as the starting point for researching government data, including the United States (www.data.gov), Australia (https://data.gov.au) and New Zealand (https://data.govt.nz), London (https://data.london.gov.uk) and New York City (https://data.cityofnewyork.us).

These sources can be a valuable resource for academics, researchers and journalists but, just as for budget information from public bodies, it is difficult to interpret what one finds unless one understands the structure of the organizations.

The UK Government publishes details of payments by national departments (the equivalent of ministries) above £25,000 and has asked other public sector organizations to publish information about every item of expenditure exceeding £500. This has contributed to Great Britain being ranked joint second, with Australia (out of 94 countries) in the *Global Open Data Index* (Open Knowledge Foundation, 2022).

The index looks at ten datasets for each country, two of them being government budget and government spending information. The assessment looks at things like whether the data are digital, are publicly available online, are free, are available in bulk and are up to date. The top-ranked country in 2022 was Taiwan, with an index score of 90 per cent. Other countries in the top ten (in order) were France, Finland, Canada, Norway, New Zealand, Brazil and Northern Ireland. You can see the full table at https://index.okfn.org/place/.

Something else is different about the public sector, too: the public expect much more from public servants than they do from private sector managers. The relationship is different. When you purchase goods or services from a profit-seeking organization then it is a discrete transaction between the two parties. As a customer you are concerned with the quality of the goods, the after-sales service and so on, but one does not expect the organization should sell you the goods or services at a discount because one is a part-owner as well as a customer. Customers are unlikely to have an opinion about the level of the chief executive's salary or whether or not they should travel in a private jet. Citizens, whether taxpayers or not, are interested in how public money is used (or abused).

Issues related to public expectations and accountability are discussed in more detail in Chapter 8.

Public sector accounting

Businesses of all kinds, save for the smallest microbusinesses, prepare statements of accounts using the accrual basis of accounting. This basis matches the timing of expenses and revenues and recognizes that, on any given date, there are assets and liabilities relating to the future. This basis of accounting has to be used if profit is to be calculated, and a significant body of accounting regulations and standards aim to assure users of accounts about the reliability and comparability of the accounting statements.

Public sector accounting practices are being brought into line with the generally accepted practices of the private sector. Roughly 30 per cent of jurisdictions use the accrual basis of accounting, and another 20 per cent intend to adopt this basis by 2025 (IFAC and CIPFA, 2021).

On the face of it, the harmonization is a sensible idea. In an age of networked governance and a blurring of distinctions between sectors it would surely be helpful to the public if all organizations' accounts were published on a consistent basis. Unfortunately, there are problems associated with it and some of these are touched upon in the following paragraphs.

A key difference to mention here is that private sector organizations prepare profit and loss accounts whereas non-profit organizations prepare either an 'income and expenditure account' or a 'statement of financial affairs'. The preparation of these statements uses accounting practice that is consistent with accounting practices in the private sector. There are, however, some important differences that are worth noting here in brief.

First, the private sector is concerned only with exchange transactions. That is, transactions where the parties exchange things they assess as being of broadly equal value. Most notably, the sale of a product requires the seller and buyer to agree on a price and there is an exchange of the product for money. Similarly, employees exchange their time and energy for money and so on.

The bulk of transactions undertaken by a government are also exchange transactions, but not all of them. Demanding and collecting taxes are not exchange transactions. The taxpayer receives nothing (directly) in return for the money they pay to the government. Similarly, transgressors who have to pay fines are not taking part in an exchange transaction.

Governments are also on the other side of non-exchange transactions when they pay grants or welfare benefits to third parties.

All of the non-exchange transactions, for government spending as well as receipts, need to be reflected in government accounts, but they need specific accounting policies and techniques since there is no equivalent in private sector accounting standards.

Another area where public sector accounting diverges from private sector accounting relates to the identification and valuation of assets that are of long-term benefit to the organization. In a business, an asset that provides a long-term benefit is valued using the present value of income that is expected to be generated by the asset. For example, production machinery in a factory will, it is expected, shape products that can be sold and an airline's aircraft is expected to generate sales revenue.

It is true that governments have some non-current assets that can be valued using the expected value of future sales. For example, the assets owned by state-owned enterprises and bridges and tunnels where tolls are levied. In general, though, when a government acquires or builds an asset for long-term benefit it does not expect to get any income in return. Indeed, far from the asset representing future income, the asset has future liabilities attached, in terms of maintaining and operating the asset. In these circumstances a government cannot, therefore, use the private sector accounting approach to value the asset and, thus, something else is required.

The ongoing process of harmonization of accounting practice between the public and private sectors and between countries is discussed in more detail in Chapter 8. You can also find a glossary of technical terms, including many accounting terms, at the back of this book.

PFM reforms

There is no single best way to manage public finances, just as there is no single best way to govern a country or manage a business. There are constant developments and improvements made to PFM practices. Allen (2013: 411) wrote: 'Interest in strengthening budgetary institutions—defined as the laws, procedures, and rules that determine and regulate the behaviour of public officials and organizations—and [PFM] can be traced back at least 2,000 years.'

What matters is what works, and this will mean improvements and reforms of PFM systems are needed from time to time. Cole (2022) quotes Keith Muhakanizi, permanent secretary in Uganda's Ministry of Finance: 'Public finance reforms matter when they change the lives of the people living in your village.'

When a country has weak PFM arrangements, its growth and the achievement of the SDGs are hindered. Bandy and Metcalfe's report (2021: 7) on a global survey of PFM practitioners showed that 'the quality of a government [...] has a profound impact on citizens'. The areas they identified for improving PFM post-COVID-19 included improving transparency and accountability of government spending; intensifying the focus on risk management; ensuring services achieve value for money; adopting accrual accounting and budgeting; and adopting e-procurement processes (Bandy and Metcalfe, 2021: 7–8).

African countries face many challenges in terms of their PFM systems. Opalo (2021) sees weak legislative oversight means spending often follows the will of the executive branch of governments, and much is lost to 'white elephant projects, corruption and general waste'. Opala (2021) also sees a strategic challenge ahead: 'Given Africa's demographic and political trajectories, the challenges confronting its public finance management systems will only get tougher.'

The Public Expenditure Framework Assessment (PEFA) is a tool to help governments evaluate and improve their PFM systems. The assessment covers seven broad areas of PFM, referred to as pillars (PEFA, 2016). The seven pillars are:

1. budget reliability;
2. transparency of public finances;
3. management of assets and liabilities;
4. policy-based fiscal strategy and budgeting;
5. predictability and control in budget execution;
6. accounting and auditing; and
7. external scrutiny and audit.

Within the 7 pillars are 31 key components called PFM indicators. These indicators are analyses of 94 characteristics, referred to as dimensions. For more details on the PFM indicators and dimensions go to the PEFA Secretariat's website (https://www.pefa.org) where you can also access all the assessment reports completed to date and many other resources.

The PEFA Secretariat's *2020 Global Report on Public Financial Management* (PEFA, 2020) is based on nearly 700 assessments of countries' PFM systems completed by 2019. It gives an insight into the state of PFM around the world before the coronavirus pandemic. The key messages of the report were that countries tend to be better at budget formulation than budget execution. Perhaps it is not a surprise that producing a good plan is easier than implementing it to achieve the intended results. That could be true for a simple plan let alone budgets for organizations of the scale and complexity of governments and other PBEs.

PEFA (2020) also reported that other relatively weak areas of PFM are budget execution, risk management, and scrutiny and transparency. On equality and inclusion, the PEFA noted that some countries had made advances in developing and implementing gender-responsive budgeting but this was not a mainstream feature of PFM in most countries. This will be covered in Chapter 2.

Within the report the PEFA Secretariat recognized that the hundreds of PEFA assessments that have been done have focused on the role, function and performance of finance ministries and not on the PFM work done in line ministries and below national government level, that is, the parts of government where public services are created and delivered. Essentially they were noting that PFM systems focused more on the first two objectives of PFM (economic sustainability and allocating resources to programmes) and less on the third one, delivery public services in a value for money way.

Any given PFM practice or technique may be very successful in the country or jurisdiction where it was developed but that development was context-specific. The new or modified practice was solving a problem that came from a previous solution (Senge, 1990), and there is no guarantee that the practice would work in another place or at another time. Developed countries have produced numerous PFM innovations and many PFM innovations have been transferred from developed countries to low-income countries. There are good reasons to adopt practices that work elsewhere, not least the avoidance of spending lots of time and money developing a custom practice. But transfers are not always successful. As Schick (2013: 74–5) noted:

> PFM innovations are not substitutes for good governance. They will not banish corruption, motivate a demoralized or indifferent civil service, ensure that funds are spent only on authorized purposes, cancel white elephant projects, and cure government of other pathologies.

Lawson (2012) concluded that PFM reforms deliver results when three conditions coincide:

- when there is a strong political commitment to their implementation;
- when reform designs and implementation models are well tailored to the institutional and capacity context; and
- when strong coordination arrangements—led by government officials—are in place to monitor and guide reforms.

Hadley et al. (2021) echoed the importance of political commitment in their report on 20 years of PFM reforms in Nigeria. They also suggested that linking PFM reforms to service delivery results is not straightforward. In part this was an example of the PEFA Secretariat conclusion about service delivery. The PFM support in Nigeria had concentrated on the 'state level while local governments play[ed] an important role in financing and delivering basic education and primary health services'.

Matt Andrews's *The Limits of Public Financial Management Reform in Development* (2013) analyses the adoption of PFM reforms in developing countries and proposes an alternative to the direct adoption of large-scale solutions. His analysis shows a reality gap, where most countries' PFM systems look better than they are: they have good laws on budgeting and transparency and so on, but their performance is not so good.

Andrews (2013) suggested that reforms should be found that fit actual problems using a technique called problem-driven iterative adaption (PDIA). In short, the technique calls for analysing the root causes of a complex problem to find entry points and possible solutions. Action is taken towards a solution but including feedback loops is important so that it is possible to reflect and learn from the actions taken, adapt the solution as necessary and act again (and again and again). This technique allows for building a solution that fits the local context. You can find a PDIA toolkit and other resources at Harvard University's Center for International Development website (https://bsc.cid.harvard.edu/PDIAtoolkit).

Looking to the future, Andrews (2022) suggests that public finance performance should be assessed in terms of the following pillars:

1. equity;
2. fiscal sustainability;
3. environmental sustainability;
4. effectiveness;
5. inclusion;
6. growth and innovation; and
7. accountability.

These have some alignment with the seven pillars of the PEFA framework listed above but they are not the same.

CONCLUSION

This book is about managing public money and this first chapter has defined the objectives of PFM and the stages that make up the PFM cycle. It has also explained what is meant by public money and where it comes from. It has also discussed how the NPM paradigm has influenced financial management in PBEs and

This chapter has also introduced the concepts of NPM and public value management and outlined some of the key differences between the public and private sectors. Those differences have an impact on some of the challenges that governments and public managers face when it comes to PFM.

One of those challenges stems from the fact that PBEs are driven by politics rather than money. The next chapter is concerned with the aspect of financial management where the interface with the political authorizing environment is most obvious: the budget process.

EXERCISES

1. The growth of internet access and social media has made it easier for misinformation to be presented as fact, whether deliberately or by accident. Would

a fact-checking service be a public or merit good? That is, what are the arguments for fact-checking to be provided to citizens as a public service?
2. Are public goods provided only by governments?
3. What do you think is the optimum level of public expenditure as a proportion of a country's GDP?

REFERENCES

Allen, R. (2013). Challenges of Reforming Budgetary Institutions in Developing Countries. In M. Cangiano, T. Curristine, & M. Lazare (Eds.), *Public Financial Management and Its Emerging Architecture* (pp. 411–30). Washington, DC: International Monetary Fund.

Andrews, M. (2013) *The Limits of Public Financial Management Reform in Development*. Cambridge, MA: Cambridge University Press.

Andrews, M. (2022). *Managing Public Finances for the Future* [Blog]. Available at: https://buildingstatecapability.com/2022/01/25/managing-public-finances-for-the-future/ (Accessed: 25 April 2022).

Bandy, G. P., & Metcalfe, A. (2021). *Rethinking Public Financial Management*. London: ACCA. Available at: https://www.accaglobal.com/gb/en/professional-insights/global-profession/rethinking-public-financial-management.html (Accessed: 25 April 2022).

BBC. (2022). *Money, Money, Money* [Podcast]. Available at: https://www.bbc.co.uk/programmes/w3ct42d7 (Accessed: 1 July 2022).

Behn, R. (2013). *Which Comes First: Resources or Results?* [Blog]. Available at: https://thebehnreport.hks.harvard.edu/files/thebehnreport/files/behnreportdec2013.pdf (Accessed: 26 April 2022).

Benington, J. (2009). Creating the Public in Order to Create Public Value? *International Journal of Public Administration*, 32(3), 232–249.

Berkeley, A., Ryan-Collins, J., Voldsgaard, A., & Wilson, N. (2022). *The Self-Financing State: An Institutional Analysis of Government Expenditure, Revenue Collection and Debt Issuance Operations in the United Kingdom*. UCL Institute for Innovation and Public Purpose Working Papers (WP 2022/08). Available at: https://www.ucl.ac.uk/bartlett/public-purpose/publications/2022/may/self-financing-state-institutional-analysis (Accessed: 30 May 2022).

Boyne, G. A. (2002). Public and Private Management: What's the Difference? *Journal of Management Studies*, 39(1), 97–122.

Bryson, J. M., Crosby, B. C., & Bloomberg, L. L. (2014). Public Value Governance: Moving Beyond Traditional Public Administration and the New Public Management. *Public Administration Review*, 74(4), 445–456. https://doi.org/10.1111/puar.12238.

CIPFA. (2011). *The Role of the Chief Financial Officer in Local Government.* London: CIPFA. Available at: https://www.cipfa.org/-/media/files/cipfa-thinks/reports/role-of-cfo-v2-2011.pdf (Accessed: 9 May 2022).

Cole, N. (2022). *Top 14 Public Finance Lessons.* Available at: https://www.cabri-sbo.org/en/media/top-14-public-finance-lessons (Accessed: 25 April 2022).

Conklin, J. (2006). *Dialogue Mapping: Building Shared Understanding of Wicked Problems.* Chichester, England: Wiley Publishing.

Coombs, H. M. and Edwards, J. R. (1990). The Evolution of the District Audit. *Financial Accountability and Management,* 6(3), 153–76.

Diefenbach, T. (2009). New Public Management in Public Sector Organizations: The Dark Sides of Managerialistic 'Enlightenment'. *Public Administration, 87*(4), 892–909.

Douglas, S., & Overmans, T. (2020). Public Value Budgeting: Propositions for the Future of Budgeting. *Journal of Public Budgeting, Accounting & Financial Management,* 32(4), 623–637. https://doi.org/10.1108/JPBAFM-05-2020-0066.

Glenday, G., & Hemming, R. (2013). Tax Design From a Public Financial Management Perspective. In R. Allen, R. Hemming, & B. H. Potter (Eds.), *The International Handbook of Public Financial Management* (pp. 416–434). Basingstoke: Palgrave Macmillan.

Hadley, S., Piron, L.-H., Williams, G., & Cummings, C. (2021). *Pfm Reforms in Nigeria: Lessons From 20 Years of UK Support.* Available at: https://blog-pfm.imf.org/pfmblog/2021/11/-pfm-reforms-in-nigeria-lessons-from-20-years-of-uk-support-.html. (Accessed: 26 April 2022).

Hedger, E., Manning, N., & Schick, A. (2020). *Beyond Doctrine: Refocusing PFM for Vital Public Objectives* [Blog]. Available at: https://blog-pfm.imf.org/pfmblog/2020/07/-beyond-doctrine-refocusing-pfm-for-vital-public-objectives-.html#_ftn2 (Accessed: 28 June 2022).

HM Treasury. (2021). *Budget 2021.* London: The Stationery Office. Available at: https://assets.publishing.service.gov.uk/government/uploads/system/uploads/attachment_data/file/966869/Budget_2021_Print.pdf (Accessed: 26 April 2022).

Hood, C. (1991). A Public Management for All Seasons? *Public Administration, 69*(1), 3–19.

Hwang, H. & Powell, W. W. (2009). The Rationalization of Charity: The Influences of Professionalism in the Non-Profit Sector. *Administrative Science Quarterly, 54*(2), 268–98.

IFAC and CIPFA. (2021). *International Public Accountability Index: 2021 Status Report.* Available at: https://www.ifac.org/publications/international-public-sector-financial-accountability-index-2021-status-report (Accessed: 10 May 2022).

IMF. (2021). *Fiscal Monitor: Database of Country Fiscal Measures in Response to the COVID-19 Pandemic*. Washington DC: IMF.

Keynes, J. M. (2010). The End of Laissez-Faire. In *Essays in Persuasion* (pp. 272–294). London: Palgrave Macmillan.

Lapsley, I. (2009). New Public Management: The Cruellest Invention of the Human Spirit? 1. *Abacus, 45*(1), 1–21.

Lapsley, I., & Wright, E. (2004). The Diffusion of Management Accounting Innovations in the Public Sector: A Research Agenda. *Management Accounting Research*, 15(3), 355–374.

Laughlin, R. (2008). A Conceptual Framework for Accounting for Public-Benefit Entities. *Public Money and Management*, 28(4), 247–254.

Lawson, A. (2012). *Evaluation of Public Financial Management Reform.* Stockholm: SIDA. Available at: https://www.oecd.org/derec/afdb/publicmanagementregorm.pdf (Accessed: 25 April 2022).

Lord Sharman of Redlynch. (2001). *Holding to Account: The Review of Audit and Accountability for Central Government.* London: HM Treasury.

Mazzucato, M., & Kaitel, R. (2019). *Getting Serious About Value.* Available at: https://www.ucl.ac.uk/bartlett/public-purpose/sites/public-purpose/files/iipp_policybrief_07_getting_serious_about_value.pdf (Accessed: 11 May 2022).

McLeay, M., Radia, A., & Thomas, R. (2014). Money Creation in the Modern Economy. *Bank of England Quarterly Bulletin*, Q1. Available at: https://www.bankofengland.co.uk/quarterly-bulletin/2014/q1/money-creation-in-the-modern-economy (Accessed: 30 May 2022).

Micklethwait, J., & Wooldridge, A. (2020). *The Virus Should Wake Up the West* [Blog]. Available at: https://www.bloomberg.com/opinion/articles/2020-04-13/coronavirus-pandemic-is-wake-up-call-to-reinvent-the-state (Accessed: 27 April 2022).

Miller, M., Hart, T., & Hadley, S. (2021). *Public Finance and Service Delivery: What's New, What's Missing, What's Next?* Working Paper 607. London: Overseas Development Institute. Available at: https://cdn.odi.org/media/documents/DPFPFMservicedeliveryProof07.pdf (Accessed: 28 April 2022).

Mintzberg, H. (1983). *Structure in Fives: Designing Effective Organizations.* Upper Saddle River, NJ: Prentice-Hall.

Moore, M. H. (1995). *Creating Public Value: Strategic Management in Government.* Boston: Harvard University Press.

Moore, M. H. (2000). Managing for Value: Organizational Strategy in For-Profit, Nonprofit, and Governmental Organizations. *Nonprofit and Voluntary Sector Quarterly, 29*(1) (Supplement), 183–204.

Moore, M. H. (2003). *The Public Value Scorecard: A Rejoinder and an Alternative to 'Strategic Performance Measurement and Management in Non-Profit Organizations' by Robert Kaplan*. Cambridge, MA: The Hauser Center for Nonprofit Organizations.

NHS Digital. (2022). *NHS Workforce Statistics - January 2022* [Webpage]. Available at: https://digital.nhs.uk/data-and-information/publications/statistical/nhs-workforce-statistics/january-2022 (Accessed: 9 May 2022).

OECD. (2021). *Government at a Glance 2021*. Available at: https://www.oecd.org/gov/government-at-a-glance-22214399.htm (Accessed: 26 April 2022).

Office of Budget Responsibility. (2022). *Public Finances Databank March 2022* [Spreadsheet File]. Available at: https://obr.uk/data/ (Accessed: 26 April 2022).

Opalo, K. (2021). *It's Time to Democratize Public Finance Management Systems in African States* [Blog]. Available at: https://www.imf.org/en/Publications/fandd/issues/2021/12/Africa-Democratize-Public-Finance-Management-Systems (Accessed: 25 April 2022).

Open Contracting Partnership. (no date). *Transforming Public Contracting Through Open Data and Smarter Engagement* [Website Article]. Available at: https://www.open-contracting.org/what-is- open-contracting/ (Accessed: 5 May 2022).

Open Knowledge Foundation. (2022). *Global Open Data Index* [Webpage]. Available at: https://index.okfn.org/place/ (Accessed: 30 April 2022).

PEFA. (2016). *PEFA 2016 Framework*. Available at: https:// www.pefa.org/resources/pefa-2016-framework (Accessed: 10 May 2022).

PEFA. (2021). *2020 Global Report on Public Financial Management*. Washington, DC: PEFA. Available at: https://www.pefa.org/global-report-2020/ (Accessed: 25 April 2022).

Rhodes, R. A., & Wanna, J. (2007). The Limits to Public Value, or Rescuing Responsible Government From the Platonic Guardians. *Australian Journal of Public Administration*, 66(4), 406–421.

Schick, A. (2013). Reflections on Two Decades of Public Financial Management Reforms. In M. Cangiano, T. Curristine, & M. Lazare (Eds.), *Public Financial Management and Its Emerging Architecture* (pp. 21–77). Washington, DC: International Monetary Fund.

Senge, P. M. (1990). *The Fifth Discipline: The Art and Practice of the Learning Organization*. London: Doubleday.

World Bank. (2022). *Expense (% of GDP)* [Data File]. Available at: https://data.worldbank.org/indicator/GC.XPN.TOTL.GD.ZS (Accessed: 30 April 2022).

FURTHER READING (AND WATCHING)

All of the chapters include suggestions for further reading and watching. Links to the following resources, and lots more, are available (for free) at www.managingpublicmoney.co.uk/extras.

In 2013 two books were published that address public financial management in great depth and are appropriate for serious students of public financial management. The first is the *International Handbook of Public Financial Management* edited by Richard Allen, Richard Hemming and Barry Potter (2013). At 850 pages this is an encyclopaedic work with chapters on everything from budgeting to auditing. Its focus is on financial management by national governments although much of what it says applies to sub-national governments and other public sector organizations.

The second book is *Public Financial Management and Its Emerging Architecture* edited by Marco Cangiano, Teresa Curristine and Michel Lazare (2013). This covers similar ground to the *International Handbook* but from the point of view of reforming public financial management practices and institutions. What is particularly useful is Allen Schick's opening chapter, *Reflections on Two Decades of Public Financial Management Reforms* (2013: 21–77).

For a different take on the field of PFM, have a look at the blog post by Hedger, Manning and Schick (2020). They refer to PFM as a 'settled science' and suggest that we will need to escape 'from some old ideas as we develop and pursue new ones' that will set up post-COVID-19 PFM systems that can grapple with climate change, inequality and economic recovery.

The Bank of England explains how money is created in an article entitled *Money Creation in the Modern Economy* (McLeay, Radia and Thomas, 2014). There is also a companion video at www.youtube.com/watch?v=CvRAqR2pAgw.

Berkeley et al. (2022) write that, for more than 150 years, the UK Government has been creating new money and purchasing power whenever it undertakes expenditure. That means government spending creates money rather than such spending being financed by collecting taxes or issuing debts.

For a different but complementary view of money there is a series of four 30-minute podcasts by the BBC (2022) called *Money, Money, Money*. They are hosted by Rachel Botsman, an expert in trust, and consider money in terms of trust, value, psychology and power.

Moore's *Creating Public Value* (1995) is worth reading because it is where the public value theory was first put forward. However, *Public Value: Theory and Practice* (Benington and Moore, 2011) is more up to date and includes discussion of practical issues faced by public managers in their work.

For a recent essay about public value you could try Mazzucato and Kaitel (2019). They argue that value is and should be created by governments in more ways than addressing market failures. Indeed, much of the value created by businesses depends on innovations and risk-taking by governments. They quote Warren Buffet, 'Society is responsible for a very significant percentage of what I've earned.'

There is a working paper by Miller, Hart and Hadley (2021) that discusses what might be missing from PFM in respect of service delivery. They call for a broader perspective to be taken in order to improve spending on public services.

There are lots of blog posts about real-life experiences of using PDIA on the Center for International Development's blog at https://buildingstatecapability.com.

If you want to know more about the cost of public services in your country or city try an online search for your national or local government's budget documentation and annual report. If you want to know more about financial management in the public sector in general terms then please read the remainder of this book.

Chapter 2

Public sector budgeting

LEARNING OBJECTIVES

After reading this chapter you will:

- understand the objectives of budgeting;
- be able to explain the strengths and weaknesses of the common approaches to preparing a budget;
- be aware of the differences between public and private sector budgeting practices; and
- recognize how budgeting influences the way public benefit entities (PBEs) are governed and operate.

KEY POINTS OF THIS CHAPTER

- Budgeting is a critical activity in PBEs.
- Budgets have multiple uses within and outside an organization.
- Whilst there are alternative, more rational budgeting approaches, organizations often use incremental budgeting because it is easily understood and produces relatively stable budgets from year to year.
- Budgeting is a more significant activity within public organizations than in private ones, taking up a considerable amount of time and resources. For politicians the budget process is how they determine the allocation of limited resources to their priorities; and for citizens the final budget tells them what their taxes will produce.
- Budgets are one of the elements of accountability for PBEs and public managers.

DOI: 10.4324/9781003250838-2

KEY TERMS

Budget-holder—a manager with responsibility for controlling income and expenditure within the approved budget for a specified organizational unit or project.

Gender budgeting—an approach to public sector budgets that promotes gender equality.

Incremental budgeting—an approach to budgeting where next year's budget is based on this year's budget adjusted for pay and price inflation and committed changes in policies.

Medium-term expenditure framework (MTEF)—an outline of the operating and capital budgets for a three- to five-year period.

Participatory budgeting—a democratic process allowing citizens to take part in the allocation of a public budget by identifying spending proposals and voting on them.

Performance budgeting—an approach to budgeting where performance information is used as a basis for the allocation of resources, with the overall aim of improving performance over time.

Zero-based budgeting (ZBB)—an approach to budgeting where each item is estimated anew each year, rather than by reference to its value in the previous budget.

This chapter focuses on the budget formulation and approval stages of the PFM cycle mentioned in Chapter 1. It aims to help you understand the different approaches a public organization might take to prepare its budgets, the advantages and disadvantages of each and some practical implications.

The chapter has four sections. The first section explains what a budget is and the specific features of budgeting in the public sector. The second section explains the various uses of budgets, and the third describes some alternative approaches to budget formulation. The fourth and final section describes some practical issues connected with budgeting in the public sector.

It is a long chapter reflecting the critical importance of budgeting in the public sector. The process of developing and approving the budget for a PBE (usually an annual process) is amongst the most important activities undertaken by its politicians and executive management. There is a general expectation that a public organization of any size has a budget and, in contrast to most other policy areas, doing nothing or slipping the budget approval/legislation deadline is not an option.

WHAT IS A BUDGET?

Put simply, a budget is a plan written in financial terms. The budget says with numbers what the organization's plans say in words (although, unfortunately for

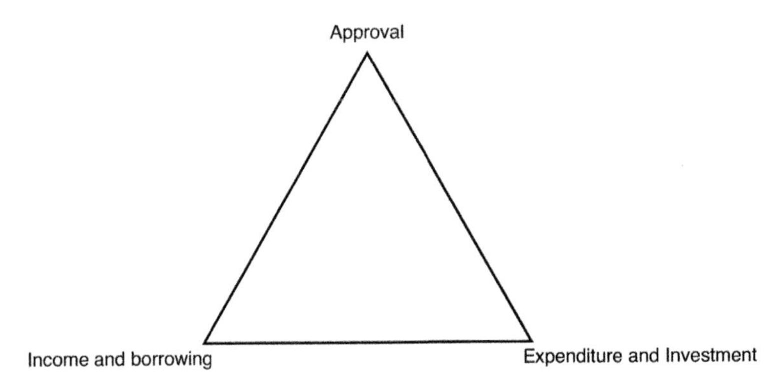

Figure 2.1 *The budget triangle.*

many people, saying things with numbers is as understandable as saying them in an ancient language). We can, of course, have longer, more complicated definitions. Smith and Lynch define a public budget this way:

> A 'budget' is a *plan* for the accomplishment of *programmes* related to *objectives* and *goals* within a definite *time* period, including an estimate of *resources required*, together with an estimate of *resources available*, usually compared with one or more *past periods* and *showing future requirements*.
>
> (Smith and Lynch, 2003: 6, italics in original)

The development of government budgeting is linked with the rise of modern states in Western Europe because the governments needed bureaucratic systems to manage the increasing tax revenues they were collecting (Allen and Krause, 2013).

A PBE's budget is important because it translates policies, commitments and goals into decisions about taxes and other revenues. The use of a budget as a plan is the primary use of a budget, but other uses are explained later in this chapter.

If a PBE's purpose is to create public value then it would be appropriate for its plans to be formulated in order to meet its purpose. That being the case, a budget that properly reflected the organization's plans would, by definition, be an expression about how the organization will create public value. The budget, therefore, would need to capture the three elements of Moore's strategic triangle (1995) at least to the extent of the organization's capability to create public value. This means that we can think of a budget triangle (see Figure 2.1) as a parallel of Moore's strategic triangle. Where Moore's triangle has operational capacity, authorizing environment and a publicly valuable purpose as its points, here the three points are, respectively:

- the level of income and borrowing, which is what determines the capacity of the organization (which must be less than the operational capacity because it does not include the co-producers' budgets);

- approval, by the organization's highest level of governance (which may or may not include publicly elected officials); and
- the planned expenditure and investment, which will be the resources that are to be converted into goods and services that are valued by the public.

FEATURES OF BUDGETING IN THE PUBLIC SECTOR

The OECD (2022) has identified ten principles of budgetary governance that are relevant to the budgets of governments and other PBEs. The principles are listed in Box 2.1.

BOX 2.1 THE TEN PRINCIPLES OF BUDGETARY GOVERNANCE

1. Manage budgets within clear, credible and predictable limits for fiscal policy.
2. Closely align budgets with the medium-term strategic priorities of government.
3. Design the capital budgeting framework in order to meet national development needs in a cost-effective and coherent manner.
4. Ensure that budget documents and data are open, transparent and accessible.
5. Provide for an inclusive, participative and realistic debate on budgetary choices.
6. Present a comprehensive, accurate and reliable account of the public finances.
7. Actively plan, manage and monitor budget execution.
8. Ensure that performance, evaluation and value for money are integral to the budget process.
9. Identify, assess and manage prudently longer-term sustainability and other fiscal risks.
10. Promote the integrity and quality of budgetary forecasts, fiscal plans and budgetary implementation through rigorous quality assurance, including independent audit.

In a government or other PBE it is the executive's responsibility to prepare and submit a draft or proposed budget and the legislature's (or governing body's) responsibility to approve the budget. There is a wide spectrum of difference in the actual arrangements: 'a reflection not only of differences in the budget system but also of the differences in political, administrative, legal and cultural arrangements' (Lienert, 2013: 63–4).

It can take several months, often more than six, to prepare the budget and the process swallows up a significant amount of resources in the process. The indicative budget calendar for Rwanda's government, for example, runs from September to the end of June, for a financial year beginning in July (Government of Rwanda, 2019: 37–43). Myanmar begins its state (regional) and union (national) government budgeting work in January, nine months ahead of the financial year beginning on 1 October.

City governments can also find themselves involved in very long budget preparation processes. Cape Town Council, for example, began work on its 2019/20 budget (the financial year beginning on 1 July 2019) in May 2018. That was 13 months' work on a one-year budget (City of Cape Town, 2019: 62).

At the national level, the minister of finance (the Chancellor of the Exchequer in the United Kingdom) uses the annual budget statement in part to state their view about key economic items to set tax policy and tax rates and to state the government's spending plans, usually analysed by government ministry or department and non-departmental public body (NDPB). After approval by Parliament the budget figures filter down into budgets for regional government offices, hospitals, local councils and so on and the national budget figures can be used as control totals.

Typically, the PBEs that comprise the public sector in the broadest sense (ministries, local governments, state-owned enterprises and so on) would have a similar process. There would be less emphasis on managing the economy in the budget formulation stage but there would be a consideration of how the economy is expected to impact on the levels of income (whether from taxes, grants or service fees) and expenditure (demography, demands from politicians, the general public or service users). It is important, too, that the budget reflects the organization's service plans. Ideally: 'The organization [should integrate] financial planning with strategic and service planning processes on a medium to long-term basis' (Audit Commission, 2009).

A PBE's finance director/chief finance officer might regard the budget process as more important than producing the statements of account at the end of each year. They and their staff are certainly more visible when engaged in the dialogue and modelling of the budget than when they are engaged in the bookkeeping work of the final accounts process.

Politics of budgeting

Budgeting in the public sector is inevitably political. At all levels of the public sector, budgeting is characterized by scarcity and uncertainty. Lienert (2013: 94) wrote: 'At its heart, budgeting is a political conflict over scarce resources,' and Anessi-Pessina et al. (2016) noted that public sector budgets are for sharing power and well as resources.

The budget process is about allocating resources to competing priorities and issues of fairness or social justice come into it. Wildavsky (1961: 187) summed it up: 'Most practical budgeting may take place in a twilight zone between politics and efficiency.' Even if the process is in a twilight zone the budget that emerges tells the public something about the political priorities. When campaigning to be vice president of the United States in 2008, Joe Biden used this: 'Don't tell me what you value. Show me your budget and I will tell you what you value.'

This is perhaps most obvious at the national government level where policies on who and what is taxed and which services will be provided inevitably redistribute resources in the economy. The redistribution might be from rich to poor or between regions, between generations, between workers and non-workers. Whatever the redistribution, it makes public budgeting critically important to citizens and businesses.

When decisions are made about the allocation of resources there will inevitably be winners and losers. This dichotomy can be clearly seen in the budget-setting processes by governments in many countries as various groups of citizens voice their support or opposition to specific budget proposals. There is, therefore, a practical limit to the amount of taxes citizens will pay in even the wealthiest of countries, placing a limit on the size of the public budgets, and yet the demand for public services will exceed what is affordable.

That budgeting is a political process is obvious and explicit in the case of national and local governments where the approval of the budget is constitutionally the duty of elected MPs or councillors. In organizations like schools, hospitals and NGOs there may not be elected representatives making up the governing body in full but the process of agreeing a plan for forthcoming year (or longer) will be political. As Wildavsky put it:

> If politics is regarded in part as conflict over whose preferences shall prevail in the determination of policy, then the budget records the outcomes of this struggle.
>
> Wildavsky (1984: 4)

One axis of conflict is between what Wildavsky (1984) referred to as spenders and guardians. Spenders want PBEs to spend more and deliver more services and guardians (referred to as conservers by Liniert, 2013) want PBEs to spend as little as possible. Any stakeholder in a budget process could adopt either of these mindsets, but Wildavsky suggested an institutional aspect. Stakeholders from the line ministries, and equivalents, are likely to be spenders because they are associated with the programmes where the spending happens. Stakeholders from the Treasury/Ministry of Finance or other central finance department are likely to be guardians, aiming to exert some overall control over the size and scope of the budget. Wildavsky saw benefits from these countervailing roles.

> Administrative agencies act as advocates of increased expenditure, and central control organs function as guardians of the treasury. Each expects the other to do its job; agencies can advocate, knowing the center will impose limits, and the center can exert control, knowing that agencies will push expenditures as hard as they can. Thus roles serve as calculating mechanisms.
>
> (Wildavsky, 1975: 7)

Form and content of a budget

Whilst PBEs could prepare budgets in any way they wish, good practice is to follow the classical rules of budgetary theory (Jones and Pendlebury (2010: 86), which are summarized in Box 2.2.

BOX 2.2 THE CLASSICAL RULES OF BUDGETARY THEORY

Unity—that there is one budget for the organization as a whole and it is against that budget that spending is controlled.

Balanced budget—the whole of the spending must be balanced by income, and ultimately the organization's expenditure (net of any income from fees and charges and ring-fenced grants) will be financed from taxation.

Non-hypothecation of income—the taxation is collected by the organization as a whole to finance the budget as a whole.

Gross expenditure principle—a budget-holder's budget will separately show the gross expenditure and the gross income from fees and charges, etc. (if relevant) so that the central financial department is determining separately how the budget-holder should be spending money from how they should be collecting income. This prevents the budget-holder from netting-off additional expenditure against additional income.

Annuality—the authorized budget is for a period of a year and the authorized expenditure must take place during that year.

Specification—the central financial department or chief finance officer specifies, in detail, the rules that budget-holders must follow and, inter alia, these rules may or may not allow an element of virement of budget items.

In a PBE the budget tends to be developed at the same level of detail as the recording of income and expenditure in the general ledger. This contributes in part to why the process takes a lot of time and resources. Allen and Krause (2013: 125) show the differences in the level of detail of budget submitted to legislatures range from fewer than 200 lines to more than 34,000 (Turkey). The right level of detail needs to be judged in context.

> It is not possible to provide guidelines for the optimal number of line items. On the one hand, when there are more than, say, 1,000 lines, the transparency of the budget's main objectives is undermined; simplification of the budget's structure may be useful. On the other hand, if appropriations are too aggregate, [...] control could be undermined unless the outcome- or programme-based budgets are also accompanied by adequate explanatory notes on planned and actual spending.
>
> (Allen and Krause, 2013: 125)

When a draft budget is presented to the legislature or governors of a PBE it is likely to be accompanied by a number of supporting documents (which may be prescribed in the relevant law or constitution, or simply be expected/requested by the legislature or governors). Lienert (2013: 73) suggests that these supporting documents would include:

- a budget policy statement that explains the strategic priorities that have been incorporated into the draft budget, ideally with an analysis of the impact on the budget of major policy changes;
- information about the main assumptions underpinning the draft budget figures (such as interest rates and forecasts for pay and price inflation);
- a statement on financial risks that could include sensitivity analysis about the main assumptions as well as information about guarantees and contingent liabilities;
- comparison of the draft budget with the budget for the current year and actual income and expenditure in the previous year; and
- a medium-term financial strategy that shows estimated income and expenditure for the next two years, if not longer.

The draft budget might also be accompanied by longer-term financial projections, covering ten years or more (Lienert, 2013: 73). This is perhaps more likely to be the case for governments that may wish to be informed about macroeconomic and demographic projections in order to consider potential future policy changes.

The budget information can be presented in objective and/or subjective terms. The objective view is where income and expenditure are analysed in terms of the outputs, programmes, services and/or projects that will be delivered. The subjective view analyses the budget in terms of inputs such as employee costs, premises costs, etc. Table 2.1 gives an example of the top level of the two views for a university. For each of the high-level groupings there would be further levels of analysis that would allow for more detail to be recorded in the financial

Table 2.1 *Objective and subjective analysis for a university*

Objective analysis	*Subjective analysis*
	Expenditure
Academic departments	Employees
Administration and support services	Premises-related expenses
Student services	Supplies and services
Residences	Transport-related expenses
Catering and conferences	Capital financing charges
	Income
	Grant income
	Income from fees and charges
	Sales
	Income from investments
	Internal recharges

system. he objective analysis by faculty could be further analysed into individual departments and then further analysed into courses. Similarly, in the subjective view, employee expenses could be analysed into teaching staff, management and support staff and then teaching staff might be analysed into salaries, employer taxes, pension contributions and training expenses.

Generally speaking, an external audience is likely to be more interested in the objective view rather than the subjective. Taxpayers are perhaps more interested in seeing when the budget is analysed into the amounts to be expended on services like education and waste collection rather than how much is to be expended on staff or premises in global terms. The subjective analysis, on the other hand, is perhaps more useful for internal audiences. For example, the top management team may be interested to know the proportion of spending that is related to staffing or premises or payments to contractors.

Equality, diversity and inclusion

Governments and PBEs are involved in the delivery of a wide range of programmes and services that we might regard as aspects of social justice. The 17 interlinked global goals of the SDGs (United Nations, n.d.) also envisage that a sustainable future involves social justice. In particular, SDG 5 is about achieving gender equality, SDG 10 aims to reduce inequality and SDG 16 is about promoting just, peaceful and inclusive societies. If these goals are to be achieved by the global community, then governments need to reflect them in their budgets. Civil society organizations, such as the International Budget Partnership (https://internationalbudget.org), are alive to this and seek to improve public budgeting in terms of credibility, equity, justice and sustainability.

On the premise that PBEs' budgets allocate resources to priorities, it follows that it should be possible to analyse published budgets to ascertain whether they actually reflect the stated priorities. At the micro level an individual might do this to discover how much has been allocated to a service or project that they are interested in. At a macro level researchers could analyse government budgets to see how consistent they are with, for example, the government's obligations under the Universal Declaration of Human Rights (www.un.org/en/documents/udhr/) or the SDGs or any other stated priority.

Gender-responsive budgeting

Gender-responsive budgeting 'seeks to include a gender perspective at all stages of the budgetary process to promote equality throughout activities carried out by governments' (Polzer, 2022). Gender budgeting is an umbrella term for the specific tools that could be used by a government or PBE to incorporate a gender perspective into budget formulation and the other stages of the PFM cycle (Galizzi, Meliou and Steccolini, 2021: 499).

Gender budgeting initiatives go back to the 1990s but it is much more recently that the concept has received greater attention, and there has been more discussion about the need to integrate it into the mainstream budgeting and financial reporting processes. However, PEFA (2021) reported gender budgeting was not a mainstream feature of PFM in most countries.

Some countries have made advances in developing and implementing gender-responsive budgeting and it has been successful in some places at some times. Galizzi, Meliou and Steccolini (2021) give agriculture as one sector where there has been some success, as well as a general increase in the awareness of gender equality as an issue in public policy and PFM.

Curristine, Tchelishvili and Weerathunga (2022) specifically note that all the countries in the G20 intergovernmental forum have implemented gender-focused financial policies but 'too few countries assess the upfront impact of policies on gender or evaluate their effectiveness ex-post'.

Gender budgeting is not the preserve of high-income countries. Sushant and Laha (2021), for example, analysed gender budgeting of government departments in India since the country's first gender budget statement was published in 2005.

The budget process is part of the culture of an organization, setting or reflecting the way things are done in the organization. Organization culture has a role to play in gender budgeting. Rubin and Bartle (2021) identified five factors that help gender budgeting to take hold in a public organization. They are:

- Key decision-makers must acknowledge gender inequities and see budget policy as a tool to promote gender equity.

- There must be a legal basis for gender equity.
- The Ministry of Finance is a crucial source of institutional support, often providing line ministries with training, guidelines and expertise to perform the necessary gender analysis.
- Gender-disaggregated data must be available to assess the differential gender impacts of policies and programmes.
- Civil society provides organizational support in the implementation of gender budgeting.

Participatory budgeting

Participatory budgeting is an approach to making budget decisions that makes sense only in respect of PBE budgets and, even then, probably only for a specific element of the budget.

Participatory budgeting goes further than just informing or consulting the general public about budget proposals. A participatory budgeting system is one that enables citizens to come up with ideas for projects to be financed from public money. The Participatory Budgeting Project (2022) explains how participatory budgeting works in five steps:

1. A steering committee representing the community **designs the process** in terms of rules and an engagement plan.
2. Residents **brainstorm ideas** and share them.
3. Volunteers **develop feasible proposals** from the ideas.
4. Residents **vote** on the proposals that best serve the community.
5. The government/public agency **fund the winning proposals** and implement them.

The projects that get the most support in an organized vote are implemented by the relevant public agency. This is explained at www.participatorybudgeting.org/how-pb-works/.

There are very many examples of participatory budgeting in Brazil, where it started in the city of Porto Alegre in 1989 and had spread to another 80 municipalities by the late 1990s (de Sousa Santos, 1998). There are examples in a wide range of OECD countries, including Belgium, Canada, Germany, Italy, Mexico, the United Kingdom and the United States (Caddy, Peixoto and McNeil, 2007; Babcock et al., 2008) and Dias (2018) has articles relating to examples on every continent (except Antarctica). And Professor Greg Clark (BBC, 2019) claimed it has been used in 30,000 cities for at least some of the budget.

Participatory budgeting is consistent with the principles of co-production and the 'public governance' paradigm. The public organization engages with local people to understand the problems and identify solutions. The outcome of the process is a budget that marries the public's views of what matters to them (i.e., what they value) with the organization's capacity. In other words, it results in a plan to create public value. The process takes time and commitment from the PBE, public managers, politicians and community members, and often it will take a full year of public meetings and so on to complete the full process.

Participatory budgeting is often done at a very local level to allocate funding to projects affecting a geographical community. The approach can work particularly well for the rationing of capital investment or a specific, earmarked fund.

The scale of a participatory budgeting can be bigger than a city ward. For example, the whole budget of the City of Vallejo in California was subject to a participatory budget exercise in 2012. The process was implemented to allocate the US$3.28 million receipts from a local sales tax. Twelve projects were chosen from over 800 for implementation in 2013/14 (the financial year began in July 2013). The largest amounts were allocated to improvements to parks and recreation facilities (US$621,500), potholes and street repairs (US$550,000), installation of a pilot closed circuit television scheme (US$450,000) and a scheme to give college scholarships in return for students doing community work for the city (US$320,000) (City of Vallejo, 2014: 22). The City Council regards the project as a great success in meeting the three goals it set: to improve the City of Vallejo, to engage the community and to transform democracy. As a result, it allocated US$2.4 million in the 2014/5 financial year for projects selected through a second cycle of participatory budgeting.

Participatory budgeting has the advantage of bringing credibility and public ownership of the budget of an organization. It also means that the budget will respond to changes in the public's demand for services. Whilst responsiveness is often seen as a good thing it may be seen as volatility and fickleness. A participative budget could result in capricious changes in the budget from year to year depending on which members of the public get involved and what is on their collective mind. This is not such a concern if the budgets that are subject to participation are discretionary, capital budgets which are, by their nature, likely to change from year to year; it would be a risk, though, if a PBE used participation to allocate its core operating budget or even to fund a multi-year project. The reason for the latter being excluded from participatory budgeting systems is the fact that it would commit some, perhaps much, of the budget in future years, effectively reducing the choices available to citizens in future rounds of participatory budgeting.

The potential problem of volatility can be exacerbated by the fact that within the scope of an organization's budget there may be a high interest in some issues and very little interest in others. This could result in the skewing of the public's attention towards some specific elements of the budget.

To enable the broadest participation a public organization needs to be able to communicate what the issues are and the implications of alternative approaches to resolving them. There is a risk of over-simplifying complex issues and thereby appearing to devalue the knowledge and experience of professionals. It is easy to imagine, for instance, that public participation in setting a police service budget would focus on creating a more visible presence of police officers patrolling the streets despite senior police officer's assertions that it would be less effective at reducing crime than less visible, intelligence-led police work.

Budgeting is more significant in the public sector than the private sector

Budgets are important in the management of any organization, but there are a number of arguments that budgeting is more important in public and third sector organizations than in profit-making organizations. There are three broad aspects of budgeting that are generally more significant in the public sector:

- budgeting as part of the accountability process;
- consultation and stakeholder participation; and
- budgeting as a financial health indicator.

Budgeting as part of the accountability process

As we shall see in Chapter 8, accountability is an extremely important factor in public financial management. There is a tendency to conceive of accountability as backwards-looking judgement; someone gives an account of what they have done after they have done it. When it comes to public money, however, there is a requirement to give an account of what you plan to do as well as what you have done. This is connected with the expectation of taxpayers to know what they are paying for but the publication and scrutiny of budgets goes beyond organizations that have tax-raising powers.

There are parts of the public sector where budgets are subject to audit and assurance checks. In the 1980s there was a spate of local authorities in the United Kingdom who refused to set balanced budgets and, as a result, all local authorities' chief finance officers are required by law to state their opinion about whether the budget being considered by the full council meeting is balanced and sustainable. This puts a professional and personal responsibility on the chief finance officer to ensure that budgets are not constructed on unrealistic assumptions. At times when significant cuts are required by local authorities the temptation can arise to defer unpleasant decisions and include in the budget a generic item of 'efficiency savings to be identified' or similar, but the requirement for the chief finance officer to state the budget is balanced mitigates against this happening. A plan would have to be in place for the savings to be realized if the amounts are to be included in the budget.

External auditors of many public organizations would include a review of expenditure against the budget as well as comparing it with the actual expenditure in previous years. This is not strictly necessary to reach an opinion about whether the organization's accounts present a fair view of its financial affairs, but it allows the auditor to form a view about the quality of the budget in the first place and the ability of the organization to control its expenditure during the financial year.

The budget of a private sector organization is an internal affair. It will be used as the basis of monitoring income and expenditure for each cost centre and profit centre and there are few circumstances where a company might share any part of its budget with external parties. It does happen, for example, in the form of a business case that might be shared with a potential lender or in a prospectus for raising finance. Also listed companies are obliged to provide profit forecasts to the Stock Exchange.

Things are different in the public sector: many organizations publish their budgets before the year commences and many also publish their performance against their budget after the year has ended. The extent of the publication of budget information varies across the public sector but the expectation is set at the top with the government's budget statements. Immediately after the Chancellor of the Exchequer has made their statement to Parliament a wealth of information is available from the Office of Budget Responsibility (https://budgetresponsibility.org.uk), including the high-level spending plans, for capital investment and operating expenditure, for each government department (in the form of Departmental Expenditure Limits). Something similar will be available in many countries after the minister of finance has delivered the budget speech to parliament/the legislature.

The other organizations in the United Kingdom with tax-raising powers are local authorities and they are required by law to include information about their budgets with the council tax and non-domestic rates bills that are issued to citizens and businesses, respectively, each March. Even where a PBE does not routinely publish any information about its budget the public could discover it through a request under the Freedom of Information Act 2000.

Another difference about PBEs is that, not only do they measure their performance against budget, but they publish it, too. Private sector organizations would monitor their performance against budget but the requirement to publish financial statements requires only the comparison of information with the previous accounting year. The public would never know, in general, what level of turnover and profit the organization had budgeted for, the exception being listed companies that would publish forecasts, and even these would be updated during the year rather than be the budgeted figures from the beginning of the year. In the public sector, however, there is a tendency to publish the actual level of expenditure against the budgeted amounts.

Consultation and stakeholder participation

The extent of public consultation about budgets differs across the public sector. There is no formal consultation by the government about the national budget. Indeed, quite the opposite occurs with the UK Chancellor's proposals being kept secret until the announcement to Parliament. In local government, however, there is a legal duty to consult representatives of non-domestic ratepayers and many local authorities have made efforts to consult with local residents, too. This might be in the form of public meetings, focus groups and online surveys. The aim of the consultation is to improve the ownership and understanding of the local authority's budget, but these goals are difficult to achieve. The funding of a PBE can be complicated and the implications of changes in the level of expenditure on services is not necessarily easy to comprehend. A lot of effort is required, therefore, to ensure that the public participants in a consultation process understand what they are being consulted about.

Also, to be blunt, if a PBE is carrying out consultation on its budget then, to be meaningful, there has to be enough time for changes to be made to the draft budget. If no changes could possibly be made then the exercise is closer to market research than consultation.

THE USE OF BUDGETS

By definition budgets are plans but they have more uses than just planning. Budgets can also be used for:

- authorizing managers to incur expenditure;
- measuring performance;
- controlling;
- communicating; and
- motivating managers.

These uses are described in more detail below.

Authorizing expenditure

Once formally approved and adopted by the organization, the budget becomes an authorizing document in the budget execution stage of the PFM cycle. The budget translates the organization's policies and strategies into financial terms but it is the managers who have to implement them, and not implement something different. The budget gives the public manager (budget-holder) the authority to spend a maximum amount on salaries, services, projects, etc. in order to meet their organization's goals and, by implication, the budget does not give them authority to spend money on anything else.

In practice, organizations have to have some emergency provisions in their budget execution procedures to cover unforeseen, emergency situations where there are imminent threats to life or property. The COVID-19 pandemic is a recent and dramatic example where public managers were faced with spending pressures not envisaged when their budgets were approved. This can be approached in different ways. Some governments and organizations would change the budget to accommodate the newly created plans for dealing with the crisis. Other governments and organizations would instead permit the public managers to spend what they need to spend, effectively giving them authority to exceed the approved budget. The IMF (2020) recognized the latter approach could be adopted for the COVID-19 crisis when it wrote, 'Do whatever it takes, but keep the receipts.' There is more about making in-year changes to a budget later in this chapter.

The delegation of financial responsibility away from accountants and administrators and to the public managers who deliver the services is a key element of NPM. This practice is evident in primary health care, in hospital wards, in schools and many other public institutions. Wherever an organization delegates responsibility it needs to do so in a clear way and the budget assists in this. The budget sets out the total amount that a manager is authorized to spend to deliver the services and/or projects that they are responsible for. There will be a spending limit for the full year but there may also be a limit for each month and, if appropriate, there might also be an income budget that the manager is expected to meet, too.

In the public sector budgets tend to be very detailed and the internal rules and regulations not only limit a manager's authorization to incur expenditure at the aggregate level of their budget but also in terms of its components. If a budget includes a provision for salaries and wages the manager is not normally allowed to hire additional staff even if they make savings in other elements of their budgets. The obvious reason for this is that the organization may wish to use the underspend for something else and it should have the opportunity to make such a decision. Therefore, the organization will have formal financial procedure rules about how to make such transfers of budget (called virements). There might be some leeway in the rules for the transfer of small amounts to be approved by a senior manager but the most significant transfers would require approval at the political level.

This is quite different from the private sector where budget virements are not commonly used (vendors of commercial accounting software have to build into their systems the functionality to manage budget transfers in order to sell their product to PBEs). The reason for this is the difference in emphasis on cost control. PBEs have to control costs within the budgeted amount as a way of limiting service delivery. Private sector businesses are not limited in that way. For them, costs are controlled in the context of their sales revenues. If they sell more products than they budgeted they will spend overspend their production budgets, too, but it would not be a problem providing the sales revenue exceeds the production costs because they would make more profit than they budgeted to make. In practice, a business can flex its budgets based on the activity volume and use the flexed budget as a tool for controlling the associated expenses.

Generally speaking, most PBEs are not in a position where their income varies as their activity volume varies and for them a static budget, rather than a flexible budget, makes more sense because it reflects the reality that their spending has to stay within its income regardless of the volume of activity. A public manager is more likely, therefore, to adjust the volume of activity to stay within the budget than seek a change to the budget. This is what leads, for example, to one hospital closing some wards or clinics towards the end of a financial year whilst another hospital can spend extra money on new equipment that was not planned in the budget.

Measuring performance

Budgets can be used for performance measurement. At the end of each month or quarter or year, it is possible to compare the expenditure actually incurred against the budgeted amount and, potentially, compare the planned outputs of services and/or goods against the actual outputs. This is the basis of the performance budgeting approach described later in this chapter.

Something that is perhaps more significant in the public sector than the private sector is the extent of analysis of performance against the budget. Private firms seldom publish their budgets (although they may be obliged to provide profit forecasts to the stock market) and when they publish their actual performance, they tend to compare it with the actual performance in the previous corresponding period. Public organizations compare their budgets with each other as evidenced by publications like CIPFA's Statistical Information Service (www.cipfa.org/services/cipfastats).

In the public sector it is common for an organization to compare its actual spending against the budget. Indeed, the International Public Sector Accounting Standards expect this comparison to be included in PBEs' annual reports (see Chapter 8). Interesting as this might be, it tells the public very little. Where actual spending is close to the budget it might be tempting to conclude that the organization had its affairs under tight control but that might or might not be the case. The actual spending in aggregate may disguise widespread overspending and underspending that happen to cancel each other out. And where there are large variations between budget estimates and actual spending, are they the result of poor budgeting, poor expenditure control or both?

Budgeting as a financial health indicator

Assessing a PBE's ability to create and manage budgets is one way to assess its overall financial management effectiveness. In the UK's Comprehensive Performance Assessment regime in the 2000s, the Audit Commission's assessment of local authorities' use of resources was based on key lines of enquiry (KLOEs) and three of the ten KLOEs related to managing finances (Audit Commission, 2009).

The PEFA framework was briefly outlined in Chapter 1. As you can see below, items 1, 2 and 3 of the seven pillars are related to the budget formulation and approval stages of the PFM cycle.

1. **Budget reliability**—the budget is realistic and is implemented as intended.
2. **Transparency of public finances**—information on PFM is comprehensive, consistent and accessible to users.
3. **Management of assets and liabilities**—public investments provide value for money, assets are recorded and managed, fiscal risks are identified and debts and guarantees are prudently planned, approved and monitored.
4. **Policy-based fiscal strategy and budgeting**—the budget is prepared with due regard to government policy.
5. **Predictability and control in budget execution**—the budget is implemented in an orderly and predictable manner and there are arrangements for the exercise of control and stewardship in the use of public funds.
6. **Accounting, recording and reporting**—adequate records and information are produced, maintained and disseminated to meet decision-making control, management and reporting purposes.
7. **External scrutiny and audit**—arrangements for scrutiny of public finances and follow up by executive are operating.

(PEFA Secretariat, 2016: 2)

Since 2001 over 300 PEFA assessments have been done in 144 countries (www.pefa.org). Almost all of the assessments have been done in low- and middle-income countries. Matt Andrews (2013a) used data from PEFA assessments to identify three types of gaps in the public financial management arrangements of developing countries:

- the de facto gap—where the laws and regulations are strong and meet good practice standards but their implementation and enforcement is weak;
- the deconcentrated gap—where central organizations like the finance ministry are strong and well-managed but decentralized/regional organizations are weaker; and
- the downstream gap—where budget development is stronger than budget execution.

Controlling

The approved budget is the basis of the control of expenditure and is thus an important element of the overall system of management control in an organization. This control can be implemented at every level of the organization because expenditure can be monitored for every business unit and project and aggregated into departments or divisions all the way up to the corporate total.

It is not sufficient to control the budget on an annual basis. Generally, the budget for a full year would be separated into monthly budgets, which enables control of expenditure closer to the time when it is incurred. The monthly budgets might be equal twelfths of the full year budget but more sophisticated systems would profile the budget across the year based on the expectation of when expenditure would be incurred. For example, a budget for heating and lighting costs would be higher in winter months and lower in the summer, whereas the budget for grounds maintenance would have the opposite profile. There is more about how this is done in Chapter 4.

Communicating

A budget is a useful communication tool. At the corporate level it can communicate the organization's plans to the public and other external stakeholders. For PBEs there is often an expectation, sometimes even a legal obligation, to provide a summary of the budget to the public. UK local authorities are required by law to present a summary of their operating and capital budgets to taxpayers as part of their council tax bill. The corporate budget may also be communicated internally to staff to help them understand the organization's plans and direction. Arguably this is most important in the change management process to help staff and service users understand the need for change.

Motivating managers

An organization may seek to use its budgets as a motivator for staff. This is perhaps more easily and directly achievable in a private sector company, such as a retail chain, where it may set budgets for each branch in the form of sales or profit targets to motivate branch managers. The company might also attach performance bonuses to the achievement of the targets.

PBEs are generally not structured in the same way as private companies and competition between teams or units to meet performance targets or the payment of bonuses for achieving performance targets is typically not part of their culture. In such organizations the budget tends to be expressed in terms of inputs and the manager is charged with delivering outputs or outcomes. There is the question of whether a manager should be motivated to spend all the budget and claim that the outputs delivered are the maximum possible or should be motivated to deliver the targeted level of output whilst spending as little as possible. This boils down to: should managers be motivated to be effective or efficient? Put like this, politicians and the public would be tempted to answer, 'Both.'

Even if an organization does not seek to use its budgets as a motivator it may have to avoid its budgets being a de-motivator. It is easy to imagine a situation where challenging economic times results in a public manager's budget being cut. Given that the public manager (probably) believes the service they deliver is important and valued by its recipients they are surely going to find it a challenge to feel motivated by a budget cut because they may infer it means their service is less important than others.

The link between motivation and performance is complex, being connected with the psychological contract, pay levels, hours worked, power and so on. The level of motivation for an individual manager that arises from the budget may depend on the extent of their inclusion and engagement in the budgeting process and their ownership of the resultant budget (even when it has been cut).

ALTERNATIVE METHODS OF BUDGETING

Producing a budget for an organization might be regarded as finding a solution to a problem. As for any other management problem there are different ways of solving it. This section describes three broad methods to budget formulation that a public organization might adopt. First, we will consider the incremental budgeting methods and then the more rational approach of zero-based budgeting. Third, performance budgeting is considered, which is an umbrella term for a number of approaches, including programme budgeting, output-based and outcome-based budgeting, with an emphasis on linking budget allocations to performance.

The distinctions between these three budgeting methods are not hard and fast and PBEs may change their approach from year to year, or even adopt hybrids that have features of more than one method.

Top-down or bottom-up budgeting?

Top-down budgeting is when senior management set the budgets and targets, with little involvement of their service managers. When a central government sets budgets and targets for local governments and other PBEs, without much involvement of the organizations, that is also a top-down approach.

Top-down budgeting enables senior management to communicate plans to staff, coordinate the activities of the organization and facilitate the setting of performance targets. Its major disadvantage is the risk of reducing motivation and commitment to the budget.

Bottom-up budgeting is when the budget is initially drafted by the individual service managers (or by the local governments/PBEs) and consolidated and refined by senior management (or central government). This approach means there is greater stakeholder involvement in the budget preparation process, which can result in greater commitment to the budget. It also benefits from the stakeholder's knowledge and experience. On the other hand, it is more time-consuming and individuals/subordinate organizations may set relatively generous or undemanding budgets for themselves.

One might expect that bottom-up budgeting gives the participants an incentive to overestimate costs. As the budget builds up from business units into divisions and departments the overestimation within it grows and grows. There is no guarantee that the top-level management will drive out all of the overestimation resulting in the final budget that is not as efficient as it could have been. Indeed, this scenario may be the case in some organizations, but Ehrhart et al. (2007: 293) found that 'there is no general tendency for top-down budget process to deliver smaller budgets' and that the sequence in which budgetary decisions are taken affects the budget that ensues.

Incremental budgeting

Incremental budgeting is probably the most basic method of budget preparation, and it is used by organizations in the public and private sectors. In terms of problem-solving, it is finding a solution by assuming that the solution that worked last time must be nearly right for this time and adjusting it here and there until it fits.

Incremental budgeting taps into the way one often thinks about the future; by looking at the past and identifying what has changed or is likely to change for the budget period. Essentially, incremental budgeting is a process where the budget for the upcoming period (usually a year) is derived by taking the budget for the current period, the 'base budget', and updating it for expected changes. The changes might include:

- the effects of new or changed policies, whether these are autonomously made by the organization or imposed on it by changes in the environment (such as a change in law or regulation);
- changes in demographics or other factors that impact on the demand for the services provided by the organization. For example, changes in the age profile of a local population affect the provision of health care services whereas changes in the number of dwellings affects the cost of collecting and disposing of refuse;
- changes in payroll costs because of pay settlements, the progression of individual members of staff along their pay grade and/or changes to cost of the employer's contributions for national insurance or pension funds;
- price inflation for goods or services used by the organization. Price inflation may be estimated as a general rate to be applied across all goods and services or separate inflation rates may be used for distinct classes of goods and services, such as a rate for fuel costs, a rate for office expenses and a rate for food supplies;
- changes in income levels that might result from changes in tax bases and tax rates, changes in the level of grants receivable by the organization, the level fees to be charged for services and/or a change in the expected level of usage of services.

A general description of the process of incremental budgeting in a PBE is set out below; first, there is an example of the bidding-type of process for preparing a capital programme and, second, an example of how the financial planning–type of process could be used for operating budgets.

Bidding approach to incremental budgeting

Bidding is the most departmental approach to budgeting. If it were being used for the development of a capital programme the organization would first identify the total estimated resources that are available to finance capital expenditure over the period of the capital programme (usually a minimum of three years but may be longer). Next, the amount of resources required by capital projects that are already included in the capital programme as commitments is deducted from the total resources, leaving the amount available for new projects.

Once the available resources are known the departments will be invited to submit bids for inclusion in the capital programme. The bids could be as simple as the name of a project and an estimate of the cost but they are likely to be developed a bit further, into an outline business case that demonstrates the need for the project and the expected benefits.

Once all the bids are received, they will be assessed by the treasury/finance department against a set of evaluation criteria. The criteria could be things like meeting legal requirements, potential to generate savings in ongoing operating expenditure, relevance to politician's official manifesto and so on until a draft capital programme is completed. The draft programme would then go through the formal governance route to be approved.

As bids usually exceed available resources the process will result in a number of bids being rejected by the treasury/finance department, although some of them could be kept on a reserve list to be added into the programme if problems arise with any of the approved projects.

Financial planning approach to incremental budgeting

The financial planning approach to incremental budgeting does not have the same free-for-all as a bidding process. It is characterized by having a medium-term expenditure framework (MTEF) or medium-term financial strategy as a guide to the process and the integrated production of capital and operating budgets. The MTEF would have been based on estimates of resources and inflation and would reflect previously determined commitments. Using the MTEF as a basis, expenditure guidelines would be produced for each ministry or department (or whatever business units comprise the organization) advising them how they should prepare their first draft of the budget for the following year. The guidelines will include assumptions to use for things like pay awards and interest rates; information about policy commitments that should be budgeted for, usually including a maximum value that will be allowed; and how to incorporate the operating costs of capital projects that are due for completion.

The first draft of the budget is often a 'standstill budget'. Strictly speaking, a standstill budget is the estimated cost of doing next year exactly what is being done this year. The first draft of the budget in the financial planning approach may not quite be a standstill budget in this strict sense because if there were new commitments (which might growth or cuts) already contained in the MTEF they will be included in the first draft of the budget. What is meant by a standstill budget in such circumstances is the budget for doing next year what was assumed in the MTEF. In other words, it is the budget before any ***new*** decisions are made.

In respect of any such new decisions, the estimated cost of changes in law, policy, demand for services and so on will be identified. These will be considered for funding if there is any space between the estimated level of resources (from taxes, grants or whatever) for the government/PBE and the standstill budget.

Often the difference is the other way around, and estimated expenditure exceeds the estimated resources. The budget therefore has to be revised and a list of savings (cuts in expenditure and/or increases in income) prepared for consideration. There may then be a process of iteration as some proposals are accepted and others rejected until, eventually, a budget arrived at that is affordable in terms of available resources and acceptable in policy terms.

Depending on the culture of the organization, its formal constitution and the stakeholders involved, the budget may be the subject of consultation with the public or other external stakeholders before it is submitted for formal approval.

Advantages of incremental budgeting

The first advantage of incremental budgeting is its relative simplicity, both to undertake and also to explain to stakeholders. The base budget should be easy to find and it has the legitimacy of having been approved by the organization's board or council in the first place. The process of adding to and taking away from the base budget amounts for new policies and other changes since the base budget was approved only needs to justify the amount being added or taken away. This also gives a sense of credibility.

Second, incremental budgeting produces a relatively stable budget. Perhaps as much as 90 per cent of the budget remains the same as the previous year. Politicians, in particular, like this stability because it saves them from having to explain radical changes to their constituents.

Disadvantages of incremental budgeting

The first disadvantage is a corollary of the first advantage listed above: there is no challenge to the base budget and the assumptions within it. Any errors and, importantly, any slack in the base budget will remain because there is (little or) no scrutiny of the base budget.

Second, incremental budgets have a high degree of inertia and it can be difficult to respond to radical changes in policy or the organization's environment when the budgeting process is concerned only with marginal changes. This can be seen in the response of organizations to dramatic reductions in funding as part of the austerity measures taken by governments since 2008. Incremental budgeting does not prioritize services very well and leads to organizations making across the board cuts to all services (an approach sometimes referred to as 'salami-slicing').

COVID-19 has changed the world in many ways and will have consequences for government spending for many years. Andrews (2021) is concerned that the tendency for governments to use incremental budgeting may not be up to the challenge: it will lead to doing more of what is currently done rather than doing new things.

> New spending usually builds incrementally on old spending, such that policies accumulate on top of existing activities instead of adding new ones. This happens because budget allocation processes are political, with spending allocations controlled by incumbent political claimants. These incumbents often even structure technical mechanisms to keep new claimants at bay.

Third, incremental budgeting is focused on inputs rather than outputs. It takes as a starting point that the organization employs so many people and uplifts the budget for the expected pay rise. This has no regard, for example, to whether there have been improvements in productivity that might give the organization the option to maintain the current level of output using few people (rather than the default of keeping the current number of people but paying them more).

The fourth weakness of incremental budgeting is its strong focus on departments/organizational units. This is perhaps stronger in the bidding version but it also applies to financial planning because the MTEF and budget guidelines will tend to be structured along departmental/organization lines. The nature of an incremental budget is to build it from the existing structure of departments and business units. Where an organization is a hierarchical bureaucracy, as PBEs classically are, draft budgets will filter up through the departmental structure to be aggregated into a corporate total from where it will be wrangled into a balanced budget for the whole organization. This means the corporate view tends to be seen as the sum of the departments rather than corporate policies and priorities being reflected by the departments.

Finally, incremental budgeting relies very much on information from line managers/ministries about the pressure on their programme or service area and associated costs. Clearly the line managers/ministries are not impartial and it will be tempting for them to seek to manipulate the process. They can do this fairly easily because of the fact that they have specialist knowledge that the finance department/ministry or finance does not have. One tactic would be to exaggerate the cost impact of a particular pressure; another would be not to admit to any known slack in the budget so that it can be kept in reserve in case the requested budget increases are not approved.

Despite its shortcomings and the alternative methods that are about to be described and which try to improve on it, incremental budgeting remains popular. As Allen Schick put it an Overseas Development Institute conference in 2013, 'the war between incrementalists and others will be over when everyone realises that incrementalism has won' (Andrews, 2013b). Nevertheless, there are alternative approaches to budgeting.

Zero-based budgeting

Zero-based budgeting (ZBB) was developed at Texas Instruments in the 1960s (Pyhrr, 1970) and, in terms of the problem-solving analogy, it is the equivalent of trying to forget how you have solved the problem before and starting with a blank sheet of paper.

Under a ZBB approach the organization will build up its budget for every activity and project from scratch every year, effectively justifying every item in the budget by reference to the organization's mission, objectives and policies. For example, a zero-based school budget would be based on the number of pupils enrolled in the school next year rather than beginning by adding a pay rise to the current cost of teachers' salaries.

Broadly, the steps in the ZBB method are:

1. **Identify decision units**—a decision unit is a single activity or a cluster of activities that can be separately identified. Depending on context a decision unit might be an institution or a department, or even a cost centre within a department. Each decision unit will have a manager (or managers) responsible for its budget, and they will need to justify all costs associated with the decision unit.
2. **Define decision packages**—decision packages are the specific activities within a decision unit. These decision packages should be in line with the overall strategy and objectives of the organization. They are effectively a bid for funding and resources from the organization, and they should contain details of how they meet their objectives, the consequences of not funding them and alternative courses of action available.

3. **Rank decision packages**—decision packages are prioritized by the decision unit managers using both financial and non-financial criteria to assess which packages best meet the aims of the decision unit and wider organization.
4. **Allocate resources**—decision packages that are higher up the ranking receive a higher level of funding, to reflect their greater potential to meet the goals of the decision units and organization. Decision packages towards the bottom of the ranking may not receive any funding at all, or if the service is statutory/essential, they will receive the minimum level of funding to provide the service.

Advantages of zero-based budgeting

ZBB addresses the key weakness of incremental budgeting by challenging everything in the base budget. That means the budget process is much more focused on policies and priorities than on inputs. It also means that the organization is less likely to resort to the salami-slicing of budgets at difficult times. Having constructed its budget by reference to priorities in difficult times the organization ought to be able to recognize the areas of its budget that are lower priority and focus its cuts on those areas. In effect, ZBB can find and cut out inefficiency within the organization and make scarce resources go further/achieve more.

Second, ZBB can foster the ownership of budgets by the managers because of their necessary involvement in constructing them. By definition, the managers will have assessed what activities they need to do to achieve the organization's objectives and estimated the cost of doing them. Thinking back to the uses of budgeting, ZBB may help create the conditions to motivate managers.

ZBB also has the advantage of enabling an organization to respond more quickly to changes in its environment or radical changes in policy because there is no assumption that anything in the current budget will be included in the new budget.

Disadvantages of zero-based budgeting

ZBB's dynamism is, of course, constrained by the frequency that an organization carries out its budgeting and this leads to ZBB's first disadvantage: it is a difficult and time-consuming process. Every budget-holder has to reconstruct their budget in accordance with the organization's priorities every year and the finance department/ministry has to coordinate all that activity and assemble the consolidated budget.

Second, for many organizations, particularly PBEs that deliver statutory public services, there are budgets that are 'locked-in'. These are aspects of their operation that are fundamental to their existence for which the ZBB approach would produce more or less the same result as an incremental approach. For example, a state school in the United Kingdom is constrained by legislation, the national curriculum, the expectations of its local education authority and the Office for Standards in Education, Children's Services and Skills (Ofsted) and its share of the total schools budget that is calculated by formula (which itself is, in practice, increased incrementally each year). In such circumstances, the school's head teacher and governors have little incentive to undertake a ZBB process because they will decide they need a certain number of teachers to meet the required pupil:teacher ratio and they will occupy the same school buildings and will have to pay the utility bills, and so.

Similarly, in the short term, a PBE is practically constrained by the assets it uses for service delivery. For example, the courts service will have hundreds of court premises located all around the country. If it were conducting a ZBB exercise it might identify that to meet its objectives it ought to have different premises. The chances are that the changes required to achieve this would be a medium- to long-term programme, which the organization would factor into its MTEF and capital programme. Meanwhile, it would have to produce operating budgets based on operating the service from the existing premises and it might as well do that using incremental budgeting.

Locked-in budgets can also result from the fact that funding of many public organizations operates in an incremental way, and ZBB is unlikely to result in significant changes in the expenditure budget year on year for no other reason than public organizations are unlikely to budget to spend differently from the income that they expect to receive.

Another issue associated with ZBB is that the process results in winners and losers each year and the chances are that the winners and losers are probably not the same each year. As Machiavelli (2009) put it: 'the innovator makes enemies of all those who prospered under the old order, and only lukewarm support is forthcoming from those who would prosper under the new.'

The organization has to manage the impact of the winners and losers. Therefore, whilst ZBB has the potential to motivate managers, it is not likely to motivate all of them all of the time.

Another possible problem for an organization that uses ZBB in a dynamic environment is that a decision package (that is, a programme or service) that is a low priority for a year or two may release/make redundant staff with valuable skills and experience only for the organization to require such skills and experience later if the decision package's priority rises. The organization will have to incur the costs of recruiting and training new staff to replace the staff that they previously released whilst also incurring costs to release staff from whichever area has then become the lower priority. Such transaction costs could be very significant.

A fourth criticism of ZBB is that stakeholders may see it as an exercise to revisit a problem that has previously been solved. A public manager may infer that ZBB ignores the experience and knowledge (or, indeed, wisdom) that went into producing existing budgets and this could lead to stakeholders not being fully committed to the ZBB process and/or striving to produce a budget that is similar to, if not the same as, the existing budget.

These disadvantages make ZBB better suited to occasional use or to focused use on specific programmes, services or functions (decision units) rather than being used for the full budget process every year.

Performance budgeting

Performance budgeting is, 'public sector funding mechanisms which use formal performance information to link funding to results (outputs and/or outcomes), with the aim of improving performance' (Robinson, 2013: 237). In terms of the problem-solving analogy, performance budgeting is a method where each year you try to find a better solution than previously whilst giving citizens a way of judging how well the solution worked.

Performance budgeting is a broad term encompassing a number of techniques/ methods and that means there is a variety of methods that may involve similar work in terms of budget formulation: one organization's programme budgeting process could be much the same as another's output- or outcome-based budgeting whilst another does priority-based budgeting.

Activity-based budgeting is also a form of performance budgeting that is an extension of the activity-based costing process described in Chapter 5. An activity-based budget is derived from the estimated cost of producing a unit of each of an organization's activities, multiplied by the expected number of units in the period. Dumfries and Galloway Council in Scotland produced an activity-based budget in 2018 and the Government of Estonia (n.d.) included it in its 2014–2020 PFM reform programme.

Performance budgeting goes further than incremental budgeting and ZBB because it explicitly incorporates performance measures and assessment. It seeks to integrate financial and performance information at the budget formulation stage of the PFM cycle so that the subsequent monitoring reports, in the budget execution stage, can also integrate budget monitoring with performance monitoring.

As it is a method for linking 'expected results with budget levels' (McGill, 2001: 377), it is well-suited for the NPM era and many governments and PBEs have adopted it, in some form or other.

> Linking budgets with performance is something that many developed and developing countries have done or are moving towards. Nearly all OECD countries have developed performance information and many have introduced procedures to integrate it into accountability, budgeting, and

> management processes. In many cases they have found it to be more difficult to use performance information in their budgeting than in their general management.
>
> (Cangiano, Curristine and Lazare, 2013: 11)

The difficulties does not mean that national governments and other PBEs are not adopting or seeking to adopt it for their PFM system. The Collaborative African Budget Initiative (CABRI) published a report in 2013 about the extent of progress by African countries in implementing performance and programme-based budgeting (PPBB). Of the 54 African countries studied two, Mauritius and South Africa, had fully functioning PPBB systems in place and 21 had made at least some progress. Twelve countries had begun reforms towards PPBB and 11 were committed to making reforms in the future by having passed a relevant law. This left only eight countries (including Eritrea, Libya, Somalia and South Sudan) that had not made any PPBB reforms (CABRI, 2013: 23).

Over in Asia, Pakistan announced in 2021 a medium-term performance-based budget covering three financial years (Afnan Alam, 2022). One reason for this change away from input-based budgeting was the negative impact that the COVID-19 pandemic had on the government's finances and public services. The hope is that the new system will make it easier for the government to deliver on policy priorities and commitments.

The OECD (2008) identified three categories of performance budgeting systems:

1. presentational performance budgeting;
2. performance-informed budgeting; and
3. direct performance budgeting.

In the first category the budget is presented along with performance information but there is no link between performance and the actual budget allocations. The performance information is contextual or background information.

Performance-informed budgeting systems allocate resources on the basis of past or future performance level. Performance information is therefore used in the budget formulation process but it is not the only factor and there is, in effect, a relatively loose, indirect link between performance and budgeting.

Direct performance budgeting

Direct performance budgeting has tight links between performance and budget decisions, with resources allocated on the basis of actual results. This type of budgeting is, however, used only in limited-service areas/sectors, such as higher education and health. This is because there needs to be some standardization in terms of results to be able to use it for resource allocation.

> If a performance budgeting system is one in which there are formal links between increments in spending and increments in results, no OECD country would claim to have introduced such a system, at least not on a government-wide basis.
>
> (CABRI, 2013: 7)

Robinson (2013) identifies four performance budgeting mechanisms that would fit into the OECD's category of direct performance budgeting systems because they link the funding to ministries/departments/programmes to the quantity of results they achieve. They are shown in Box 2.3.

BOX 2.3 TYPES OF DIRECTLY LINKED PERFORMANCE BUDGETS

Formula funding—where unit costs of outputs are used in a formula where the PBE decides the number of outputs to be provided and the budget for the provider unit is the number of outputs multiplied by the unit cost per output. If the volume of outputs is more or fewer than planned the budget is not changed.

Purchaser-provider contracts—where the budget is based on the principle of payment by results. The PBE sets a price for an output and pays the provider unit for the quantity of outputs actually produced. If the provider produces more or fewer outputs its budget rises or falls accordingly. This transfers some of the risk to the provider unit but the purchaser may have to impose a ceiling on the amount it will pay. It can also provide an incentive for the provider unit to control its costs to be less than the unit price so that it makes a surplus rather than a deficit.

Bonus funding—where departments or programmes have a core budget that covers most of their operational costs and they can 'earn' supplementary funding for achieving specified performance targets. This is akin to the performance-related pay that employees might enjoy (more commonly in the private sector than the public sector). It tends to be used to reward performance against targets which are not stable enough or controlled by the PBE to be used as the basis for the formula funding or purchaser-provider mechanisms.

Budget-linked targets—where performance targets are set for outputs or outcomes at the same time as the budget is determined. The target might be set for achievement in just one year or set as medium-term targets that are linked to the medium-term budgets.

(Source: Robinson, 2013: 241–4)

There are many examples of **formula funding budgeting** mechanisms and they tend to be in the education and health sectors. The technique can be applied to universities and higher education colleges where their funding is based on the number of students taught or, sometimes, the number of students graduating. This can work in higher education because it rewards the institution for attracting and retaining students. Generally, formula funding would work less well for primary and secondary education because it is compulsory.

The United Kingdom's NHS has operated on the basis of **purchaser-provider contracts** for decades; it has remained the basic principle for funding primary and secondary health care even though there have been numerous restructures implemented. In fact, the system is a version of the diagnostic-related group funding system for hospitals which is used in more than 20 countries (Robinson, 2013: 241). Under this type of system there are prices paid for completed treatments for patients (i.e., the price covers everything from admission to discharge). There are more than a thousand treatment types and the price for each varies according to its complexity.

The health system in Rwanda operates a **bonus funding** mechanism. The government pays each facility a needs payment each month based on population it serves and the level of poverty. The facilities also receive a performance payment each quarter based on level of activity they have achieved weighted by a quality score (which is a percentage figure based on a combination of 13 factors, including cleanliness and financial management as well as some clinical factors). This system has contributed to an improvement in health services and health outcomes despite the total value of inputs remaining relatively low (Picanyol, 2012).

In the United Kingdom the public service agreements operated by the government from 1998 to 2007 were an example of **budget-linked targets**. The government had in mind some ambitious improvements in public services and there was a negotiation between the Treasury and spending ministries, local authorities, police authorities and so on to agree on what amounted to performance contracts where both parties agreed what level of service improvement would be achieved and the associated funding level.

The direct performance budgeting mechanisms in Box 2.3 have advantages over incremental budgeting and ZBB but work better in certain service areas than others. To have such performance budgets you need the PBE to have the capacity to estimate the effects of marginal changes in expenditures on results. This requires knowledge of fixed and variable costs (see Chapter 5) and being able to allocate them to units of output. For example, formula funding requires unit cost information to link changes in budget with changes in outputs or outcomes. This is possible for services that are standardized and produced in reasonable quantity. For instance, a vaccination programme could (should) know how many more people will be vaccinated if the budget were increased by X? Unit costs are much more difficult for services that are non-standard and irregular, which of course many public services are (Robinson, 2013: 241).

Without that sort of information a PBE is just guessing that allocating extra money to a programme or department will yield better and/or more outputs. As with incremental budgeting, information asymmetry works here if the central finance ministry/department do not know the unit costs or the marginal impact an increase or decrease in the budget would yield. If asked, a public manager is likely to overestimate their needs for extra funding rather than risk not having enough resources to deliver. Arguably, spending managers have a greater incentive to hold on to their data, distort it, etc. if performance is tightly linked to budget allocation than under conventional incremental budgeting.

It would be difficult for a national government to use direct performance budgeting comprehensively across all of their services because not all services meet the requirements of standardization or have suitable performance measures. PBEs with narrower scopes of service areas than national governments might be able to make one of, or a combination of, the mechanisms work for all of their activities.

Advantages of performance budgeting

Performance budgeting's major advantage is its strategic focus on results on a corporate level. There is some evidence of it contributing to improved performance, such as the Rwandan health care example described earlier, although overall the evidence of its impact on performance is widely debated.

One aspect where performance budgeting helps is its formalization of performance targets, whether at an organizational or at an individual level. Having clarity about performance expectations can help to motivate public managers.

Performance budgeting is consistent with the doctrines of NPM and is seen as good practice. National governments may choose to implement it solely for its expected benefits but, in lower-income countries for instance, they may also be influenced by the signal it sends to aid agencies and donors. CABRI (2013: 23) identified that 46 out of 54 African countries have or were moving towards a system of performance budgeting in 2012.

Disadvantages of performance budgeting

First, performance budgeting is difficult and costly to implement. It is likely to require more extensive budget documentation and, of course, it requires the relevant performance information to be collected, reported and monitored (and possibly audited). The level of difficulty increases where outcomes rather than outputs are being measured.

The cost of performance budgeting has to be balanced against the gains (actual or expected) the PBE will enjoy, which are themselves debatable.

> Experience outside Africa has shown that, for most government expenditures, the links between budget allocations and performance are unclear. For example, the extent to which education performance improves, if at all, when education budget spending increases by, say, 10 per cent is unknown.
>
> (CABRI, 2013: 40)

Performance budgeting can be seen as a luxury approach. It takes a lot of time and resources to develop and managed performance budgets and when time or money is short, PBEs may be tempted to suspend their performance budgeting in favour of something simpler. As Schick (2013: 69) put it: 'Performance metrics and programme budgets are not high on the "to do" list for deadline-sensitive budget cutters.'

A second disadvantage is what happens when a programme or department fails to meet its target. Should good performing programmes, departments and units get more funding in the future as a reward for meeting their targets or less funding as a way of stretching their targets? And should the poor performers get less funding because of their poor performance or more funding in order to help them improve their results? And whatever is done, the designers of the budget system also have to include a method of capping the total cost of services; otherwise, the budgeting system may encourage public managers to increase their performance in terms of outputs to a level that the PBE cannot afford.

In practice, these difficult questions will lead PBEs and public managers to prefer not to have tight links between budgets and performance. As Curristine and Flynn pointed out: 'Countries tend not to mechanically reduce or increase agency or programme budgets based solely on performance results. Priority programmes, even those performing poorly, are unlikely to see funding reduced' (2013: 235).

Also, as mentioned earlier, linking budgets to results can create an incentive to public managers to manipulate data rather than improve performance. The distorting effects that setting performance targets can have are covered in Chapter 7 (see Table 7.2 for a summary).

Finally, of course, there is no point budgeting for results if you do not also manage for results and this is one of the main issues discussed in Chapter 7.

Hybrid approaches to budgeting

The previous three sections described three major methods of budgeting. In practice, organizations can and do develop ad hoc, hybrid budget methods. This may be because they recognize the weaknesses in the methods outlined above and seek to mix and match features from different methods in order to get a better result. An organization might, for instance, carry out ZBB on a rolling programme so that each year most of the budget is formulated incrementally but a proportion of the budget is challenged and re-built from scratch. Or, at times of crisis, an organization may identify a set of services or departments (because, for instance, they are voluntary or discretionary, or because they have historically had problems of overspending) and carry out ZBB on those.

An alternative hybrid is to create a priorities fund (perhaps by top-slicing an amount from other areas of the budget) and have an annual process of allocating the fund to key projects or new initiatives. This brings a performance budgeting approach to a small proportion of the budget. Often such arrangements are only for the setting-up and testing of initiatives. If the initiative is successful, its long-term operating costs have to be absorbed into the base budget, presumably at the expense of a lower priority item, so that the priority fund can be used for other new initiatives

BUDGETS AND BUDGETING: SOME PRACTICAL ISSUES

Whatever the flaws and issues with a budget methodology, the process of budgeting is important to PBEs. Budgeting forces public managers and politicians to think about their services, users' needs and wants, the wider environment, risk, policies and so on when making decisions about what to do. The remainder of this chapter looks at some of the practical issues a public manager might encounter when budgeting. These practical issues are:

- balancing a budget;
- the limitations of a budget;
- the assumptions used to prepare the budget;
- budgeting for risk and uncertainty;
- making changes to an approved budget;
- medium- and long-term budgets; and
- cash-basis budgeting.

Balancing a budget

A balanced budget does not necessarily mean that income equals expenditure. Generally speaking, an organization would budget for its planned income to exceed its planned expenditure in order to generate a (small) surplus, which could be kept in reserve to give the organization some contingency money to deal with unforeseen events.

Sometimes an organization may plan for its expenditure to exceed its income without the result being disastrous. Such a budget, termed a deficit budget, might be prudent and sustainable for an organization when taking a view over a number of years. If, for example, an organization has built up its reserves then it would have to have a deficit budget for the year or years where it used the reserves, perhaps to invest in new premises or equipment. In fact, in the United Kingdom the Charity Commission expects all charities not to have excessive reserves and therefore an individual charity may need to have a deficit budget from time to time in order to manage the level of its reserves. A similar thing can happen with local authority schools where they receive a delegated budget share each year and are frowned upon by their local authorities if their reserves become too high (say greater than 10 per cent of their annual budget).

In fact, such deficit budgets are common at national government level. For example, look back at Figure 1.1 in Chapter 1. It shows the United Kingdom has had a deficit budget in 44 of the 50 years between 1971 and 2021, and the last time there was a surplus was 2000/1. On average over that 50-year period the United Kingdom's annual budget deficit was about 3.6 per cent of GDP.

A key issue for governments' and public organizations' plans, then, is sustainability over the medium and long term. It becomes important that an organization's budgeting considers a longer period than simply the upcoming year and that its budgets balance out income and expenditure over the medium term. The exception to this might be where an organization knows that it is going out of existence, which happens to public organizations more often than we might expect if you consider school closures, reorganizations of local authorities and mergers of hospitals. Even in such circumstances the organization would be expected to run down its affairs in an orderly and prudent manner. In fact, auditors and others would be on the lookout for profligacy or extravagance by a public organization that was approaching its demise.

The limitations of a budget

The public manager should beware that the translation of a set of narrative plans and strategies into numbers may give an illusion of accuracy that is not justified. This is especially true if the numbers are expressed in whole units of currency rather than being rounded to hundreds or even thousands.

A budget needs to be calculated at a level that is commensurate with the scale of the organization, the service or project and the nature of the expense or income item. A small charity might budget very closely. It might have an exact figure for the grant it is due to receive from a donor organization that it can include in its budget, but for other items it might make estimates to the nearest ten pounds.

Multi-billion-pound government departments ought to adopt a different approach, budgeting in round thousands of pounds and possibly not budgeting for items that are below a minimum level (say £500 or £1,000).

Budget assumptions

To understand the key assumptions a budget is based on, a public manager does not need to be numerate or to understand how Excel works, they just need to be able to talk to whoever compiled their budget for inclusion in the financial system. What the public manager needs to focus on is agreeing that their budget is based on reasonable assumptions. If they can do that, then during the year they simply have to manage their services and/or projects in line with the assumptions and the numbers will look after themselves. If the assumptions prove to be too optimistic then the public manager will have to take some corrective action (see Chapter 4) and if the assumptions prove too pessimistic then they will enjoy a windfall.

For example, if the budget is based on pay rises being 3 per cent, then any settlement above 3 per cent will give the public manager a problem. They might tackle it by keeping some posts vacant for longer than they would like or by cutting back spending on training or increasing the charges levied for the service. Every situation is different and the public manager, not the accountant, is best placed to decide which alternative best solves the problem.

Table 2.2 lists some common things where assumptions would be made in the preparation of a budget. One important assumption to be very clear about is the number and grading of posts that the budget is based on. Beware of the accountant basing the budget on a structure that is different from the number and grade of staff that are actually in the public manager's team(s). A second problem can occur where the accountant assumes that all staff are paid at the mid-point of their grade. This is convenient for the accountant and, on average across the organization it may level out, but where a team has a high proportion of staff who have reached the top of their grades then the budget for staffing will be calculated

Table 2.2 *Common budget assumptions*

For operating budgets	*For capital budgets*
Pay rises	Timing of payments to major contractors
Number and grades of staff	Number and grade of own staff working on the project
Average level of vacancies (sometimes called slippage rate or staff turnover rate)	Estimated slippage from approved project timetable
Price inflation for goods and services (be especially concerned about the rate used for fuel, utility and contracts for outsourced services)	Price inflation on payments to contractors
Interest rate for loans	Level of contingency
Growth or reduction in user demand for service	
Price rises for charges made to users	
Sales volume for charges to users	
Level of bad debts	

at perhaps 5 per cent lower than the annual salary bill giving the public manager an immediate problem.

Agreeing assumptions with the accountant is not a one-time, one-way process. It is iterative. The public manager can expect the accountant to know the bigger picture of the organization's finances and the finance director's expectations about pay and price rises, what the politicians/trustees will find acceptable. What the public manager brings to the table is their knowledge of the demand for their services, what needs to improve and what can be left alone. The negotiation and agreement of assumptions is a process that, ultimately, pulls the public manager's plans for their service or project into line with the budget. Once the budget is approved it is down to the public manager to deliver the results.

Budgeting for risk and uncertainty

A public manager has to have in place strategies and plans for managing risks relating to their services or projects. Drennan and McConnell (2007: 91) identify four actions (the 4Ts) that a public manager can take regarding each and every risk:

- **terminate it**—find a way of operating or managing that means the risk no longer exists;
- **transfer it**—find a way of operating where a third party takes on the risk (e.g., by outsourcing or by paying insurance premiums);
- **treat it**—find ways to reduce the likelihood of the risk occurring and/or reduce the impact of the risk if it does occur; and
- **tolerate it**—accept it is a risk that cannot feasibly be treated in an affordable way and live with it.

The strategies and plans adopted by the public manager in response to the identified risks would need to be reflected in their budget. For risks that are terminated, there is, by definition, nothing to include in the budget. Transferred risks may be reflected in the budget depending on how the risk is transferred and to whom. Insurance is a kind of transfer of risks and the budget would include the insurance premiums. There could be policy excesses associated with the insurance policies that the public manager needs to be aware of. If risks are transferred to suppliers, then the price for their goods and services should include a factor for the risks they face.

For treated risks, the cost of the treatment would need to be incorporated in the budget, both the initial cost and any ongoing costs. For example, the installation of a security system to prevent theft of equipment from an office would have ongoing operating and maintenance costs to be included in the budget.

This leaves all the risks that the public manager has to tolerate, either because it is not possible to manage the risk (changes in the population or acts of God) or the cost of treating the risk is prohibitive, given the likelihood and impact of the risk happening. There are basically two explicit ways of dealing with this and one covert way.

First, the budget could include a contingency item. This could be an amount based on a percentage of the total expenditure, the percentage reflecting the level of uncertainty in the budget figures. It is commonly used in capital projects as an allowance (say 5 per cent or 10 per cent) for changes in specification and/or prices over the course of the project. It is practical, too, in preventing capital projects being held up every time the project manager seeks a (relatively) small revision to the budget.

A contingency item is seldom included in the operating budget allocated to a public manager; instead, if a contingency is used for operating budgets it would tend to be at the corporate level where its use can be controlled by the finance director or politicians.

The second explicit approach is to create one or more reserves by putting aside some funds each year. The reserves can then be used to finance planned or unplanned expenditure, just as an individual's savings account could be used for a planned purchase (to buy a new car) or unplanned, unforeseen expenses (to pay for repairs to their house). The level of reserves to be maintained by an organization is a matter of judgement by the board, just like the contingency approach does.

The covert way an organization or individual public manager can budget for uncertainty is by overestimation of all or some items in the budget. By building some slack into their budget the public manager has a cushion against unforeseen events and, if towards the end of the year nothing unexpected has happened, they could use the unspent money on new equipment, etc. Whilst this approach is contrary to the expectation of transparency and could have potentially dysfunctional effects on the organization, it would be naive not to recognize that it happens.

Making changes to an approved budget

The public manager also needs to remember that the real world will throw up unforeseen events and the public manager will have to adapt their plans and activities in response. The public manager's budget is a snapshot based on the plans as they were at a certain point in time. Even if the budget were perfect on the first day of the financial year it would soon be out of date, maybe by the end of the first week. Certainly, by the second half of the financial year, things will have happened that were not envisaged at the time the budget was approved: staff will have left or been promoted, a supplier's prices will have changed, the weather will have affected fuel usage and so on. If the organization produces a mid-year revised budget the known changes can be incorporated into it, but, even then, it is simply a second snapshot that will also be out of date before the end of the financial year.

It is the budget-holder's job to make changes to their plans to keep their use of resources within the limit of the approved budget. They do not have to do that on their own, though. They could seek help and advice from their line manager (and once they have involved their line manager the problem ceases to be theirs alone and becomes a shared problem) or their peer colleagues or their accountant. Given the effort put into agreement of the budget assumptions the accountant would be well placed to use their understanding of the service or project to identify potential solutions. A bonus from this approach is that if the public manager and the accountant are working together on the problem, the accountant is not in a position to criticize the manager for poor budget management.

Sometimes the issues cannot be resolved by moving things around and a change to the approved budget is needed. The COVID-19 pandemic will have caused many governments and PBEs to change their budgets, possibly more than once in the same financial year.

Many public organizations have a formal process for making changes to budgets. In general, the total budget for the organization has to balance so the changes that can be made are transfers—the increases in budget lines have to be matched by decreases in other budget lines. (In some countries these budget transfers are called virements).

As well as setting thresholds for the financial value of budget transfers that can be approved at various levels within the organization there is usually a requirement that the budget transfer does not result in the commitment to additional expenditure in future years. This is to prevent the occurrence of situations such as a one-off saving being transferred to the salaries budget and a new member of staff recruited on a permanent contract.

Of course, moving budgets around does not address an underlying or structural budget problem and, at some point, the actual cause of over- and underspending will have to be tackled.

Medium- and long-term budgets

The preceding descriptions of budgeting have been described with the formulation of annual budgets in mind. However:

> Outcomes can often be overlooked or downplayed in the annual budget process as measurable changes in outcomes happen over a time period that is far greater than a year. The medium-term financial strategy, however, is able to provide a focus on outcomes to help improve longer term decision

> making. A by-product is that the medium-term financial strategy can allow early intervention strategies to come to the fore along with a greater challenge around service delivery.
>
> (Scott, 2016)

PBEs are expected to have medium-term financial strategies covering at least three years but possibly five and some organizations would also have long-term plans covering ten years or more. Medium-term budgeting is accepted as good practice amongst governments although there is no single model for preparing or presenting a medium-term budgeting framework (MTBF). There were fewer than 20 countries with MTBFs in 1990 but by 2008 there were more than 130 (Schick, 2013).

Medium- and long-term strategies set out the organization's intentions over the coming years. They reflect binding commitments (such as the terms of private finance initiative contracts that have been entered into), but they do not commit the government or PBE to stick rigidly to the expenditure plans contained within them. This has to be the case because a change of government or political control or some other unforeseen event may cause the organization to change its priorities and policies and, therefore, its financial plans.

The case for taking a medium-term approach to budgeting is founded on the fact that an annual budget perspective does not properly take into account the costs and benefits of public programmes that run over many years. Annual budgeting, particularly if it is incremental budgeting, encourages politicians and managers to focus on their short-term interests rather than the long-term interests of society.

> Budgeting in most countries focuses on preparing an annual plan for revenue and expenditure, but an understanding of fiscal developments beyond this relatively short time horizon is important for the ability to make the right choices. Budget decisions made today generally have consequences for several years to come, and events expected to occur in two or three years' time may call for action today. This realization has prompted many countries to introduce medium-term budget frameworks.
>
> (Harris et al., 2013: 137)

Strategy 'emerges more from a pragmatic process of bodging, learning and compromise than from a rational series of great leaps forward' (Mintzberg, 1994 cited by Whittington, 2001). Medium- and long-term financial strategies are outline budgets, setting out estimates of income and expenditure at a high level. They are broad plans, not detailed ones. They, too, are likely to be the result of bodging, learning and compromise.

The update of medium- and long-term financial strategies would be a product of the budgeting process alongside the annual budget. Given the interconnection of them it would be sensible for the medium- and long-term strategies to be approved at the same time as the annual budget. Also, budgets for capital expenditure projects that span more than one financial year (such as major construction works) can be included within a medium-term capital programme, ensuring that sufficient funding is available to finish the project.

There are practical issues connected with producing medium- and long-term budgets. The first is the uncertainty about future income levels and the cost of goods and services is amplified. A business that generates its income from sales might have market information to support its estimates of sales revenue in the coming years, but public sector organizations rely, for the most part, on grants and charities on donations.

Future funding levels are not the only difficulty in producing a long- or medium-term strategy. Regard has to be had about price inflation, pay awards, interest rates and potential changes in the law. Low-income countries that are highly sensitive to swings in commodity prices, interest rates and donor aid may find it particularly difficult to implement medium-term budget frameworks effectively because of the problems of forecasting their available resources in future years.

One major issue that governments and PBEs should incorporate into their medium- and long-term financial plans is climate change. In 2021 the UNDP issued its *Guidance Note on Budgeting for Climate Change* It has three main principles: build on existing systems and practices to ensure sustainability; align efforts with the budget cycle; and clearly define roles and responsibilities.

For the budget preparation stage, the UNDP (2021) recommends including climate change issues in the budget by requiring the spending agencies to prepare their budget submissions through a climate lens. Budgets that include performance information over the medium term can provide a platform for integrating climate change issues into the budget process.

Cash-basis budgeting

The cash basis of accounting is a method where transactions are recorded in financial statements on the date, and at the value, when the exchange of money takes place. This has the advantage of being based on factual events but it means that many assets and liabilities are not recorded in the financial statements because no money has, yet, changed hands.

Businesses do not use cash-basis accounting because profit cannot be calculated without taking into account the assets and liabilities, such as sales and purchases made on credit. They use accrual-basis accounting and this approach is becoming more common amongst governments and PBEs (IFAC and CIPFA, 2021). (There is more about the bases of accounting and the implications for PBEs in Chapter 8.)

Reichard and van Helden (2016) noted that, whilst governments in many Western countries have transferred their cash-based accounting systems into accrual-based systems for financial reporting purposes, they have retained cash-based budgeting systems. This is a problem in two ways. Internally, it makes it difficult for budget-holders and those who oversee them to manage because the budget focuses them on the cash flow aspects of what they are doing (that is, what matters most is when money changes hands) rather than considering the full economic impact of their decisions. This undermines the main benefit of using accrual-basis accounting in the first place.

External users of financial information also have the problem of reconciling the budget information with the financial reports. If those financial reports are produced under International Public Sector Accounting Standards (IPSASs) then there is an accounting standard, IPSAS 24, which requires a reconciliation of the budgeted and actual income and expenditure.

Reichard and van Helden (2016: 61) concluded 'that in most cases a stepwise adoption of accrual elements in the budget is recommended' whilst acknowledging that this would have implications for reconciling budget and actual information until the adoption of accrual-based budgeting is completed. Bandy and Metcalfe (2021) also recommended that governments and PBEs adopt accrual-based budgeting as well as accrual-based reporting as part of the development of PFM after COVID-19.

CONCLUSION

This chapter has focused on the budget formulation and approval stages of the PFM cycle. It has described several alternative methods for preparing budgets and identified some of the practical issues that a public manager may encounter in connection with budgeting. It is easy for the annual budgeting process to be an end in itself and to lose sight of the fact that the organization exists to create public value by achieving its objectives and not to produce attractive budget documents and reports.

PBEs' budgets are predominantly about spending money, but, to execute the budget, the PBE needs some income, whether from taxes, other sources or both. That is the focus of the next chapter.

EXERCISES

1. Thinking about the budget for your organization, programme, project or service area, what are the main assumptions it is based on?
2. What are the reasons for and aims of preparing a capital budget that is separate from an organization's operating budget?

REFERENCES

Afnan Alam, M. (2022). *Evaluating Pakistan's Performance Based Budget* [Blog]. Available at: https://blog-pfm.imf.org/pfmblog/2022/01/-evaluating-pakistans-performance-based-budget-.html (Accessed: 17 May 2022).

Allen, R., & Krause, P. (2013). The role, responsibilities, structure and evolution of central finance agencies. In R. Allen, R. Hemming, & B. H. Potter (Eds.), *The International Handbook of Public Financial Management* (pp. 98–115). Basingstoke: Palgrave Macmillan.

Andrews, M. (2013a). *The Limits of Public Financial Management Reform in Development*. Cambridge, MA: Cambridge University Press.

Andrews, M. [@governwell]. (2013b). #cape2013 Schick: The War Between Incrementalists and Others Will Be Over When Everyone Realises That Incrementalism Has Won [Tweet], 14 November. Available at: https://twitter.com/governwell/status/401000523652153344.

Andrews, M. (2021). *Creating Space for Better Post-Covid Public Policy Spending* [Blog]. Available at: https://buildingstatecapability.com/2021/12/08/creating-space-for-better-post-covid-public-policy-spending/ (Accessed: 20 May 2022).

Anessi-Pessina, E., Barbera, C., Sicilia, M., & Steccolini, I. (2016). Public sector budgeting: A European review of accounting and public management journals. *Accounting, Auditing & Accountability Journal*, 29(3), 491–519. https://doi.org/10.1108/AAAJ-11-2013-1532.

Audit Commission. (2009). *Use of Resources Framework: Overall Approach and Key Lines of Enquiry*. London: Audit Commission.

Babcock, C., Brannan, E., Gupta, P., & Shah, S. (2008). *Western Participatory Practices: Observations on Experience*. Washington, DC: World Bank.

Bandy, G. P., & Metcalfe, A. (2021). *Rethinking Public Financial Management*. London: ACCA. Available at: https://www.accaglobal.com/gb/en/professional-insights/global-profession/rethinking-public-financial-management.html (Accessed: 25 April 2022).

BBC. (2019). *Participatory Budgeting, Paris, France* [Radio Show]. Available at: https://www.bbc.co.uk/programmes/w3csz41t (Accessed: 20 May 2022).

Biden, J. (2008). *Show Me Your Budget and I'll Tell You What You Value* [Video]. Available at: https://www.youtube.com/watch?v=vuLwjFmESrg (Accessed: 19 May 2022).

CABRI. (2013). *Performance and Programme-Based Budgeting in Africa: A Status Report*. Pretoria: CABRI.

Caddy, J., Peixoto, T., & McNeil, M. (2007). *Beyond Public Scrutiny: Stocktaking of Social Accountability in OECD Countries*. Washington, DC: International Bank for Development and Reconstruction/The World Bank.

Cangiano, M., Curristine, T., & Lazare, M. (2013). Introduction: The emerging architecture of public financial management. In M. Cangiano, T. Curristine, & M. Lazare (Eds.), *Public Financial Management and Its Emerging Architecture* (pp. 1–17). Washington, DC: International Monetary Fund.

City of Cape Town. (2019). *2019/20-2021/2 Budget (Annexure A)*. Cape Town: City of Cape Town.

City of Vallejo. (2014). *Participatory Budgeting in Vallejo: Innovation in Democracy and Community Engagement: A Summary of Cycle 1*. Vallejo, CA: City of Vallejo. http://bit.ly/1kmistJ.

Curristine, T., & Flynn, S. (2013). In Search of Results: Strengthening Public Sector Performance. In M. Cangiano, T. Curristine, & M. Lazare (Eds.), *Public Financial Management and Its Emerging Architecture* (pp. 225–58). Washington, DC: International Monetary Fund.

Curristine, T., Tchelishvili, N., & Weerathunga, S. (2022). *Gender Budgeting is More Widespread But Implementation Remains a Challenge* [Online Article]. Available at: https://blogs.imf.org/2022/03/08/gender-budgeting-is-more-widespread-but-implementation-remains-a-challenge/ (Accessed: 17 May 2022).

de Sousa Santos, B. (1998). Participatory budgeting in Porto Alegre: Toward a redistributive democracy. *Politics and Society*, 26, 461–510.

Dias, N. (Ed.). (2018). *Hope for Democracy: 30 Years of Participatory Budgeting Worldwide*. Faro, Portugal: Oficina. Available at: https://www.oficina.org.pt (Accessed: 20 May 2022).

Drennan, L. T., & McConnell, A. (2007). *Risk and Crisis Management in the Public Sector*. Abingdon: Routledge.

Dumfries & Galloway Council. (2018). *Activity Based Budget Estimates 2018/19*. Available at: https://www.dumgal.gov.uk/media/20503/Activity-Based-Budget-Estimates-2018-19/pdf/Activity_Based_Budget_1819_Final.pdf (Accessed: 25 May 2022).

Ehrhart, K. M., Gardner, R., Von Hagen, J., & Keser, C. (2007). Budget processes: Theory and experimental evidence. *Games and Economic Behavior*, 59(2), 279–295.

Galizzi, G., Meliou, E., & Steccolini, I. (2021). Theme: Experiences and challenges with gender budgeting and accounting. Moving towards gender-responsive forms of accountability. *Public Money & Management*, 41(7), 499–501. https://doi.org/10.1080/09540962.2021.1971862.

Government of Estonia. (n.d.). *Performance Based Budgeting* [Webpage]. Available at: https://www.rahandusministeerium.ee/en/objectivesactivities

/state-budget-and-economy/performance-based-budgeting (Accessed: 25 May 2022).

Government of Rwanda. (2019). *Manual of Public Financial Management (PFM) Policies and Procedures.* Kigali: Ministry of Finance & Economic Planning.

Harris, J., Hughes, R., Ljungman, G., & Sateriale, C. (2013). Medium-term budget frameworks in advanced economies: objectives, design, and performance. In M. Cangiano, T. Curristine, & M. Lazare (Eds.), *Public Financial Management and Its Emerging Architecture* (pp. 137–174). Washington, DC: International Monetary Fund.

IFAC & CIPFA. (2021). *International Public Accountability Index: 2021 Status Report.* Available at: https://www.ifac.org/system/files/publications/files/IFAC-CIPFA-International-Public-Sector-Accountability-Index.pdf (Accessed: 23 May 2022).

IMF. (2020). *Fiscal Monitor April 2020* [Website]. Available at: https://www.imf.org/en/Publications/FM/Issues/2020/04/06/fiscal-monitor-april-2020 (Accessed: 19 May 2022).

Jones, R., & Pendlebury, M. (2010). *Public Sector Accounting* (6th ed.). Harlow: Pearson Education.

Lienert, I. (2013). Role of the legislature in budget process. In R. Allen, R. Hemming, & B. H. Potter (Eds.), *The International Handbook of Public Financial Management* (pp. 116–136). Basingstoke: Palgrave Macmillan.

Machiavelli, N. (2009) *The Prince* [Translated by Tim Parks]. London: Penguin Classics.

McGill, R. (2001). Performance budgeting. *International Journal of Public Sector Management,* 14(5), 376–390. https://doi.org/10.1108/09513550110404633.

Moore, M. H. (1995). *Creating Public Value: Strategic Management in Government.* Cambridge, MA: Harvard University Press.

OECD. (2008). *Performance Budgeting: A Users' Guide.* Available at: https://www.oecd.org/gov/budgeting/Performance-Budgeting-Guide.pdf (Accessed: 20 May 2022).

OECD. (2022). *Principles of Budgetary Governance.* Available at: https://www.oecd.org/gov/budgeting/principles-budgetary-governance.htm (Accessed: 17 May 2022).

Participatory Budgeting Project. (2022). *What is PB?* Available at: https://www.participatorybudgeting.org/what-is-pb/ (Accessed: 22 May 2022).

PEFA. (2021). *2020 Global Report on Public Financial Management.* Washington, DC: PEFA. Available at: https://www.pefa.org/global-report-2020/ (Accessed: 25 April 2022).

PEFA Secretariat. (2016). *Framework for Assessing Public Financial Management*. Washington DC: World Bank.

Picanyol, C. (2012). *Case Study: Financing and Monitoring for Results in the Health Sector in Rwanda*. Oxford: Oxford Policy Management.

Polzer, T. (2022). *Gender Agenda* [Online Article]. Available at: https://www.publicfinancefocus.org/viewpoints/2022/04/gender-agenda (Accessed: 17 May 2022).

Pyhrr, P. A. (1970). Zero-Base Budgeting. *Harvard Business Review, 48*(6), 111–21.

Reichard, C., & van Helden, J. (2016). Why cash-based budgeting still prevails in an era of accrual-based reporting in the public sector. *Accounting Finance & Governance Review*, 23(1/2), 43–65.

Robinson, M. (2013). Performance budgeting. In R. Allen, R. Hemming, & B. H. Potter (Eds.), *The International Handbook of Public Financial Management* (pp. 237–258). Basingstoke: Palgrave Macmillan.

Robinson, M. (2021). *The Illusion of Outcome-Based Budgeting* [Blog]. Available at: https://blog.pfmresults.com/the-illusion-of-outcome-based-budgeting/ (Accessed: 17 May 2022).

Robinson, M (2022). *Attacking Budgetary Incrementalism* [Blog]. Available at: https://blog.pfmresults.com/attacking-budgetary-incrementalism/ (Accessed: 17 May 2022).

Rubin, M. M., & Bartle, J. R. (2021) Debate: Gender responsive budgeting—Moving toward equity for women and men. *Public Money & Management*, 41(7), 502–503. https://doi.org/10.1080/09540962.2021.1951467.

Schick, A. (2013). Reflections on two decades of public financial management reforms. In M. Cangiano, T. Curristine, & M. Lazare (Eds.), *Public Financial Management and Its Emerging Architecture* (pp. 21–77). Washington, DC: International Monetary Fund.

Scott, A. (2016). Why medium term financial strategies make sense. *Public Finance*, June. Available at: https://www.publicfinance.co.uk/opinion/2016/06/why-medium-term-financial-strategies-make-sense (Accessed: 25 May 2022).

Smith, R. W., & Lynch, T. D. (2003). *Public Budgeting in America* (5th ed.). Upper Saddle River, NJ: Pearson Prentice Hall.

Sushant, & Laha, M. (2021). Game changer or accounting practice? Gender responsive budgeting in India. *Public Money & Management*, 41(7), 539–547. https://doi.org/10.1080/09540962.2021.1965401.

TED. (2021). *How to Share Public Money Fairly* [Video]. Available at: https://www.ted.com/talks/maja_bosnic_how_to_share_public_money_fairly (Accessed: 17 May 2022).

UNDP. (2021). *Budgeting for Climate Change: A Guidance Note for Governments to Integrate Climate Change into Budgeting*. Available at: https://www.undp.org/publications/budgeting-climate-change-guidance-note-governments-integrate-climate-change-budgeting (Accessed: 17 May 2022).

United Nations. (n.d.). *The 17 Goals* [Webpage]. Available at: https://sdgs.un.org/goals (Accessed: 20 May 2022).

Whittington, R. (2001). *What is Strategy and Does it Matter?* Andover: Cengage Learning.

Wildavsky, A. (1961). Political implications of budgetary reform. *Public Administration Review*, 21(1), 183–190.

Wildavsky, A. (1975). *Budgeting: A Comparative Theory of Budgetary Processes*. Boston/Toronto: Little, Brown & Company.

Wildavsky, A. (1984). *The Politics of the Budgetary Process* (4th ed.). Harlow: Pearson Education.

FURTHER READING (AND WATCHING)

Links to the following resources, and lots more, are available at www.managingpublicmoney.co.uk/extras.

The OECD has a budget practices and procedures database that can be found at www.oecd.org/gov/budget/database/.

For some reading about performance budgeting look at the report by CABRI (2013), which includes a summary of performance budgeting practices in OECD countries as well as its analysis of the progress made by African countries. It also includes case studies on Burkina Faso, Tunisia, Uganda and Mozambique. CABRI have also published on their website the papers and presentations from their 2012 conference on performance budgeting (https://bit.ly/1fzwpJ2) which includes more case studies.

Marc Robinson is an expert in performance budgeting (see, for example, Robinson, 2021 and 2022). Aside from academic publications, he also writes a blog (https://blog.pfmresults.com) that is worth bookmarking.

There are a number of places you could find out more about participatory budgeting. The websites of Participedia (https://participedia.net), the Participatory Budgeting Project, based in New York (www.participatorybudgeting.org), and the PB Network, based in the United Kingdom (www.pbnetwork.org.uk), are sources of practical information, news and resources on participatory budgeting around the world. The Participatory Budgeting Project has a webpage of short, explanatory videos at www.participatorybudgeting.org/run-pb/videos-articles/.

There is a TED talk by Maja Bosnia titled *How to Share Public Money Fairly* that introduces what gender-responsive budgeting is and why it matters in 12 minutes (TED, 2021).

Finally, if you want to try your hand at balancing a budget you could search online for budget simulators like the one for the US federal government at https://us.abalancingact.com/2022-federal-budget.

Chapter 3

Taxation and other sources of income

LEARNING OBJECTIVES

After reading this chapter you should:

- understand the main reasons why governments impose taxes;
- know the meaning of terms such as direct and indirect taxes and progressive, flat-rate and regressive taxes;
- be able to analyse taxes in terms of characteristics like efficiency, equity, buoyancy and feasibility;
- understand the reasons for financing some public services through fees and charges rather than taxation; and
- be able to choose between alternative methods for determining the price to charge for a service.

KEY POINTS OF THIS CHAPTER

- Governments have the power to demand and collect taxes from citizens, businesses and others.
- A tax is levied on a person, whether a natural person or a legal person such as a corporation. A duty is levied on a thing.
- Taxes can be used for regulation, for economic stimulation and for redistribution as well as raising revenue for government.
- There are four types of taxes: income taxes, consumption taxes, wealth taxes and poll taxes.
- Some public services can legitimately and feasibly be financed by charging fees to the direct recipients of the service.

DOI: 10.4324/9781003250838-3

- Governments can use taxes for purposes other than raising money to pay for public services.
- Public managers need to be assured that taxes (and other income) are being collected efficiently otherwise the viability of the organization will be jeopardized.

KEY TERMS

Direct tax—a tax where the legal taxpayer and the economic taxpayer are the same person (whether a natural person or a corporate body).
Economic taxpayer—the person who ultimately bears the burden of the tax.
Flat-rate tax—a tax with a constant tax rate applied across the whole tax base.
Indirect tax—a tax where the legal taxpayer is not the economic taxpayer.
Legal taxpayer—the person who is liable to make the payment of tax to the government.
Non-exchange transaction—a transaction where one party receives something of value without giving value in return.
Progressive tax—a tax where the marginal rate of tax increases as the tax base increases.
Regressive tax—a tax where the marginal rate of tax falls as the tax base increases.
Tax base—the value of assets, property or transactions that are subject to a particular tax.
Tax rate—the amount that is applied to a tax base to determine the amount of tax that is payable for a given period. The rate of tax can be regressive, neutral or progressive.

This chapter discusses the various forms of income available to governments and public benefit entities (PBEs). For governments the principal source of income is taxation, something which is available only to government. Some PBEs, such as lower tier governments, might have tax-raising powers, but for the most part PBEs receive income in the form of grants, donations and fees. This is quite different from the private sector, where fees from sales are the principal, perhaps only, source of income a business would have. Regardless of sector, all organizations need to generate sufficient income over a period of time (from whichever sources) to finance the organization's expenditure if it is to remain sustainable.

The chapter begins with a definition of taxation and explains a number of different types of taxes and some associated theoretical aspects of taxation. The chapter then focuses on various other forms of income that can be used to finance public services such as fees and charges, grants, gifts and donations. The final part of the chapter considers some practical financial management issues, such as methods of collection that public managers ought to be familiar with.

WHAT IS A TAX?

President Franklin D. Roosevelt (1936) said: 'Taxes, after all, are the due that we pay for the privileges of membership of an organized society.' Swain and Reed (2010: 38) defined taxes as the 'involuntary extraction of resources' to finance a government's expenditure.

Generally, there is not a direct correlation between the taxes paid by a specific taxpayer to government (nationally or locally) and the services used/received by the taxpayer. Sometimes a tax is collected and used exclusively for a specified service and these are called hypothecated taxes. More usually a government raises income through a variety of taxes (because a spread of taxes means that the government is not over-dependent on one or two taxes).

If the total raised from taxes (together with other fees and charges) is less than the total spent on the delivery of public services, then the government or PBE has a deficit in its cash flow and must borrow money (or create some money) to cover the deficit. It is, therefore, strategically very important for a government to maintain a sustainable balance between its spending plans and its income from taxes and other fees and charges in order to keep its total borrowing at a manageable level (albeit what is manageable for one government might not be manageable for another).

A tax is not the same thing as a fee. The difference relates to the degree of correlation between the payment and services. A fee is the charge attached to an exchange transaction; a transaction where the two parties exchange things of equal, or approximately equal, value. A fee, therefore, has to be paid only when there are associated goods or services to be delivered by the other party.

A tax, on the other hand, 'has to be paid regardless of any services provided by the public sector entity' (Bergmann, 2009: 30). It is the classic example of a non-exchange transaction since the value of public services that a citizen receives has nothing to do with the amount of tax they are assessed to pay.

As an illustration of this difference, most roads are generally provided by government and are free to use. Taxpayers pay taxes regardless of whether they travel on the roads or not; indeed, they pay whether they have access to a vehicle or not. However, where toll roads exist, the toll is a fee payable only by the drivers of vehicles who use that stretch of toll road.

This works the other way around, too. Taxpayers can choose not to use public services but this does not excuse them from their liabilities to pay taxes. For example, if parents decide to send their children to a private sector, fee-paying school they do not get any reduction in their taxes to reflect the fact that they are not making use of public sector schools.

Some of the other sources of income for PBEs are also non-exchange transactions. Grants, gifts, donations and fines all involve the transfer of money from one party to another without yielding benefits in exchange, directly or indirectly.

Taxes are often referred to by different terms, such as duties, excise and customs. In short, a tax is levied on a person (whether a natural person or a legal person such as a company) and relates to their income or property or some other appropriate tax base.

A duty, on the other hand, is levied on a thing, such as a commodity or a transaction or an estate. Some duties are levied based on the value of the thing that is the tax base, such as a stamp duty payable on the value of a real estate transaction.

Excise duties are levied on the quantity of the commodity or goods rather than the value. The excise duty payable on petrol is on the basis of the number of litres or gallons that are bought not the price paid for the fuel. Many governments impose excise duties on alcohol, tobacco, petrol (gasoline) and diesel, which are products that could be over-consumed.

A customs duty is payable for the transport of goods across political borders, and, depending on the states involved, the transporter may have to pay both an export and an import duty. One advantage of customs duties is that they are relatively easy to impose if a government has control of its borders.

Customs duties are not payable when crossing every border. The European Union (EU) is an example of a customs union, which means that customs duties are not levied on the transfer of goods between the countries within the European Union. The West African Economic and Monetary Union, the Andean Community, the Caribbean Community and the Southern Common Market are other examples. The terms of leaving the EU agreed by the United Kingdom means it is no longer part of the EU customs union, but it is in a customs union with the Crown Dependencies (that is, the Isle of Man, Guernsey and Jersey).

For simplicity, unless otherwise stated, throughout the rest of this book the term 'tax' will be used to denote any kind of tax or duty.

Who pays tax?

No taxation without representation is a famous political slogan from the era of the American Revolutionary War. The notion that taxpayers should have the power to elect and unelect those who decide what taxes should be imposed seems very reasonable. However, taxes are actually paid by more than just the members of society who can vote (Daly, 2021). Businesses pay taxes; tourists pay taxes; children pay taxes; the deceased pay taxes—or at least their estates do. Nevertheless, Roosevelt's comment at the top of this chapter more or less holds. Citizens and businesses rely on the government for law and order, security, infrastructure and vital services like education and the price of having these provided, directly or indirectly, by government is the tax that has to be paid.

Tax expenditures

Tax expenditure is the use of reliefs, allowances and so on to meet policy goals such as creating jobs, attracting foreign investment or greening the economy, but 'they are often opaque, costly, and ineffective as well as politically motivated' (International Budget Partnership, 2022).

Tax expenditures reduce the total receipts from a tax and there are several problems with tax expenditures. First, they tend not to be transparent, and often they are not included in the budget as an expenditure 'above the line' but netted off the income. Tax expenditure also tends to benefit the rich rather than the poor because the rich have higher marginal tax rates. For example, in the United Kingdom individuals who give to charity can elect for their donation to be subject to the Gift Aid scheme. This allows the charity to recover from HM Treasury an extra 25 per cent of the donation being the equivalent of the basic rate of tax that had been paid by the individual. However, if the individual is a higher rate taxpayer they will be able to claim a credit on their taxes for the difference between the higher rate and basic rate of tax on their charitable donations. The end result of this is that richer people get a benefit from giving to charity that poorer people do not. Another example is the discount on council tax for second homes of up to 50 per cent. Each local authority makes its own policy decision about this discount but where it is offered it clearly benefits richer people only.

The difficulty for many governments is that tax expenditures are a form of tax cut (although perhaps not explicitly presented in that way) so if it were to scale them back or abolish them, they would be seen by the public as tax increases. Politicians therefore have an incentive to keep them in place. The International Budget Partnership (2022), on the other hand, sees rationalizing tax expenditures as a way of increasing the revenue available to governments to tackle the issues flowing from the coronavirus pandemic.

Regional and local taxes

Many countries have fiscal policies where some taxes are determined and collected at regional or district level, to finance regional or local government services. How each country does this is a matter for itself. In South Africa, for example, Chapter 3 of the constitution provides for the national, provincial and local 'spheres of government' to work cooperatively. Paragraph 214 (a) says that there should be an 'equitable division of revenue raised nationally among the national, provincial and local spheres of government' (Republic of South Africa, 1996). The constitution provides for each sphere to have tax-raising powers. The levying of rates on property is reserved for the local government sphere and income taxes, value-added taxes, general sales taxes and customs duties are reserved for the national government. The provincial sphere has considerable flexibility to impose any other taxes itself or to impose a flat-rate surcharge on any national tax except the taxes mentioned above, which are national government-only taxes.

The Council of Europe has a *Charter on Local Self-Government* that recognizes central government may need to control regional and local bodies but the Charter also encapsulates the principle that regional and local bodies should not be deprived of the financial resources to carry out their functions. The Charter also provides, in Article 9, 'Part at least of the financial resources of local authorities shall derive from local taxes and charges of which, within the limits of statute, they have the power to determine the rate' (Council of Europe, 1985).

In the United Kingdom, central government exercises control over the level of the council tax levied by English local authorities in an indirect way by offering grants to councils that keep their tax rises low and requiring them to have a local referendum for any tax rises that are proposed to be above a prescribed amount. The Scottish Parliament and Welsh Assembly operate their own controls over the council tax rises made by local authorities in their countries.

Tax avoidance

An obvious impact of taxation is that there will be an incentive not to pay it. Tax evasion is unlawful and governments implement systems to prevent and detect such non-payers. Tax mitigation, which is the management of financial affairs within the constraints of the tax regime to minimize the amount of tax that is payable, is not unlawful.

For high-worth individuals and multinational companies, the amounts of tax that can be avoided (mitigated) is an incentive to incur the cost of putting in place and then operating suitable arrangements. These costs might relate to the services of professional tax advisors, setting up of companies and trusts in tax havens, making tax-deductible donations to charities and having to ensure that rules about residency are not breached.

Bill Bryson (2013) gives the following anecdote about Calvin Coolidge's treasury secretary, Andrew Mellon:

> According to the historian Arthur M. Schlesinger, Jr, with a single piece of legislation Mellon gave himself a greater tax cut than that enjoyed by almost the entire populace of Nebraska put together. Mellon had the Internal Revenue Service send its best men to prepare his tax returns for him with a

> view to keeping them as small as possible. The head of the IRS even helpfully provided a list of loopholes for Mellon to exploit.

The whole issue of tax avoidance has been more prominent recently. Cobham and Janský (2017) estimated the global loss of tax through tax avoidance was $500 billion a year.

In 2013 the UK's Public Accounts Committee had a particular focus on the issue and called senior managers from Starbucks, Google and Amazon to hearing to explain why they paid so little in corporation tax despite having substantial businesses in the country. And in 2008, when campaigning to be a senator, Elizabeth Warren explained her view about why businesses should pay a fair share of tax, as good corporate citizens.

> There is nobody in this country who got rich on their own. Nobody. You built a factory out there—good for you. But I want to be clear. You moved your goods to market on roads the rest of us paid for. You hired workers the rest of us paid to educate. You were safe in your factory because of police forces and fire forces that the rest of us paid for. You didn't have to worry that marauding bands would come and seize everything at your factory. Now look. You built a factory and it turned into something terrific or a great idea—God bless! Keep a hunk of it. But part of the underlying social contract is you take a hunk of that and pay forward for the next kid who comes along.
>
> (Warren, 2011)

Governments design tax regimes to compete with each other so they cannot blame high-worth individuals and companies for shopping around. And if a company avoids tax, the argument goes, its owners would pay more tax because they would receive higher dividends and make greater capital gains when they sold their shares. This might be the case, but there is no guarantee that the owners—whether they are real people or organizations like insurance companies and pensions funds—would be resident in the same territory and actually pay their tax to that government.

The second argument is that companies drive economic activity and even if they pay little by way of corporation tax there are sales taxes, payroll taxes and so on that are paid to the government as a result of the company's activities. Whilst this may be true, other people would argue that the company is enjoying the benefits of public services, such as law and order, transport, the education of its workforce, towards which it is not paying taxes.

The tax competition between countries is not accepted by everyone as a good thing. Shaxson and O'Hagan (2013) outlined the negatives in a paper about the myths of tax competition. They state that such competition shifts wealth upwards as the owners of capital pay less tax, often causing the overall tax system to be regressive, demanding more tax from low- and middle-income families than the wealthiest. There can also be a distortion of markets as multinationals that are benefitting from moving profits to low-tax jurisdictions have an unfair advantage over smaller, locally based businesses. This is not competition based on product quality, efficiency and innovation; rather, it is based on the vagaries of the international tax system.

Like many things in life, it is a matter of finding a reasonable balance, one that satisfies the government and the governed. This means there should be a balance in terms of the tax bases that are taxed, the buoyancy and predictability of tax yields, the impact on citizens according to their levels of income, their use of services and their locations.

In 2021, championed by the president of the United States, Joseph Biden, the OECD agreed on a plan for international corporate tax reforms that would see 141 countries have a minimum tax rate of 15 per cent from 2023. This is called the *OECD/G20 Inclusive Framework on Base Erosion and Profit Shifting* (OECD, 2022). This is an important step in modernizing the tax system to reflect the nature of a globalized economy. The framework will particularly benefit low income and developing countries by removing the incentive to shift profits to other jurisdictions. It does not, however, mean that tax avoidance will be completely eliminated (Steel and Nair, 2021).

In 2013 the UK's General Anti-Abuse Rule (GAAR) came into force. This is a regulation intended to stop businesses and individuals from using devices that have no other purpose but to reduce liability for tax. The GAAR Guidance includes: 'Taxation is not to be treated as a game where taxpayers can indulge in any ingenious scheme in order to eliminate or reduce their tax liability' (HM Treasury, 2021: 6). Specifically, the GAAR applies to Income Tax, Corporation Tax, Capital Gains Tax, Inheritance Tax, Petroleum Revenue Tax, Stamp Duty Land Tax and Annual Residential Property Tax. However, just because something is not covered by the GAAR does not mean the government will not use other anti-avoidance methods to enforce tax liabilities.

Finally, a different way of looking at tax avoidance. As the saying goes, you can catch more flies with honey than vinegar. Perhaps governments would do better by focusing on praising, publicly, the taxpayers who fulfil their obligations to give an extra incentive for people and businesses not to avoid their taxes (Kirkup, 2020).

Tax evasion

Whilst tax mitigation is legal (provided it is not abusive avoidance), tax evasion is not. The difference is that the former is the proactive management of tax affairs in order to reduce your liability for taxes; the latter is misrepresentation of your affairs to tax authorities.

Like other frauds it is difficult to evaluate how much tax evasion takes place. In 2020 the Tax Justice Network estimated that $427 billion in tax is lost every year to tax abuse by corporations and private individuals (Mansour, 2020).

Another measure is the 'tax gap' being the difference between the amount of income that should be reported to the tax authorities and the amount that actually is reported. Murphy (2011) calculated that the tax gap in 145 countries (covering 98 per cent of the global GDP) amounted to 18 per cent of global GDP (i.e., $1 in every $6 is not subject to taxation) and the total amount of tax evaded was US$3.1 trillion.

In absolute terms, the biggest losers are countries with large economies and relatively high average tax rates. Murphy (2011) also compared his estimates of the value of tax evaded in each country with its budget for public health care as a way to demonstrate the scale of evasion in each country. He identified 119 countries where the value of tax evaded was more than 50 per cent of their health care spending, and in ten of those countries the ratio was more than 200 per cent. The highest ratios were Bolivia (419 per cent), Russia (311 per cent) and Papua New Guinea (305 per cent).

In 2020/1 the UK's HM Revenue and Customs (2021) estimated the tax gap in the United Kingdom at 5.3 per cent of the tax due, which will translate to something like 2 per cent of GDP.

WHY LEVY TAXES?

The explanation in Chapter 1 about public goods and merit goods gives us the first and perhaps most obvious reason for imposing taxes on citizens and businesses: to raise money to cover the cost of providing goods and services to the public.

The classical way of explaining the need for taxes is to state that governments have to collect taxes from citizens (and all the other taxpayers mentioned above) in order to have enough money to spend on services. This is how things would have to be if there was a fixed amount of money in the system and it was not possible to incur expenditure on credit. In that situation, the government would have to take some money out of the hands of citizens and businesses in order to pay civil servants and all the other expenses.

Government spending does not work quite like this in modern times. Governments use fiat money and this can be created at a stroke; and there is also plenty of scope for governments to borrow money. The notion that governments collect taxes and then spend the money on public services is, according to modern monetary theory (MMT), the wrong way around. The MMT view is that governments spend money on public services first and then use taxation to remove the cash they have injected into the economy in order to manage inflation (Murphy, 2020).

Whichever of these views of the connection between government spending and taxation you find persuasive, they each give governments a reason (need) to generate revenue from taxation in order for the government and economy to be sustainable.

There are, also, three other reasons for imposing taxes: regulation, economic stabilization and redistribution of income. Each is covered in more detail below.

Regulation

Taxes can be used to manage the consumption of something (Swain and Reed, 2010: 38). Environmental taxes, for example, can be imposed in order to incentivize individuals and organizations to change their behaviour, perhaps to consume less of a product with negative externalities such as pollution. Taxes which achieve this by internalizing the externalities of a transaction are called Pigouvian taxes, being named for the economist Arthur Pigou (Bergmann, 2009: 132).

> Excises can therefore be justified as being corrective, or Pigouvian, in that they intentionally distort consumption choices in ways that are judged socially desirable.
>
> (Glenday and Hemming, 2013: 419)

Environmental taxes—taxes on goods, such as diesel, or services, such as flying, with a proven negative impact on the environment—are examples where taxes are used to regulate behaviour.

A carbon tax is a tax on fossil fuels, especially those used by motor vehicles, intended to reduce the emission of carbon dioxide. It is increasingly clear that reducing the burning of fossil fuels is an important step in dealing with climate change and carbon taxes could be helpful in regulating the behaviour of citizens and businesses.

Carbon taxes can be effective. Hájek et al. (2019) found raising carbon tax on fossil fuels by €1 per tonne can result in the reduction of carbon dioxide of 11.58 kg per person per year. Just because they would be effective does not, however, mean that carbon taxes are easy for governments to implement. At the time of writing this book, the conflict between Russia and Ukraine is having a dramatic impact on the price of oil around the world. This works its way through the economy to higher prices at petrol (gasoline) pumps and governments are under pressure to take action to reduce those prices. This indicates how hard it would be, either now or in the future, for governments to impose taxes that would increase the cost of fuel for motorists.

The Soft Drinks Industry Levy implemented in the United Kingdom in 2018 is a tax designed to regulate behaviour: to reduce the amount of sugar consumed by children in order to reduce the levels of obesity in children. The levy was imposed on drinks manufacturers and, for the most part, they changed their recipes to reduce the sugar content rather than see the retail price of their drinks increase and/or their profit margins reduced. The levy raises relatively little (£301 million in 2020/1 [HM Revenue & Customs, 2022a]) but seems to be having a positive impact on the consumption of sugar. Pell et al. (2021) found the levy was responsible for 'changes in both the volume of, and sugar purchased in, drinks in many categories' and sugar decreased by 9.8 per cent (29.8 g) per household.

Landfill Tax was the first environmental tax in the United Kingdom. It is designed to incentivize waste producers either to produce less waste or to find alternative (cleaner and cheaper) methods of disposal. Figure 3.1 suggests the tax is working with the total amount of waste taken to landfill sites falling by 40 per cent over the 24 years shown in the graph. In fact, it has fallen by 51 per cent from the 86.9 million tonnes that went to landfill in 1998/9 (Office of National Statistics, 2021).

Another example of an environmental tax is a levy on single-use plastic shopping bags. In Ireland there has been such a tax since 2002 and it has been very effective in reducing the number of bags used in the country, with a fall from 328 bags per person in 2002 to 14 bags per person in 2014 (Department of the Environment, Heritage and Local Government, 2014). England, Wales, Northern Ireland, Botswana, Germany and Denmark are other examples of countries with a plastic bag levy.

Of course, imposing a tax is not the only way a government can tackle the issue of proliferation of plastic bags. Rwanda has completely banned plastic bags (Clavel, 2014) as have South Africa, China and Taiwan. And Kenya's law against them includes fines of up to US$40,000 (Ndiso, 2017).

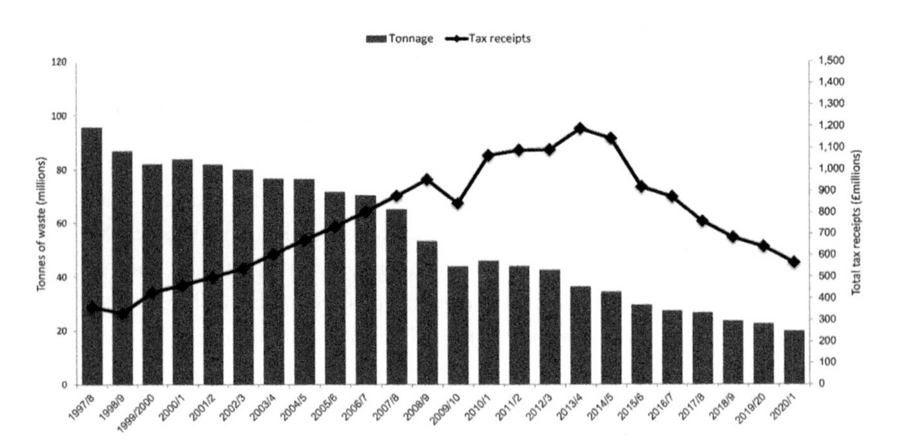

Figure 3.1 *Landfill tax in the United Kingdom, 1997 to 2021.*

Economic stabilization

Taxes can be used to stimulate investment and growth, at a national level or sub-nationally. This could be achieved in many different ways, including by having lower overall taxes so individuals have more money to save, by giving tax relief on the interest earned from savings and by giving tax relief for investment in a certain location.

A government might also want to protect some or all of its domestic industries from overseas competition and this can be done by applying import duties on competing goods, to give domestically made goods an advantage (although international trade agreements may limit the scope for this).

Towns and cities compete against each other for inward investment, especially for major developments like factories, airports and retail centres. Depending on the legislation in each jurisdiction there may be scope for the towns and cities to offer tax breaks to investors. Even if there are no special tax breaks on offer, investors will consider the levels of taxation they would pay in each location as part of their overall economic option appraisal.

There are many policies other than tax policy (such as interest rate policy and payment of welfare benefits) that governments can implement to manage their economies and perhaps these are more commonly seen. The COVID-19 pandemic was a time when governments did make changes to their tax policies in order to sustain the economy. In the United Kingdom, for example, there was a holiday on the stamp duty payable for purchasing homes in order to protect the housing market. There was also a temporary reduction in value-added tax (VAT) payable in hospitality services to help that industry recover from the lockdown.

Redistribution of income

Free market economics can result in the unequal distribution of resources. Competition creates losers as well as winners.

The prevention of human suffering that can result from such unequal distribution is a justification for the provision of a minimum level of public services (Swain and Reed, 2010:196). It is also a justification for a government to use policies to redistribute resources. Tax policies are often designed so that those who have the greatest ability to pay to have the highest burden as a way of achieving this (see progressive rates of tax later in this chapter). Taxes on wealth such as inheritance tax are also redistributive since they limit the build-up of wealth.

The European Union (EU) uses the European Regional Development Fund and its Cohesion Fund as instruments to reduce the disparities between the various regions and member states of the EU. For the period 2021 to 2027, the EU has allocated €392 billion to these funds (European Commission, 2021).

#

On occasion a government will devise a brand-new tax, giving it the opportunity to design the tax to suit whichever purpose (or combination of purposes) is relevant. It is conceivable, and perhaps likely, that when a government imposes each new tax, it does so for a discrete purpose (that is, Tax A is to raise income, Tax B is for regulation and so on) but over time all new taxes become established, part of the whole system of taxes and part of the political decision-making process. This means that the purpose of the tax may evolve, perhaps developing a hybrid purpose. It is, if nothing else, easier for a government that wishes to implement a policy change to consider whether it can achieve the desired effect by adjusting an existing tax rather than creating a new one. An example of this is the changes to the standard rate of value-added tax (VAT) in the United Kingdom between 2008 and 2011.

The basic rate of VAT in the United Kingdom had been 17.5 per cent since 1991 but was lowered to 15 per cent (the rate it had been from 1979 until 1991) in December 2008 for a fixed period of 13 months. The reason for this was to stimulate the economy in response to the global recession by reducing the retail price of many goods and services. In June 2010 the Chancellor of the Exchequer, George Osborne, announced that the standard rate would rise to 20 per cent from January 2011, a change in the rate that was expected to yield an additional £13 billion a year. Announcing the increase in June 2010 Osborne said, 'That is thirteen billion pounds we don't have to find from extra spending cuts or income-tax rises' (House of Commons Library, 2013), indicating that the purpose of the increase was to generate income.

TYPES OF TAXES

Taxation is a subject rife with jargon. This section explains various types of taxes and what is meant by terms like direct, indirect, progressive, regressive, equitable, efficient and buoyant when used to describe a tax. First, taxes can be classified into four types: income, consumption, wealth and poll taxes.

Income taxes

Income taxes are taxes levied on earnings and, in this context, income would include earnings from overseas interests and income from investments and savings as well as the salary or wages received from paid work. Examples include personal income tax for individuals and corporation tax for businesses.

The forerunner of modern income taxes was the income tax levied in Great Britain (not Ireland) in 1799 to raise money to finance the Napoleonic wars. The law that enabled it was repealed in 1802, but income tax returned in 1803 until the end of the wars in 1815 (HM Revenues & Customs, 2013). Income tax was reintroduced in 1842 and although there was talk of abolition in the second half of the nineteenth century it has remained a feature of government finances ever since. In the 1860s it raised less than 10 per cent of government budget but in 2021/2 it is estimated to raise £198 billion (24 per cent of the total government receipts of £820 billion) (HM Treasury, 2021). In fact, in the United Kingdom income tax is approved only for one year, and it has to be reenacted every year as part of the Finance Act (HM Revenues and Customs, 2013). Nevertheless, it seems unlikely that a UK government would cease to impose an income tax in its annual budget if only because it would have to increase the rates of other taxes and/or find alternative sources of income if it were to avoid budget cuts of almost £200 billion.

In the United States, income tax was proposed to finance the 1812 war but not implemented. A federal income tax was in place from 1862 but was repealed in 1872. A further attempt at a federal income tax law in 1894 was later declared unconstitutional. It was the Sixteenth Amendment to the Constitution, ratified in 1913, that finally made it clear that the federal government could levy an income tax:

> The Congress shall have power to lay and collect taxes on incomes, from whatever source derived, without apportionment among the several States and without regard to any census or enumeration.
>
> (Sixteenth Amendment to the US Constitution, 1913)

The key advantage of income taxes is that they are clearly linked to the ability to pay. However, whilst in the nineteenth century income taxes may have been stated in simple terms—in 1799 in Great Britain income tax was 10 per cent on income over £60, with some relief up to £200 (HM Revenue and Customs, 2013)—modern income tax legislation is very complicated with multiple rates of tax and lots of exemptions and exclusions. This is partly because the scope of such taxes has expanded to make greater numbers of citizens liable for income tax. Swain and Reed (2010: 46) illustrate this by showing that in 1939 in the United States only 9 million individuals paid federal income tax but 43 million individuals did by 1945. In the 2019 tax year, there were 157.8 individual tax returns, declaring $12.1 trillion in income and yielding $1.5 trillion in income tax (Internal Revenue Service, 2021: 19).

By comparison, in the United Kingdom there were 10 million people liable for income tax in 1939; 15 million by 1944 (HM Revenues and Customs, 2013) and it is estimated to be 32.2 million in 2021/2 (HM Revenues and Customs, 2021b). Of these, about 13 per cent pay income tax at the highest rate.

Income tax is often thought of as a national government tax but there are countries, such as Norway and Sweden, where there is local/municipal income tax as well as national/federal income tax. In 2010 all the states of the United States except Alaska, Florida, Nevada, South Dakota, Texas, Washington and Wyoming had some form of state income tax (Swain and Reed, 2010: 47).

Consumption taxes

Consumption taxes are taxes on what a person spends, such as value-added taxes, sales taxes, stamp duty on the purchase of land and customs and excise duties. A consumption tax is more straightforward than income tax because it is easier to measure the tax base and there are fewer exemptions and exclusions to be administered. It can be argued consumption taxes are superior to income taxes in terms of fairness because they treat everyone the same way (Metcalf, cited by Swain and Reed, 2010: 47). Some might argue that treating everyone equally is not the same as treating everyone fairly.

There are weaknesses in consumption taxes, too. They are regressive (see later) because the impact of such a tax on basic commodities like food and fuel will impact disproportionately on poorer people. There can also be problems in countries where different rates of tax are operated in neighbouring locations, such as different levels of sales tax in American States because consumers may travel across the border to benefit from the lower tax rate.

Value-added tax

A value-added tax (VAT) is a tax that is levied on the value added at each stage of the manufacture and supply of goods and services. A VAT operates throughout a supply chain. At each stage of production of the goods or services the producer is liable to pay to the government the tax on the value of the output they have produced (reflected in the selling price to their customer), but they claim back the tax that they paid on their inputs. This pattern continues all the way along the supply chain until the goods or services reach their final consumer who bears the full amount of the tax (because, by definition, they do not add value to the product and sell it on to someone else).

Value-added taxes are becoming more widespread, with examples operating in the Nordic countries, Australia, New Zealand, Japan, Canada, South America, India and South Africa. In addition, all EU countries are required to operate a VAT system. A European Commission directive (2006) sets out the framework of the scheme but each nation's government determines the level of VAT, within upper and lower limits. and the precise scope of goods and services that are liable to VAT. Table 3.1 shows the standard rate of VAT for a sample of the EU countries in January 2022 and Table 3.2 shows the standard rate for a sample of non-EU countries.

Wealth taxes

These are taxes on what is owned, which might be tangible wealth, such as real estate, and personal belongings like jewellery, or intangible wealth like stocks and shares. Examples of wealth taxes are capital gains tax and inheritance tax.

Table 3.1 *Sample of standard VAT rates in the EU 2022*

Country	*Rate %*
Hungary	27
Sweden	25
Denmark	25
Poland	23
Portugal	23
Ireland	23
Italy	22
Netherlands	21
Spain	21
Belgium	21
Germany	19
Malta	18
Luxembourg	17

Source: Avalara (2022).

Table 3.2 *Sample of standard VAT rates in non-EU 2022*

Country	*Rate %*
Argentina	27
Iceland	24
Uruguay	22
United Kingdom	20
Chile	19
Kenya	16
Mexico	16
New Zealand	15
South Africa	15
Australia	10
Indonesia	10
Switzerland	7.7
Sri Lanka	8
Bahrain	5
Taiwan	5
Andorra	4.5

Source: Avalara (2022)

Wealth taxes, on the face of it, would ensure that richer people pay more tax than poorer people and might be a way of redistributing resources within society. A problem with them is the difficulty of assessing the tax base. As some aspects of wealth, like moveable property, are difficult to assess for taxes there is a tendency to tax only wealth that is tangible and difficult to hide from the government. This approach makes the tax inequitable. If there are two equally wealthy people and one stores their wealth in assets that are outside the scope of taxation (diamonds, say) but the other does not (owning houses and cars, say), then the amount of tax they pay would be considerably different. A second issue is that being wealthy is not quite the same as being able to pay a tax bill. A person inheriting property does not necessarily have the cash to pay the tax and, as a result, may be forced to sell the property or obtain a mortgage on it in order to settle the estates tax bill.

Wealth taxes were much more popular in the nineteenth century. At the end of that century over 30 of the states in the United States levied taxes on all property but the administrative difficulties and costs means that only Florida levied such a tax in 2010 (Swain and Reed, 2010: 48).

Taxes on personal property are still in operation in many jurisdictions, but they tend to be limited to property that has to be registered or licensed, such as cars, trucks and boats, because it is difficult to hide such property from the tax collection authorities.

Poll taxes

A poll tax (or a 'head tax' or 'capitation tax') is a tax on an individual for being an individual (that is, the person is the tax base). Such taxes can be very unpopular because they impact on the poor much more harshly than the rich. The last time that a poll tax was implemented in Great Britain, as the Community Charge—in 1989 for Scotland, 1990 for England and Wales—it resulted in civil unrest. The riots and non-payment campaigns in 1990 were a contributor to the resignation of Prime Minister Margaret Thatcher in November 1990. Subsequently, the Community Charge was reduced by £140 per head in 1991 and completely replaced by the council tax in April 1993. The previous implementation of a poll tax, 600 years earlier in 1380, contributed to the Peasants' Revolt, which was largely unsuccessful but did achieve the abolition of the poll tax. It could be another 600 years before the United Kingdom has another one.

In the United States, the term poll tax is used differently, referring to a fee payable to be able to vote in an election. Technically a fee rather than a tax, nonetheless from the 1890s to the 1960s they were 'a legal way to keep African Americans from voting in southern states'. They were abolished from federal elections in 1964 by the Twenty-Fourth Amendment of the US Constitution and the Supreme Court ruled them unconstitutional in state elections in 1966 (National Museum of American History, 2022).

Direct and indirect taxes

To understand the difference between direct and indirect taxes it is necessary to appreciate the difference between the legal taxpayer and the economic taxpayer of any tax. The legal taxpayer is the person who is liable to pay the tax to the government. This is the person who receives the tax bill or assessment and who would be subject to recovery action for non-payment (for example, receiving reminders and facing prosecution in court). The economic taxpayer is the person who ultimately bears the burden of the tax; the person who is ultimately out of pocket.

A ***direct tax*** is one where the legal taxpayer and the economic taxpayer are the same person (or corporate body). Many taxes, such as personal and corporate income taxes, are direct taxes.

An ***indirect tax*** is a tax where the legal taxpayer pays the tax to the government but the burden is passed on to the economic taxpayer, possibly through a chain of people. VAT is an example of an indirect tax that works in this way (as explained above). Fuel and alcohol duties are other examples of indirect taxes: these duties are paid by the fuel companies, and the breweries and distilleries but the burden is passed on to the consumers through the retail prices of the products.

Progressive, regressive and flat-rate taxes

To assess and collect a tax a government needs to define a tax base (whether that be earnings, assets, spending, units, whatever) and prescribe at least one rate of tax to be applied to the tax base for a given period. All sorts of things can be used as a tax base. Throughout history there have been taxes on salt, cooking oil, windows, molasses and sugar, alcohol and oil products as well as on income, property holdings, inheritances and general purchases.

Tax rates are typically stated as percentages to be applied to the value of the tax base and governments tend to determine the tax rate that will apply for the full financial year but this is not always the case. In the United Kingdom (other than in Northern Ireland where rates are still payable), the council tax in each local authority area is assessed as a standard amount for all properties within the same tax band so it is not a common percentage of the value of the properties it applies to. Often, too, governments will design a tax so that different rates of tax are applicable for different sizes of tax base.

The effect of these differences in rates across the tax base can be described by using the terms progressive, regressive and flat-rate taxes.

Progressive taxes

A progressive tax is one where the marginal tax rate becomes higher for taxpayers with larger tax bases. Income tax in the United Kingdom is a progressive tax. The marginal rate of tax paid by an individual increases as their annual earnings exceeds stated thresholds. In the United Kingdom in 2022/3 there is a tax rate of 0 per cent on the first £12,570 of taxable income. From £12,571 to £50,270 the rate is 20 per cent. A rate of 40 per cent is payable on taxable income from £50,271 up to £150,000 and all taxable income above this level is taxed at 45 per cent (HM Revenue & Customs, 2022b).

A progressive rate of tax can be seen as fair since it places a greater tax burden on those better able to afford it, in keeping with the use of taxes as a way of redistributing wealth amongst citizens. Whilst this may be the case, governments have to have some regard to the disincentive effect that higher rates of tax may have. In the 1960s the United Kingdom's highest rate of tax was 95 per cent, prompting the 'super-rich' to consider tax exile status and other ways to reduce their overall tax bill (and amongst other things prompting George Harrison to write *Taxman* in 1966). The very high marginal tax rates seen in the 1950s and 1960s have been replaced with top tax rates of around 40 per cent in OECD countries and 20 to 40 per cent in developing countries.

Regressive taxes

A regressive tax is one where the marginal rate of tax paid by a taxpayer with a larger tax base is lower than for a taxpayer with a smaller tax base. Sales taxes are regressive, especially if they are applied to commodities like basic foodstuffs because rich and poor people might buy broadly the same amount of food and therefore pay broadly the same amount of tax in total. The amount of tax paid, therefore, would be a larger proportion of the poorer person's disposable income than it is of the richer person's.

The Community Charge described above is an example of a regressive tax. The liability for each adult was the same regardless of income or means. This could be a significantly high proportion of a poor person's total income whilst being a negligibly small proportion of a rich person's income.

Regressive taxes have been criticized because they embody a social injustice by placing a disproportionate tax burden on poorer people.

Flat-rate taxes

In between progressive and regressive taxes, it is possible to have a flat-rate tax, where all taxpayers are taxed at the same marginal rate regardless of their tax base.

Those in favour of flat-rate income taxes argue that this is fairer than a progressive rate of tax because it does not punish those who are high achievers. It is also argued that such income taxes are simpler and therefore easier to collect. This latter point is questionable since the complexity of income taxes is defining what constitutes taxable income: the actual rates to be applied are very simple to do (Murphy, 2017).

In 2022 many countries have flat-rate income taxes, including Bolivia (13 per cent), Greenland (45 per cent), Hungary (16 per cent), Kazakhstan (10 per cent), Mongolia (13 per cent) and Russia (13 per cent).

There are countries where the national/federal income tax is graduated but a flat-rate tax is used at the local level. This is the case with prefectures in Japan and the counties in Norway. And whilst US federal taxes and most state income taxes are progressive, some states, including Colorado, Illinois, Indiana, Pennsylvania and Utah, have flat-rate income taxes.

If flat-rate taxes are fairer and encourage economic growth, why are they not used in all countries? Critics would argue that flat tax rates effectively redistribute wealth at the expense of people on middle incomes. Under progressive tax regimes, the richest pay a higher marginal rate of tax and would benefit significantly from the change to a flat rate of tax. The poorest are likely to benefit from basic tax-free allowances leaving the middle earners to pay more (unless the government is willing to accept a lower total yield from tax and cut its spending on services instead).

Hypothecated taxes

A hypothecated tax is a tax which is raised for a specific purpose, i.e., the money raised from this tax can be used only for a stated purpose. This can give a direct link between the tax paid by a taxpayer and a public service and is one way that a public sector organization could be funded.

This approach could be attractive in some circumstances, but there are some issues related to it. First, what does the public sector organization do if the yield from the tax does not cover the cost of the service? The second issue is the opposite: what would the public sector organization do if it has a surplus of tax revenue since, by definition, the money can be spent only for the specified purpose? Because of these potential problems, governments generally prefer the flexibility of not tying any of their taxes to specific projects or services.

As well as being progressive, regressive or flat rate, taxes can also be assessed in terms of their equity, efficiency, neutrality, buoyancy, simplicity and feasibility.

Equity

The fairness of a tax (or at least the perceived fairness of it) is crucial to its collectability. Governments rely on citizens' cooperation in the payment of taxes and this is strained when citizens believe a tax to be unfair. As Jean Baptiste Colbert, Controller-General of Finances in Louis XIV's France from 1665 to 1683, put it: 'The art of taxation consists in so plucking the goose as to obtain the largest amount of feathers with the least amount of hissing' (Brooks, 2010).

As mentioned already, in the United Kingdom the Community Charge, which was in practice a poll tax, met with a campaign of non-payment and ultimately led to rioting in 1990. In the eighteenth century the unfairness of taxes was at the heart of the war of independence of the United States.

It is desirable, then, for governments to impose taxes that are equitable and there are two dimensions of equity to consider: horizontal equity and vertical equity. **Horizontal equity** means that people in similar economic circumstances are treated similarly (i.e., people with a similar ability to pay have a similar amount to pay). **Vertical equity** means that people with a greater ability to pay have to pay more. Hatgioannides, Karanassou and Sala (2017) state: 'The overarching policy question is the following: in the current era of fiscal consolidation, should the rich be taxed more? Our evidence suggests unequivocally yes.'

Ideally a tax is both horizontally and vertically equitable and some taxes are, such as income tax. Other taxes are equitable in only one dimension. Sales taxes, as mentioned earlier, have horizontal but not vertical equity and so does a poll tax.

A government should have regard to the spread of taxes across the population of taxpayers, both of people and also of businesses. For reasons of equity a government would not want to gather a disproportionate amount of its income from a small group or class of taxpayer unless its intention is to use tax as a means of redistribution. Even in such a case the government should concern itself with monitoring the effectiveness of its policy. It might also be concerned about the regional fairness of its taxes, perhaps seeking to use taxes as a way of redistributing wealth amongst its richer and poorer regions.

There is also the concept of **benefit equity**: that the amount of tax a person (or business) pays is related to the amount of benefit they receive. This is difficult to assess when taxes are non exchange transactions and not hypothecated to designated services but it is possible for individuals and corporate bodies to evaluate their total tax bill against the total of services they receive. If they believe there is an imbalance it is for them to decide whether to relocate to another territory or take some other action that will redress the balance.

Finally, there is **intergenerational equity** (Jones and Pendlebury, 2010: 9). Typically, this concept is discussed in connection with government borrowing to pay for projects and services that the current generation of taxpayers will benefit from but future generations of taxpayers will pay for because they will be paying taxes to settle the loans and interest. This might be a reasonable and fair thing to do if the money is borrowed to pay for a project that the future generations will benefit from (a high-speed railway, say) but not so reasonable if the money is used for current spending rather than for long-term investments.

Of course, there might be a 'win some, lose some' argument about this concept. Today's taxpayers may be paying the loans that were used to provide public assets for previous generations (roads, schools, hospitals, etc.), but they may also be benefitting from new assets that future generations will pay for. Indeed, if a public asset is expected to last for, say, 50 years then there is an argument that financing the asset's construction with a 50-year loan would be equitable because taxpayers will be required to pay sufficient taxes over the 50 years to repay the loan but during that time they will be benefitting from the use of the asset.

The concept of intergenerational equity can also be used to consider how education, especially university-level education, should be paid for. A graduate can expect, on average, to enjoy better earnings, have a better standard of living, better health and live longer than a non-graduate. The question is, should current taxpayers meet the cost of educating a student? One answer, of course, is not to finance university education from taxes at all, but to impose fees. An alternative is to have some form of graduate tax, which means that the graduate would pay additional taxes in the future to reflect the extra benefits that they enjoyed by having three or four years of university education.

Efficiency

Another factor to be considered when assessing a tax is its efficiency, in terms of its neutrality and its administrative efficiency (i.e., ease of collection). A neutral tax is one that does not distort the economy by causing individuals or businesses to make different decisions about goods or inputs or locations, and so on from the decisions they would make if the tax was not imposed.

Administrative efficiency is very important for the practical collection of a tax. Designing a tax which is equitable and progressive is all well and good but the tax also needs to be assessed and collected. Administrative efficiency can be calculated by dividing the total cost of collection by the total yield from the tax.

Income from salaries and wages is relatively easy to track but cash income from tips and private transactions are harder to identify and assess. As already mentioned, there is a problem with wealth taxes because wealth can be hidden or there can be difficulties in assessing the tax base. Real estate valuations are expensive to undertake, for instance, so taxes like property rates might not be revalued every year (Swain and Reed, 2010: 40) leading to inaccuracies and disparities. In the United Kingdom, domestic properties have not been revalued for council tax purposes since the initial valuations were done in 1992. This means that newly built properties have to be valued at what they would have been worth if they had been built in 1992.

A stamp duty, by contrast, is a property tax that is easier to identify and collect because it is due at the point of sale of a property and is assessed on the value of the sale.

In part the problems of tracking the liability for taxes can be addressed by deducting the tax at source. In the UK deduction at source goes back to the income tax of 1803 when banks were obliged to deduct tax from interest on bonds.

Since 1944 the United Kingdom has operated a pay-as-you-earn system for income tax, making the collection of income tax very efficient, costing 1p for every pound collected in 2012/3 (HM Revenues and Customs, 2013: 61). This low cost of collection is partly because the pay-as- you-earn system (PAYE) places some of the burden of collection on employers.

The overall cost of collecting (national) taxes in the United Kingdom in 2020/1 was 0.59 pence per £1 (HM Revenues and Customs, 2021: 8). There had been a steady improving trend to the cost of collection through to 2019/20 when it was 0.52 pence per £1 collected. The 2020/1 performance was clearly affected by COVID-19 in terms of both costs for HMRC and yield of taxes. Table 3.3 shows the cost of collecting some of the main taxes in the United Kingdom in 2011/2 and 2020/1.

In the United States, the Internal Revenue Service reported its cost of collection for the 2020/1 fiscal year as 33 cents per $100 collected and it collected $4.11 trillion. There has been a steady improvement since 1993 when the cost was 60 cents per $100 (Internal Revenue Service, 2022: 72).

An alternative way to assess efficiency is to compare the effective tax base of a tax (i.e., the amount collected) against the theoretical tax base (i.e., the maximum the tax could yield). The effective tax base is usually lower than the theoretical tax base because of tax expenditures such as reliefs and allowances. Another reason for the difference is that there will be sectors of the tax base that are too difficult or costly to administer. For example, it is common to exclude people on low incomes from income tax and small businesses from registering for sales taxes or VAT, both of which reduce the effective tax base. This makes sense on a practical and equitable basis but in countries where a high proportion

Table 3.3 *Cost of collecting UK taxes*

Tax	*2011/2 pence/£*	*2020/1 pence/£*
Income tax	1.02	0.73
Corporation tax	0.73	0.57
National insurance contributions	0.28	0.12
VAT	0.63	0.63
Administering tax credits	1.55	1.71
Overall cost	**0.63**	**0.52**

Source: HM Revenues and Customs (2021).

of people and businesses fall into these categories it significantly diminishes the actual amount of tax that can be collected versus the theoretical maximum. This is a more significant issue in developing countries where a greater proportion of the workforce is self-employed or casually employed and earning very low incomes and where many businesses are too small to be registered for VAT or sales taxes.

Neutrality

As mentioned earlier in this chapter, governments can use individual taxes to regulate consumption and influence behaviour but governments should also have regard to the negative or unintended effects of taxation. There is tension between using taxes to achieve social or political objectives and having a 'neutral' tax, one which does not have undesired consequences.

Taxes distort the operation of markets. If a tax is due on a product or service then the price paid by the buyer will be higher than the seller receives. In theory, this will lead to a reduction in demand for the product/ service. A government, however, can use the money raised from such taxes to stimulate demand or provide subsidies and tax relief for strategically important industries.

In theory, taxes on products like tobacco and alcohol and services like gambling reduce the demand for them, which a government may regard as good for the collective public health and it would benefit from lower health care costs. However, the addictive nature of these products and services means taxes on tobacco and alcohol may be increased without necessarily reducing demand, enabling the government to receive extra money. This potentially puts a government in the awkward position of wanting citizens to consume less of such harmful products but being accustomed to receiving a significant amount of income from the sale of the products that any reduction would create a gap in the budget. Also, if the level of taxes makes the products too expensive for some people, then they may choose to evade the tax by buying tobacco or alcohol through the informal economy (i.e., unlawfully), giving the government an additional problem to tackle.

Taxes that are at different rates in different jurisdictions or regions can result in consumers buying goods elsewhere. The internet makes this even more feasible, both to research prices in other places and to place orders. If the additional costs in terms of transportation, import duties, etc. are less than the price saving then a rational consumer would then buy the goods elsewhere and import them to their home location. If taxes apply on some goods but not others then consumers may substitute the untaxed goods. Governments can stimulate this if, for example, imported goods were taxed but not home-produced goods then the latter would be relatively more attractively priced.

Buoyancy

Buoyancy is the ratio of the percentage change in yield of a tax and the percentage change in the tax base. If this ratio were close to one (or higher than one) then the tax is very buoyant, rising or falling quickly when the tax base rises or falls.

Income tax and corporation tax are buoyant. If earnings or profits increase in the economy then so does the government's tax yield. For other taxes, there is a time lag before changes in the tax base result in a change in the yield, and this would cause the tax buoyancy calculation to result in a figure lower than one. Domestic property taxes, for instance, tend to have the tax base recalculated periodically (if at all, in the case of the tax base for the United Kingdom's council tax, which has not been revalued since it was introduced in 1992) so the yield from them is less buoyant.

A buoyant tax has the advantage for governments that as the tax base rises the government will receive more income, but there can be problems in a time of recession because the government's income from the buoyant tax would fall and yet this might correspond with an increase in demand for spending by government (on welfare benefits, say). This may drive the government to increase the rate of tax in order to generate more income from the smaller tax base, or it may have to cut its spending.

It may also be more difficult at budget time to estimate the income that a government will receive from a buoyant tax if the tax base is dynamic or volatile and therefore difficult to predict. Taxes on oil extraction might fall into this category, for example. At the other end of the spectrum, some taxes have a tax base that is (almost) fixed and estimating the yield is such easier. A tax on real property where market values are stable might be like this.

Given the different levels of buoyancy that taxes have a government might want to diversify its sources of income. If all its taxes were income tax then this is good when the economy is growing, wages are rising and businesses are reporting high profits, but things could become very difficult during periods where economic growth is slow, or even falling. At that time the government would see the yield from its taxes falling at the very time it might want to spend more in order to give the economy a boost. South Sudan is a country which has this sort of problem. Its government gets over 90 per cent of its income from oil, making its annual budgets susceptible to changes in oil prices, which are outside of its control.

Botswana is an example of a country that has been consciously trying to diversify its economy so that it is less reliant on minerals (diamonds, copper, nickel). The government recognized that it needs to have an economy that is sustainable after the minerals run out (or become too expensive to extract). It adopted an Economic Diversification Drive for 2009–2016 with the aim of the country being dependent on all sectors of the economy. In 2012 the country's GDP growth was 4.1 per cent despite a decline of 7 per cent in the mining sector (mining was worth 20 per cent of GDP in 2012). This is because the non-mining and utilities sectors grew by an average 6.2 per cent in 2012, and they had grown by 7.8 per cent in 2011 (Matambo, 2014: 4).

Tax elasticity is a related concept to buoyancy. The total tax elasticity of a country is the proportional change in total tax revenue to the change in GDP. Governments would like their tax elasticity to be greater than or equal to one so that the revenue from taxes grows at least as fast as the overall economy. Each government's context is different so each would have to design its taxes appropriately to achieve an overall elastic tax system. One tactic is to tax fast-growing sectors of the economy more than slow-growing sectors; another is to have progressive income taxes with a broad tax base because people and businesses will pay more tax as they become wealthier.

Simplicity

Albert Einstein said, 'Everything should be as simple as it can be, but not simpler' (cited by Sessions, 1950). The simpler a tax's definition is, the easier it is for taxpayers to understand, both in general terms and in terms of their own liability to pay. One of the incentives for the United Kingdom to create the Office for Tax Simplification (OTS) was to make the United Kingdom more attractive to investors.

Toynbee (2021) poses the question of whether people would vote for taxes to be fairer if they understood them better. She makes a reference to TaxLab (https://ifs.org.uk/taxlab/), an information service operated by the Institute for Fiscal Studies that explains the UK tax system in an impartial way, providing a portal for charts and other downloadable data.

It would seem, then, that there could be benefits for governments having tax systems that are as simple as possible. There are citizens who feel this way, too, forming lobby groups like the Taxpayers' Alliance in the United Kingdom and Americans for Tax Reform in the United States.

Unfortunately, simple tax systems have two major problems. First, simplicity and fairness are often inversely related. A poll tax is simple but on the last two occasions that it has been tried in the United Kingdom its inherent unfairness has resulted in strident protests. Second, simple taxes are easier for taxpayers to avoid or evade.

The response to the first issue might be to introduce some exemptions or relief for some taxpayers in order to make the tax fairer but this, of course, is making them less simple. The response to the second is to draft the tax legislation tightly in the first place and then seek to close any loopholes that become apparent from monitoring taxpayers' behaviour. This is rather like the way that anti-virus software works. The software includes definitions of all known viruses and has to be constantly updated by its engineers whenever a new virus is discovered.

All of this adds layer upon layer of complexity and makes tax laws long and complicated. In 2012, the OTS published a report which clarified that the UK tax code amounted to 6,102 pages (Turnbull-Hall and Thomas, 2012).

The OTS created a tax complexity index (OTS, 2015). The index has ten different complexity factors, six for 'intrinsic complexity' and four for 'impact of complexity' (see Box 3.1). The taxes that have the highest index are various aspects of corporation tax and income tax. At the other end of the spectrum, Landfill Tax and Air Passenger Duty have low scores for complexity.

BOX 3.1 THE TAX COMPLEXITY INDEX

The tax complexity index has two parts: underlying complexity and impact of complexity. The former has six components and the latter has four components, as described below.

Underlying complexity

- numbers of exemptions plus the number of reliefs (as these tend to make matters more complex for taxpayers and the HMRC);
- the number of finance acts with changes to the area (since 2010);
- the Gunning-Fog readability index (which gives an indication of how easy the text is to read);
- number of pages of legislation (which is an objective measure although it is a proxy because some complex tax policies might be expressed very briefly and less complex policies written at length);
- complexity of HMRC guidance; and
- complexity of information requirement to make a return.

Impact of complexity

- number of taxpayers (because more taxpayers means more impact);
- aggregated compliance burden for a taxpayer and HMRC;
- average ability of taxpayers; and
- revenue at risk due to error, failure to take reasonable care and avoidance.

Long and complex tax laws and regulations are not unique to the United Kingdom. For example, in 2005 the federal Income Tax Code was estimated to have over 7 million words (Hodge, Moody and Warcholik, 2005).

Feasibility

A tax has to be feasible in two ways: it has to be practically feasible and politically feasible.

Practical feasibility

Perhaps it goes without saying that a tax needs to be collectible but this is an important consideration. Practical feasibility also relates to the assessment of a taxpayer's liability in the first place. In 1976 the Layfield Committee considered the structure and financing of local government in the United Kingdom. The Committee recommended the introduction of a local income tax as a supplement to the existing local property tax rather than as a replacement, but they nullified this by recognizing that there were not practical arrangements to be able to collect it.

Modern computer systems with massive databases and multiple access channels now make it possible to keep track of the liability and payments of millions of taxpayers so the practical feasibility of a local income tax is less of a concern than it was over 40 years ago. Even so, collection of a local income tax in the United Kingdom would be difficult because many people earn their income (and thus pay tax through the PAYE system) away from the local authority district where they live. Depending on how a local income tax was designed and implemented employers might have to deduct local income tax from its employees' pay at tens or hundreds of different rates and pay the money over to tens or hundreds of different local councils. Whilst computers may make that possible it is potentially expensive for employers and councils.

One advantage of customs duties is that they are relatively easy to impose if a government has reasonable control of its borders. They are also one way to impose tax on a country's informal economy (the illicit economy of undeclared work, etc. that runs alongside the official economy) because if goods produced in the informal economy ultimately cross the borders there will be a customs declaration to make. This is in contrast to, for example, a person doing some informal labouring work for cash, which would be hard for a government to assess and collect personal income tax unless the person declared their earnings.

Another aspect of practical feasibility is the potential for taxpayers to avoid the tax. This is discussed in a separate section towards the end of this chapter.

Political feasibility

A government needs to be able to get sufficient support for (a) the introduction of a tax and (b) the periodic setting of the rate(s) of the tax. A tax therefore needs to be politically feasible.

It is a matter of judgement about what level of tax is acceptable to people and to business, in terms of the total tax paid but also the extent to which their activities are subject to tax. Having a tax proposal in a party's manifesto may not be enough to ensure the political feasibility of a tax. In the 2007 elections, the Scottish Nationalist Party became the largest party in the Scottish Parliament and their leader became First Minister in a minority government. The introduction of a local income tax in Scotland (an extra 3 pence in the pound that would be passed on to local government) had been a key element of the SNP's manifesto for that election but because they were unable to gain enough support from non-SNP MSPs for their 2009/10 budget proposals the policy was dropped in February 2009 (Carroll, 2009).

Swain and Reed (2010: 41) give another example. In the 1980s Florida sought to extend the scope of its sales tax to professional services like lawyers and accountants but the outcry from these firms and companies was so severe that the expansion of the tax was repealed.

OTHER SOURCES OF GOVERNMENT INCOME

Relatively few PBEs have tax-raising powers and fewer still, if any, are financed solely from the taxes they raise. PBEs, in general, obtain additional funding for their activities from one or more of the following:

- fees and charges;
- grants;
- donations and gifts;
- sale of assets;
- fines;
- rental income;
- interest and investment income;
- fines; and
- lotteries.

Fees and charges

Depending on the public body in question there may be very little or very significant scope to raise income from fees and charges.

As explained at the start of this chapter a tax differs from a fee for a service or a product because a tax is a non-exchange transaction. Governments can, and do, provide some goods and services in direct exchange for the payment of a fee. These include things like:

- passport and visa applications;
- tolls for using certain highways, tunnels and bridges; and
- tickets for travel on public transport.

Fees and charges are also the main form of income/revenue (perhaps the only form of income/revenue) for state-owned enterprises, like railways and utility companies.

There are a number of reasons why a PBE might charge users for services:

- to raise additional money to pay for services that are beyond the level that grants and donations and taxes can provide;
- to hypothecate some income to provide a specific service;
- to ration a service by discouraging excessive, extravagant or frivolous consumption that might happen if the service were provided for free;
- to improve management by having a clear signal between inputs and outputs (as private sector organizations do); and
- to regulate demand for a service that would otherwise be in the private sector, by creating a government monopoly (Jones and Pendlebury, 2010: 104).

Where a PBE has the power to charge for (some or all of) its services it has to determine its policy for charging and then, if it decides to levy charges, from time to time it would need to review and revise the charges.

There are some principles to underpin decisions about charging users in the public sector. Where the good or service is a pure public good (see Chapter 1), then it should be financed by general taxation. Where the good or service benefits an identifiable, specific group or a group causes negative externalities, then there is a case for imposing fees to be payable by that group (and the charges may or may not be hypothecated). In some cases, user charges may be too difficult or expensive to be implemented in which case specific taxes could be levied as a 'second best' solution (Potter, 2013: 499).

The introduction or increase of a charge for a service might be seen by the public as a hidden tax (Bergmann, 2009: 32). As explained earlier a tax is a non-exchange transaction whereas a fee is chargeable in exchange for the provision of a good or service but the public who use the service may see the introduction of a charge as an extra payment they make to government. Even if the fee were introduced in a package of measures that included an equal reduction in taxes there might be some individuals who gain by having a lower overall bill and others who lose, seeing their total bill increase.

Fees, rather than taxes, can also be used to regulate the consumption of public services. A national park that is free to enter may attract more visitors than it can manage if its pathways are not to be eroded. By imposing an entry fee, the demand to visit will be reduced (and at the same time the money raised could be used for the maintenance of the park). Differential fees can be imposed, too, to regulate or influence behaviour. A city council may design the fees for its city centre car parks so that they are attractive for shoppers who stay for a short time but prohibitive for office workers who wish to park for a full day. The intention is to incentivise workers to use public transport instead of a private vehicle.

What price to charge

When goods or services are provided for a fee, how should the level of the fee be determined? This depends in part on what the objective is. Is it to recover 100 per cent of the cost of the service or to make a profit? Is it, instead, to act as a deterrent or to ration the services? Or maybe it is to tackle inequality in access to a service by having alternative prices? In setting charges, generally PBEs would set them at a level that reflects the benefits enjoyed by the user rather than trying to maximize the yield (because they are not profit-seeking organizations). Sometimes, though, there are issues about the ability to pay which might reduce the fee in some way (such as lower fees for students from poor families).

Three broad approaches to price-setting—market pricing, cost-plus pricing and incremental pricing—are discussed below.

Market pricing

First, the public body could adopt the prices charged by other organizations providing the same or similar services. The other parties could be private sector organizations operating in the same market (for example, car park operators, leisure centres, private health care providers), or they could be other public bodies. The latter may occur because the public bodies do not want a differential in their charges to cause the public to move from one body to the other.

Taking the prices charged by other organizations has the advantage that it is easy to do and it does not distort the market for the product or service. On the other hand, it means that the charge is not related to the cost of production and the public body might make a surplus (i.e., a profit) or loss on each product or service 'sold'. This might be acceptable if the body's policy were to obtain some income as general support to its activities. It might also be fine because taking the market price yields the level of surplus that the body wants anyway.

A common technique in the private sector is price discrimination (or differential pricing). This is where the organization sells goods and services which are very similar (or even identical) at different prices in different markets. The difference in the prices does not reflect differences in production costs. For example, there is very little difference in production costs between business class and economy class flights—the former has larger seats, more legroom and more food choices but the journey takes the same amount of time—but the former might be sold at three or four times the price of the latter. Airlines can do this because the tickets are sold in different markets. Business class tickets are sold, to be blunt, to people who are spending their company's money and not their own and there is an element of extra value from the business class service that they want.

The aim of price discrimination is to price the customer based on the value they expect to receive from the product or service not on what it costs to produce it. As Ben Graham put it: 'Price is what you pay; value is what you get' (Ben Graham cited by Buffett, 2009). This applies to purchases big and small.

Robert Crandall, former chief executive of American Airlines, is quoted by Baker (2011, location 1866): 'If I have 2,000 customers on a given route and 400 different prices, I'm obviously short 1,600 prices.' Price discrimination is not confined to airlines and the travel industry: many retailers offer premium products that cost much more than the basic products, as do many online services; cinemas and theatres have lower prices for afternoon shows than the evening shows; pharmaceutical companies charge lower prices in low-income countries.

PBEs who are considering the pricing of their services may at first shun differential pricing as a private sector marketing technique, but it is not uncommon for PBEs to offer lower prices to students, the elderly and/or people on welfare benefits. It is, therefore, a technique for public managers to understand and use where it suits their policy objectives.

Cost-plus pricing

The second option for charging is to levy a charge that is a prescribed mark-up on the cost of producing the goods or service. This can be done two ways. Either the marginal cost of producing one unit of the goods/service can be calculated and the mark-up rate devised to be large enough to recover the body's overheads; or the full cost of producing one unit, including overheads, is calculated and the mark-up rate would equal the 'profit margin' required to yield the desired surplus.

Sometimes it is important that a surplus is made because it will be used to support the delivery of other products or services. This can be the case for charities where a subsidiary company is set up to be a profit-seeking, trading entity but any profits it makes are gifted to the parent charity to support whatever the charity's objectives are. The reasons for doing this are twofold:

- Charitable aims do not encompass trading so if a charity traded in its own name (in a material way) it might lose its charitable status and the tax advantages, etc. that go with that.
- If the profits are gifted under a covenant, they are not subject to tax, meaning the parent charity gets the full benefit of the profits made by the trading subsidiary.

The basis of devising the cost of which the mark-up rate is to be added can dramatically alter the resultant price. This is all about how overheads are taken into account in the calculation of the unit costs, and Chapter 5 includes a discussion of the traditional method of absorption costing and the more recent development of activity-based costing.

Incremental pricing

The third way of setting prices is to take last year's price and add an inflationary increase to it. This method fits well with an incremental budgeting process (see Chapter 2). It has the same advantages as incremental budgeting, being easy to understand and stable, but it suffers the same drawback, that there is no challenge to the original price. This means there is no challenge of the policy of charging for goods and services or of the realistic level of income that should be derived from the charges.

Often an organization will set a guideline that the budget for income will be increased by a prescribed percentage. It might be assumed that the fees will need to be increased by the same percentage but the size of the increase depends on the price elasticity of the goods or service.

Price elasticity

Price elasticity describes the relationship between the change in the price of a product and the total income yielded. In a free market a firm might expect that an increase in its price will see a drop in sales as some customers choose to buy from a competing firm or decide that, from their point of view, the product is not worth the new price. A number of factors come into this, including the existence and extent of competition and the potential for consumers to substitute an alternative product (for example, to buy margarine instead of butter). The greater the potential for customers to go elsewhere, the greater the price elasticity of the product.

A public manager can develop an understanding of the price elasticity for any fees and charges that they are responsible for by reviewing the effect previous price increases had on the income yield. This understanding will enable the public manager to identify the level of price increase needed to yield a required increase in income and vice versa.

Often a public sector body has a monopoly on the provision of services in its area of operation so by definition there is no competition. Levying charges for monopoly services is unusual; they would more likely be financed by taxes or duties. If fees and charges were levied for such monopoly services then the consumer would have little choice but to pay the increased price or not use the service, making the fee relatively inelastic.

Grants

The principal source of funding for many PBEs is a grant from government or an NGO. Grants can be unconditional, meaning that the money may be spent by the organization on anything within its remit; or conditional, where there are conditions or stipulations attached to the grant that restricts its use for specified activities or functions. Conditional grants are sometimes called ring-fenced grants or earmarked grants and they enable the grantor (which might be a national government, a supranational organization like the EU, an NGO like an aid agency, or some other PBE) to be assured that the money it gives is applied in the way that they wish.

The imposition of terms and conditions on grants, with associated requirements to provide regular reports on its use and audit certificates, make the grants more like contracts (and thus exchange transactions).

Funding by formula

A grant could be for an arbitrary amount of money or it could be negotiated in some way between the giver and the receiver. Often, though, the grant will be based on a formula. This could be a unit-based formula, such as a grant of $N will be paid for every job created by the recipient. Or the formula could be a more complicated one using metrics such as population, demographics, number of service users, average cost of providing services, land area, road length and so on.

One advantage of formula-based grants is the fact that once the formula for calculating the grant is set, it is a fairly simple and easy way of allocating resources, as the relevant numbers simply need to be plugged into the formula. This can be helpful for the grant receiver as much as the grant giver because it enables the receiver to better estimate its income in future periods. This can help greatly with strategic planning and sustainability.

When a grant is based on a reasonable formula, it can be perceived as a fair means of funding. However, as a general rule, simplicity and fairness are inversely related. A simple formula for allocating funding to local government might be to base it on the population in each local government area. This is about as simple as it can be but the chances are that some local governments will see it as unfair. Local government areas with a disproportionately high number of school children or a high number of elderly people will argue that they need more money for schools or for social care. The central government could decide that its funding formula needs to be based on the population in different age bands. This formula is more complicated but, probably, a bit fairer.

However, it could be made fairer by adding in other factors. The density of the population might be a factor because densely populated cities argue they need more money per person than a sparsely populated rural area. Then, perhaps a factor that recognizes the relative wealth or poverty of different areas could be added, or crime levels, or population health indicators.

Like many aspects of public financial management, in the end, the science will have to give way to art: someone will have to judge what is the right balance between simplicity and fairness.

Donations and gifts

Donations and gifts are more likely to be a significant source of income to NGOs and charities than PBEs involved in delivery of government services. Some charities are funded by an endowment but many have to be active in fundraising, seeking donations from supporters.

There are some PBEs that are not charities that might receive donations. Hospitals, for example, might receive bequests from patients they have cared for or donations given in memory of such patients. For organizations that receive ad hoc donations which amount to a small part of their total income it might be prudent not to include an estimate of such income in budget projections unless there is evidence of a trend of donations that allow for reasonable estimates and predictions to be made.

For organizations that are more reliant on donations, there is the issue of forecasting the income for each year, which obviously becomes more uncertain the further forward an organization is planning. As donations are a non-exchange transaction, the level of income will not be related to the services the organization produces. Such organizations need to have strategies and plans that are flexible enough to adapt to situations where the income from donations exceeds or falls short of its budget expectations.

Asset sales

Another way to raise income is to sell assets. The obvious issue with this source of income is that the PBE has to have some assets it does not want or need and such surplus assets can be sold only once.

It is sensible for a PBE not to use the sale proceeds from selling an asset to finance operating expenditure but to use it to finance capital projects or to pay off long-term loans. Whilst some PBEs will be constrained in this way, many are not, and, in difficult times, they may be tempted to sell assets to raise cash to meet running expenses. If a PBE is in a situation where its ongoing operating expenditure is greater than its operating income, an asset sale might provide a short-term solution pending the management implementing a longer-term sustainable strategy (i.e., cutting spending or raising income), but at some stage, the underlying funding problems have to be addressed if the PBE is to be sustainable.

Given that any asset that a PBE sells is by definition a public asset, there is an expectation that the sale will be at the best price obtainable. Anything less than this might raise suspicions of wrongdoing. To obtain the best price in an open and transparent way might mean that the assets are sold at auction or by open tender rather than by the private negotiation between buyer and seller.

Rental income

Governments and PBEs often own lots of land and buildings and can, therefore, obtain income from renting these assets to tenants. Public sector organizations generally are not in the business of investing in property solely to rent it out for profit: there are private sector businesses that do this and it is not really appropriate for government to compete against them. Rents are, therefore, likely to be earned only from letting out surplus land and buildings and probably amounts to a small element of the total annual income.

Interest and investment income

If an organization has cash that is not needed immediately then it can invest it. This investment might be only for one night or for several months, perhaps even a year. The safest investment of this spare cash would be in government bonds (gilt-edged bonds), but it might instead be lent to banks, building societies or other PBEs. The interest earned will be income which the organization can use to finance its expenditure.

A private sector organization might invest in stocks, shares, properties and so on. Such investments are taking a risk with the owners' money in the hope (expectation) of being rewarded with a good return on the investment. In the public sector there may need to be more caution about this sort of investment because it is public money that is being put at risk. In recognition of this, the scope of permitted investments might be proscribed by law, or even forbidden for some organizations. In the United Kingdom, local authorities can invest only for periods up to one year and, although the investment may be overseas, it must be denominated in sterling (so that there is no foreign exchange risk).

There are examples of public organizations losing considerable sums from poor investments. In 1991 the Bank of Commerce and Credit International (BCCI) collapsed and the Western Isles Council in Scotland lost £24 million. In the short term, the Council had to borrow extra money in order to meet its commitments, although over the next decade or so it recovered from the bank over 90 per cent of what it was owed.

The BCCI scandal prompted the issue of guidance on good practice for investments (for example, CIPFA's *Treasury Management in the Public Services*, 2011). Essentially good practice requires organizations to have proper governance of its treasury management activities, with an annually agreed treasury management policy and strategy and regular reports about the activity in terms of deals made, interest earned and exposure. And even with all that guidance, in 2008 a number of UK public bodies, including the Audit Commission, had money invested in Icelandic banks when they collapsed.

Fines

If a fine or penalty is imposed on someone, whether for committing a criminal or civil offence, it is neither a fee nor a tax. It is, though, a flow of money from the 'offender' to the public service organization that enforced the rule that was broken. A fine is, therefore, a non-exchange transaction.

In the overall scheme of public finances, the amount paid in fines will be very small, but it could be a significant source of funding for some public sector organizations, whether that be the courts, police forces, local councils or others. In general, fines are probably not levied to raise a significant amount of income, but it might be sensible for the organization to monitor the administrative costs of collection against the amount collected.

Lotteries

Lotteries are a form of gambling where tickets are sold and prizes awarded to the winning ticket(s). In countries where gambling is legal, it is in the public interest to regulate the number of lotteries and who operates them. As a result, many countries have national lotteries, including the United Kingdom. The United States does not have a national lottery but most of its states operate their own lotteries.

The total income from selling lottery tickets has to cover the cost of administering the lottery and funding the prizes. Any surplus that remains is net income to the government.

The terms of the lottery may determine how the net income is used. The United Kingdom's National Lottery is operated under a franchise agreement. From the ticket sales of £8.4 billion in 2020/1, about 58 per cent was awarded in prizes, 12 per cent was paid in duty to the government, 3 per cent went to commission to retailers as commission and around 4 per cent covered the lottery operators costs and profits. This left 28 per cent (£1.9 billion) to be paid to 'Good Causes' (National Lottery, 2022). There are 12 specialist organizations (relating to health, education, environment, arts, sports and heritage) that make the decisions about which applications for funding should be successful. Since the National Lottery began in 1994 it has supported 660,000 projects with £45 billion (and the government will have collected about £20 billion in duty).

BORROWING

If a government or PBE spends, or plans to spend, more money than it receives, or expects to receive, then it needs to bridge the gap somehow. If it has reserves (savings) from earlier years it could use that money to bridge the gap. The alternative is to borrow money. (Not all PBEs have the right to borrow money but when they do it can be an important source of funding.)

In order to borrow, a government issues bonds. A bond is a type of debt where the interest rate and length are fixed, and the length could be months or years. Financial institutions, companies and individuals invest in these, effectively lending their money to the government. Bonds can subsequently be traded on markets by their holders, so their market value at any point in time may differ from their face value.

Social impact bonds are a recent innovation for government borrowing and different from traditional bonds. See Box 3.2 for an explanation.

BOX 3.2 SOCIAL IMPACT BONDS

Social impact bonds (SIBs) are a particular kind of borrowing by PBEs where the money is used to finance social welfare services and projects. They are relatively new: the first was launched in the United Kingdom in 2010, and the first in a developing country was in Colombia in 2017.

SIBs are based on 'payment by results'. There is, therefore, a contract between the lender and borrower where the return that the lender receives is dependent on the performance of the programme or project financed by the bond.

An example is *Empleando Futuro,* a SIB to provide skills training and employment support to vulnerable, unemployed individuals in Bogotá, Cali and Pereira. The upfront capital commitment was 835 million COP (US$290,000) with a potential maximum payment to investors of 2.9 billion COP (US$1.0 million). The project ran from March 2017 to December 2018. It involved 1,855 people and 899 were placed into formal jobs. Of those, 677 retained their jobs for at least three months and 309 held their jobs for six months or more. The nominal return to investors was 8.2 per cent (Government Outcomes Lab, 2022).

Social Finance publishes the *Impact Bond Global Database*. In 2022 there were 138 impact bond schemes with a capital value of over $440 million, having an impact on 1.7 million people (Social Finance, 2022). A further 70 bonds were being developed in countries as different as Argentina, India, Japan and Uganda.

The interest rates on government bonds have to be attractive to people and institutions. That means they will need to be comparable with rates available from the private sector and other governments, although if the government is seen as creditworthy, they can be a little lower due to the lower investment risk involved.

The classical view is that when a government's borrowing is too high there will be a negative impact on economic activity (just as would be the case if there were high levels of taxation). The reason this happens is that significant levels of government borrowing are likely to make domestic interest rates very attractive to the international investment markets, who will need to buy the currency to invest in the government's bonds. If the currency has a floating exchange rate, this increased demand for it pushes up exchange rates, making the currency more expensive to buy overseas. This, in turn, will make the country's exports more expensive and its imports cheaper. This depresses economic activity, as production of the exported goods and goods that compete with imports will fall, and the international balance of payments will go into deficit.

Kelton argues government debt should be seen as investment into the economy rather than a cumulate deficit in government income. Her short Twitter thread (Kelton, 2018) explains government borrowing like this. When a government receives less in tax than it spends it issues bonds. The buyers of those bonds (denominated in the government's own currency) swap their currency, which is not interest-bearing, for the interest-bearing bonds. This is swapping one kind of debt, currency, for another, bonds. Under modern monetary theory (MMT), the government could have an overdraft at its central bank instead of issuing the bonds, but there are some benefits from issuing the bonds. These include:

- managing/influencing the interest rates operating in the economy;
- creating a safe place for people (and institutions like pension funds) to save their money; and
- providing a mechanism for banks to secure their deposits.

The practical constraint on government spending, according to MMT, is not the size of deficits and debts but inflation. If inflation is too high, then a government would need to take more money out of the economy, as taxation, in order to prevent people from bidding-up prices.

Government debt and GDP

When an individual goes to a bank for a personal loan or a mortgage the bank will ask the individual to provide details of their income and committed monthly payments. This is so that the bank can review the individual's situation and creditworthiness and determine how much money, if any, it is prepared to lend the individual. The bank knows that the higher the loan repayments are as a percentage of the individual's income the more risk there will be of the individual defaulting on the loan.

The same holds true for businesses, non-profit organizations and national governments. If interest payments are too high then it puts the long-term sustainability of the organization or government at risk. The situation for governments is not quite the same because governments can do something that individuals, businesses and most PBEs cannot: they can create the money they need to pay back the loan. The MMT view is that the amount of debt is not an issue if inflation is under control. The classical view suggests there is a limit to what is sustainable for a government to be able to repay.

Borrowing can be productive for economic growth of developing countries as long as the economic returns from the extra government spending are higher than the cost of repaying the borrowed money. If a government gets into a situation of having a high and unsustainable level of debt, then it not only damages economic growth and the high level of debt and interest payments will reduce the amount of money available for the government to spend on public services and development in future years.

The ratio of public debt to GDP is a key economic measure. The total global government debt was already increasing before the dramatic extra spending to respond to the COVID-19 pandemic. In 2020 the global total of public (that is, government) debt reached 99 per cent of global GDP, approximately US$87 trillion (Gaspar, Medas and Perelli, 2021). The growth of government debt in advanced economies since before the 2008 global financial crisis is stark. In 2007, on average advanced economies had government debt of about 70 per cent of GDP and by 2020 it was an average of 124 per cent of GDP.

A World Bank study (Grennes, Caner, and Koehler-Geib, 2010) showed that a public debt to GDP ratio above 77 per cent had a negative impact on a country's economic growth, and the tipping point was lower, at 64 per cent, for emerging economies. Besides this possible negative impact on growth, a high ratio of debt to GDP could be an indicator that a country may have difficult paying off its debts.

Table 3.4 shows the ratio of general government debt to GDP for a sample of countries at the end of 2018 and end of 2021. This shows a wide difference between countries and also the impact of COVID-19 (whether because of spending being financed by borrowing and/or changes to GDP).

The benchmark ratios of 64 and 77 per cent are not hard rules. Table 3.4 shows Japan's ratio is more than 250 per cent, but its government is not seen as being at very high risk of defaulting on its debts, partly because most of the debt is owed to its own citizens rather than to institutional investors.

Moving away from sovereign governments, it is not so easy to use a rule of thumb about the proportion of income that is paid in interest for PBEs. This is because some PBEs do not have the power to borrow money at all, effectively having to pay for everything from their income from grants, fees and charges. Such organizations might enter into leases and hire purchase agreements, though, and the counterparties to these arrangements need to assure themselves that the organization will have the wherewithal in future years to meet the payments.

For public bodies that do have the power to borrow money from banks and similar lenders, their borrowing powers are likely to be constrained in some way so that central government can control the aggregate level of public sector borrowing.

Table 3.4 *Government debt to GDP ratios 2018 and 2021*

	At nominal values 2018	*At market values 2018*	*At nominal values 2021*	*At market values 2021*
Australia	65.0	31.5	86.0	42.7
Brazil	75.9	n/a	78.3	n/a
Colombia	50.3	n/a	63.4	n/a
Denmark	42.5	31.1	45.3	33.1
Germany	60.9	49.8	69.3	58.7
Indonesia	29.2	n/a	38.3	n/a
Ireland	72.2	46.2	62.3	40.7
Japan	234.9	197.1	259.1	217.6
Mexico	37.7	n/a	43.2	n/a
Spain	102.6	94.6	127.6	116.9
Sweden	55.2	27.8	58.1	24.9
Thailand	40.4	n/a	54.0	n/a
United Kingdom	91.3	97.3	168.0	117.8
United States	137.5	n/a	150.2	n/a

Source: World Bank (2022).

Government borrowing is generally secured against future taxes, which means that taxpayers bear the risk of their governments defaulting on its debts, not the banks, institutions or other countries that lend the money. This is the case for national and local government in Europe and for the US federal government. However, state and local governments in the United States borrow money with an explicit statement that it is not default-free. This means that the lenders are bearing the risk of not being paid back and that is why there is a much greater emphasis placed on the credit-rating of American state and local governments (Jones and Pendlebury, 2010: 9).

The dramatic increase in total public sector debt post the coronavirus pandemic was mentioned earlier in this section. Most of that debt will be repaid by governments in full and on time, but some of it will not be. Beers et al. (2021: 3) stated that 0.5 per cent of sovereign debt was in default in 2020. This amounts to over US$440 billion and, clearly, is bad news for the lenders.

CONCLUSION

A PBE cannot create public value if it does not have any resources and the most flexible resource is money. The money may come from taxes—payments that taxpayers are obliged to make regardless of which public services they may benefit from—or from fees, grants, donations, gifts and fines. PBEs may also borrow money to cover the shortfall between their receipts and expenditure.

A government's tax policy may be designed to achieve social and political goals as well as to raise money. To do this the government would have to take into account the features of the taxes it imposes, in terms of the tax rate, yield, equity, neutrality, flexibility, buoyancy, efficiency and feasibility.

Having considered where the money comes from, the next chapter looks at controlling expenditure.

EXERCISES

1. Identify two or three taxes from your country or region and consider their strengths and weaknesses in terms of equity, efficiency, buoyancy, feasibility, flexibility. Think of ways that the weaknesses could be reduced.
2. If a government collects a toll from people who cross a bridge, is that a tax?
3. Governments could pay for every service that they wish to provide through taxes if they wanted, why do they impose fees or charges on some of the services they provide?
4. Is it fair for a government to use borrowed money to cover a deficit because future generations of taxpayers will have to repay the loans?
5. In many countries, alcohol is legally permitted for adults. Moderate, responsible drinking might be acceptable but heavy drinking causes health and social problems. One way to tackle this is to increase the price of alcohol by having a minimum retail price per unit of alcohol in order to reduce the amount individuals can consume. What do you think would be the benefits and costs, in financial terms, of implementing a minimum alcohol price?

REFERENCES

Avalara. (2022). *International VAT and GST Rates* [Webpage]. Available at: https://www.avalara.com/vatlive/en/vat-rates/international-vat-and-gst-rates.html (Accessed: 27 May 2022).

Baker, R. J. (2011). *Implementing Value Pricing: A Radical Business Model for Professional Firms* (Kindle ed.). Hoboken, NJ: Wiley.

Bastagli, F. (2013). Tax evasion: Ten terms you need to know [Online article]. ODI. Available at: https://odi.org/en/insights/tax-evasion-ten-terms-you-need-to-know/ (Accessed: 26 May 2022).

BBC. (2020). *Why We Need to Debunk the 'Deficit Myth'* [Video]. Available at: https://www.bbc.com/reel/video/p08jbbry/why-we-need-to-debunk-the-deficit-myth- (Accessed: 30 May 2022).

Beers, D., Jones, E., Quiviger, Z and Walsh, J. F. (2021). *BoC–BoE Sovereign Default Database: What's new in 2021?* London: Bank of England. Available at: https://www.bankofengland.co.uk/-/media/boe/files/statistics/research-datasets/whats-new-in-2021.pdf (Accessed: 25 April 2022).

Bergmann, A. (2009). *Public Sector Financial Management.* Harlow: FT Prentice Hall.

Brooks, A. C. (2010, April 14). 'Spreading the wealth' isn't fair. *Wall Street Journal.* Available at: https://www.wsj.com/articles/SB10001424052702304168004575177910000899010 (Accessed: 30 May 2022).

Bryson, B. (2013). *One Summer: America, 1927.* London: Doubleday.

Buffet, W. E. (2009). *To the Shareholders of Berkshire Hathaway Inc.* Available at: https://www.berkshirehathaway.com/letters/2008ltr.pdf (Accessed: 6 June 2022).

Carroll, S. (2009). Alex Salmond drops flat-rate local income tax plan. *The Guardian,* 11 February.

CIPFA. (2011). *Treasury Management in the Public Services.* London: CIPFA.

Clavel, É. (2014, February 15). Think you can't live without plastic bags? Consider this: Rwanda did it. *The Guardian.* Available at: https://www.theguardian.com/commentisfree/2014/feb/15/rwanda-banned-plastic-bags-so-can-we (Accessed: 7 June 2022).

Cobham, A., & Janský, P. (2017). *Global Distribution of Revenue Loss From Tax Avoidance: Re-Estimation and Country Results.* WIDER Working Paper 2017/55. Available at: https://www.wider.unu.edu/sites/default/files/wp2017-55.pdf (Accessed: 7 June 2022).

Council of Europe. (1985). *European Charter of Local Self-Government.* Available at: http://conventions.coe.int/Treaty/EN/Treaties/Html/122.htm (Accessed: 7 June 2022).

Daly, S. (2021). *No Taxation Without Representation: The Fragile Link Between Taxation and Representation* [Online Article]. Available at: https://taxatlincolnox.wordpress.com/2021/06/18/no-taxation-without-representation-the-fragile-link-between-taxation-and-representation/ (Accessed: 30 May 2022).

Department of the Environment, Heritage and Local Government Ireland. (2014). *Plastic Bags* [Web Page]. Available at: https://www.gov.ie/en/publication/28528-plastic-bags/ (Accessed: 30 May 2022).

European Commission. (2006). *Council Directive 2006/112/EC* [Web Page]. Available at: https://eur-lex.europa.eu/LexUriServ/LexUriServ.do?uri=CONSLEG:2006L0112:20100409:EN:PDF (Accessed: 6 June 2022).

European Commission. (2021). *European Regional Development and Cohesion Funds (2021–2027)* Available at: https://eur-lex.europa.eu/EN/legal-content/summary/european-regional-development-and-cohesion-funds-2021-2027.html (Accessed: 6 June 2022).

Gaspar, V., Medas, P., & Perelli, R. (2021). *Global Debt Reaches a Record $226 Trillion* [Blog]. Available at: https://blogs.imf.org/2021/12/15/global-debt-reaches-a-record-226-trillion/ (Accessed: 25 April 2022).

Glenday, G., & Hemming, R. (2013). Tax design from a public financial management perspective. In R. Allen, R. Hemming, & B. H. Potter (Eds.), *The International Handbook of Public Financial Management* (pp. 416–434). Basingstoke: Palgrave Macmillan.

Government Outcomes Lab. (2022). *Colombia Workforce Development Social Impact Bond - EMPLEANDO FUTURO* [Webpage]. Available at: https://golab.bsg.ox.ac.uk/knowledge-bank/case-studies/colombia-workforce-sib/ (Accessed: 7 June 2022).

Grennes, T., Caner, M., & Koehler-Geib, F. (2010). *Finding* the *Tipping Point—When Sovereign Debt Turns Bad.* Washington, DC: World Bank. Available at: https://elibrary.worldbank.org/doi/epdf/10.1596/1813-9450-5391 (Accessed: 7 June 2022).

Hájek, M., Zimmermannová, J., Helman, K., & Rozenský, L. (2019). Analysis of carbon tax efficiency in energy industries of selected EU countries. *Energy Policy*, 134. https://doi.org/10.1016/j.enpol.2019.110955.

Harrison, G. (1966). *Taxman.* London: Northern Songs Limited.

Hatgioannides, J., Karanassou, M., & Sala, H. (2017). Should the rich be taxed more? The Fiscal inequality coefficient. *Review of Income and Wealth.* Available at: https://openaccess.city.ac.uk/id/eprint/18086/ (Accessed: 26 May 2022).

HM Revenues & Customs. (2013a). *A Tax to Beat Napoleon* [Web Page]. Available at: https://webarchive.nationalarchives.gov.uk/ukgwa/+/http://www.hmrc.gov.uk/history/taxhis1.htm (Accessed: 6 June 2022).

HM Revenues & Customs. (2013b). *Pocket Guide 2013.* London: HMRC. Available at: https://assets.publishing.service.gov.uk/government/uploads/system/uploads/attachment_data/file/292030/4006_Pocket_Guide_2013_update_v2_accessible.pdf (Accessed: 27 May 2022).

HM Revenues & Customs. (2019). *2018–19 Annual Report and Accounts.* London: HMRC.

HM Revenues & Customs. (2021a). *2020–21 Annual Report and Accounts.* London: HMRC.

HM Revenues & Customs. (2021b). Table 2.1 *Number of Individual Income Tax Payers.* Available at: https://www.gov.uk/government/statistics/number-of-individual-income-taxpayers-by-marginal-rate-gender-and-age (Accessed: 6 June 2022).

HM Revenues & Customs. (2021c). *General Anti-Abuse Rule (GAAR) Guidance.* [July 2021 edition]. Available at: https://www.gov.uk/government/publications/tax-avoidance-general-anti-abuse-rules (Accessed: 7 June 2022).

HM Revenues & Customs. (2022a). *Soft Drinks Industry Levy Statistics Commentary 2021* [Webpage]. Available at: https://www.gov.uk/government/statistics/soft-drinks-industry-levy-statistics/soft-drinks-industry-levy-statistics-commentary-2021 (Accessed: 6 June 2022).

HM Revenues & Customs. (2022b). *Income Tax Rates and Personal Allowances* [Webpage]. Available at: https://www.gov.uk/income-tax-rates (Accessed: 6 June 2022).

HM Treasury. (2021). *Budget 2021*. London: The Stationery Office. Available at: https://assets.publishing.service.gov.uk/government/uploads/system/uploads/attachment_data/file/966869/Budget_2021_Print.pdf (Accessed: 26 April 2022).

Hodge, S. A., Moody, J. S., & Warcholik, W. P. (2005) *The Rising Cost of Complying With the Federal Income Tax*. Tax Foundation Special Report No. 138. Available at: https://taxfoundation.org/rising-cost-complying-federal-income-tax (Accessed: 6 June 2022).

House of Commons Library. (2013). *VAT: The New 20% Standard Rate*. Available at: https://commonslibrary.parliament.uk/research-briefings/sn05620/ (Accessed: 6 June 2022).

Internal Revenue Service. (2021). *Statistics of Income: Individual Income Tax Returns Complete Report 2019*. Available at: https://www.irs.gov/pub/irs-pdf/p1304.pdf (Accessed: 6 June 2022).

Internal Revenue Service. (2022). *Internal Revenue Service Data Book 2021*. Available at: https://www.irs.gov/pub/irs-pdf/p55b.pdf (Accessed: 6 June 2022).

International Budget Partnership. (2022). *Is It Time to Rationalize Tax Expenditures?* [Online Article]. Available at: https://internationalbudget.org/2022/04/is-it-time-to-rationalize-tax-expenditures/ (Accessed: 7 June 2022).

Jones, R., & Pendlebury, M. (2010). *Public Sector Accounting* (6th ed.). Harlow: Pearson Education.

Keen, M., & Slemrod, J. (2021). *Rebellion, Rascals, and Revenue: Tax Follies and Wisdom Through the Ages*. Princeton and Oxford: Princeton University Press.

Kelton, S. (2018). Government borrowing (debt) is not like private borrowing (debt). Let me explain. *Twitter*, 15 September. Available at: https://twitter.com/StephanieKelton/status/1041042774278189056 (Accessed: 7 June 2022).

Kelton, S. (2021). *The Big Myth of Government Deficits [TED]*. Available at: https://www.ted.com/talks/stephanie_kelton_the_big_myth_of_government_deficits. (Accessed: 25 April 2022).

Kirkup, J. (2020). *Stop Shaming Tax Avoiders* [Online Article]. Available at: https://unherd.com/2020/05/could-coronavirus-stop-tax-avoidance/ (Accessed: 26 May 2022).

Mansour, M. B. (2020). *$427bn Lost to Tax Havens Every Year: Landmark Study Reveals Countries' Losses and Worst Offenders* [Online Article]. Available at: https://www.taxjustice.net/2020/11/20/427bn-lost-to-tax-havens-every-year-landmark-study-reveals-countries-losses-and-worst-offenders/ (Accessed: 26 May 2022).

Matambo, O. K. (2014). *2014 Budget Speech*. Gabarone: Government Printing and Publishing Service. Available at: https://www.bankofbotswana.bw/sites/default/files/publications/budget_speech_2014.pdf (Accessed: 27 May 2022).

Murphy, R. (2011). *The Cost of Tax Abuse*. Chesham: Tax Justice Network. Available at: https://taxjustice.net/reports/the-cost-of-tax-abuse/ (Accessed: 8 June 2022).

Murphy, R. (2017). *Boris Johnson Can Have Flat Taxes or Democracy, But Not Both. Which One Does He Prefer?* [Blog]. Available at: http://www.taxresearch.org.uk/Blog/2017/10/04/boris-johnson-can-have-flat-taxes-or-democracy-but-not-both-which-one-does-he-prefer/ (Accessed: 6 June 2022).

Murphy, R. (2020). *MMT: A Primer* [Blog]. Available at: https://www.taxresearch.org.uk/blog/2020/12/02/mmt-a-primer/ (Accessed: 30 May 2022).

National Lottery. (2022). *Where the Money Goes* [Webpage]. Available at: https://www.national-lottery.co.uk/life-changing/where-the-money-goes (Accessed: 6 June 2022).

National Museum of American History. (2022). *Poll Taxes* [Webpage]. Available at: https://americanhistory.si.edu/democracy-exhibition/vote-voice/keeping-vote/state-rules-federal-rules/poll-taxes (Accessed: 6 June 2022).

Ndiso, J. (2017). Kenya just imposed the world's toughest law against plastic bags. *The Independent*, 28 August. Available at: https://www.independent.co.uk/news/world/africa/kenya-just-imposed-the-world-s-toughest-law-against-plastic-bags-a7916146.html (Accessed: 26 May 2022).

OECD. (2021). *Building Fairer Societies Through Global Tax Co-Operation* [Video]. Available at: https://www.youtube.com/watch?v=KEh2aYw546A (Accessed: 7 June 2022).

OECD. (2022). *International Collaboration to End Tax Avoidance* [Webpage]. Available at: https://www.oecd.org/tax/beps/ (Accessed: 7 June 2022).

Office for National Statistics. (2021). *Environmental Taxes Bulletin Tables (June 2021)* [Spreadsheet]. Available at: https://www.gov.uk/government/statistics/environmental-taxes-bulletin (Accessed: 27 May 2022).

Office of Tax Simplification. (2015). *Office of Tax Simplification Complexity Index*. Available at: https://www.gov.uk/government/publications/office-of-tax-simplification-complexity-index (Accessed: 27 May 2022).

Pell, D., Mytton, O., Penney, T. L., Briggs, A., Cummins, S., Penn-Jones, C., Rayner, M., Rutter, H., Scarborough, P., Sharp, S. J., Smith, R. D., White, M., & Adams, J.(2021). Changes in soft drinks purchased by British households associated with the UK soft drinks industry levy: Controlled interrupted time series analysis. *BMJ*, 372. https://doi.org/10.1136/bmj.n254.

Potter, B. H. (2013). User charging. In R. Allen, R. Hemming, B. H. Potter, & Potter (Eds.), *The International Handbook of Public Financial Management* (pp. 496–512). Basingstoke: Palgrave Macmillan.

Republic of South Africa. (1996). *Constitution of the Republic of South Africa. No. 108 of 1996.*

Roosevelt, F. D. (1936). *Address at Worcester, Mass. 21 October 1936.* [Web page] Available at: https://www.presidency.ucsb.edu/documents/address-worcester-mass (Accessed: 25 May 2022).

Sessions, R. (1950). How a 'difficult' composer gets that way. *New York Times,* 8 January 8, p. 89.

Shaxson & O'Hagan. (2013). *A Competitive Tax System is a Better Tax System.* London: New Economics Foundation. Available at: https://www.taxjustice.net/wp-content/uploads/2014/04/Mythbusters-2013-competitive-tax-system-is-bad-tax-system-.pdf (Accessed: 7 June 2022).

Sixteenth Amendment to the U.S. Constitution: Federal Income Tax. (1913). Available at: https://www.archives.gov/founding-docs/amendments-11-27#xvi (Accessed: 6 June 2022).

Social Finance. (2022). *Impact Bond Global Database* [Webpage]. Available at: https://sibdatabase.socialfinance.org.uk (Accessed: 26 May 2022).

Steel, I., & Nair, V. (2021). *International Corporate Tax Reforms: What Could the OECD Deal Mean for Lower-Income Countries?* London: ODI. Available at: https://cdn.odi.org/media/documents/ODI-SH-InternationalCorporateTaxReforms-WP-2710.pdf (Accessed: 26 May 2022).

Stiglitz, J. E. (2000). *Economics of the Public Sector* (3rd ed.). New York: W. W. Norton.

Swain, J. W., & Reed, B. J. (2010). *Budgeting for Public Managers.* Armonk, NY: ME Sharpe Inc.

Toynbee, P. (2021). If the British understood taxes better, perhaps we would vote for them to be fairer. *The Guardian,* 14 June. Available at: https://www.theguardian.com/commentisfree/2021/jun/14/understood-taxes-better-vote-fairer-taxlab (Accessed: 26 May 2022).

Turnbull-Hall, C., & Thomas, R. (2012). *Length of Tax Legislation as a Measure of Complexity.* London: Office of Tax Simplification. Available at: https://bit.ly/1moCeYa.

Warren, E. (2011). *Elizabeth Warren on Debt Crisis, Fair Taxation* [Video]. Available at: https://www.youtube.com/watch?v=htX2usfqMEs (Accessed: 7 June 2022).

World Bank. (2022). *Quarterly Public Sector Debt* [Webpage]. Available at: https://databank.worldbank.org/source/quarterly-public-sector-debt# (Accessed: 7 June 2022).

FURTHER READING (AND WATCHING)

Links to the following resources, and lots more, are available at www.managingpublicmoney.co.uk/extras.

The theory of taxation is a key aspect of economics so a textbook that has a public sector focus, such as Stiglitz's *Economics of the Public Sector* (2000), would give an economist's perspective on the issues. Also, the Glenday and Hemming chapter in *The International Handbook of Public Financial Management* (2013) is a good introduction to the issues of tax design.

Keen and Slemrod's *Rebellion, Rascals, and Revenue* (2021) offers a more entertaining take on the history of taxation.

For a comprehensive glossary of tax terms check out those from the OECD at www.oecd.org/ctp/glossaryoftaxterms.htm.

To learn more about the taxes in your country, such as the amounts they yield and the cost of collection, etc., review the documents you can find on the website of your national treasury. For the United Kingdom, the starting point would be www.hm-treasury.gov.uk; for federal taxes in the United States, you could start at the Office of Management and Budget at www.whitehouse.gov/omb/ or look at the Internal Revenue Service, www.irs.gov, for tax statistics.

If you want to learn more about MMT, you could try the short video, *Why We Need to Debunk the 'Deficit Myth'* made by the BBC (2020) and featuring Stephanie Kelton. Stephanie Kelton is one of the prominent voices of MMT and you can see her speaking about the myth of government deficits at a TED conference in August 2021 (Kelton, 2021).

The IMF maintains the Global Debt Database (www.imf.org/external/datamapper/datasets/GDD) with numerous datasets relating to private and public debts in 190 economies.

Francesca Bastagli's article for the ODI explains ten terms that will help penetrate 'the dark arts of tax evasion' (Watkins, cited by Bastagli, 2013). There is a video on the BBC news website that gives a quick explanation of how companies can avoid corporation tax (https://bbc.in/1s2eAnD). The OECD also have a short video, *Building Fairer Societies through Global Tax Co-operation*, about the work done over the last ten or more years to address the problem of global tax avoidance (OECD, 2021).

Chapter 4

Budget execution

LEARNING OBJECTIVES

After reading this chapter you should:

- know the stages of the budget execution phase of the PFM cycle;
- understand the concept of internal control and appreciate the importance for public benefit entities (PBEs) to have an effective system of internal control;
- understand the importance of timely budgetary control information and recognize the key components of a budgetary control report; and
- be aware of the typical financial risks that PBEs face.

KEY POINTS OF THIS CHAPTER

- The stages of budget execution (the actual collecting and spending of public money) are authorization, commitment, receipt and verification, payment, and accounting and reporting.
- It is management's responsibility to operate an effective system of internal control.
- A public manager who is a budget-holder needs timely, relevant and accurate information to be able to monitor and control the income and expenditure they are responsible for.
- Relatively few risks can be managed by taking out an insurance policy.
- Fraud and corruption are not unique to the public sector. It is management's responsibility to create and maintain systems to prevent and detect fraud and corruption (and not the responsibility of auditors).

DOI: 10.4324/9781003250838-4

KEY TERMS

Appropriation—the formal release of money from the central finance ministry or department to spending ministries or departments so that they can spend their budget.

Budgetary control—the process of managing income and expenditure in accordance with the approved budget.

Budget-holder—a manager who is given responsibility for controlling the expenditure for one or more business units or projects.

Cash flow—the total amount of money paid out and received.

Corruption—the dishonest or fraudulent conduct for private gain by those in power.

Detect control—a type of internal control that detects an error or irregularity has occurred.

Fraud—the use of deception to gain an unfair or illegal advantage.

Internal control system—the system of checks and other control measures that ensure that the organization meets its objectives.

Prevent control—a type of internal control that prevents an error or irregularity occurring.

Statement on internal control—a published statement made by 'those charged with governance' of an organization which sets out their opinion about the effectiveness of the organization's system of internal control and details proposals for addressing any weaknesses.

Treasury single account—a system of linked bank accounts that allows centralized management of cash balances.

Having prepared a budget for the year and got the taxes and/or other income approved, it is time to deliver. This is the budget execution phase of the PFM cycle described in Chapter 1. This chapter outlines various general aspects of budget execution, and it is applicable across the spectrum from small charities right up to very large government ministries. Chapters 5 and 6 then look at specific aspects of budget execution: using financial information to make decisions and public procurement, respectively.

This chapter begins by outlining the stages of budget execution. This is followed by a section explaining the concept of internal control in general before looking in more detail at a very important component of internal control: budgetary control. The fourth section is about managing cash flow and the fifth is about financial risks. The final section discusses fraud and corruption.

BUDGET EXECUTION

Preparing and approving budgets is a fundamentally important process in public sector organizations but having a great budget does not mean the planned services and projects will be delivered. A government needs to be effective at budget execution if it is to meet its objectives.

Budget execution, or implementation if you prefer, requires the government to get money into the hands of civil servants, doctors, teachers and soldiers and all the other people on its payroll, and also settle all the invoices from suppliers. A government that cannot pay teachers' salaries, for example, will struggle to have a good education service: indeed, it may struggle to have any education service at all.

The key objectives of the budget execution phase of the PFM cycle are

- complying with the budget, to ensure delivery of the government's agenda, given that the budget is (or should be) a financial expression of the government's agenda;
- managing expenditure to prevent overspending on projects or programmes; and to ensure any underspending is also controlled;
- making changes to the budget based on regular monitoring and analysis; and
- communication among the sub-units of the government or PBE about the budget.

The budget execution process is driven by budget officers. These are usually found in the finance ministry or central finance department and they have a 'thankless task' (Welham, Hadley and Miller, 2019a) because they 'are the staff who answer the phone when a spending ministry wants something: whether that be clarification on guidance, permission to spend on a sensitive area, or more money.' Budget officers (whatever their actual job titles) are needed because when a budget is approved/legislated the spending does not just happen.

The details of the work done by budget officers differs across governments and PBEs—Welham, Hadley and Miller (2019b) looked at five countries: the Netherlands, the United Kingdom, Slovenia, Malaysia and Myanmar—but there are common stages of the budget execution phase of the PFM cycle.

STAGES OF BUDGET EXECUTION

Authorization

Once the budget has been approved, the spending ministries and agencies need to be authorized to spend money in line with the budget. The authorization could be to permit the whole year's budget to be spent but often the authorization may be valid only for a month or a quarter. The authorization also may not be pro rata, perhaps allowing 20 per cent to be spent in the first quarter rather than 25 per cent.

The need for the authorization stage is to manage cash flow. Governments need to have a system of control where the aggregate spending of ministries and other publicly funded organizations (such as railways, utilities, local government and so on) can be controlled. If the level of spending exceeds, the budgeted amount or the income from taxes is not fully collected then the government will be forced to borrow more than it planned and in the long term this can lead to economic problems. Governments, therefore, operate a combination of legislative controls that limit the powers and duties of public organizations, such as restricting the ability to take out long-term loans; imposing conditions on the grants and fiscal transfers they make to PBEs aid; and requiring frequent reports on income and expenditure to be submitted to them. The ultimate control, though, is controlling the flow of cash from the government's treasury using a system of authorizations (or appropriations). In theory, at least, a government can limit the spending of an organization by not giving it any more money. In practice, if a PBE were financially mismanaged and became insolvent the chances are that the organization's creditors would expect the government to honour the debts so it would have to provide enough cash to pay off the debts, at least.

Where the parliament/legislature has not yet formally approved the budget before the budget year starts, it is normal to allow the government to start spending on a temporary authorization, often restricted to a certain limit of the previous year's expenditure for the same month.

In most countries any unspent amount of the operating budget cannot be carried forward to the following year. Some countries, including Australia, Canada, most Scandinavian countries and the United Kingdom, have systems that permit a small percentage of the budget to be carried forward. In countries like these where there is good overall control of aggregate expenditure, the use of carry-forwards of budgets encourages more efficient and effective use of the resources. In countries where aggregate control of expenditure is weak it is better not to allow carry-forwards in order to improve fiscal discipline.

The authorization of capital budgets (that is, budgets for things like major construction projects) can often be carried forward as long as the total amount is unchanged, to allow for delays and rephasing of the capital projects.

In decentralized budget execution arrangements, the authorization stage is also the stage where the government releases funds to the spending ministries and agencies. The release of money is called an appropriation. In some cases, the release of funds from the finance ministry to the line ministries has to be further allocated to subordinate spending agencies.

Commitment

The commitment stage is the point where a future obligation to pay for something is incurred. A commitment can be in the form of placing an order or awarding a project for the goods to be received or services to be rendered. Commitments are not just related to the procurement of goods or services from suppliers. The monthly salary bill for government employees and the interest payments due on debts are also commitments. Indeed, at the point a civil servant is hired or a bond is issued the government is making a relatively long-term commitment to make payments.

Commitments need to be recorded in the financial information system so that they can be monitored and the payments made correctly as and when they are due. It is important for the government to have financial systems to monitor the extent of commitments because it is expected that all such commitments will become actual expenditure once the goods or services have been delivered. The monitoring of this information can help in cash management and planning for borrowing.

If commitments are not monitored there is a risk that the government, or some ministries/departments/programmes at least, will over-commit their budget causing a problem when all the invoices arrive and there is not enough money to pay them.

Of course, the existence of a commitment does not guarantee that the goods/services or project will be delivered/executed as expected and the ultimate payment may be made for a different amount and/or at a different time.

The time lag between the commitments being made and the related payments can be a problem, especially if it stretched beyond the current financial year. This is not uncommon for particularly capital projects, such as constructing roads, bridges, schools and hospitals or implementing major computer systems.

Receipt and verification

Th receipt and verification stage of budget execution is critical because it is where the relevant spending ministry or agency or programme certifies that the goods or services have been received in accordance with the original specifications. It is appropriate for the spending ministry or agency to do this since they are in a position to know what was required from the supplier and to know whether it has been delivered.

In accounting terms, once the delivery is verified there is a liability to pay the agreed price and if the accounts are kept on an accrual basis this is the point where the expenditure is recognized (more on accrual accounting in Chapter 8). Verifying delivery is therefore tantamount to authorizing the payment of the bill, but in some countries this will be recorded as a payment order. In francophone systems, for example, after being verified a bill is passed to a payment officer, usually at the Ministry of Finance (MoF), with a request that the bill be paid.

Payment

This is the stage where the payment is made, whether in cash, by cheque or electronically. In some budget execution systems these payments will all be made centrally by the finance ministry/department but in decentralized systems the ministries and agencies may have their own bank accounts into which the treasury/finance ministry has paid their appropriations so that they can then make the necessary payments.

Accounting and reporting

Accounting is a system of recording, analysing and summarizing the transactions that occur as a result of an organization's activities. One of the key objectives of internal control (see next section of this chapter) is to ensure that complete and accurate accounts are maintained. It is critically important for the overall management of public finances that all transactions are correctly recorded in the financial management information system (FMIS).

In governments where accounts are kept on the cash basis when the payment is made it will be recorded in the accounts as expenditure. Where accounts are kept on an accrual basis expenditure is recognized at the point when the delivery was verified and a liability created. The payment of the bill extinguishes the liability.

Budget execution good practice

Good practice in public sector budget execution involves the following:

- having a **realistic and credible budget** since having a good budget is the basis of the whole function. Over-optimistic estimates can lead to multiple problems throughout the budget execution process;
- the timely and **predictable release of funds to spending ministries** and departments so that they are able to make payments to staff and suppliers in an orderly, controlled way;
- **effective cash flow management systems** so that money is available when and where it is needed, whilst minimizing the cost of borrowing (see cash flow management later in this chapter);
- **effective expenditure controls**, whether centralized or decentralized, in order to prevent the loss of public money through waste, theft or fraud (see Box 4.1);
- a system of **in-year budget changes** to allow the organization to address internal and/or external events in a managed way;
- **good quality information** about spending and receipts to use in decision making; and
- the **integration of budgeting and accounting** so that there is consistency in the information, especially where the information is published.

BOX 4.1 CENTRALIZED AND DECENTRALIZED BUDGET EXECUTION

Centralized budget execution means funds are managed by the ministry of (or from the central finance unit of a PBE). The key features of the centralized approach are:

- the pooling of funds at central level results in better cashflow control/ management;
- less (or no) funds are in the hands of the line ministries or departments;
- additional controls on payments can be implemented by the finance ministry or central finance team as well as verifications carried out by line ministries;
- the finance ministry can see the big picture that can help in resource prioritization at national/central level;
- there is uniformity of processes and procedures across all ministries and agencies (and departments); and
- there is a transparent and simplified audit trail.

Decentralized budget execution distributes budgeted funds to each line ministry and agency (or business unit of a PBE) and they have to manage their cash flow and make the payments to staff and suppliers. The key features of this approach are:

- line ministries are more empowered with direct access to the funds they need to deliver their work;
- projects, programmes and payments can be executed more quickly; and
- fewer controls compared to centralized budget execution.

INTERNAL CONTROL

The management of an organization need to be in control of it and this requires a system of internal control that has the following aims:

- to safeguard the organization's assets (which means money, of course, but also the buildings, equipment, data, intellectual property, raw materials, components, etc. that it owns and uses) from loss through error, theft, fraud, abuse, mismanagement or waste;
- to ensure the organization's complies with relevant laws and regulations and its own internal policies;

- to ensure there are complete and accurate records; and
- to produce financial and other performance reports that are timely and accurate.

Until relatively recently internal control was seen as concerning only financial systems. Now, however, it is regarded as relevant to the wider activities of an organization than its financial processes. For example, to achieve its objectives an organization (probably) needs to recruit and train people with the right qualities and qualifications. Hiring the wrong people could prove costly in both financial and performance terms and, therefore, it is appropriate that the controls operating on the recruitment and selection process are seen as part of the overall system of internal control.

The system of internal controls in an organization includes management activities like supervising junior staff and checking their work, and automated controls like validation checks on computer systems that prevent, for example, letters to be entered in a data field that should have numerals in it. Box 4.2 describes the five interrelated components of internal control.

BOX 4.2 THE COMPONENTS OF INTERNAL CONTROL SYSTEMS

Internal control consists of five interrelated components that apply to all aspects of an organization's operation (European Commission, 2006: 43):

- the control environment;
- risk assessment;
- control activities;
- information and communication; and
- monitoring.

The **control environment** is the culture of the organization regarding the control of its resources and is the foundation of the system of internal control. **Risk assessment** is the process of identifying what could go wrong in terms of the organization achieving its objectives and deciding on appropriate responses. The **control activities** are all the procedures and measures that the organization puts in place as part of its response to the risk assessment. The **communication** of good quality **information**, internally and externally, is important for meeting internal control objectives (for example, staff need to know what the organization's policies are). Finally, there should be ongoing **monitoring** of the operation of internal controls and from time to time there should be evaluations, which are likely to be conducted by internal and external auditors but could be performed by management itself.

There are two schools of thought about how internal control systems operate: Napoleonic and Nordic (Bergmann, 2009: 116). The Napoleonic school takes a centralized approach to the approval of transactions, effectively meaning that every transaction is approved by a financial controller (as well as perhaps being approved by the relevant public manager). The Nordic school, on the other hand, is a more devolved approach where the public manager is held accountable for every transaction, even for transactions where they have themselves delegated the responsibility. Government and other public bodies may construct their internal control systems to suit their purposes but they are likely to reflect the culture and norms of their place.

The Napoleonic approach to control probably improves compliance and reduces misconduct but it is 'relatively complicated, uneconomic and time-consuming' and the respective responsibilities of the central controllers and the 'front-line' managers are unclear (Bergmann, 2009: 117). The Napoleonic approach is common in France and southern Europe. The Nordic approach is more consistent with the Westminster model of government found in the United Kingdom, Australia, New Zealand and Canada. It is also more consistent with the new public management's practice of devolving financial responsibility to public managers rather than having centralized control. However, the reduced degree of central control means that the system requires more trust to be placed in more people who are far removed from the centre.

Internal controls can be written down within a PBE's operational rules and procedures, covering things like spending and receiving money, recruiting staff, procuring supplies and so on. Such rules might be termed financial regulations, financial procedure rules, standing orders or something similar and should be available to all managers who are involved in, or responsible for, financial transactions. Typically, the financial regulations describe the internal controls at a general level. They make clear the responsibilities of the chief finance officer and other staff and politicians, board members, governors or trustees (as appropriate). There would also be practical information about the authorization of individuals in terms of, for example, the maximum value of a purchase order that they may place without competitive tendering or the process for adding a new employee to the payroll.

Writing down the financial procedure rules is not enough. Public managers need to heed Schick's observation: 'when there are no rules, there is no impulse to evade them, but when government constrains financial actions or outcomes, wily spenders may have ample incentive to hide uncomfortable facts from central agencies' (2013: 37). The kinds of things Schick has in mind were having off-budget accounts, delaying payments, not reporting arrears and being unduly optimistic in forecasts. Being mindful of the potential for non-compliance means that public managers have to put in place arrangements for checking that the rules are being followed. This can include not only internal audit reviews (see Chapter 9), but also other checks carried out by the manager or programmed into systems.

Prevent and detect controls

The types of internal controls that can be implemented fall into two categories: prevent controls and detect controls.

Prevent controls

As the adage goes, prevention is better than cure and so it is preferable for an organization to design its internal control systems so that errors and thefts are prevented. Examples of prevent controls include:

- the authorization of orders for goods and services and the setting up of new recruits on the payroll system;
- authorization for the sale or disposal of assets;
- separation of duties so that no single person can carry out all the stages of a process;
- adequate supervision of staff, especially if they are handling money;
- physical controls, such as locks and fences;
- identity and password controls on computer systems;
- automatic controls that can verify the inputs to computer systems and ensure all necessary data fields are complete and validated before a transaction can be entered; and
- controls over the development, testing and implementation of computer systems.

Detect controls

In an ideal system there would be a set of controls that meant that it was perfectly controlled, with no errors, waste or theft. In practice, the human interface with systems introduces the potential for things to go wrong and for that reason organizations need to have some controls to detect when things have gone wrong. Examples of detect controls include:

- the reconciliation of banks accounts to the accounting system;
- budget monitoring reports;
- reporting to and sign off by line managers;
- spot checks of a junior's work by a supervisor, whether as a routine or on an ad hoc basis;

- computerized data-matching techniques that can identify anomalous transactions;
- stock takes;
- closed-circuit television monitoring; and
- alarms.

The cost of control

Every internal control has a cost. It could be a one-off cost such as fitting a lock to a door or an ongoing cost in the form, for instance, of additional staff being employed to perform the control. The organization's management therefore have to consider the cost of a control against its benefit (the likelihood that it will prevent or detect errors and irregularities). Whilst it might be reasonable to hire security guards to collect cash from the organization's premises and deliver it to the bank, it would be excessive to use security guards to protect the contents of a stationery cupboard.

In an environment where there are multiple controls it is possible that there may be some controls that overlap with each other, effectively introducing extra costs without giving sufficient extra benefits. Public managers, and auditors, may be able to identify solutions to such overlaps in order to have as efficient a system of internal control as possible.

Controls should be reviewed from time to time to ensure they are still effective and proportionate. This might particularly be the case where a control is applied based on the value of a transaction. Consider an organization that requires purchase orders over a certain value to be approved by a director. When this control was first implemented there might have been only a few such transactions a month. But the effect of price inflation over time means that more and more orders require the director's approval, taking up more of their time and potentially holding up the placing of orders with suppliers. It might be appropriate, therefore, for the threshold value to be reassessed from time to time to maintain a sensible balance between cost and risk.

Three key internal controls

It is management's responsibility to have and operate internal controls to protect the organization's assets. There are many, many internal controls that an organization may choose to operate but there are three that are particularly important for any organization—separation of duties, control of commitments and bank reconciliation—which are explained below.

Separation of duties

Separation of duties means organizing operating processes so that no single person carries out the whole of a financial process in order to have a check for errors and to prevent frauds. For example, the person who authorizes an order for supplies should not be the person who makes the payment to the supplier; the person who processes salary payments should not be the person who sets up new employees in the payroll system.

PBEs should set up their processes, where possible, to have different people perform each of the following three roles in respect of each transaction:

- **authorizing officer**—who initiates the transaction and makes the commitment;
- **accountant**—who makes the payment; and
- **financial controller**—who checks everything about the transaction to ensure that it was carried out properly.

Separating duties in this way is not a guarantee that nothing can go wrong because (a) humans sometimes make genuine mistakes and (b) sometimes they collude with each other. These are risks that managers should bear in mind, but they will have more assurance from a system in which duties are separated than where they are not.

In small organizations with few people, it can be difficult to have three people involved in all the processes. In this situation managers should try to arrange their staff's duties so that there is separation of duties on the most important transactions, such as adding new employees to payroll. Even two people being involved is better than just one.

Control of commitments

The second crucial internal control is the control of commitments such as the placing of purchase orders. If a vendor receives an order and duly delivers the goods or services they are entitled to be paid, regardless of whether the order was properly authorized and/or there is room in the budget. PBEs can get into severe difficulties if their public managers enter into more commitments than they can afford so it is important that the PBEs maintain control over their commitments. Modern FMISs can help with this because they can be programmed with controls which can check that sufficient budget is available before an order can be placed. However, PBEs need to put in place other mechanisms to capture the extent of their commitments, such as the reporting by a social worker every time they decide that a citizen is entitled to social care the estimated cost and duration of the care package.

Bank reconciliation

The third crucial internal control is bank reconciliation. This control does not prevent a mistake or a fraud but it will detect if the organization has made payments from its bank account(s) that have not been processed through the accounting system or where the amounts are different. It would find, for example, incidences where the value of a cheque has been altered after it was issued.

As a key internal control, it should be carried out frequently because the longer the delay in detecting an error has been made or a fraud has been perpetrated the harder it will be to resolve. The frequency depends on the size of the organization and the volume and value of bank transactions. A large organization would reconcile its accounts daily but small organizations with few transactions might not have the capacity for daily reconciliations and do them weekly, or even monthly.

Statement on internal control

From time to time, corporate scandals occur that prompt governments to take action to prevent recurrences. Examples include Enron in 2001, Worldcom in 2002 and Carillion in 2017/8. The resulting changes imposed on private sector corporations after such scandals sometimes have an impact on practice in the public sector, too. One such was the Sarbanes-Oxley Act 2002. This is a US federal law officially called the Public Company Accounting Reform and Investor Protection Act. Since it was introduced in 2002 it has had a significant influence not only on American companies, but also on the public and non-profit sectors in the United States and around the world. It is section 404 of the Act which is of particular importance. This section requires an entity's management to assess the effectiveness of its internal control system and report on it regularly. Furthermore, the external auditors are required to audit the management's assessment.

For public sector and charitable organizations in the United Kingdom there has been a requirement since the early 2000s for their statements of accounts to include a statement on internal control. This is a statement made by 'those charged with governance,' which means the equivalent of the board of directors of a private sector organization. The statement would include sections on:

- the scope of responsibilities (of the persons making the statement);
- the purpose of the system of internal control;
- the risk and control framework;
- a review of the effectiveness of the system of internal control; and
- if there are any, a description of significant internal control issues and what is proposed to be done about them.

In this context those charged with governance might be the whole board of trustees or politicians or it may be a sub-committee, such as a finance committee or audit committee. It might, for some organizations, be a combination of executive officers and non-executive board members. Whoever it is, it is a significant matter for them to make the necessary enquiries and read the relevant reports to be able to satisfy themselves that they believe the system of internal control is effective or not.

BUDGETARY CONTROL

Within the overall system of internal control, the control of income and expenditure—commonly, budgetary control—is crucially important. The budget is the financial expression of the organization's plans and maintaining the level of income and expenditure in line with the budget is obviously important in the short term, but it also has ramifications for the longer-term financial sustainability of the organization.

Sometimes a PBE operates budgetary control solely at its corporate level. This might be appropriate in small organizations where there are few employees or volunteers and all transactions are therefore approved by the board or finance committee. More likely, though, in larger organizations budgetary control is operated on a delegated basis, with summarized reports being considered at senior levels. Having said that, in such organizations there might be situations where the centralized chief finance officer or financial controller imposes a centralized system, perhaps on a temporary basis. This sort of approach can be effective when an organization is facing a short-term crisis because it allows the organization to impose a constraint on incurring new expenditure until the crisis has passed. For example, a government ministry may have a recruitment freeze or a hospital may close some wards for the last part of a financial year in order to avoid overspending its budget.

The role of a budget-holder

A budget-holder is a manager who is given responsibility for controlling the expenditure for one or more services or projects. They will be authorized to spend the approved budget on their programme, service or project and, by implication, they are not authorized to overspend the approved budget amount.

One of the basic principles of budgetary theory is that there should be a set of rules for budget-holders to follow. It is important that budget-holders have read and understand the rules that apply to them.

Monitoring income and expenditure

Typically, organizations operate on a monthly cycle of reporting. At the end of each month, reports are produced from the accounting system for each unit of the organization and they are supplied to the relevant budget-holders. The reports show the income and expenditure incurred so far in the financial year alongside the budgeted income and expenditure and calculate the variances as the difference between actual and budget.

A positive variance (or favourable variance) is where actual spending is less than the budget, or actual income is higher than budgeted. Conversely, a negative variance is where spending exceeds the budget, or income is under budget.

Of course, public managers are employed primarily to be skilled teachers, nurses, social workers, criminal investigators, fire fighters, planners, engineers, soldiers, etc. and they are not necessarily going to be skilled financial managers. They may require, therefore, training in their budget-holding role as well as ongoing advice and support from financial managers.

In some organizations budget-holders might have a meeting with a management accountant each month to review the budget monitoring report together. In others the budget-holders might be expected to be more self-sufficient. Either way there should be some feedback from the budget-holder to the central finance team about their plans and proposals to address any issues identified from the budget monitoring reports. Often this feedback will be in the form of the budget-holder's forecast of the spending to the end of the financial year. The finance team can aggregate all the budget-holder feedback and forecasts into a forecast for the whole organization.

From the budget-holder's point of view, a common frustration is that the devolution of financial responsibility to them is too firmly constrained. They may have a budget that is mostly comprised of employee costs over which they have little influence because they need approval from senior management to recruit someone into a vacancy. And often, public sector pay scales and pay rises are negotiated collectively, possibly at the organization level but possibly at a national level, and it is not easy to change someone's salary, to reward them for good performance, say, or to prevent them from leaving the organization (which are common managerial tactics in the private sector).

It is helpful for budget control systems, therefore, to distinguish between controllable and uncontrollable items within a budget-holder's budget. The controllability principle means budget-holders are held responsible only for those budget lines that they can significantly influence. This means:

- if the budget-holder can control the quantity and price paid for a product or service, then the product or service would be classed as controllable and they are responsible for all the expenditure incurred for that product or service;
- if the budget-holder can control the quantity of the product or service but not the price, then only the variance between budget and actual for usage (not price) should be identified as being the budget-holder's responsibility; and
- if the budget-holder cannot control the quantity used or price paid (which is often the case for the recharges from central support departments allocated to their budget), then the costs are uncontrollable and the budget-holder should not be held accountable for them.

Format of budget monitoring reports

The form and content of the externally published statements of accounts are prescribed by generally accepted accounting practices or international financial reporting standards, but the contents of internal financial reports are not. The FMIS needs to be able to produce information for external reporting and internal reporting so naturally it helps if the two formats are broadly similar, but the FMIS could be configured to produce internal reports to match the management structure even if that differed from the external reporting requirements.

Table 4.1 is an illustration of the format of the budgetary control report that a budget-holder might expect to receive soon after the end of each month. How soon after the month end depends on the accounting processes that the organization operates. It would not be uncommon for this to be within a few working days of the end of the month, perhaps with the reports e-mailed directly from the FMIS, but it might take much longer. The problem is, of course, that if it takes three or four weeks to produce a monthly report the budget-holder might regard the information as out of date and wait for the next one. At best this results in a delay in the budget-holder taking any necessary corrective action but it could be much worse. It is another example of the challenge of the human interface with systems of internal control.

Profiling of budgets

Note that Table 4.1 identifies the budget for the month and for the year to date. The simplest way to calculate the budget for the month is to divide the approved budget for the year into twelfths and for many items within the budget this may give a reasonable estimate of the incidence of the expenditure or income throughout the year. Salaries, for example, fall into 12 equal payments (except where pay rises are awarded mid-way during the year). Other items of expenditure might be seasonal—the cost of heating and lighting buildings is higher in the winter than in the summer—or 'lumpy', such as the expenditure on agency teachers which might be estimated for each month based on how many teaching days there are. There will be, nevertheless, some budget lines where the incidence is difficult to predict, such as emergency repairs and maintenance of buildings, where the default profile of 12th would be used.

Table 4.2 has some examples of expenditure profiles to illustrate how the pattern may differ for different items of expenditure. Profiles can be calculated from data that the budget-holder has (such as the number of school days in each month mentioned above) or from reviewing expenditure in previous years to identify the broad pattern of expenditure from month to month.

What is important about budget profiles is that the budget-holder recognizes that the budget for each month and the cumulative budget for the year to date are

Table 4.1 *Example of a budgetary control report*

Budget monitoring report							
Financial year	20xx						
Period	3						
Budget-holder	*Name*						
	Approved	*Current month*			*Year to date*		
	Budget	*Budget*	*Actual*	*Variance*	*Budget*	*Actual*	*Variance*
Service area division							
Cost centre 1							
Employees							
Salaries	480,000.00	40,000.00	40,572.00	–572.00	120,000.00	119,554.60	445.40
Agency staff	25,000.00	2,083.33	1,534.23	549.10	6,250.00	3,975.45	2,274.55
Pensions	67,200.00	5,600.00	5,630.08	–80.08	16,800.00	16,737.64	62.36
Premises							
Rent	7,530.00	627.50	0.00	627.50	1,880.00	0.00	1,880.00
Fuel, light and heating	1,200.00	60.00	149.50	–89.50	168.00	149.50	18.50
Supplies and services							
Stationery	0.00	0.00	0.00	0.00	0.00	112.46	–112.46
Printing	35,600.00	17,800.00	20,800.00	–3,000.00	17,800.00	20,800.00	–3,000.00
Telephones etc.	1,500.00	125.00	0.00	125.00	375.00	199.80	175.20

Total expenditure	618,030.00	66,295.83	68,735.81	−2,439.98	163,273.00	161,529.45	1,743.55
Fees and charges							
Sales income	−500.00	−41.67	0.00	−41.67	−125.00	−99.00	−26.00
Miscellaneous income	0.00	0.00	0.00	0.00	0.00	−12.50	12.50
Grants							
Specific grant 1	−46,780.00	−15,593.33	−15,593.33	0.00	−15,593.33	−15,593.33	−0.00
Specific grant 2	−85,000.00	0.00	0.00	0.00	0.00	0.00	0.00
Total income	−132,280.00	−15,635.00	−15,593.33	−41.67	−15,718.33	−15,704.83	−13.50
Net expenditure	750,310.00	81,930.83	84,329.14	−2,398.31	178,991.33	177,234.28	1,757.05

Table 4.2 *Examples of budget profiles*

Month	*Staff salaries (%)*	*Grounds maintenance (%)*	*Fuel (%)*	*School term-time expenses (%)*	*Year-end expense (%)*
January	8.33	0.00	15.00	7.50	0.00
February	8.33	0.00	15.00	10.00	0.00
March	8.33	5.00	15.00	10.50	0.00
April	8.33	10.00	5.00	7.50	0.00
May	8.33	15.00	5.00	10.00	0.00
June	8.33	20.00	4.00	10.00	0.00
July	8.33	20.00	3.00	7.50	0.00
August	8.33	20.00	3.00	0.00	0.00
September	8.33	10.00	5.00	10.00	0.00
October	8.33	0.00	8.00	10.00	0.00
November	8.33	0.00	12.00	10.00	0.00
December	8.33	0.00	15.00	7.50	100.00
Total	**100.00**	**100.00**	**100.00**	**100.00**	**100.00**

simply estimates of how the approved budget would be expended (or received). It is the full budget for the year that the budget-holder should not overspend; the incidence of expenditure over the first 11 months may vary dramatically from the profiled budgets, but what really matters is the position at the end of the 12th month.

It is the budget-holder's responsibility to understand the nature of the items in their budget and what the position will be by the end of the financial year. In some budgetary control systems, the accounting system can calculate a forecast for the full year by assuming that the expenditure pattern incurred in the year to date continues throughout the remainder of the year. Such a calculation might be helpful but the accounting system would not know what the budget-holder knows about their situation and plans so it is better for the budget-holder to prepare their own forecast (or projection, if you like) for the full financial year. This forecast will help the budget-holder identify if they should be taking any corrective action. Ideally, the budget-holder will be required to inform the central finance department about their forecast so that they are either assured that the budget-holder has everything under control or that there are problems.

There are two issues relating to forecasting that are worth mentioning here. The first is the method by which a budget-holder might carry out a forecasting exercise and the second is how bias may be present.

There are three broad methods of forecasting: opinion, trend and causal (Swain and Reed, 2010: 173). Opinion-based forecasting is the quickest, easiest and cheapest method, especially if the only opinion sought is the budget-holder's own. Trend forecasting uses historical data to try to predict what will happen in the future. At its simplest this could be the sort of pro-rata calculations that the accounting system might do based on expenditure in the year to date. However, there are more complicated techniques, such as using moving averages or taking averages from the same month over a number of previous years that could be employed if the data are available. Causal forecasting can be carried out when there is a causal relationship between expenditure (or income) and some other item of data. For example, the cost of a COVID-19 vaccination programme is related to the size of population, stratified by age band if the programme offers different vaccines at different ages.

The second issue is bias. Forecasting is necessarily an uncertain activity and the forecaster knows that they are unlikely to be precisely correct. They may seek to adjust their forecasts, therefore, to recognize the potential for error. A cautious or prudent forecaster might deliberately take a slightly pessimistic view and overstate their forecasts of expenditure and understate any forecasts of income. This approach means that any error in the forecasts that subsequently materializes is likely to be good news (that is, in their favour). There are times, though, when a public manager might make a more optimistic forecast. They might do this because they wish to portray a problem not to be as serious as it appears, or perhaps because they believe in a certain service or project and wish to spend more money on it. Partly as a result of this, one of the functions of the central finance department/ministry is to monitor the forecasts against what actually happens, to build up knowledge about which budget-holders are the cautious or pessimists and which are optimists and factor this into their corporate assessment of the organization's financial position.

Managing the bottom line

Public sector budgets can be very detailed, with budget estimates for every line item of expenditure and income in every cost centre or business unit. Added to that, the organization's rules may say that a manager may not incur ***any*** expenditure for which there is not a budget. If such a rule were interpreted as applying to each line item, then it would make the practical operation of the organization difficult because however good the estimates are there will naturally be some variation.

In practice, then, budget-holders are often expected to manage their budgets so that the 'bottom line' is achieved. In these terms, the bottom line means the budgeted gross expenditure net of the income that is directly and uniquely associated with the cost centre. By adopting such a regime, a budget-holder has some flexibility in terms of overspending some items and underspending others. These matching over- and underspends might be related, such as an underspending on salaries because of vacancies being used to offset the overspend on temporary, agency employees to pick up the work. Equally they may be unrelated, such as an overspend on travelling expenses being offset by reducing the expenditure on office equipment.

Managing the bottom-line approach might not be applied at the level of each cost centre but for whole divisions or departments of the organization. On the face of it, this seems reasonable, since it is placing a responsibility on a senior manager to make sure that any budgets in their division or department that are overspent are balanced by others that are underspent. A potential problem with this approach is that it can disguise problems that become apparent only when a reorganization takes place.

Consider a department where Unit A always overspends and Unit B always underspends by an equivalent amount. As far as managing the bottom line is concerned, the director is happy and the rest of the organization either does not know or does not mind about it. But then there is a reorganization where the director loses Unit B and gains Unit C, whose manager always hits their budget and the director now has a problem to balance their new budget. Can they actually reduce the spending of Unit A? Will they have to squeeze Unit C to make savings in order to bail out Unit A? If the latter approach were tried the manager of Unit C might be very resistant. Meanwhile, elsewhere in the organization the director who gained Unit B cannot believe their luck because now they have a unit that always underspends its budget allowing them to spend more money on Unit D, their favourite unit. In these scenarios the organization would have been better off if someone had looked at the causes of Unit A's and Unit B's under- and overspending and either fixed them or made permanent changes to their budgets so that they reflected the reality of the situation.

This scenario would be even worse if there were a restructuring of public services within a city and units were being transferred into and out of separate PBEs. Again, some will be winners and others will be losers. This can also be an issue in privatization or outsourcing of an element of a PBE. In that case, the private company that is 'receiving' the business unit will be keen to carry out due diligence to establish what the level of expenditure and income really is rather than relying on the budget estimates. If historically it has been an underspent budget, then the outsourcer has an easy win to make savings; if it has been an overspent budget, the outsourcer will reflect the actual cost in their pricing and the PBE could find that their expenditure on the service appears to rise as a result of the outsourcing. (It only appears to rise when compared to the budget, which is inadequate, but not when compared to the amount the service actually costs.)

Taking corrective action

Budgetary control means more than simply looking at monthly budget monitoring reports. Control requires action to be taken when things do not go according to plan. Receiving a monthly budgetary report and glancing at the figures in the bottom right-hand corner is at best a monitoring process. A budgetary control process requires budget-holders to use the information in the report and other information that they have, to identify problems and potential problems and to take corrective action.

Senior managers may be responsible for large budgets that are controlled on a month-to-month basis by junior and middle managers. These senior managers can decide to take a management by exception approach to managing the overall budget. What this means is that each of the junior and middle managers is given freedom to make decisions and manage their own budgets by themselves. When an unusual or exceptional budget variance occurs that the junior/middle manager cannot manage or resolve alone, then they pass the decision up to the next level. Management by exception can be applied in other aspects of management and its strength is that it enables managers to spend their time working effectively on areas where they can have the most impact.

A useful rule of thumb for budget-holders is to consider their budget in the light of the Pareto principle (sometimes called the 80:20 rule). The Pareto principle says that 80 per cent of effects come from 20 per cent of causes. In terms of budgetary control, this would suggest that 80 per cent of the value of budget variances is likely to come from 20 per cent of the budget lines with variances. If a budget-holder focuses their attention on making sure the 20 per cent of the budget lines that is most at risk of being overspent they stand a good chance of managing the whole budget. The key task for the budget-holder is, therefore, to understand their budget well enough to know which are the 20 per cent of line items on which they should focus their attention.

What action a budget-holder takes when things do not go as planned depends on the situation. First, is the budget being underspent or overspent? If it is underspent, they may be able to use the budget they have saved to pay for something that was not planned in the budget. Often this kind of change to the budget is permitted only within certain parameters. A public sector organization's financial rules will usually require underspent budgets above a stated threshold to be reported to the central finance team/ministry so that a corporate decision can be made about whether and how to use the budget saving.

If the budget is being overspent the budget-holder might be able to contain expenditure by deferring some items until the next year, not recruiting to vacant staff positions or finding cheaper suppliers. They might even be able to increase income or they might be able to make a change to the budget by transferring some budget from elsewhere.

In general, the total cost of a service is influenced by the volume of outputs that are produced, the quality of those outputs and the efficiency of the process of producing them. To reduce the total cost, therefore, means the budget-holder can try one or a combination of reducing the volume of outputs, reducing the quality of outputs (that is, the standard of service to be delivered) or improving the production process. And there are basically three ways that volume of outputs can be reduced:

- reduce the scope of the service;
- reduce the demand for the service; and
- increase the qualifying threshold for access to the service.

An individual budget-holder may or may not have the power to make these changes because they might need a temporary or permanent change in policy. If they do not have the power then they would have to take up the issue with their 'authorizing environment'.

The implications of exceeding the budget

The internal rules and regulations of an organization are likely to state that a budget-holder shall not incur expenditure without an approved budget to cover the amount. There might be a specific exclusion from this for emergency expenditure (expenditure in response to an imminent threat to lives or property) where the approach is spend first, deal with the consequences later (as was evidently the case as governments and PBEs responded to the coronavirus pandemic in 2020).

Just like a speed limit on a road sign does not prevent a vehicle from travelling too fast, the existence of a rule does not prevent overspending of budgets (or the under-recovery of income, which has the same adverse result for a budget-holder and the organization). The scale of overspending might often be just a few per cent of the value of the budget and arguably, therefore, within the margin or of error within the budget estimates anyway, but sometimes the scale is enormous. The Scottish Parliament building in Edinburgh was initially budgeted in 1997 to cost between £10 million and £50 million depending on the option chosen, but it was finally completed in 2004 (three years behind schedule) for £431 million (White and Sidhu, 2005).

Sometimes the overspending is the result of poor or non-existent control but at other times it may be the result of wilful action. Spending money to deal with an emergency may fall into this latter category, just as police, fire and ambulance vehicles exceed the speed limits to protect life and property. However, it could happen because:

- the budget was inadequate in the first place, not being sufficient even to cover the items of expenditure that the organization was committed to;
- the budget-holder may have made a miscalculation about the budget available to meet a commitment but was obliged to pay for it when it was delivered;
- budgets are moving targets (Bland, 2009) and sometimes plans go awry despite the best efforts of public managers, perhaps because of changes in the economy, the operating environment or other external factors; or

- the budget-holder might take a Machiavellian view that if they overspend by a few per cent there will be other budget-holders in the organization who underspend and, therefore, in overall terms everything will balance out.

The first of the above list can be a particular problem where budgets are prepared from the top-down (see Chapter 2) without the involvement of the budget-holders because (a) the finance department may not know all of the relevant policy and operational issues that lead to the organization being committed to certain items of expenditure and (b) it is easier for the budget-holder to avoid taking ownership and responsibility for their budget.

Of course, whatever the reasons for a budget being overspent there are consequences for the organization, and perhaps for the responsible public manager, too. As suggested in the third bullet point just above, for the organization as a whole there may be compensating underspent budgets, meaning that, in overall terms, the organization can stay within its total budget.

For subsequent years the organization might wish to review its budget allocations, taking funding from underspending budgets and allocating it to overspending ones. If this were done the organization would have to consider whether it was rewarding poor behaviour (overspending) whilst simultaneously punishing good behaviour (underspending). It might find that in future more of its budget-holders overspend in order to get more money in the future budget increases. This could be a particular concern if the organization uses a performance budgeting approach (see Chapter 2).

Returning to Moore's concept of the strategic triangle (1995: 22), by overspending the budget a public manager would fall out of line with the wishes of the authorizing environment, since they authorized only a certain level of spending. If, through the process of budgetary control a public manager identifies that overspending may occur it would be part of their constant balancing of the three parts of the strategic triangle to resolve it. They could seek a new authorization in the form of a revision to the budget, perhaps formally made by budget transfers (virements) or perhaps just an informal understanding with the politicians or other authorizers. This is why it is important for budgetary control systems to include a process of reporting upwards through the managerial structure of the organization.

On a personal level, a budget-holder who is responsible for overspending their budget may face disciplinary action by the organization. This depends, though, on the culture of the organization they work for. Some organizations may take a very hard line about it, whereas others tolerate or condone overspending, even when it has serious implications for the organization as a whole.

In some countries an errant public manager may face more than losing their job. In South Africa, for instance, the Public Finance Management Act 1999 (as amended) regulates the financial management of national and provincial government institutions. Section 38 requires every institution and every department of the institutions to appoint an 'accounting officer' to be responsible for the financial affairs of the institution or department. Section 38 (1) (h) requires them to take disciplinary action against any staff who contravene the provisions of the Act, commits an act to undermine the internal control system or 'makes or permits an unauthorized expenditure, irregular expenditure or fruitless and wasteful expenditure.' Not only that, section 81 states that breaches of section 38 (and some other sections) are 'financial misconduct' and grounds for dismissal. Section 86 goes further; 'an accounting officer is guilty of an offence and liable on conviction to a fine, or to imprisonment for a period not exceeding five years, if that accounting officer wilfully or in a grossly negligent way fails to comply with a provision of section 38, 39 or 40.'

Year-end spending

A phenomenon that occurs towards the end of the financial year can be an urgent rush to spend whatever amount remains unspent in the budget. This might mean buying goods that would otherwise have been bought in the following financial year, which on the face of it is a reasonable thing to do. However, there will be budget-holders using up their budgets on non-essential purchases, quite possibly wasting public money rather than saving the money so that it can be spent on something more useful in the future.

There are a number of possible explanations for why this phenomenon occurs. One is that prudent budget-holders might deliberately hold back on expenditure in the early part of the financial year as a way of cushioning their programme, service or project from unforeseen problems. In the private sector a manager might aim to have spent only 48 per cent of the budget by the halfway point of the year but earned 52 per cent of their income target. If no problems occurred in the second half of the year the manager will have exceeded their profit target. It is not quite the same in the public sector. A public manager cannot get a bonus for exceeding a profit target and faces the prospect of criticism for underspending. Against such a background, a budget-holder might adopt a strategy to use the money they have saved in the final weeks of the financial year rather than post an underspend for the full year.

Another possible explanation concerns budgets for one-off projects. The chances are that the budget would have been approved only a matter of days before the financial year commenced and thus there was little prospect of new projects commencing on the first day of the financial year. If the funding for the project was for a single year, then the budget-holder knows that there will not be funding in the following year's budget to complete the project so they try to complete it before the year end. This could be good because it puts staff and contractors under pressure to deliver; however, it could be bad if it leads to the PBE paying in advance for work that has not been done or some other arrangement or stratagem is employed to circumvent the rules. If they cannot do that, they may seek to spend this year's budget on things that would have been in the following year's budget in order to give themselves room in the following year's budget to finish the project.

Third, the budget-holder could fear that if their budget is not fully spent this year then the next year's budget will be reduced. This is a legitimate fear because the central finance department that monitors expenditure during the year will treat over- and underspending areas of the budget as signals about where the budget may be too tight or too loose, respectively. It might also be a legitimate fear because the organization may be as displeased about underspending as it is about overspending. At times where organizations' total budgets are reducing it must be still more likely that underspent budgets are reduced.

Whatever the reasons that lead to the rush of spending, the pressure for this can be so strong that organizations undertake transactions that are foolish or wasteful (and sometimes fraudulent). It is, therefore, in an organization's interests to make arrangements that reduce the likelihood of this sort of spending. There are a number of different ways that the issue can be tackled, including:

- having tighter procurement systems that make it more difficult for budget-holders to make purchases towards the end of the year unless they can demonstrate the need;
- factoring a manager's budget performance into their annual performance assessment;
- allowing budget-holders to make budget transfers (called virements) during the year so that they can adjust between tight and loose budgets; and
- allowing for the carry forward of a percentage or even all of an underspending so that it can be used sensibly in the following year rather than rashly in the current year. This sort of arrangement rewards underspending but it might also be designed so that overspendings are carried forward in order to have a stick as well as a carrot.

All of the above might work well in some organizations but each of them has a downside. Tighter procurement can prevent some managers from acquiring what they need when they need it. It might also just serve to pull the rush forward a bit; managers placing their orders in month 10 in order to avoid the tighter rules that apply in months 11 and 12.

If budget performance is a factor in a public manager's annual assessment, then they will have a motive for arguing that any overspend is not their fault whilst any underspending is entirely the result of their managerial ability, regardless of what the real causes are.

The use of budget transfers is perhaps acceptable up to a point, but some transfers might run counter to the intentions of the organization's board or political leaders so there needs to be some oversight and control of them rather than a free for all.

Finally, allowing the carrying forward of unspent budget amounts can be helpful (see for example, Douglas and Franklin, 2006) in encouraging managers not to take a short-term view but there can be problems if, for example, some budget-holders feel that their budgets are too tight and they are struggling to make ends meet whilst they see colleagues with looser budgets enjoying the ability to spend the money they did not need in the first place. Also, if the regime also insists that overspent amounts are carried forward, it can put services with inadequate budgets into a spiral of decline as the carried forward overspend means they have to cut their budgets, which then gives them a more difficult budget to meet so they overspend again, and so on.

MANAGING CASH FLOW

A PBE needs to be aware of its cash position because it needs enough cash at the right time to pay employees and suppliers. It is crucially important for any organization to monitor the level of its bank account(s) and for all but the smallest of organizations this would probably be done on a daily basis. As mentioned earlier in this chapter, a PBE also needs a way of controlling the spending by its sub-units and divisions, such as by a system of budget appropriations.

In the private sector, it is possible for profitable companies to become bankrupt. A company might sell its product at a profit but if the customers do not pay for what they buy the company will eventually find itself unable to pay its own staff and/or suppliers. This is why the liquidity ratio of a company (see Glossary) can be important because it demonstrates how well the company is placed to pay its debts in the short term.

In a PBE, in parallel with the system of budgetary control, the central finance department will need to forecast the inflow and outflow of cash and ensure that its cash balances never fall below zero (or exceed the overdraft limit if there is one). Larger organizations have more flexibility than smaller ones to manage when payments are made and organizations that are funded by buoyant taxes (see Chapter 3) or government grants have more reliable and predictable cash inflows than organizations that rely on ad hoc donations for a significant proportion of their income.

Treasury single account

Managing public money through the use of a treasury single account (TSA)—a linked set of government bank accounts that gives a consolidated view of the government's cash resources—is strongly recommended by global institutions as good practice in public financial management. A TSA could be, literally, a single bank account for all payments and receipts but it is usually a set of linked bank accounts, which make it possible for the treasury to have a consolidated view of the total cash in the accounts at any point in time.

The primary objective of a TSA is to ensure effective aggregate control over government cash balances. The consolidation of cash resources through a TSA arrangement minimizes borrowing costs. If ministries and agencies have separate accounts then some could be in surplus on any given day whilst others are overdrawn. The overdrafts will incur costs but if all the balances were aggregated the surpluses would offset some (perhaps all) of the overdrafts and the costs would be lower (or nil). There are advantages of TSAs, including:

- reducing transaction costs during budget execution, such as lower overall bank fees because there are fewer accounts;
- facilitating the reconciliation between banking and accounting data;
- having complete, up-to-date information on the government's cash resources;
- better control of the appropriation of funds to line ministries and agencies;
- better cash management, including cash flow forecasting; and
- lower liquidity reserve needs because the volatility of cash flows through the treasury are reduced and a smaller cash reserve/buffer is needed to meet unexpected events.

Collecting the cash is critical

A government or PBE needs to receive cash (whether as income or through borrowing) before it can make payments. Collecting income, therefore, is an important aspect of budget execution.

The best way to collect income is to require payment at the time-of-service delivery, or in advance. For many of the fees and charges that a PBE collects, such as entry fees to leisure centres and museums, this might be a feasible option and it would be in the organization's interest not to extend credit terms to the service users. For collecting taxes and other regularly paid bills the use of electronic payment methods like direct debit reduce the potential for arrears to build up (as well as being a much cheaper method of collection in terms of administration costs).

For some sources of income, a PBE might consider withdrawal of the service to the person until the debt has been paid. This is what a private sector organization would do. In the private sector, it would not be sensible to continue supplying goods and services to a customer that has not paid for previous supplies since it jeopardizes the financial position of the vendor.

In a public service context, there might be other considerations that complicate the situation and lead the PBE to continue to provide services to non-payers. There may be a moral reason that prevents the service from being withdrawn. If an elderly person has not paid for their care in a publicly run care home, removing them from the care home might cause greater suffering and hardship, especially if there are no relatives to care for them. The chances are that the person will require housing and care somewhere and that would place a burden on another part of the public sector. In these circumstances, if the person has assets such as a house, the PBE can look at the potential to place a charge over the assets so that the debts are paid from the proceeds of the sale of the asset.

Alternatively, removal of one public service might create a demand on another public service. Evicting a tenant from social housing may cause the person to be homeless and they would require other services, such as hostel accommodation.

For non-payment of taxes and other non-exchange items like fines there is no service or product to be withheld pending payment. The organization could try to withhold all services from the non-payer but this is fraught with difficulties. First, the organization would need to identify the person as a non-payer, which is fairly easy if they have received a bill and not paid it but it would be difficult to identify those non-payers who have not even been assessed for the tax. Second, would it be fair, for example, to prevent the children of a non-payer from attending school? Third, some public services are enjoyed by residents and visitors without charge (for example, highways and public libraries), so it would not make sense to deprive a non-payer of them. Finally, there are public goods like street lighting that are not excludable in the first place. All in all, an attempt to deprive a non-payer from using many (let alone all) public services is not feasible. This means, therefore, the governments and other tax-raising PBEs require powers to enforce the payment of taxes. There are numerous ways that a PBE might try to recover the debt before taking legal action (such as the issuing of reminders and warning notices and allowing for the debt to be settled in instalments), but for some taxpayers these methods do not result in payment of the debt and the courts have to be involved.

Debtors' prisons were a feature of Dickensian Britain but for most civil debts there is no longer the power for the courts to commit the debtor to prison. That is not the case for council tax debtors (as it was not for community charge debtors) where there is scope in the law for the debtor to be committed to prison if they are judged to be guilty of 'wilful refusal or culpable neglect' in respect of their council tax debt (Local Government Finance Act 1992, Schedule 4, Para 8 [1] [c]).

Whilst this sanction is ultimately available for a local authority to seek, in one way it is unhelpful: the court action is costly and there is a chance that the court will remit the debt so that the local authority does not actually receive the money that was the subject of the action. Nevertheless, such action might be taken in some cases as a signal to others that non-payment of council tax is unacceptable.

RISK MANAGEMENT

This chapter so far has been about control. Risk management—identifying possible future events that could have a negative impact on the achievement of the organization's objectives—might be regarded as trying to control the uncontrollable.

Risk is inherent in everything that every organization does. Risk management is about making decisions that take into account the risks and opportunities (and costs and benefits). The UK Government's *Orange Book: Management of Risk – Principles and Concepts*, says:

> At its most effective, risk management is as much about evaluating the uncertainties and implications within options as it is about managing impacts once choices are made. It is about being realistic in the assessment of the risks to projects and programmes and in the consideration of the effectiveness of the actions taken to manage these risks.
>
> (HM Treasury, 2020: 2)

Bandy and Metcalfe's research into the response of governments to the coronavirus pandemic led them to conclude 'that emergency plans in many places were not robust enough for the challenge of Covid-19' (2021: 29). As a result, they recommend that effective risk management practices should be embedded in all the institutions that are part of the PFM process (2021: 8). Brandt and Valdez (2019), writing before the coronavirus pandemic, said something similar: that more attention should be placed on what the leaders in government (public managers) should do to manage and address risks that could result in government failure. They suggested that the leaders should 'practice and embrace enterprise risk management or ERM'.

ERM identifies top risks to achieving an organization's objectives. Management can then assess the likelihood and impact that might result if the risks crystallize and make informed and deliberate risk response decisions. ERM is applied at a corporate (that is, the enterprise) level, rather than on individual projects or programmes, and it is intended to be a continuous process rather than carried out on an ad hoc basis.

Dealing with uncertainty in the budget process was considered in Chapter 2 and this section considers briefly the financial risks that a PBE might face. Financial risks fall into two categories:

- risks relating to decision making and financial management; and
- risks relating to the cost of the loss or damage that the organization suffers if an unexpected event happens (Drennan and McConnell, 2007: 98).

The first group of risks relate to transactions such as taking out loans, making investments, making judgements about things like future inflation rates, bad debts, theft and fraud. The potential losses from these sorts of risks are potentially enormous, as the example of the PBEs who had money loaned out to Icelandic banks in 2008 when they collapsed amply demonstrates. Whilst much of the money might be recovered eventually, there is still a huge cost associated with the process of recovery and possible budget cuts have to be made in the interim until the money is recovered. There is also the risk of damage to the reputation of the affected PBEs and a loss of confidence in them.

As mentioned in Chapter 2, for each risk an organization can decide to tolerate it, terminate it, transfer it or treat it. One of the ways a risk may be transferred is to take out an insurance policy. The types of risks that can be insured are, 'primarily pure, physical risks, where statistical records exist of past experience in that particular area' (Drennan and McConnell, 2007: 5). In this context a 'pure' risk is one that, if it happens, has a negative impact. In practice, a public organization is able to get insurance cover for risks like fire; flood; explosion; crimes like theft, vandalism, arson and fraud; loss of earnings; pollution; accidents and injury to employees and the public; accidental damage to property, professional negligence; and product liability (Drennan and McConnell, 2007: 99).

Even when insurance policies are used the insurer may impose an excess or deductible, which means the PBE remains liable for a specified amount of the loss(es). The insurer might also insist on the organization putting in place specific measures to reduce the risk as a condition of the insurance policy. For instance, the insurer may require physical access controls on office buildings to reduce the potential for computer equipment to be stolen, or fences around premises, or training of staff in something. Such stipulations add costs to the PBE over and above the insurance premiums.

An alternative strategy that is available to larger organizations is to set up a self-insurance fund where money is paid into the fund every month/year (akin to paying premiums to an insurance firm) and the fund can be used to cover losses as and when they occur. This does what an insurance policy does in terms of smoothing the financial impact of risks, but whereas an insurance policy has the certainty of the insurance premium (providing the insurer does not go bust), self-insurance does not have a cap. A run of losses could extinguish the fund and the organization may need to find resources from elsewhere.

Dealing with a crisis

One of the objectives of PFM mentioned in Chapter 1 was to ensure fiscal sustainability. In part, this objective is met by having good medium- and long-term plans, good forecasts and adequate contingency funds. Even so, circumstances arise from time to time that put an organization or government into a greater or lesser degree of financial distress.

Levine (1985) identified a two-by-two classification of 'fiscal stress' depending on whether its duration is short or long term and whether its severity were high

Table 4.3 *Strategies for dealing with financial stress*

		Duration	
		Short term	*Long term*
Intensity	Low	Crunch Recruitment freeze Spending freeze Reduce overtime Reduce spending on training and travel Use reserves	Squeeze Release agency and temp workers Renegotiate contracts with suppliers and partners Undertake efficiency reviews Find partners to share expenses
	High	Crisis Defer repairs and maintenance Delay capital projects Temporary closure of services/facilities Increase fees and charges	Crush Increase taxes (if possible) Redundancies Cut pay and/or other benefits Use (more) volunteers Close down services/facilities Cancel capital projects Sell off or transfer assets

Source: Adapted from Levine (1985) and Bland (2009).

or low. This results in the distinction of crushes, crises, squeezes and crunches. Table 4.3 combines Levine's work with Bland's (2009) to identify possible strategies to deal with each of the four scenarios.

When it comes to dealing with a crush, crisis or whatever, organizations in similar circumstances could have different strategies. For example, a charity could look for bigger donors and/or cut its administration costs, but an organization with tax-raising powers could look to increase tax rates and/or tax bases.

Non-profit organizations may face the ultimate disaster from a period of financial stress: bankruptcy and liquidation. Even during financial crashes it is unlikely for a government organization to be liquidated. This includes those PBEs that are operated as commercial companies (such as utility providers and railway operators) because it would cause other creditors to lose confidence in the government. Nevertheless, a PBE that is insolvent (this means it does not have enough money and assets unable to pay its debts) would need to be addressed. In the United Kingdom this might be through the government installing an intervention team but in other countries (such as the United States) the organization may be able to file for bankruptcy in order to reschedule the payment of its debts.

FRAUD AND CORRUPTION

The primary responsibility for preventing and detecting fraud and corruption (and other losses of public money) lies with the public manager, so it is part of the budget execution phase.

Fraud

In simple terms a fraud is theft but unlike a house burglary or stealing a car, a fraud involves an element of deception or trickery. Levi et al. (2007: iii) gives a layperson's definition of a fraud: 'I tell you a lie, you give me the money.' This captures one aspect of deception, the telling of a lie, but the deception might be carried out by failing to disclose some information. An example of this would be a fraud where the family of a deceased person does not tell the government about the death in order to continue to receive the deceased's government pension.

There are a vast number of ways that frauds can be committed. In the United Kingdom, the National Fraud and Cyber Crime Reporting Agency (Actionfraud) has an A to Z of more than 100 types of fraud on its website at https://www.actionfraud.police.uk/a-z-of-fraud-category.

The number and value of frauds is rising. Gee and Button (2021: 6) estimate the global level of fraud to be 6.4 per cent of GDP (or $5.4 trillion).

Specifically for the United Kingdom, the National Crime Agency (2022) says that 'Fraud is the most commonly experienced crime.' In 2021 the Victims Commissioner (2021) estimated 4.6 million people a year are affected by fraud, and fraud accounts for 39 per cent of all crimes in the United Kingdom. Scams during the COVID-19 pandemic increased the level of fraud by almost 20 per cent in the UK (Office for National Statistics, cited by Gee and Button, 2021: 7).

The level of fraud in the United Kingdom in 2005 was estimated to be about £10 billion, of which about two-thirds related to frauds perpetrated against the public sector (Levi et al., 2007: 3). The picture was much the same in the 2013 report. Fraud against the private sector was estimated at £21.2 billion and fraud against the public sector was £20.6 billion. By 2021 it is estimated that the financial losses are £137 billion a year (Gee and Button, 2021: 7).

Corruption

Corruption is dishonest or fraudulent conduct by those in power. Transparency International defines it as 'the abuse of entrusted power for private gain' (www.transparency.org/en/what-is-corruption). Corruption often involves bribery which is the giving of money or something else of value to someone to induce them to act in a certain way.

Corruption could happen in any part of the public sector but Mauro, Medas and Fournier (2019) suggest that it is more prevalent in extractive industries like oil and minerals, because of the vast amounts of money and profits involved, and state-owned enterprises, where the managers may be unduly influenced by politicians.

Public procurement is another of Mauro, Medas and Fournier's corruption 'hotspots' (2019), particular very high-value projects, such as infrastructure construction and defence systems. The most common forms of corruption in procurement are:

- bribes to officials to obtain contracts;
- collusion/price-rigging by bidders;
- facilitation payments paid to officials to obtain licences, certificates, etc. that they need; and
- bribes to gain acceptance of substandard work or materials (Sanchez, 2013: 315).

Sanchez (2013) reports on Kenny (2006) suggesting that the real damage of corruption is not the narrow financial impact it has on a project but the longer-term economic costs because it reduces the rate of return on public investment and possibly increases the long-term maintenance costs.

Mauro, Medas and Fournier (2019) echo this in their article describing the social costs that accompany the direct financial losses of tax revenue. Corruption can reduce (eliminate?) trust in the government, which could have consequential impacts, such as reducing the willingness of taxpayers to pay their taxes.

Corruption works in small ways as well as in the award of big contracts. Often poor people are disproportionately affected by it because they have to pay bribes to public officials in order to receive public services.

Transparency International is an NGO that campaigns for the eradication of corruption and it publishes annually its *Corruption Perceptions Index* (CPI). The countries that were the top and bottom deciles of the 2021 rankings are shown in Table 4.4.

The CPI is produced from surveys of country experts and business leaders. Transparency International's reasons for producing and publishing it is to raise awareness about the levels of corruption around the world and to prompt action. Despite its fame and the frequency of its use in newspaper articles, users of the CPI should take care in drawing conclusions from it. Søreide (2006), for example, criticizes the CPI for presenting complex issues in a simple way that implies a level of precision that is unjustified. Table 4.4 includes the composite scores for the sample of countries and they separate some countries by only one point. However, there is a margin of error associated with the score for every country, which means that an individual country's actual ranking might be 20 or more places higher or lower (Søreide, 2006: 10).

What can be done about fraud and corruption?

It is, of course, better to prevent a fraud than to detect it after it has happened. Reducing fraud and corruption would have many benefits. Mauro, Medas and

Table 4.4 *Rankings in the 2021 Corruptions Perceptions Index*

Rank	Country	Score	Rank	Country	Score
1	Denmark	88	164	Comoros	20
1	New Zealand	88	164	Haiti	20
1	Finland	88	164	Chad	20
4	Sweden	85	164	Nicaragua	20
4	Norway	85	164	Sudan	20
4	Singapore	85	169	Burundi	19
7	Switzerland	84	169	DR Congo	19
8	Netherlands	82	169	Turkmenistan	19
9	Luxembourg	81	172	Equatorial Guinea	17
10	Germany	80	172	Libya	17
11	United Kingdom	75	174	Afghanistan	16
12	Hong Kong	76	174	North Korea	16
13	Austria	74	174	Yemen	16
13	Canada	74	177	Venezuela	14
13	Estonia	74	178	Somalia	13
13	Ireland	74	178	Syria	13
13	Iceland	74	180	South Sudan	11

Source: Transparency International (2022).

Fournier (2019) noted: 'Countries that reduce corruption significantly are rewarded with surges in tax revenue.' Aside from this, governments could expect to get better value for money on their spending, and citizens could have better public services and facilities. However, 'Success requires political will, perseverance, and a commitment to continuously upgrade institutions over many years' (Mauro, Medas and Fournier, 2019).

The nature of fraud is that it is a concealed crime, and Gee (2010) reports that detection rates are seldom better than one in 30. Against the background of fraudsters being difficult to detect, an organization is likely to get a better return by using its resources preventing frauds rather than detecting them and in order to prevent them an organization needs to understand what causes fraud.

There are a number of factors that can contribute to fraud happening. These include the culture of the organization, low employee morale, employee dissatisfaction with their salary and working conditions, obsolete systems that cannot accommodate new transaction types or increases in transaction volumes. More fundamentally, research has shown that there are three factors in place—the fraud triangle (Cressey, 1951; Albrecht, 2014)—when people commit fraud. This is illustrated in Figure 4.1.

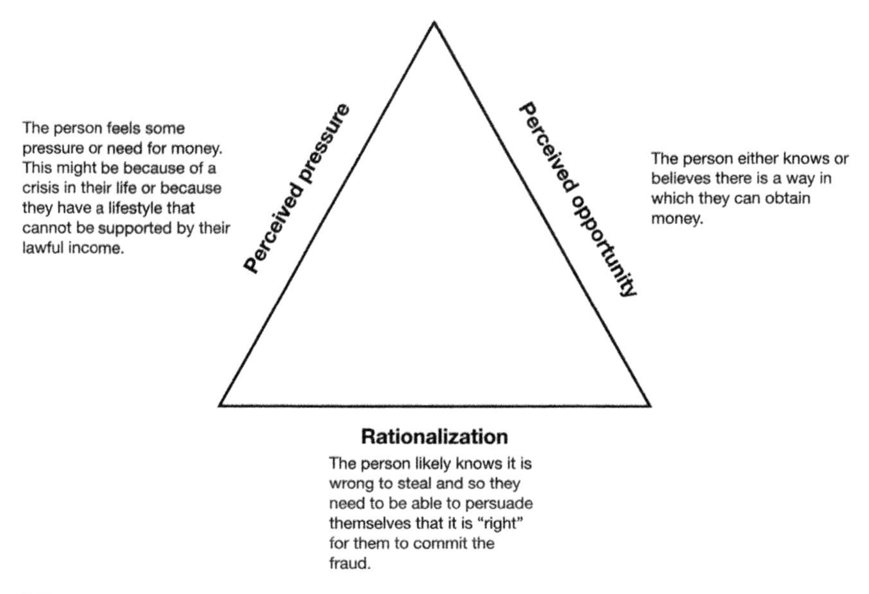

Figure 4.1 *The fraud triangle.*

There are things that a government or PBE can do within its PFM system to address some or all of the factors in the fraud triangle. Effective internal controls systems reduce the opportunity for people to steal money or other valuable assets.

The perceived pressure that a potential fraudster feels may or may not be something that an organization can directly influence. If the pressure is the result of a drug or gambling addiction that may not be something that the organization directly created. However, if the pressure is the result of not paying salaries on time, then it is something that the organization could, and should, address.

The third factor, rationalization, can be addressed by an organization having an anti-fraud culture (Hough, 2021). By having clear, consistent messages that fraud is unacceptable and leaders who visibly lead with integrity, treating everyone fairly, will make rationalization much harder. If the culture allows or tolerates poor behaviour and fraud it becomes easier for people to convince themselves that it is fine to commit fraud. Indeed, they may find themselves finding it difficult not to comply with the norm.

Jessen-Thiessen and McDonald (2018) wrote an interesting article about applying behavioural insights theory (commonly referred to as nudge theory) to tackling corruption. They recognize it is difficult because ethical decisions are a battle between morality and self-interest. They wrote: 'Integrity is a matter of self-respect. Public sector staff should be reminded regularly of the trust placed in them and the integrity expected of them.'

One of the perhaps counter-intuitive aspects of their article is that sharing responsibility reduces guilt and makes it easier for people to do nothing to fix what is wrong. They advocate, therefore, policies that evoke individual responsibility and make it easier for individuals to report misconduct. Nnadi (2020) wrote an article putting forward the view that policies that encourage and protect whistleblowers could solve the problem of corruption in Africa if financial rewards are attached, as is the case in Nigeria. Behn (2017) describes a different kind of reward for whistleblowers: that managers should take them to lunch and make sure other people know about. If they do not do this, they 'have all sent a message: We don't tolerate whistleblowers.'

CONCLUSION

Budget execution is the phase of the PFM cycle that gets stuff done, in terms of both collecting revenue and spending money on projects, programmes and services.

To do all this effectively and efficiently, the management of a PBE has to put in place a system of internal control. These controls can either prevent or detect errors, losses and waste; and they impose a cost of the organization at the same time.

Budgetary control is a critical component of the internal control system. The consequences of poor control of income and expenditure can be the failure of the organization to achieve its goals efficiently, if at all.

Internal control systems can be extremely well designed but ultimately prove to be ineffective because of the way people interface with them. This suggests that the decision making by public managers is important and that is the subject of the next chapter.

EXERCISES

1. In your context, identify some prevent and detect controls. Discuss how effective they are, whether they could be improved and whether they could be replaced or even abandoned.
2. One of the risks associated with budget execution is non-compliance with rules and regulations. What are some of the actions a government could take to mitigate this risk?
3. As a budget-holder in a PBE should you underspend your budget? Give reasons for your answer.
4. What are some reasons for a government to include the treasury function within its Ministry of Finance rather than transferring it to an independent agency?

REFERENCES

Albrecht, W. S. (2014). Iconic fraud triangle endures. *Fraud Magazine*, July/August. Available at: https://www.fraud-magazine.com/article.aspx?id=4294983342 (Accessed: 13 June 2022).

Anderson, L., & Yuko, E. (2019). *How to Be a Whistleblower* [Online Article]. Available at: https://lifehacker.com/how-to-be-a-whistleblower-1794921442 (Accessed: 13 June 2022).

Auditor General for Scotland. (2004). *Management of the Holyrood Building Project*. Edinburgh: Audit Scotland.

Bandy, G. P., & Metcalfe, A. (2021). *Rethinking Public Financial Management*. London: ACCA. Available at: https://www.accaglobal.com/gb/en/professional-insights/global-profession/rethinking-public-financial-management.html (Accessed: 25 April 2022).

Behn, R. (2017). *Take a Whistleblower to Lunch* [Online Article]. Available at: https://thebehnreport.hks.harvard.edu/files/thebehnreport/files/behnreport_2017-8_aug.pdf (Accessed: 17 June 2022).

Bergmann, A. (2009). *Public Sector Financial Management*. Harlow: FT Prentice Hall.

Bland, R. (2009). Managing your budget: Making tough decisions in tough times. *Public Management*, 91(3), 6–10.

Brandt, T., & Valdez, B. (2019). *Getting Ahead of Risks Before They Become Government Failures: An Imperative for Agency Leaders to Embrace Enterprise Risk Management*. Washington, DC: Association for Federal Enterprise Risk Management. Available at: https://govwhitepapers.com/whitepapers/getting-ahead-of-risks-before-they-become-government-failures-an-imperative-for-agency-leaders-to-embrace-enterprise-risk-management (Accessed: 13 June 2022).

Cressey, D. R. (1951). Why Do Trusted Persons Commit Fraud? A Social-Psychological Study of Defalcators. *Journal of Accountancy*, *92*(5), 576–581.

Djongue, L. K., Ramangalahy, S., & Wendling, C. (2021). *Modernizing Cash Management in Mali* [Blog]. Available at: https://blog-pfm.imf.org/pfmblog/2021/01/-modernizing-cash-management-in-mali-.html (Accessed: 17 June 2022).

Douglas, J. W., & Franklin, A. L. (2006). Putting the brakes on the rush to spend down end-of-year balances: Carryover money in Oklahoma state agencies. *Public Budgeting and Finance*, 26(3), 46–64.

Drennan, L. T., & McConnell, A. (2007). *Risk and Crisis Management in the Public Sector*. Abingdon: Routledge.

European Commission. (2006). *Welcome to the World of PIFC*. Brussels: Publications Office.

Gee, J. (2010, January 28). Bad medicine. *Public Finance*. London: CIPFA.

Gee, J., & Button, M. (2021). *The Financial Cost of Fraud 2021*. London:Crowe. Available at: https://www.crowe.com/uk/insights/financial-cost-fraud-data-2021 (Accessed: 14 June 2022).

Giles, S. (2012). *Managing Fraud Risk: A Practical Guide for Directors and Managers*. Chichester: Wiley.

HM Treasury. (2020). *Orange Book: Management of Risk – Principles and Concepts*. London: The Stationery Office. Available at: https://assets.publishing.service.gov.uk/government/uploads/system/uploads/attachment_data/file/866117/6.6266_HMT_Orange_Book_Update_v6_WEB.PDF (Accessed: 17 June 2022).

Hough, L. (2021). *Organisational Culture and Corruption: Focus on the Practical* [Online Article]. Available at: https://www.publicfinancefocus.org/viewpoints/2021/02/organisational-culture-and-corruption-focus-practical (Accessed: 17 June 2022).

Jessen-Thiessen, L., & McDonald, L. (2018). *A Nudge in the Right Direction: Applying Behavioural Insights to Public Integrity* [Online Article]. Available at: https://oecdonthelevel.com/2018/03/12/a-nudge-in-the-right-direction-applying-behavioural-insights-to-public-integrity/ (Accessed: 17 June 2022).

June, R., Chowdhury, A., Heller, N., & Werve, J. (2008). *A Users' Guide to Measuring Corruption*. Oslo: UNDP Oslo Governance Centre. Available at: https://www.undp.org/publications/users-guide-measuring-corruption (Accessed: 17 June 2022).

Levi, M., Burrows, J., Fleming, M. H. & Hopkins, M. (2007). *The Nature, Extent and Economic Impact of Fraud in the UK*. London: Association of Chief Police Officers. Available at: https://orca.cardiff.ac.uk/id/eprint/48242/ (Accessed: 13 June 2022).

Levine, C. H. (1985). Police management in the 1980s: From decrementalism to strategic thinking. *Public Administration Review*, 45(November), 691–700.

Mauro, P., Medas, P. & Fournier, J.-M. (2019) The Cost of Corruption. *Finance and Development*, (September), 26–29.

Moore, M. H. (1995). *Creating Public Value: Strategic Management in Government*. Boston: Harvard University Press.

National Crime Agency. (2022). *Fraud* [Webpage]. Available at: https://www.nationalcrimeagency.gov.uk/what-we-do/crime-threats/fraud-and-economic-crime (Accessed: 14 June 2022).

Nnadi, M. (2020). Whistleblower policy: A panacea for financial corruption in Africa [Online Article]. Available at: https://www.publicfinancefocus.org/

viewpoints/2020/05/whistleblower-policy-panacea-financial-corruption-africa (Accessed: 13 June 2022).

Oman, C. and Arndt, C. (2006). *Uses and Abuses of Governance Indicators, Development Centre Studies*. Paris: OECD Publishing. Available at: https://doi.org/10.1787/9789264026865-en (Accessed: 13 June 2022).

Pattanayak, S., & Fainboim, I. (2011). *Treasury Single Account: An Essential Tool for Government Cash Management*. Washington, DC: International Monetary Fund.

Sanchez, A. (2013). The role of procurement. In R. Allen, R. Hemming, & B. Potter (Eds.), *The International Handbook of Public Financial Management* (pp. 312–335). Palgrave Macmillan.

Sarda, M. (2019). *Implementing a Treasury Single Account in Niger* [Blog]. Available at: https://blog-pfm.imf.org/pfmblog/2019/05/implementing-a-treasury-single-account-in-niger.html (Accessed: 17 June 2022).

Schick, A. (2013). Reflections on two decades of public financial management reforms. In M. Cangiano, T. Curristine, & M. Lazare (Eds.), *Public Financial Management and Its Emerging Architecture* (pp. 21–77). Washington, DC: International Monetary Fund.

Søreide, T. (2006). *Is It Wrong to Rank? A Critical Assessment of Corruption Indices*. CMI Working Papers:WP 2006: 1. Bergen, Norway: Chr. Michelsen Institute. Available at: https://open.cmi.no/cmi-xmlui/handle/11250/2435939 (Accessed: 17 June 2022).

Swain, J. W., & Reed, B. J. (2010). *Budgeting for Public Managers*. Armonk, NY: ME Sharpe Inc.

TED. (2014). *Peter Eigen: How to Expose the Corrupt* [Video]. Available at: https://www.ted.com/talks/peter_eigen_how_to_expose_the_corrupt (Accessed: 17 June 2022).

Transparency International. (2022). *Corruption Perceptions Index 2021* [Webpage]. Available at: https://www.transparency.org/en/cpi/2021 (Accessed: 14 June 2022).

Victims Commissioner. (2021). *Fraud Surged by 24% Under Covid* [Online Article]. Available at: https://victimscommissioner.org.uk/news/who-suffers-fraud/ (Accessed: 14 June 2022).

Walley, P., Found, P., & Williams, S. (2019). Failure demand: A concept evaluation in UK primary care. *International Journal of Health Care Quality Assurance*, 32(1), 21–33.

Walley, P., & Jennison-Phillips, A. (no date). *Demand Management in the Public Sector: Developments and Issues*. Available at: https://www.open.ac.uk/centres/policing/sites/www.open.ac.uk.centres.policing/files/files/Outputs/Demand_management_in_the_public_sector_developments_and_issues.pdf (Accessed: 13 June 2022).

Walley, P., & Radnor, Z. (2006). Lean on me.... *Public Finance*, 27 July. Available at: https://www.publicfinance.co.uk/2006/07/lean-me-zoe-radnor-and-paul-walley (Accessed: 17 June 2022).

Welham, B., Hadley, S., & Miller, M. (2019a). *Life at the Sharp End – Controlling Public Spending* [Blog]. Available at: https://blog-pfm.imf.org/pfmblog/2019/06/life-at-the-sharp-end-controlling-public-spending.html (Accessed: 13 June 2022).

Welham, B., Hadley, S., & Miller, M. (2019b). *The Role of the Budget Officer in Controlling Public Spending* (Working Paper 559). London: Overseas Development Institute. Available at: https://odi.org/en/publications/the-role-of-the-budget-officer-in-controlling-public-spending/ (Accessed: 16 June 2022).

White, I., & Sidhu, I. (2005, January). *Building the Scottish Parliament, the Holyrood Project.* House of Commons Library. Available at: https://commonslibrary.parliament.uk/research-briefings/sn03357/ (Accessed: 16 June 2022).

FURTHER READING (AND WATCHING)

Links to the following resources, and lots more, are available at www.managingpublicmoney.co.uk/extras.

To read the full story behind the building of the Scottish Parliament, see the website of the Holyrood Inquiry at www.holyroodinquiry.org or the Auditor General for Scotland's report (2004).

The section on budgetary control mentions a number of ways that the cost of a public service could be reduced. One of those is reducing demand for the service. Walley and Jennison-Phillips (no date) wrote a literature study on demand management in the public sector that you could check out. The articles by Walley and Radnor (2006) and Walley, Found and Williams (2019) also discuss failure demand. This is the demand for service that is the result of a failure by the organization and if it could be reduced or eliminated then all of the associated cost could be saved.

The IMF's Fiscal Affairs Department has published a comprehensive manual on implementing the treasury single account mechanism (Pattanayak and Fainboim, 2011). Of a more management size are several blog posts specifically about Mali's and Niger's experiences of implementing TSAs (Djongue, Ramangalahy and Wendling, 2021; Sarda, 2019).

Steve Giles's book, *Managing Fraud Risk* (2012), is not specifically about the public sector, but it covers topics that are still relevant to public managers, including responsibilities, governance, controls and prevention, fraud detection and investigation as well as a chapter on ethics.

Peter Eigen is the founder of Transparency International and he gave a short presentation at a TED (Technology, Entertainment, Design) conference in Berlin in 2009 where he explained why he believes it is important for corruption to be eradicated, so that all people can benefit from public investment (TED, 2014).

Given the criticisms of Transparency International's Corruptions Perceptions Index you might also be interested in a UNDP publication, *A Users' Guide to Measuring Corruption*, that makes recommendations about good practice when measuring corruption (June et al., 2008) and Arndt and Oman's book, *Uses and Abuses of Governance Indicators* (2006).

The Jessen-Thiessen and McDonald article (2018) mentioned in the chapter relates to a set of behavioural insights published by the OECD. The insights can be found at www.oecd.org/governance/ethics/behavioural-insights-integrity/.

The OECD has produced information on fighting corruption in the public sector which is split into three themes: integrity in public procurement (www.oecd.org/gov/ethics/integrityinpublicprocurement), managing conflicts of interest (www.oecd.org/gov/ethics/conflictofinterest) and lobbying (www.oecd.org/gov/ethics/lobbying) with links to toolboxes and other resources.

Lastly, Lifehacker has published an article on how to be a whistleblower (see Anderson and Yuko, 2019).

Chapter 5

Using financial information to make decisions

LEARNING OBJECTIVES

After reading this chapter you should:

- be able to distinguish between different types of costs and how changes in the volume of outputs affects total cost;
- appreciate the importance of understanding costs in financial decision making;
- identify which cost (and income) items are relevant to a decision;
- understand the time value of money and how to carry out project appraisals using the discounted cash flow method; and
- understand the principles of reasonableness in decision making.

KEY POINTS OF THIS CHAPTER

- Costs (and income) can be classified in a number of ways based on their behaviour.
- There are alternative ways of allocating overheads and the method used can affect subsequent decisions.
- Decisions involving the payment and/or receipt of money in the future should take into account the time value of money.
- Non-financial factors may be the most critical ones for some decisions.

DOI: 10.4324/9781003250838-5

KEY TERMS

Activity-based costing—a method for allocating overheads to products/services by identifying the activities that cause the costs to be incurred.

Cost—the resources consumed to buy or produce a product or service.

Cost-benefit analysis—an analysis of a project or programme that takes into account, in monetary terms, the costs incurred and the benefits received by the community as a whole, over the long term.

Cost-effectiveness analysis—an analysis of a project or programme that takes into account the costs incurred in the achievement of a specified output (i.e., the effect that results from the expenditure).

Discount rate—the percentage value used to discount future cash flows when calculating present value.

Fixed costs—costs that remain constant in the short-term regardless of the volume of production such as the rent of premises and the salaries of head office staff.

Net present value (NPV)—the sum of the present values of all the cash inflows relating to a project minus the present values of all the cash outflows.

Opportunity cost—not a cost that is incurred, but the value of the benefits foregone by not selecting the best alternative option from the option that is chosen.

Overheads—the costs incurred by an organization (such as head office expenses) that are not easily traceable to individual products or services.

Present value—the value of a future amount expressed in terms of today's money.

Time value of money—the principle that a sum of money today is worth more to the holder than the same sum of money at a future date.

Variable costs—cost items that vary in proportion to the volume of production, such as the components used on a production line.

Making decisions is a fundamental part of a manager's role regardless of their sector. Depending on the manager's role and the context, their decisions may be mundane, operational ones or major strategic decisions about objectives and policies. Financial information is likely to be one of the considerations in most decisions, if not all of them. Even the most mundane decisions about, for example, purchasing low value goods might require consideration of the budget availability to cover the expenditure.

Budget control was covered in Chapter 4 so this chapter focuses on longer-term decisions relating to alternative courses of action. These are investment decisions, whether they be literally decisions about the investment of money in a financial asset, such as a bond, or the more common decision about whether to invest in a project or programme.

The basic framework for making decisions is:

- list the alternative courses of action that are available (which could include a 'do nothing' option);
- identify the costs and income/benefits for each alternative;
- identify relevant non-financial factors for each alternative; and
- appraise the alternatives and decide which one is preferred.

The first section of this chapter clarifies what is meant by the term 'costs' as distinct from 'expenses' and the second section explains how costs can be classified according to their behaviour in relation to an organization's activity volume. The third section outlines two alternative methods for deriving the full cost of a product or service. The fourth section explains common approaches to the project appraisal with an emphasis on using the discounted cash flow approach. The final section outlines some practical issues relating to decision making in the public sector.

WHAT IS A COST?

A cost is the accumulation of the resources used to produce a good or a service, expressed in money terms (because that is a common denominator to allow intangibles like time to be included). In business the cost of producing a product is a factor in deciding on a selling price that would yield an acceptable profit. In the public sector generally there is no pricing decision to make but knowing the cost of creating a public service is still helpful for decision-makers to know.

There are at least six reasons why a public manager may wish to know the cost of a service or product:

- to identify if a profit/surplus is being achieved;
- to set a price (as discussed in Chapter 3);
- to plan or budget;
- to account for where resources have gone;
- to make or substantiate a claim (for example, for a grant application or an insurance claim); and
- to be able to place a value on stocks (or inventory) of goods for external financial reports.

The work to produce these costs and to give advice on them to managers fall within the field of management accounting. This field is internally facing, with its primary focus being to support decision making. (The field of financial accounting is concerned with producing financial statements and has more of an external focus.)

Costs are different from expenses, although related. A business or PBE's expenses are all the goods and services that it buys. These expenses will be captured by the organization's accounting system and can be verified as facts. For all the expenses there will be payslips and invoices and receipts associated with them.

Cost is not the same as value. Value is what customers (in business) or service users (in public sector) perceive to be the benefits of the product or service that they buy (or receive). Whether the cost of producing a public good or service is worth the value that it generates for people is critically important and is the subject matter of Chapter 7.

Costs are derived from the expenses by allocating them to the products, functions or activities in which the organization is interested. In a manufacturing business this might be the individual product lines it manufactures; however, the same expenses could instead be allocated into costs of functions such as production, distribution and marketing. Similarly, PBEs could have alternative costing views of themselves. A hospital could identify costs for all of the various treatments/therapies it provides, but it could also have functional costs of inpatients, outpatients, emergency medicine, catering, cleaning, management and so on. And with the right systems in place, it could analyse its costs down to the level of each patient.

At the aggregate level of an organization, or sub-unit of an organization, the total of all the costs for a period must equal the total expenses for that period.

CLASSIFICATION OF COSTS

The (management) accounting profession uses the noun 'cost' with many prefixes, each having a specific meaning. Some of those terms, such as opportunity cost, are used by non-financial managers without necessarily knowing the specific, technical meaning. This section explains the most common and important terms and there are others (such as 'historic cost') that have been included in the Glossary at the back of this book.

Fixed costs

Fixed costs are those items of expenditure that do not vary as the volume of output (the amount of goods or services produced) varies. In a hospital, for instance, the expenses of property taxes and equipment maintenance contracts would be fixed costs, having to be paid in full regardless of how many patients are treated. The nature of fixed costs means that as the volume of outputs increases the average cost per unit of outputs decreases.

Fixed costs are fixed for the short to medium term, not forever. It is possible for a fixed cost to remain constant for a very long time but generally an organization can change its fixed costs. It may take time and resources to make the changes and they are not automatically related to the volume of output. Staying with the hospital example above, it might be possible to build an extension to deal with an increased volume of output, or to vacate some premises to reduce its costs.

The cost of the chief executive and senior management of the hospital is also a fixed cost, in the short term at least. Over a longer timescale there could be changes in the senior management structure that would change the value of such a fixed cost but would not convert it to a variable because whatever the cost of the revised management structure it would not vary in proportion to the volume of patients treated.

Variable costs

Variable costs are those costs that increase proportionately as the volume of output increases and decrease as the volume falls. An increase or decrease of ten per cent of output would increase or decrease variable costs by ten per cent also. Examples of variable costs are things like the raw materials and components used in a manufacturing process. Back to the hospital example, the cost of food varies as the number of patients staying in the hospital varies.

Figure 5.1 illustrates how the total cost changes as the volume of output changes for both fixed and variable costs. There are some costs that behave differently, having elements of both fixed and variable cost, which means that as the volume of output increases, they do not increase in the same proportion. The two types of mixed cost are illustrated in Figure 5.2.

Mixed costs

Mixed costs have a mix of fixed and variable elements. Semi-variable costs differ from variable costs in that there is a minimum cost incurred even when the volume of output is zero. Utilities tend to fall into this category because there is a fixed charge for connection to the service that is payable regardless of the level of consumption. Motor vehicle expenses are semi-variable costs, too: there are the costs of registration and insurance to be paid whether the vehicle is driven or not, whilst the cost of fuel and tyres varies in line with the distance travelled.

Semi-fixed costs are items that are fixed for a range of volumes but then jump up or down by a quantum amount when the volume moves out of this range. An example of this is the team leader in a call centre. As the volume of calls being handled increases the cost of customer advisors is a variable cost as the management can adjust the hours worked by advisors and recruit extra advisors to balance the workload. Eventually it reaches the point where an additional team leader is needed to supervise the customer advisors, thus increasing the fixed cost by the amount of the team leader's salary and benefits.

Fixed and variable income

All of the above prefixes could be applied to income as well as cost:

- Fixed income—such as a grant that is received as core funding for the organization regardless of its activity level.
- Variable income—such as fees and charges for services that are variable because the more services provided the more fee income is earned.
- Semi-fixed income—such as an organization with a contract to supply services that might be paid on the basis of volume bands, so if the volume of services supplied is between A and B the fee that is earned is X but if the volume rises above B the fee rises to X + Y.
- Semi-variable income—such as a service charge where there is a fixed element received as a retainer and a variable amount earned from the volume of services actually provided. There probably are not many services provided on this basis by PBEs other than utilities but, in theory, it could be applied to other services.

Cost structure

Cost structure refers to the particular relationship of fixed, variable and mixed costs in an organization, department or project. A prison, for example, has a high level of fixed costs because few elements of its costs change if there are more or fewer prisoners inside. Alternatively, a social housing provider's internal repairs and maintenance unit would have a cost structure that has a higher level of variable costs because the number of staff hours used and the cost of materials will increase or decrease in line with the volume of repairs completed.

Understanding the cost structure helps a manager make decisions because they will know the extent to which their costs, and income, will change if the volume of outputs increases or decreases by any given amount. The charts in Figures 5.1 and 5.2 also illustrate why understanding the cost structure is important when looking for expenditure cuts.

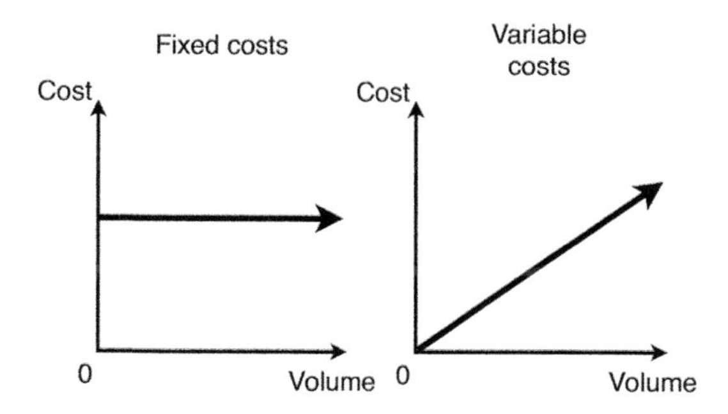

Figure 5.1 *Fixed and variable costs.*

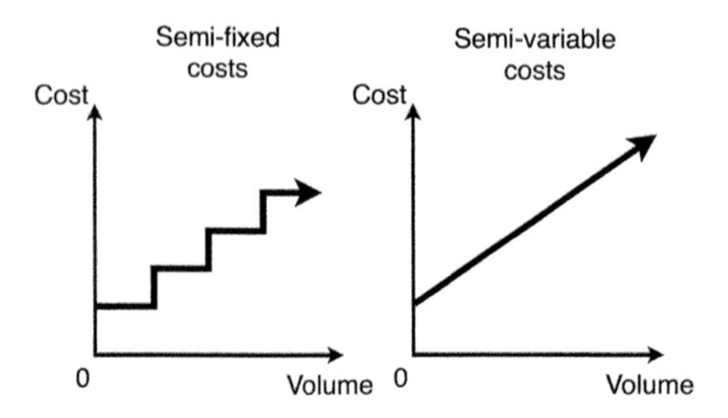

Figure 5.2 *Semi-fixed and semi-variable costs.*

An organization's fixed costs cannot be avoided in the short term, and they may prove difficult to reduce even in the medium to long term, so the focus will be on reducing variable costs (and this is the basis of the strategies mentioned in Chapter 4 for dealing with a financial 'crunch' or 'crisis'). A by-product of an approach that reduces variable costs is that the average cost per unit of output will rise because the same amount of fixed cost is incurred in producing the lower volume of output.

For example, the public transport department in a city government post-COVID-19 can give us some insights into thinking about cost structures. Public transport has very high fixed costs because of the investment in the infrastructure and vehicles. The proportions differ between subway, tram and bus systems of transport but nevertheless there will be a lot of capital invested in the system.

The variable and semi-variable costs of public transport relate to the actual number of trains, trams or buses that are operated. Prior to the COVID-19 pandemic these vehicles may have been full or substantially full generating a good deal of income even if, overall, there was a subsidy from the city government. The lockdowns imposed during the pandemic dramatically reduced passenger numbers and the associated income, forcing the city government to increase its subsidy.

Post-COVID-19, city governments are faced with a dilemma. There are high fixed costs to be met in the short to medium term and passenger numbers that have not returned to pre-COVID-19 levels. This may tempt the city government to increase fares in order to bring the subsidy to its pre-COVID-19 level. Fare rises, however, may reduce passenger numbers further, putting the government under more pressure to cut services and sell off assets. The alternative view might be to recognize the investment is a sunk cost and it would be better if the trains/trams/buses were full and, therefore, fares should be reduced (or even abolished).

Another example relates to ICT services. Large organizations can and do build and operate their own data centres where all their computer systems are housed and operated. Such data centres have a significant fixed cost element to their cost structure. More recently, it has become technologically and economically possible for organizations to outsource their ICT needs to specialist companies that operate massive data centres. The contracts for these services can be based on the amount of data processed, and organizations that choose to outsource their data processing can switch much of the cost from being a fixed cost to a variable cost.

Direct and indirect costs

The direct costs of a product or service are the costs that can be directly traced to it in an economically feasible way. The components and raw materials used in the production of a commodity can usually be traced to it, as can the cost of labour directly involved in the production/manufacturing process. It may be possible to trace the use of materials like glue and fixings to a product, but, in many cases, the amount would be trivial and/or it would not be feasible to do so and instead such costs are collected as supplies and treated as an indirect cost.

Indirect costs, also called overheads, are all the costs that cannot be directly traced to a product or service. These would include the cost of management and supervision, premises and facilities management, stationery, energy usage and the depreciation charge for plant and equipment.

If an organization has unused assets that incur costs, then these too would be an overhead but the costs are unlikely to be allocated to outputs since the asset is not involved in the production of the outputs. Nevertheless, there is clearly an incentive to dispose of unused assets, although sometimes there are practical or political barriers to doing so and thus the organization continues to bear the cost as part of its overheads.

The techniques of costing explained later are, in essence, techniques for allocating the indirect costs to an organization's products or services in order to derive a figure for the full cost of each product. This can be expressed as an equation.

$$\text{Full cost of product} = \text{Direct labour cost} + \text{Direct materials cost} + \text{Share of indirect costs}$$

Relevant costs and sunk costs

When making short-term decisions it is not necessary to consider every single item of cost for every available option because many costs will be unaffected by the decision. The relevant costs (and benefits) for a short-term decision are the **future** costs (and benefits) that are **avoidable** depending on which option is chosen.

Any costs that are past (i.e., costs that have already been incurred or committed) are not affected by a decision about the future and are therefore not relevant to the decision. These are called **sunk costs**.

Consider a hypothetical government ICT project. The project has been running in a ministry for several years and is way over budget. A new minister is faced with the decision on whether to finance the completion of the project or sanction its termination. It would be tempting for the minister to be influenced by the millions already spent on the project but they are sunk costs and not relevant for the decision they have to make. Instead, they should be considering only the uncommitted future costs, and benefits, of the two available options.

In the short term, fixed costs will generally be committed and unavoidable and therefore not relevant for a decision. However, fixed costs would be relevant for a longer-term decision where it is possible for fixed costs to be changed or eliminated (i.e., avoided in part or full). So, for example, a decision about rationalizing a PBE's estate would take into account fixed costs for the buildings that could be sold, sub-let, demolished or otherwise vacated.

Opportunity cost

The final type of cost to be explained in this section is not a cost of the use in the same way as the preceding items. An opportunity cost is not the value of resources consumed in the production of something. Instead, it is the value of the benefits that would have been received from the best alternative option from the one that was selected. So, if a government department has a vacant office that it could either use to accommodate a new team or rent it to a tenant and it chooses to use it for the new team then the rent it could have received from the new tenant is the opportunity cost.

Box 5.1 summarizes the various types of cost discussed in this section.

BOX 5.1 SUMMARY OF COST CATEGORIES

Fixed cost—a cost item that remains constant in the short term regardless of the volume of production.

Variable cost—a cost item that varies in proportion to the volume of production.

Semi-fixed cost—a cost item that is fixed for a given volume of activity but at some critical level increases to a new level.

Semi-variable cost—a cost item that includes a fixed component and a component that varies with the volume of production.

Direct cost—a cost item that can be easily traced to a product or service.

Indirect cost—a cost items that cannot be easily traced to a product or service (also called overheads).
Relevant cost—future expenses that have not yet been committed.
Sunk cost—an expense that has already been made or is committed.
Opportunity cost—the potential benefits foregone when one option is chosen from a range of alternatives.

COSTING METHODS

Costing is a generic term for the process of identifying the cost of something. The direct costs of producing a product or service could be easy to establish if there is a reasonable accounting system in place. This sum, however, understates the resources consumed in creating the product or service because it does not include any of the indirect expenses incurred by the organization. To get a fuller estimate of the full cost of creating the product (it will only be an estimate because there is no absolute figure for the full cost), there needs to be a method for allocated indirect expenses to products and services.

The process of costing developed in the industrial age as manufacturers became larger and made many products. The owners/managers of these manufacturers wanted to know how much it cost to make each product and thus to know which products were most profitable. There is evidence of its use at Josiah Wedgwood's potteries in the 1770s (Fleischman, Hoskin and Macve, 1995) and at Boulton and Watt's foundry in the 1790s (McKendrick, 1970). Despite its roots in manufacturing the techniques have been developed to relate to service industries and have been adopted by PBEs.

Costing techniques may be of particular benefit for manufacturing businesses but they are used in PBEs, even ones that produce services rather than goods. However, their usefulness in PBEs is more limited because:

- the techniques deal with outputs rather than outcomes, because outputs are more easily measured, whilst PBEs are often more interested in the outcomes the outputs produce;
- PBEs tend to have a smaller proportion of variable costs than manufacturers; and
- in general, there is no income to match against a product or service's costs.

A costing exercise does not change the total cost, it allocates only the total to products/services. Because of this, in a small organization or one that produces a single product or service, costing techniques are unlikely to add any value.

Similarly, using costing techniques in a PBE that produces multiple services can lead to a better understanding of the cost of each service, but if the information is not used for decision making, then it would not be worth the PBE spending much time and money developing a complex costing system.

There are alternative methods of costing something and this chapter will focus first on absorption costing which might be regarded as the traditional approach and then it will briefly explain activity-based costing (ABC) (Cooper and Kaplan, 1988). Before that, a word of caution:

> It is a mistake to aim at an unattainable precision. It is better to be vaguely right than precisely wrong.
>
> (Read, 2009)

It is very unlikely that it will be feasible to trace every element of cost to a product as a direct cost and the apportionment of overheads inevitably involves a degree of estimation. In carrying out a costing exercise, therefore, there has to be sufficient accuracy in the data and calculations for the results to be meaningful without seeking an excessive, and probably unjustified, level of precision.

There are various issues in overhead allocation besides the level of accuracy. There's the fairness of the allocation (which is often directly related to the level of accuracy); the complexity of the method of allocation and therefore its understandability for non-financial managers; and the potential for unintended consequences such as a manager seeking to avoid an overhead charge for the human resources department by buying the service directly from a third party and in the process increasing the total cost of human resources work for the organization.

The methods of costing differ in the way that overhead expenses are allocated or apportioned to outputs. Examples of overhead expenses include managers and supervisors (including their assistants, secretaries and incidental expenses); policy and strategy teams; governance and democracy costs; support services like payroll, accounting, ICT, human resources and facilities management; and premises costs.

Traditional (or absorption) costing

In this method of costing the direct costs of producing the service or commodity are charged directly to the relevant cost centre. This is a straightforward function of an accounting system. The indirect costs (sometimes called overheads) are collected in separate cost centres and then allocated (or apportioned) to all of the organization's services/commodities.

The allocation of overheads is usually calculated by reference to a common basis such as the number of direct employees producing each service, or the amount of office space occupied by the employees. It is good practice if the basis of allocation is a reasonable approximation to the service's usage of the overhead.

For example, the allocation of the cost of the payroll service on the basis of the number of employees producing each service is more reasonable than an allocation based on the total direct cost of each service (because the latter would be skewed if there were a service employing very few people but spending a lot of money on contracted suppliers).

The allocation bases used tend to be inputs to the service/commodity, such as floor space occupied, number of employees, number of minutes or hours of labour or machinery used. This is because the inputs are common across the services/commodities but the outputs are not. In a hospital, the average time spent in an operating theatre to carry out different surgical procedures can be used to allocate the cost of running the operating theatre to the various medical specialties. It would not be feasible to do this using outputs because how does a hip replacement compare to a heart transplant?

Often in large organizations overheads are allocated in stages. First, the highest level of management overheads is allocated to the departments or divisions, where they are rolled up with the department's own overheads and allocated to the units within the department and so on until the costs reach each service or product. For example, in a city council the cost of running the city hall building would be allocated to the departments of sanitation and education based on the amount of space the senior managers of each department used within the building. The education department will then include the charge for city hall within its overheads and allocate them to the schools on some basis (pupil numbers, perhaps).

Outsourcing of a service takes away some of the problem of allocating overheads to every service. The outsourced supplier's overheads will be wrapped up in its prices and as the volume of work they carry out increases or decreases the total price will change in accordance with the terms of the contract. It is a matter for the supplier to deal with the consequences of its income rising or falling in terms of overheads.

Activity-based costing

Activity-based costing (ABC) is a more sophisticated approach to allocating an organization's overheads. It was developed by Cooper and Kaplan (1988) and seeks to trace (allocate) overheads to outputs by understanding how the production of the output drives the cost of support activities. This can result in answers that are significantly different from the answers derived using absorption costing, although an organization would have to decide whether the improvement is worth the cost of operating an ABC system.

The ABC methodology has four stages:

- identify the major activities that take place;
- determine the cost driver for each of the major activities;

- create a 'cost pool' to collect the costs for each major activity; and
- allocate the costs from each 'cost pool' to products according to each product's demand for each activity.

As an example, Table 5.1 shows the activities and cost drivers for a master's degree.

In the context of a home for elderly persons, some of the major activities would be admitting new residents, cleaning, catering and providing an occupational health service. The cost drivers for these activities (in a specified period) might be the number of residents admitted, the number of occupied rooms, the number of residents and the number of people requiring occupational health care, respectively. By collecting the costs of each of the four support activities and data on the drivers, it is possible to calculate a cost of admission per person admitted, cost of cleaning per occupied room per day, cost of catering per resident per day and cost of occupational health per resident using the service.

The key advantages of ABC are that it highlights the misplaced emphasis of absorption costing on volume-related allocations of overheads by focusing on the causes of overhead costs. It can encourage collaboration and cooperation between departments and provide useful control information for managers.

Balanced against these advantages, ABC requires many more cost pools and cost drivers to be identified than absorption costing and it relies heavily on past data and detailed time-recording information by staff to identify how long they spend on various activities. In large organizations this can be a massive amount of data requiring full-time staff to collect and process it. Furthermore, the changeover to ABC can result in conflict because the new basis of overhead allocation may result in the stated full cost of some products to be much higher than they were under the absorption costing approach. This can be a particular problem if a product's price has been based on a markup on the cost because the organization may not wish to implement a price increase as a result of a change in accounting practice.

A development from ABC is activity-based management (ABM). This is a management approach where information from ABC is used to help management

Table 5.1 *Example of cost drivers for a master's degree*

Activity	*Cost driver*
Student admissions	Number of students
Module design and preparation	Number of modules
Produce documentation	Number of students
Delivery of modules (e.g., lectures)	Number of hours
Assessment	Number of students

focus on how they can improve the organization's activities. Kaplan and Cooper (1998) divide ABM into strategic ABM—using ABC information to decide which products to produce and which activities to use—and operational ABM—using ABC information to improve efficiency. ABM, too, has been adopted by PBEs (for example, McChlery, McKendrick and Rolfe, 2007; Cokins, 2006).

ABC's inventors have acknowledged its complexity and the difficulty of maintaining the system.

> In the classroom, activity-based costing looks like a great way to manage a company's limited resources. But many managers who have tried to implement ABC in their organizations on any significant scale have abandoned the attempt in the face of rising costs and employee irritation.
>
> (Kaplan and Anderson, 2004: 131)

Kaplan and Anderson do not think organizations should abandon ABC (2004: 132); they suggest organizations should consider a simpler version they call time-driven ABC. This version avoids the expensive and time-consuming work in surveying employees to find out how they utilize their time on different activities and instead uses managers' estimates of employees' productive time to establish a productive cost per hour (or per minute) to multiply against standard timings to get the costs for each activity driver. It is simpler and easier to implement and maintain, and it would be for each organization to determine whether its benefits for them exceeded its cost.

PROJECT APPRAISAL TECHNIQUES

Making a decision about which project ideas should be implemented and which should not is an important aspect of a manager's job. In general terms, in the private sector, such a decision will be about a project where there is cash paid out up front (an investment) and cash is received in the future (a return). A project would be implemented where the return exceeds the investment having taken into account the risks in the project and the fit with the organization's goals, and subject to the organization having enough funds for the investment.

Some public sector projects might also follow the general private sector model: for instance, building a toll road would have long-term net income streams in return for the initial investment in construction. More often, though, a public sector project would have no income at all. What a project might do instead is reduce expenditure in future years and this can be treated as the equivalent of a cash inflow (although really it is a reduced cash outflow). As an example, if a police force invested in a new, centralized, large custody suite and closed several smaller ones, it would save the costs of running the smaller custody suites and these would be offset against the cost of building and operating the new centralized suite. Projects of this kind can be called 'invest to save' projects, and the acid test is whether the value of the savings outweighs the investment.

Sometimes, though, the public sector is appraising a project that only costs money, both to create and then to operate, such as the building of a new school. For such projects the appraisal is one of comparing alternative delivery options to select which is best. In such circumstances one might conclude that the 'do nothing' option would be best since there would not be any spending but there may be reasons why the organization has to take action. In the example of a new school, it might be that there is an increase in children of school age or it might be to replace a dilapidated school and the education authority expects future pupils to benefit from a better education experience (i.e., there will be more public value created). Most public projects, such as building non-toll roads, bridges, prisons and parks and buying expensive specialist equipment like body scanners for hospitals, are cost-only projects like this.

A public manager might be required to appraise a range of very different projects. These could include capital projects (such as a construction project or a major ICT development) or operating expenditure projects (such as an organization development programme or giving a grant to a third party) or, possibly, investments using financial instruments and the following techniques would operate equally on any of them.

The basic approach to appraisal, as outlined in *The Green Book: Central Government Guidance on Appraisal and Evaluation* (HM Treasury, 2022), begins with the rationale for intervention (that is, the reasons why an investment or change is needed in the first place). Appraisal then requires a list of the viable alternative courses of action (perhaps first as a longlist and then as a shortlist) and estimating the costs and the benefits of each option and converting them into financial terms. These data can then be assessed using any (or all) of the following three techniques, although the NPV method is most likely to be appropriate.

Payback method

The payback method is the simplest method of project appraisal. The cash outflows and inflows are listed and the manager identifies the point in time when the cumulative total of inflows equals the total outflow. The advantage of this method is that it is quick and easy to do, it is easily understood and it emphasizes liquidity.

If the aim of a project is to payback its initial investment, then this method is relevant and when comparing more than one project the one that has the earliest payback period would be favoured. A simple example is shown in Box 5.3.

BOX 5.2 THE PAYBACK METHOD: AN EXAMPLE

A government department has a project to refurbish some unused offices at a cost of £90,000. Staff can be relocated to the refurbished offices in six months' time saving the rent of £40,000 a year for the remainder of a lease that ends in 3.5 years' time. When will the project reach the payback point?

Year		*Cash outflow/ inflow* £	*Cumulative outflow* £
0	Refurbishment cost	–90,000	–90,000
1	Half year's rent	20,000	–70,000
2	Full year's rent	40,000	–30,000
3	Full year's rent	40,000	10,000
4	Half year's rent	20,000	30,000

The table shows that payback occurs during the third year; in fact, after two years and nine months.

Often, however, as mentioned above, a public sector project is not expected to yield any cash receipts or reduce future payments: the cash outflow is expected to be 'paid back' through the public value it creates. If a project's benefits can be monetized then they could be shown as inflows and the benefit payback period calculated (see Chapter 7 for ideas about how intangible benefits can be monetized). Even so, the payback method's key weakness is that it does not take account of the timing of the outflows and inflows and the time value of money. It should be used only for the simplest of projects or to make a broad assessment of the feasibility of a project before developing the idea further.

Accounting rate of return (ARR) method

This method of appraising a project is conducted by calculating the profit that would be earned from each project and requires, therefore, depreciation and other accruals to be taken into account. It is calculated as the average annual profit from the investment divided by the average investment (after depreciation) to earn that profit.

The ARR method does not take into account when cash will be paid out or received. It is clearly of little use in the non-profit public sector and it has little to commend it in the for-profit sector. For that reason, it is not discussed further.

Net present value (NPV) method

The NPV method uses the discount cash flow technique to make an informed comparison of projects that may have different durations by assessing whether they achieve a minimum rate of return.

Note that the net present value (NPV) technique that follows may also be relevant to cost-benefit analyses in general (see Chapter 7) and evaluating bids received in competitive tendering exercises (see Chapter 6).

The key advantage of using the NPV method is that it recognizes the time value of money. This is the principle that a sum of money today is worth more to the holder than the same sum of money at a future date. If offered £100 today or £100 in one year's time a rational person would opt for £100 today because they could either spend it now rather than having to wait a year, or they could invest it and have £100 plus interest at the end of the year. However, if the same person were offered £100 today or £110 in a year's time, they would have to calculate whether they value the £110 at the end of the year more than £100 today. If, for example, they could invest the money only at 6 per cent interest, then after a year they would have £106 so it would be rational to opt for the offer of £110 in a year's time. This is because, at 6 per cent interest they would have to invest £103.77 to have £110 by the end of one year. The present value of £110 in one year's time, using a 6 per cent discount rate is £103.77. In this example 6 per cent is the person's opportunity cost of capital—the best rate of return they could get if they accepted £100 today—and this rate is used as the discount rate to translate the £110 to its present value.

The general formula for calculating the present value (PV) from a future value (FV) is:

$$PV = FV \div \left\{(1+r)^n\right\}$$

where **n** is the number of periods into the future that the future value occurs and **r** is the discount rate for each period expressed as a decimal fraction. If you have a series of cash flows over a number of periods you can calculate the present value of each cash flow.

Knowing how to calculate the factor can be useful but calculating the present value of single values and series of values is a standard function in spreadsheet applications, making the construction of project appraisal models much simpler, and available to non-financial managers who are comfortable with spreadsheet software.

To calculate the net present value for a project requires the cash outflows and inflows to be calculated for each period just like the payback method; however, then the present value for each of these outflows and inflows is calculated using the appropriate discount rate. Adding together all the present values will yield the net present value (NPV). A simple example is shown in Box 5.3.

BOX 5.3 THE NPV METHOD: AN EXAMPLE

What is the net present value (NPV) of the project described in Box 5.3 using a discount rate of 5 per cent?

Year		*Cash outflow/ inflow £*	*Discount factor*	*Present value £*
0	Refurbishment cost	–90,000	1.000	–90,000
1	Half year's rent	20,000	0.952	19,040
2	Full year's rent	40,000	0.907	36,280
3	Full year's rent	40,000	0.864	34,560
4	Half year's rent	20,000	0.823	16,460
	Net present value			**16,340**

The project has a substantial positive NPV using a 5 per cent discount rate. In fact, it would have a positive NPV for any discount rate up to 12.48 per cent, which is the internal rate of return (IRR) for the project. For any discount rate greater than 12.48 per cent the project would have a negative NPV.

The decision rule is that if the NPV is positive then the project is acceptable because it shows that the sum of present values of cash inflows (or savings, or benefits) exceeds the present values of all the cash outflows. If the NPV is negative the project should be rejected because this means that the present value of the cash inflows amounts to less than the value of the outflows. If two or more projects are being compared then the project with the highest, positive NPV should be favoured. That being said, there may be other, non-financial factors that should be considered before reaching a final decision and these are discussed later in this chapter.

For simplicity it is usually assumed that the cash flows occur on the final day of each period. This is clearly unlikely to be the case in a real-life project, but in most cases the more complex mathematics to deal with flows within each of the period makes little difference and so the period-end assumption is generally acceptable.

If, instead of annual periods, the cash outflows and inflows were analysed into monthly periods then the discount rate would have to be calculated appropriately from the annual discount rate. For instance, a 6 per cent annual discount rate is equivalent to a 0.487 per cent monthly discount rate. (It is not 0.5 per cent, 6 divided by 12, because the monthly discount rate is compounded over the 12 months to reach 6 per cent.) Another example: an annual discount rate of 10 per cent is equivalent to a monthly discount rate of 0.797 per cent.

Internal rate of return

The internal rate of return (IRR) for a project is the discount rate that produces an NPV of zero. The IRR can be easily derived from an NPV spreadsheet model by adjusting the discount rate on a trial-and-error basis until the NPV is zero. (If you are proficient with spreadsheet applications, you could use the 'goal seek' function to do this.) If the IRR exceeds the organization's cost of capital or target rate of return for projects then it is an acceptable project.

Dealing with inflation

For all of the above methods it is easier to exclude inflation from inflows and outflows. If inflation is expected to impact all the items of cost and income equally each year of the project or programme, ignoring it will not distort the decision and it avoids having to estimate price rises that might be 5, 10 or 20 years in the future. However, if it is expected that different rates of inflation will apply, either to different cost items, such as salaries and wages rising faster than the inflation for goods and services, or at different periods of the project, then it would be appropriate to make some adjustments for inflation. This is done by applying the expected inflation rates to each item and/or period over the course of the project and then using a discount rate that allows for inflation (a 'nominal' discount rate rather than a 'real' discount rate).

How to select the discount rate

The discount rate used in present value calculations is absolutely critical. If the rate is too high, valid projects would be rejected; if too low, unworthy projects would go ahead. One way, of course, would be to guess a rate, perhaps to reflect your intuition about the riskiness of the project/investment; or perhaps in order to get the answer you desire.

To be more scientific, theory says the discount rate to use is the opportunity cost of capital—the expected rate of return on the best alternative option to the project being considered. It is akin to the concept of opportunity cost mentioned earlier in this chapter.

In the private sector a company might use its cost of capital as the discount rate because this is a benchmark of the minimum return on investment that the company's shareholders expect. If a project achieves a positive NPV using the cost of capital as a discount rate then it is acceptable from the shareholders' point of view.

There are different ways to ascertain the cost of capital for a business. One way is to calculate the weighted average cost of capital, which is (basically) the average rate that the company pays in dividends to shareholders and interest on loans and bonds. The capital asset pricing model approach is slightly different, calculating the rate of return an investor would expect in return for investing in the company using information about market rates of return and the company's historic performance. Either way these are relatively easy to obtain (or calculate from a company's balance sheet), and they have some legitimacy with shareholders and investors.

Things are not so straightforward in the public sector, with academics debating the merits of alternative bases for the appropriate way to estimate the opportunity cost of capital since the 1960s at least (Lind, 1982 cited by Grout, 2005). In the public sector there are some organizations, such as local councils, that are allowed to borrow money from institutions and they could, therefore, identify their average cost of long-term borrowing. Other PBEs might identify that instead of investing the money in the project, they could invest it in a government bond earning, say, 5 per cent a year. If they did then they might regard 5 per cent as the appropriate discount rate for the project (although the effect of inflation should be excluded to get the real discount rate).

The choice of discount rate might be straightforward if the public manager's organization has a policy stating the rate that must be used. In the United Kingdom, the government has issued guidance on project appraisal (HM Treasury, 2022: 116), which prescribes that central government departments use a 'social time preference rate' (STPR) (2022: 45) of 3.5 per cent (it is a real rate so should be applied to cash flows that ignore inflation) for projects up to 30 years. Rates of 3.0 per cent and 2.5 per cent are proposed for projects of 31 to 75 years and 76 to 125 years, respectively. Whilst the rates are mandated only for central government bodies, they are used by other PBEs because they have legitimacy, and a PBE might feel on safer ground using them rather than calculating its own rate for each project.

The US federal government's Office of Management and Budget (OMB) issues a set of rates, both nominal and real, for use in evaluating cost-effectiveness, lease purchase and related analyses (OMB, 2022). The rates for calendar year 2022 are shown in Table 5.2 (and the rates for each year since 1979 can be found

Table 5.2 *US federal guidance on discount rates for 2022*

Period (years)	*Nominal discount rate (%)*	*Real discount rate (%)*
3	1.3	−1.2
5	1.6	−0.6
7	1.9	−0.3
10	2.1	0.0
20	2.5	0.4
30	2.6	0.5

Source: OMB (2022).

at www.whitehouse.gov/wp-content/uploads/2022/05/discount-history.pdf). The fact that some of the discount rates are negative is curious. They suggest that rather than the government's alternative to the investment being a benefit it would be a cost (presumably because of forecasts of deflation rather than inflation).

Sensitivity analysis

The choice of discount rate is absolutely crucial to the results of NPV calculations and the above indicated that there are numerous ways of coming up with a discount rate to use. Rather than deciding on a discount rate, plugging it into the calculations and making a decision based solely on what figure pops out at the end, it is a sensible idea to perform some sensitivity analysis.

Sensitivity analysis is the re-performance of calculations having changed the value of one of the assumptions. In the context of NPV calculations, not only can sensitivity analysis be performed by changing the discount rate up and down, but also on the other assumptions about the costs, savings, interest rates for financing the project, project start and end dates and the overall duration. If the NPV calculations are built into a computer model in a spreadsheet it is relatively easy to change the values of assumptions in turn and record the answers that result.

The variables that can be subject to sensitivity analysis represent risks to the project and the sensitivity analysis can, therefore, enable the public manager to understand the range of losses that might occur and their impact on the overall cost (in real terms as well as present value) and the viability of the project.

If the sensitivity analysis shows that a project returns a positive NPV when relatively large changes are made to the core assumptions, then the public manager may conclude that the project will be worthwhile in most circumstances that could arise and a decision to implement it is relatively robust. If, on the other hand, the NPV flips between positive and negative values when only small changes are made to the assumptions then the public manager may conclude that the project's financial viability is borderline. By itself that might not be grounds for rejection, but it would probably mean that non-financial factors relating to the project would become more significant in the overall decision.

Non-financial factors

Non-financial factors should not be ignored in a project appraisal. As mentioned before, financial management is an art rather than a science. The numbers may indicate a positive or negative NPV for a project, but there may be other factors that the public manager needs to take into account before reaching their decision. These might include:

- political manifesto commitments;
- employees' opinions;
- customer or service user relationships;
- legislation and regulations (such as health and safety at work obligations);
- reputation (whether a positive or a negative impact); and
- the implications for future projects.

Another relevant, non-financial factor is the length of the project. For projects that are 25 or 30 years long the cash flows that occur towards the end of the project would be discounted to very small amounts and would make little impact in the NPV. However, those cash flows might be very significant as far as the project delivery is concerned. This is generally not a problem for private sector projects because only inflows are a long way off and such inflows having very low present values is prudent; it means that a decision to invest is not heavily influenced by revenue (i.e., sales income) that is far into the future. Some public sector projects would have a similar profile where the cash outflows are upfront and only inflows (or savings) occur in the distant future but there is a potential issue though for projects—typically infrastructure projects—where there are outflows (costs) to be incurred far into the future (for maintenance, say) which are discounted heavily and therefore marginalized in the project appraisal decision.

For example, in a waste disposal project where the costs of environmental remediation of landfill sites are to be deferred until year 25, the PBE might be concerned that problems might arise as a result of not doing the remedial works earlier. An alternative option for the same project might involve paying for the remediation at regular intervals throughout the life of the project. The NPV of this option would be higher but it might be regarded by the PBE as preferable because it lowers the risk of problems over the project's lifetime.

FINANCIAL DECISION MAKING: SOME PRACTICAL ISSUES

Spurious accuracy

Spurious accuracy is the claiming of a greater level of accuracy in calculations than is justified by the inputs to the calculations.

Here is an example. A school is budgeted to spend £2,050,000 a year and is estimated to have 920 pupils. Simple division of the budget by the pupil numbers would say it costs £2,216.22 per pupil per year to attend the school. This level is unjustified given the rounded figures used to calculate it and, as a rule of thumb, the answer should be stated with the fewest number of significant figures as the numbers that it is derived from. In this example the budgeted spend has three significant figures and the pupil numbers has. Using the lower of these suggests the answer should be shown with two significant figures, that is £2,200 per pupil per year.

The issue with generating answers with spurious accuracy is that when a figure is stated to the penny or cent it gives the impression of a level of precision that may not be justified. This may result in the public manager (and any other person) finding the figure more credible than if it were rounded up or down. Often such 'precise' figures are simply the result of computer calculations that have not been rounded but occasionally an accountant may knowingly use such figures to increase the persuasiveness of their advice and public managers should be alert to this possibility.

Getting advice

To get all the information they require, or to be helped to understand the information they have, a public manager may seek advice from their organization's management accounting function (if there is one) or from other finance professionals who are authorized to give advice. The extent of advice sought depends on the public manager's knowledge and experience, but there will be some technical stuff about, for instance, the tax consequences of alternatives that a non-financial public manager is unlikely to understand fully. Similarly, a non-financial public manager may or may not have the skills and knowledge needed to build a spreadsheet financial model of the options and may look to experts to do this for them.

All in all, public managers should remember that advice is just that and that the decision to be made is theirs to make. In making the decision, however, they need to act reasonably for it to be lawful.

Reasonableness of decisions

PBEs must abide by the law and therefore their decision-making processes need to result in lawful decisions. In the United Kingdom and elsewhere this means that any decision that is made must be reasonable.

The concept of reasonableness can be rather slippery to describe, but fortunately, as far as decision making by public bodies in the United Kingdom is concerned, the highest court in the land has set out some principles that define the features of a reasonable decision.

The Wednesbury principles of reasonableness

These principles derive from the judgement by the Court of Appeal in 1947 in the case of Associated Provincial Picture Houses versus Wednesbury Corporation. The case concerned the licensing of a cinema by the Wednesbury Corporation in which they stipulated that no under fifteens would be allowed entry to the cinema on Sundays whether accompanied with an adult or not. The Court stated that it would only intervene in a bad administrative decision on the grounds of unreasonableness. By implication, therefore, if a public body made a reasonable decision that subsequently turned out to be a mistake or in some other way a bad decision, there would be no grounds for the courts to be involved. This is because the courts are not in a position to judge whether a public body made the 'correct' decision because there very often is no such thing, but the courts may judge whether a decision was properly reached.

The final judgement in this case set out three principles that would determine if a decision were reasonable. The principles mean that the decision-maker should:

1. take into account all factors that ought to be taken into account;
2. not take into account any factors that ought not to be taken into account; and
3. not be so unreasonable that no reasonable authority would ever consider imposing it.

For a recent example of this in action, the High Court used these principles to declare as unlawful the UK Government's policy in March/April 2020 of discharging elderly people from hospital into care homes without testing them for COVID-19 or requiring them to be isolated from other residents. The effect of this policy was very high rates of transmission of COVID-19 in care homes during the early weeks of the coronavirus pandemic.

The judges declared the policy unlawful 'because the drafters of [the policy] documents failed to take into account the risk to elderly and vulnerable residents from non-symptomatic transmission.' (cited by Booth, 2022). The judges took the view that the risk of transmission was a relevant factor in making decisions about the policy.

It is difficult to conceive of a decision by a PBE where money, whether in terms of expenditure or income or budgets or accounting, would not be captured in the first principle, as one of the factors that ought to be taken into account. If a public manager made a decision to pursue a course of action without any regard for the financial implications, it would very likely be an unreasonable decision. Indeed, such a decision might even be regarded as reckless.

CONCLUSION

Making decisions is an important aspect of the role of a public manager. To be effective at this, public managers ought to have a reasonable understanding of how costs behave and the cost structure of their programme, project or service.

Some decisions require option appraisals to be completed. The process of appraisal is:

- clarify the rationale for intervention;
- draw up a list of the viable alternative courses of action (perhaps first as a longlist and then as a shortlist);
- estimate the costs and the benefits of each option; and
- assess the costs and benefits using the payback method, the accounting rate of return method or the net present value method (as appropriate).

In carrying out appraisals and making decisions public manager should be aware of the reasonableness of the decisions they make. The next chapter focuses on a particular set of decisions that are commonly made by public managers: decisions about procuring goods and services.

EXERCISES

1. Thinking about a service or organization you are familiar with, what are the fixed costs and the variable costs? What, if any, are the semi-fixed or semi-variable costs?
2. In what circumstances would it not be necessary to use net present value technique to appraise a project?
3. A number of non-financial factors that might be relevant in making a decision were listed in the chapter. What other factors can you think of that might be relevant to a public project you are familiar with?

REFERENCES

Arts Council England. (2016). *Measuring the Economic Benefits of Arts and Culture*. Available at: https://www.artscouncil.org.uk/publication/measuring-economic-benefits-arts-and-culture (Accessed: 23 June 2022).

Asian Development Bank. (2013). *Cost-Benefit Analysis for Development: A Practical Guide*. Available at: https://www.adb.org/sites/default/files/institutional-document/33788/files/cost-benefit-analysis-development.pdf (Accessed: 23 June 2022).

Australia Government. (2015). *ICT Business Case Guide*. Available at: https://www.finance.gov.au/sites/default/files/2019-11/ICT_Business_Case_Guide.pdf (Accessed: 23 June 2022).

Booth, R. (2022). Covid care home discharge policy was unlawful, says court. *The Guardian* (27 April). Available at: https://www.theguardian.com/world/2022/apr/27/covid-discharging-untested-patients-into-care-homes-was-unlawful-says-court (Accessed: 23 June 2022).

CIPFA. (2015). *Top Tips for Business Cases* [Video]. Available at: https://www.youtube.com/watch?v=ULsPGuLz1dw (Accessed: 23 June 2022).

Cokins, G. (2006). *Activity-Based Cost Management in Government* (2nd ed.). Vienna, VA: Management Concepts.

Cokins, G. (2015). *A Need for Better Cost Information in the Public Sector* [Online Article]. Available at: https://www.ifac.org/knowledge-gateway/preparing-future-ready-professionals/discussion/need-better-cost-information-public-sector (Accessed: 21 June 2022).

Cooper, R., & Kaplan, R. S. (1988). Measure costs right: Make the right decisions. *Harvard Business Review, 66*(5), 96–103.

European Investment Bank. (2013). *The Economic Appraisal of Investment Projects at the EIB*. Available at: https://www.eib.org/en/publications/economic-appraisal-of-investment-projects (Accessed: 23 June 2022).

Fleischman, R. K., Hoskin, K. W., & Macve, R. H. (1995). The Boulton and Watt case: The crux of alternative approaches to accounting history? *Accounting and Business Research, 25*, 162–176.

Grout, P. A. (2005). Value-for-money measurement in public-private partnerships. *EIB Papers, 10*(2), 32–56.

HM Treasury. (2022). *The Green Book 2022*.London: TSO. Available at: https://www.gov.uk/government/publications/the-green-book-appraisal-and-evaluation-in-central-governent/the-green-book-2020 (Accessed: 22 June 2022).

Kaplan, R. S., & Anderson, S. R. (2004). Time-driven activity-based costing. *Harvard Business Review, 82*(11), 131–138.

Kaplan, R. S., & Cooper, R. (1998). *Cost and Effect: Using Integrated Cost Systems to Drive Profitability and Performance*. Boston, MA: Harvard Business School Press.

McChlery, S., McKendrick, J., & Rolfe, T. (2007). Activity-based management systems in higher education. *Public Money and Management, 27*(5), 315–322.

McKendrick, N. (1970). Josiah Wedgwood and cost accounting in the industrial revolution. *The Economic History Review, 23*(1), 45–67.

OMB. (2022). *Circular A-94 Appendix C Revised March 15, 2022* [Webpage]. Washington, DC. Available at: https://www.whitehouse.gov/wp-content/uploads/2022/05/Appendix-C.pdf (Accessed: 21 June 2022).

Prowle, M. (2020). *Management Accounting in Public Service Decision Making*. Abingdon: Routledge.

Seddon, J. (2008). *Systems Thinking in the Public Sector: The Failure of the Reform Regime and a Manifesto for a Better Way*. Axminster: Triarchy Press.

Tayles, M., & Drury, C. (2020). *Management and Cost Accounting* (11th ed.). Andover: Cengage Learning EMEA.

UNESCO. (2004). *Cost-Benefit Analysis in Educational Planning* (4th ed.). Available at: https://unesdoc.unesco.org/ark:/48223/pf0000139042 (Accessed: 23 June 2022).

Waka Kotahi NZ Transport Agency. (2020). *Monetised Benefits and Costs Manual*. Available at: https://www.nzta.govt.nz/resources/monetised-benefits-and-costs-manual/ (Accessed: 23 June 2022).

FURTHER READING (AND WATCHING)

Links to the following resources, and lots more, are available at www.managingpublicmoney.co.uk/extras.

To learn more about cost behaviour and costing try a management accounting textbook for business, such as Tayles and Drury's (2020) *Management and Cost Accounting*. An alternative with a public sector focus is *Management Accounting in Public Service Decision Making* (Prowle, 2020).

Cooper and Kaplan's (1998) *Harvard Business Review* article is a good introduction to the concept of ABC, but for those who want to learn about it in more depth there is the book, *Cost and Effect: Using Integrated Cost Systems to Drive Profitability and Performance* (Kaplan and Cooper, 1998). For something more specific to PBEs, there is Cokins's book: *Activity-Based Cost Management in Government* (Cokins, 2006). And if you are short of time, he wrote a series of four blog posts based on the book that are available on the IFAC website (Cokins, 2015).

Seddon (2008) provides a counterview of ABC, stating that it is 'at best a redundant activity and at worst will mislead' (2008: 183).

There are many examples of public sector project appraisal guidance published by governments and others on the internet. This includes general examples from the European Investment Bank (2013) and Asian Development Bank (2013). There are also guides for specific sectors, such as educational planning (UNESCO, 2004); culture (Arts Council England, 2016); land transport (Waka Kotahi NZ Transport Agency, 2020); and ICT (Australia Government, 2015).

These resources, and the UK Treasury's *The Green Book* that was mentioned in the chapter, imply that all the relevant information would be collected into a business case for decision-makers to consider. CIPFA (2015) published a webinar, *Top Tips for Business Cases*, that might be of interest if you have to write one.

Chapter 6

Public procurement

LEARNING OBJECTIVES

After reading this chapter you should:

- recognize good practice in commissioning and procuring goods, works and services by PBEs;
- understand the commissioning cycle;
- be able to define a public–private partnership and explain the various kinds of partnership arrangements that might be used;
- understand how the use of outsourcing impacts a PBE's financial management arrangements; and
- identify risks relating to outsourcing and partnerships.

KEY POINTS OF THIS CHAPTER

- The five rights of procurement are obtaining the right quantity and quality of goods, works or services, at the right time, in the right place and at the right price.
- A total of 30 per cent, on average, of government budgets is spent on goods and services procured from the private sector.
- There are many forms of partnership arrangements for involving third parties in the delivery of public services and projects.
- Public managers should be aware of the financial management issues connected with the commissioning of partnership arrangements, operating them and exiting them.

DOI: 10.4324/9781003250838-6

- The written agreement between partners is intended to document the allocation of risk between the partners as well as their obligations to each other and the price(s) to be paid.

KEY TERMS

Commissioning—the management function that determines the broad parameters of how public services should be delivered, that is, which services to produce internally and which to procure from a partner or contractor.

Outsourcing—the appointment of a third party to carry out a function on behalf of the client organization under the terms of a contract.

Procurement—the process of acquiring goods, works and/or services from third parties.

Public–private partnership (PPP)—a long-term arrangement where private sector organizations take on risk and responsibility for the delivery of a public project, usually involving the creation or enhancement of a fixed asset.

Public–public partnership—two or more PBEs that collaborate to achieve a joint objective.

Specification—a description of requirements and standards to which the goods, works or services should conform.

Tender—a formal offer to carry out works or to supply goods or services for a stated price.

Although the use of the private sector to deliver public services is a distinctive feature of NPM (Hood, 1991: 5) it is a practice that dates back much further than the late 1970s. For example, in the eighteenth century, tax collection in England was outsourced to private tax collectors and the similar practice of tax farming dates to Roman times, at least. This is a system of tax collection where private individuals would pay a sum to the government for the right to collect taxes for a certain region and period of time and then hope to collect a greater sum in money and goods from the taxpayers.

In the 1970s and 1980s the approach to expanding the private sector's involvement in public services was through privatization and competitive tendering. The former process was the 'selling-off' of publicly owned enterprises, often utilities that had been regarded as natural monopolies. This was done on a large scale in Australia, New Zealand and the United Kingdom (Broadbent and Laughlin, 2003: 334), whereas in the United States the utilities were generally already in private hands but there was a process of deregulation (Baker, 2003: 446).

Whilst there are many aspects of public service that public managers and politicians would feel uncomfortable about the private sector being involved in (such as aspects of national security, policing and justice), the fact is that private sector companies have experience and know-how in most of what PBEs do. They provide personal services like health care, they run prisons, they provide logistics support to armed forces in war zones, and they develop computer systems to store and process highly sensitive data.

The Open Contracting Partnership (2020) estimated that 30 per cent of government spending is spent on contracts with companies. This equates to about $13 trillion a year spent on goods, works and contracts. And 16 countries spend over $10 trillion of that total (in descending order: China, United States, Japan, Germany, India, France, United Kingdom, Indonesia, Canada, Italy, South Korea, Australia, Brazil, Netherlands, Russia and Spain).

This chapter deals with financial management issues in the logical sequence of steps of commissioning and procurement of a contract, managing the contract during its lifetime and exiting it. But before that, the reasons why a PBE might want to use a private sector supplier are considered and the different kinds of partnership that a public manager may encounter.

REASONS TO USE THE PRIVATE SECTOR IN PUBLIC SERVICES

Greve (2008: 7–13) gives five reasons why a PBE might wish to procure goods, works or services from the private sector:

- to address a lack of capacity
- to save money
- to transfer risk
- to comply with law or regulation
- to access skills, technology and/or finance (Greve, 2008: 7–13).

These reasons are discussed over the following pages.

Lack of capacity

First, there are things that any organization would buy rather than make, usually because they simply do not have the ability or desire to make them. Things like stationery, ICT equipment and vehicles all fall into the category. Indeed, the breadth of public services means that almost anything might be bought by a PBE somewhere.

PBEs do not just need to buy goods that they cannot make; they also procure works, such as the construction of infrastructure networks and buildings, and services, such as specialist legal advice. The procurement of services has gone beyond the procurement of services like consulting, which are inputs to the PBE, to procuring the actual delivery of services to the public.

At the root of these decisions about procurement is a value for money assessment of when it would make sense to buy-in the goods or works or services from a contractor, and when it would be cheaper and/or more effective to do the work inside the PBE.

This is not the only way that lack of capacity results in the use of the private sector. Organizations in crisis often find they do not have the managerial capacity to fix the underlying problems. There are different ways of addressing this, including recruitment of new managers, the use of interim managers and consultants or secondments from other organizations. One option for bringing in extra capacity is to outsource the service (to specialist and experiences providers).

A key issue in procuring a partnership in these circumstances is that the bidding companies know that there are problems in the service being outsourced and they may use this as a lever in negotiations to press for lower service standards to be imposed. Public managers may have to factor this into their commissioning and procurement plans. There may also be additional challenges in managing the contracts and contractors if there is little or no relevant expertise inside the PBE.

Saving money

In simple terms a contractor or partner can offer efficiency gains through reduced administration costs, lower direct project costs and improved incentive structures (Bergmann, 2010: 143). Jensen and Stonecash suggest that savings can arise from 'substitution of capital for labour, more efficient work practices, economies of scale, innovation and labour shedding and increases in work intensity' (2005: 772–3).

Whilst these may all be seen as positive reasons—they are about reducing waste in one way or another—Jensen and Stonecash (2005: 773) also discuss two other potential ways to save money: quality shading and redistribution. The former is the deterioration of quality after the service has been outsourced and the latter is the achievement of savings by reducing the employees' conditions and benefits. These two methods of saving money might be seen as negative and PBEs may take steps in their commissioning activity to prevent them.

In the burst of public sector outsourcing in the 1980s there was a widely held view that outsourcing would save 20 per cent. Jensen and Stonecash (2005) comment that Domberger, Meadowcroft and Thompson's findings of an average saving of 22 per cent when a contract was awarded to the private sector was accompanied by the finding that there was an average saving of 17 per cent when the service was retained 'in-house' by the PBE. This seems to support the view that PBE's benefit from exposure to competition even if ultimately they do not outsource the service. Greve (2008: 8) explains that Domberger, Meadowcroft and Thompson's findings of savings either side of 20 per cent seems to have contributed to 20 per cent savings being used as a rule of thumb for contracting out.

Even where there are initial savings identified by a PBE, by comparing its existing costs against the initial prices set out in the contract with the winning bidder, there is the issue of whether that level of savings continues throughout the lifetime of the contract. Jensen and Stonecash cite Krugman's (2002) observation:

> It's common for private contractors to bid low to get the business, then push their prices up once the government work force has been disbanded. Projections of a 20 or 30 [per cent] cost saving across the board are silly — and one suspects that the officials making those projections know that.
>
> Jensen and Stonecash (2005: 775)

Risk sharing

The third reason listed above as an incentive for outsourcing or partnering is to transfer risk. As mentioned in Chapter 2 if a risk cannot be eliminated the next best strategy is to transfer it to a third party. Where risks are proposed to be transferred to an outsourced contractor or a partner, they would be well advised to consider their ability to manage the risk before accepting it. Where there is a commercial arrangement in place in the partnership then the partner can make an allowance for the transferred risks in its price. What the PBE ends up with in such a situation is like an insurance premium: they transfer away the uncertainty of the risk in exchange for the certainty of paying the partner's price. Where the partner is better able to manage the risk than the PBE could then this arrangement should result in an efficient allocation of risk between the partners (that is, the total extra amount paid by the PBE to the partner over the term is less than it would expect the risk to have cost it over the same period).

Complying with the law

Governments who have policies for promoting the use of the private sector in public services can, if they wish, legislate to make sure that there are opportunities for the private sector to be awarded contracts in certain sectors or service areas.

In the United Kingdom in the 1980s and 1990s, complying with the law would have been a major reason for putting public services out to tender. There was compulsory competitive tendering legislation in both the NHS and local government that covered a range of functions, from catering and cleaning, sports centre management, highway maintenance, refuse collection and fleet management to support services like finance and human resources.

Competitive tendering, confusingly it was also referred to as privatization at the time, was the requirement of government and local government organizations to subject specified services to market testing. Only if the public organization could deliver the services more competitively than private sector bidders would it be allowed to provide the service itself and, in doing so, it had to maintain an internal organizational divide between the client and the contractor function. This was so that separate accounts could be produced for the contractor function that demonstrated that it was able to break even or make a 'profit' by charging the prices in its 'contract' (this term was used but technically an organization cannot have a contract with itself).

The compulsory requirement to subject services to competition was abolished for local government in 1997, but there are requirements for local authorities to achieve value for money in their work that force them to consider market testing as an option for the delivery of front line and support services. Competition remains fundamental to NHS and throughout its frequent restructures in the last 20 years there has remained a purchaser-provider split within it.

Accessing skills, technology or finance

The fifth reason in Greve's list was to gain access to skills, technology and/or finance. If a PBE identifies a gap in its skills or technology then seeking a partner who has those skills or technologies is one of the possible strategic responses. Depending on the PBE's circumstances it may be quicker or easier or cheaper to commission a partnership than to procure the skills and technology directly.

Using partnerships to access finance may often be a result of government constraints that restrict the PBE's funding for certain projects unless, for example, they are delivered in partnership or there is a minimum contribution from the private sector. If working in partnership is the only way to get funding for projects that are desirable for a PBE, then it may enter one despite any misgivings. This practice is probably the basis of the opinion of an interviewee quoted by Greasley, Watson and Patel (2008: 309), who said a public–private partnership is 'a mutual loathing in pursuit of government funds.'

On a positive note, there are advances in the field of ICT management, such as cloud computing, that specialized companies can offer to PBEs at a marginal cost which would be better value for money than the PBE seeking to build, operate and maintain their own data centres. Such deals also offer the potential for PBEs to change their cost structure by reducing the proportion of their ICT costs that are fixed costs because the use of cloud computing is a variable (or semi-variable) cost (see Chapter 4 for a reminder of the meaning of these terms).

Similarly, shared service centres are better able to invest in skills and technology because of their economy of scale. This gives PBEs an incentive to join in with shared service centres rather than each trying to do their own thing.

TYPES OF PARTNERSHIP ARRANGEMENTS

There are many possible arrangements for the private sector to be involved with a PBE in the delivery of public services and projects. A PBE may also have partnerships with other PBEs, whether a government body or a charity or a social enterprise. Table 6.1 illustrates the spectrum of possible partnership arrangements running from the PBE having a simple service contract with a contractor through

Table 6.1 *The spectrum of partnerships*

Type of arrangement	*Features*
Service contract	A conventional contract where the private sector partner supplies a service in accordance with a specification in return for a fee.
Management contract	A contract that vests the operational control of a service or facility to a private sector partner. This arrangement might be used, for example, to operate a publicly owned sports arena or similar facility.
Design and build	Often used in construction where the contractor is provided with an outline project brief but is required to produce the detailed designs and then construct the building or road, etc.
Service concession	An arrangement (similar to a licence) that grants the private sector partner the right to operate a service or facility for an agreed period of time in return for a fee (which could be defined as a percentage of the income from the concession).
Design-build-operate-maintain	Takes the design and build concept further with the private sector partner subsequently operating and maintaining the asset they designed and built.
Design-build-finance-operate (DBFO)	This is the classic arrangement for a PFI contract where the private sector partner also provides the capital finance for the project. The private sector partner would usually maintain the asset as well as operate it. The complexity of these arrangements means that the private sector partner is often a consortium of companies each providing one aspect of the DBFO.
Build-own-operate-transfer (BOOT)	An arrangement where the private sector partner is involved in a project in a similar way to a DBFO but at the end of an agreed period (perhaps 25 years or more) the asset is transferred to the PBE.
Build-own-operate (BOO)	A project arrangement like a BOOT project except that the asset does not transfer to the PBE.
Privatization	The (permanent) transfer of publicly owned organizations into the private sector (such as the government sell-off of utility companies in the United Kingdom and Australia in the 1980s).

Source: Adapted from Bergmann (2009: 139).

to the full privatization of a PBE by transferring it into private ownership. The arrangements lower down in the table involve a greater degree of private sector risk and responsibility.

The terms the partners agree for their partnership need to be in writing, for the protection of both parties. The document may be called a contract or a programme agreement, project agreement, joint venture agreement or something else. The documentation for an agreement might be little more than an exchange of letters between the partners or, such as in the case of major projects, it may have dozens of separate documents and schedules, running to thousands of pages. The simple exchange of letters is more likely when the partnership is an agreement for two PBEs to work together on a common issue than if there were a competitive procurement process to select the partner. Essentially, whatever the documentation is called it forms the contract between the partners.

The basis of a contract is that there has to be an offer from one party that is accepted by another party and there has to be an exchange of consideration. In a simple example, a company offers to provide a refuse collection service to a local council on the terms set out in a draft contract, the council accepts the offer and the consideration is the price that the council will pay in return for the company's delivery the service. One can see contracts and partnerships as an exchange of promises: the partner promises to deliver the service and the PBE promises to pay for it.

Written agreements also set out the sharing of risks between the partners—or at least they do in an ideal world. If an agreement is silent about a risk issue, perhaps because it had not been contemplated as a risk at the time the agreement was made, then the parties will have to work something out between them if the risk materializes. Unfortunately for the public manager the chances are that the cost of risks which are not included in the documentation, either explicitly or by implication, will fall on their PBE. This could be a direct impact or it could be indirect because to agree a change to the partnership agreement will require a quid pro quo: the partner will expect something in return for taking on a risk that it had not allowed for at the time it entered the agreement and often that something is a price increase. There are other things a public manager might be able to bring into such a negotiation, such as a change in the specification or a relaxation of the performance targets or an extension of the length of the agreement, but, if all else fails, they could pay for the partner to take on the risk. Such a deal would be a sensible thing to do only if the public manager judges that the amount they have to pay for the partner to take on the risk is value for money. The amount of risk taken on by the partner is a critical difference between the various forms of partnership that are described below and would be a factor in the PBE's decision on what sort of partnership to commission in the first place.

Public–private partnerships

Public–private partnership (PPP) is something of an umbrella term for a variety of arrangements and there is not a common definition across countries. PPPs fill the space between traditional procurement at one end and privatization at the other (Grimsey and Lewis, 2005: 346). Van Ham and Koppenjan (2001: 598) define them as 'co-operation of some durability between public and private actors in which they jointly develop products and services and share risks, costs and resources which are connected with these products or services.'

Kappeler and Nemoz (2010) cite the European Commission's statement that PPPs are characterized by:

> The relatively long duration of the relationship, involving cooperation between the public partner and the private partner on different aspects of a planned project [...]; the method of funding the project, in part from the private sector, sometimes by means of complex arrangements between the various players [...]; the important role of the economic operator, who participates at different stages in the project (design, completion, implementation, funding) [...]; the distribution of risks between the public partner and the private partner, to whom the risks generally borne by the public sector are transferred.
>
> Kappeler and Nemoz (2010: 4)

There are two types of public–private partnership: social and economic (Greve, 2008: 119). Strategic partnering as described above fits with the definition of social partnership being a longer-term arrangement to produce goods and services and to 'share risks and resources and gains' but without the private partner being involved in the long-term financing of the arrangement.

The economic partnership is the type that is more dominant in the literature and is discussed in the remainder of this section. In terms of Table 6.1, economic PPPs describe the arrangements from design-build-operate-maintain downwards, but hey might in some contexts include design and build and long-term concessions, too. What they have in common is they are arrangements that are principally concerned with projects which would be deemed capital expenditure if the PBE undertook them in the traditional fashion (i.e., commissioning a design from an architect or engineer, appointing a contractor to deliver what has been designed and raising loans or other funds to pay for it). PPPs have changed the public sector landscape by giving the PBE alternative ways of getting, using and paying for infrastructure and facilities.

PPPs are not (usually) joint ventures in the way two companies might collaborate to produce a new product or penetrate a certain market. PBEs do set up joint ventures with private sector partners but the joint venture entities tend to get their income from a contract or agreement with the 'parent' PBE rather than finding their income from elsewhere (such as by competing in an open market). Partly this is because there are issues about trading by PBEs or charities. Having the power to charge for the supply of services in a monopoly situation is much different from trading. Trading carries much more risk in terms of finding customers, marketing and pricing and these are risks that the taxpayers or donors may not be happy for the organization to take on.

The key difference between a PPP project and a traditionally delivered project is that a PPP provider not only constructs or enhances the asset, but also subsequently provides the services that are associated with that asset for a substantially long period. So, for a new school the PPP provider would provide a range of facilities management services within the school and would allow the education authority to use the school buildings in return for an annual fee (called a 'unitary charge'). If some of the classrooms were unavailable or otherwise unfit for use then the education authority would not have to pay the full fee/unitary charge and this risk acts as the incentive for the PPP provider to maintain the school in good condition throughout the lifetime of the agreement (which might be 25 or 30 years). Verweij and van Meerkerk (2021) analysed public–private partnerships (PPPs) and concluded that the design-build-finance-manage contracts were better value than traditional design and construct contracts.

Public–public partnerships

Public–public partnerships are rather different from PPPs. As the name implies, they involve the cooperation of two or more PBEs but they tend to be used for delivery of services rather than capital projects.

There may be many reasons for entering a public-public partnership rather than a PPP. One reason might be that a partnership with another public organization is politically more acceptable than a partnership with a private company or consortium. This might be about cultural fit or because in a public-public partnership none of the partners is seeking a financial profit from the arrangement, and therefore the total costs might be lower. It might also be because the private sector has little experience and know-how to offer. This would be the case in services that are wholly public, such as specialist aspects of police investigations, where an individual police force may feel it can get more efficiency by collaborating with other police forces than with a private company.

Strategic partnering

Strategic partnering is a form of partnership where a set of (usually but not necessarily) related services are bundled together into one partnership agreement and the contract is likely to be of a longer duration than might be the case if individual contracts had been awarded for each service. By bundling services together, the PBE hopes to benefit from the economies of scale the partner can bring and also to have simpler contract management arrangements because the partner has to manage the interfaces between the bundled services. The possible downside with this approach is that the partner may not be equally good at all the services: where a PBE takes a 'best of breed' approach instead it would appoint expert contractors for each service (but it would have a lot of separate contracts to manage).

A strategic partnering arrangement might involve the creation of a joint venture company, but, if not, there would be some form of joint governance over the activities of the partnership. In bundling together a set of services like this, the PBE is looking for added value in terms of streamlined management and governance of the contracted services and a more productive, less adversarial relationship between the partners. This added value has to offset, at least, the likelihood that the strategic partner's offer will be weaker/more expensive for some services than the PBE could have achieved if it had adopted a best of breed approach.

THE COMMISSIONING CYCLE

The terms 'commissioning, procurement and purchasing' might be seen as interchangeable as they are variations on the concept of placing an order for goods or services, but they are different. For the purposes of this book commissioning is the strategic management function where decisions are made about the way that services will be delivered. It is a commissioning role to determine whether to make or to buy certain goods and services—in the public sector, this is perhaps better phrased 'produce or procure'—and determines the high-level service specification where the commissioners want the service to be procured externally. Procurement, then, is a more tactical function, involved in fleshing out the specification, sourcing suitable suppliers or partners and settling the terms of contracts with the successful bidder. Finally, purchasing is an operational function, where goods and services are obtained from the appropriate contracted suppliers or through ad hoc purchases.

Commissioning is the process of achieving appropriate outcomes by assessing the needs of people or users in an area, designing and specifying the services to meet those needs and choosing the delivery mechanism to secure an appropriate service whilst making the best use of total available resources.

Commissioning is concerned with achieving outcomes. If politicians and managers want to deliver a specific outcome, first they have to work out how best to achieve the outcome, within the constraints of the available resources. They may decide the best approach would be the direct delivery of a programme using public servants or they may choose, instead, to commission the programme of work to be delivered by a third party, perhaps an NGO.

The four stages of the commissioning cycle are:

1. **Analysis**—where the commissioner (a public manager or committee or whatever) considers what is needed to and the environment in which the service providers are operating. This will include collecting and analysing data about existing service provision, demographic changes, public wishes and so on.
2. **Planning**—where the options for providing the service are identified and evaluated. These options are likely to include provision by third parties as well as ways that the organization could do the work itself.
3. **Doing**—where the chosen option from the planning stage is executed. This may require exiting from the current method of provision as well as setting up the new provision.
4. **Reviewing**—which includes monitoring the service provision and managing performance. Data and reports from this stage will contribute to the analysis stage in the next cycle.

A commissioning cycle could be completed every year, with the analysis and planning stages feeding into the budget planning stage of the PFM cycle. However, reviewing and changing service/programme delivery every year is likely to be unhelpful and involve a lot of transaction costs. This is especially the case if there is a multi-year contract in place with the service provider. The period of the commissioning cycle would therefore be better if it was adjusted to match the subject of the commissioning process. This might be many years rather than one.

THE PROCUREMENT PROCESS

Procuring a supplier/partner becomes increasingly complex and costly as one moves along the spectrum described in Table 6.1. As Romzek and Johnston put it, 'successful contracting requires an extraordinary amount of planning, negotiation and on-going collaboration among contracting partners' (2002: 448). As well as taking a long time—two or three years not being unusual for PPP deals—it is expensive in terms of the organization's managers' time and professional advisors' fees. As a guideline, the procurement process for a partnership might be 1 to 2 per cent of the total value of the contract. As some PPPs run into billions of pounds, euros or dollars the upfront cost to the PBE could be in the tens of millions.

In public procurement the following four fundamental principles should be upheld:

- **integrity**—is a prerequisite throughout the whole process, in order to guarantee trust and confidence in both the process and the final result;
- **transparency**—information should be accessible to all except if there are legitimate and lawful purposes behind keeping certain information private;
- **accountability**—those in charge of a procurement should be answerable for the decisions made during the procurement process; and
- **value for money**—there has to be a balance between price and quality and the tender that offers the best balance should be accepted.

Beyond these principles, the remainder of this section describes some key elements of the procurement process: the use of open competition, specifying requirements as outputs, types of contracts, payment arrangements, procurement risks and evaluation of bids.

Use of open competition

In most cases it would not be seen as appropriate for a PBE to negotiate in private with a single organization and then announce that a deal has been done (the exception being in emergency situations such as the coronavirus pandemic) because of the risk of poor value for money being attached. No matter how open about the deal the PBE was, subsequently there would always be the possibility that a different organization could have agreed to a deal that was better value for money. Indeed, competitor organizations that feel aggrieved about the missed opportunity might take legal action. This is why, usually, PBEs (usually) procure contracts by engaging in competition.

Competitive procurement involves inviting tenders from potential suppliers. The cost of going through a formal competitive procurement process means that, for practical reasons, a PBE will have a threshold contract value below which a simpler, faster method of procurement can be used. The value of the threshold will depend on the PBE's context and assessment of the balance of cost of the procurement against the value of what is being procured.

When work needs to be undertaken by an external supplier, potential suppliers are invited to submit bids, or tenders, to become the contractor for this work. This process can be referred to as "going out to tender for" whatever is required.

Alternatives to open competition

There are some situations where open competition might not result in the best value for money being obtained by a PBE. As mentioned above, for low value purchases (particularly of commodities where there is a functioning marketplace) it may not be worth the costs and time of running a competitive process.

Other situations where open competition might not be appropriate for a PBE to use include:

- where there is or could be a threat to national security (such as the procurement of defence systems)
- where the PBE is seeking goods or services where there is only one possible supplier (such as enhancing proprietary software already used by the PBE)
- where a framework contract is in place, allowing the PBE to select a supplier based on the competitive process used to create the framework contract (possibly by a different PBE)

Finally, in emergencies, especially where lives are at risk, a government or PBE may decide that it needs to act much faster than competitive procurement would allow. This was evident all over the world during the coronavirus of 2020. As the IMF put it at the time (Wending et al., 2020): 'Do whatever it takes, but keep the receipts.'

Specification of requirements

The absolutely critical thing is for the PBE to know what it wants before it procures anything (Kettl, 1993). Amirkhanyan, Kim and Lambright (2007: 707) said PBEs 'must know: 1. what service it wants to buy, 2. who it wants to buy the service from and 3. the quality of what it has purchased.' This seems obvious but in political organizations it might not be straightforward for a public manager to state what is wanted.

It is good practice for the service specification to be in output terms (as recommended by Behn and Kant, 1999: 479). This approach means that the supplier/contractor is required to design and implement appropriate methods to deliver the outputs and it is at risk for its performance in terms of achieving all the outputs.

The recipe for an output specification is to write each statement of requirements (you could have hundreds of these within a major specification) like this:

> Who will do what, when and how performance will be measured.

One of the key advantages of using an output specification is that it is shorter and easier to write than an input specification because less detail is needed. Take a parks maintenance service: one of the outputs in an output specification is that the grass is kept shorter than a prescribed length. In an input specification there would need to be detailed procedures for how to cut the grass, what to do with the clippings and a planned schedule for grass-cutting and what to do if it is raining when the grass should be cut. And the result of all this is that sometimes the grass will be cut when it does not need to be cut and at other times it will be longer than is desired.

As well as describing the outputs to be delivered the specification should include:

- the time period over which the contract applies;
- obligations or responsibilities of both supplier and client;
- arrangements for payment of fees;
- performance monitoring arrangements to be operated to ensure that the service provided is of an adequate standard;
- details of the consequences if the suppliers fails to meet the performance standards;
- other significant terms and conditions of the contract; and
- an explanation of how the bid/tender will be evaluated.

As well as describing what the results of the contract should be, the specification can also make clear which risks are the responsibility of which party.

There are some risks that are non-transferrable as far as a PBE is concerned, such as the risk of a change in political leadership in democratic organizations and changes in the law (that are not foreseen or foreseeable at the time the partnership was entered into, at least). There are other risks that are theoretically transferrable but which would not be good value for money if they were transferred. For example, if a private sector partner were employed to administer a welfare benefit scheme it could be required to take the risk of the volume of claimants increasing without any upper limit. In such a case, to limit their exposure to this risk, they might base their price on a workload that is at the upper limit of the volume that might reasonably occur or at a level that they estimate there is less than 5 per cent chance of being exceeded. Most of the time during the contract the actual demand for the benefit would be lower than the volume that the price is based on, meaning that the PBE would be paying for more service than is needed and the partner would be making a much higher profit than its work really deserves. Not only that, it could also use the spare capacity in its systems to earn revenue from other customers (although a PBE ought to include terms in the contract that entitle the PBE to a share of such revenue). In this scenario, therefore, it would be better value for money for the PBE to bear the risk of volume changes.

Table 6.2 shows some risks that a PBE is likely to retain in a partnership and some risks that would usually be expected to transfer to a partner. In practice, all risks would be subject to negotiation and agreement between the partners.

Given the moves towards measuring outcomes as well as outputs (see Chapter 7), a PBE might want to use outcomes rather than outputs as the basis of a contract specification. On the one hand, an outcome specification might

Table 6.2 *Typical allocation of risks*

Risks typically retained by a PBE	*Risks typically transferred to a partner*
• Faults or mistakes in project/ service specifications • Changes in laws and regulations that were unknown at the commencement of the partnership • Changes in political control • Changes in the specification of the services and/or projects • Changes in the organization's funding (from taxes, government grants or other sources) • Claims made by employees and customers relating to the period before the partnership • Residual value of constructed assets	• Site-related risks like ground conditions, pollution, planning permission • Delays and failures in construction phase of project • Design and management of processes, systems and methods of working to deliver the specified outputs for the services and/ or projects • Contractual defaults (e.g., failure to meet performance targets) • Recruitment, training, retention and performance of staff • Managing the supply chain, including the performance of suppliers • Pay rises and price inflation • Levels of income from user charges • Demand from users • Purchase, repair, maintenance and replacement of any equipment needed to deliver the partnership's services • Claims made by employees and customers relating to the period of the partnership

be more concise and even easier to write than an output specification. On the other hand, it might be difficult to find a partner willing to take on the level of risk that would be associated with undertaking to achieve the outcomes unless there were mechanisms to allow for events out of their control. For example, let us consider a PBE that wants to improve the safety on a stretch of highway in a town. Awarding a conventional contract to install safety features based on the PBE's design is reasonable for a partner to commit to. A contract to design, build and maintain the road, incorporating new safety features, between points A and B is fine, too, since they will be able to assess how much work is involved and put a price on it. To design, build and maintain the road between A and B and guarantee a reduction in fatalities (i.e., meet the outcome) may be difficult for a partner to commit to because the design and condition of a road are not the only reason deaths occur. The partner cannot control, for instance, fog and ice or whether drivers are drunk, and they would be unhappy if factors outside of their control meant they were not paid their full price for their work. The partner could mitigate this by adding a premium to their price, but this may make the project poor value for money for the PBE since the premium will make the whole project more expensive.

Types of contracts

A contract is basically an exchange of promises. The supplier promises to deliver the goods or services as specified in the agreement and the client promises to pay the agreed price. When it comes to spending public money on goods or services, it is best if there is a written contract in place in advance. The contract sets out the details of the goods to be delivered or the service to be provided, the responsibilities of the parties involved and various other terms and conditions.

Contracts can be broadly divided into the following categories:

1. firm price—means that the supplier bears the risk of increases or decreases in cost for a specified period of time;
2. fixed price—is similar to firm price except that price variations made to deal with inflation and/or exchange rate movements;
3. cost-plus—is a contract where the price paid is an agreed markup on the costs incurred by the supplier in completing the works or services;
4. time and materials—is an agreement where an hourly/daily/monthly rate is paid for each hour/day/month of input provided by the supplier, plus reimbursement of the direct costs of materials used by the supplier (the hourly/daily/monthly rates could be different for different grades of input); and
5. framework agreements—is an agreement with multiple potential suppliers that govern the terms and prices of contracts to be awarded by the client organization over a specified period of time.

There is no hard and fast rule governing the type of contract to be used for any particular situation. The contract type is chosen that best satisfies the needs. One important factor in deciding which type of contract to use is to think about how you want to pay for the goods or services and how much risk you are prepared to take. A firm price contract gives you certainty about how much you will pay but the supplier may include a premium in their price to cover the risk they are taking in delivering at that price. A time and materials contract could work out cheaper if the supplier is efficient but could work out much more expensive if they are wasteful. This suggests the PBE should monitor the supplier's performance to ensure they are not wasting time (or overcharging for time not actually spent on the PBE's contract).

Payment mechanisms

In a procurement process the bidders state their prices for undertaking the specified work and/or achieving the specified levels of performance. This 'bid price' will be based on the estimated volumes and so on provided to the bidder and the payment mechanism is the set of clauses and schedules within the contract that describe exactly how the payments to the partner should be calculated and paid.

Payments broadly fall into two types. There are milestone payments that are paid when the partner has achieved a specific package of work. These are useful in project agreements because there will be milestones in the project plan and all that is needed is to apportion the full price for the project into amounts that correspond to each milestone. The partner has an incentive to reach milestones in order to be paid, but the PBE can add an extra incentive by having 'long stop dates' for some or all milestones. Failure to meet a long stop date would allow the PBE to terminate the contract and/or pay a reduced fee and/or claim damages (depending on the terms of the contract).

The second type of payment is a periodic payment, the period most likely being a calendar month but it could be weekly or quarterly or annually. This type of payment suits service delivery partnerships because it pays for the services as they are delivered.

Of course, sometimes a contract will have components that are projects and components that are services and it might be agreed between the partners that a combination of payments would be made: the regular monthly payments would be supplemented by milestone payments as and when milestones are achieved.

The terms of the payment mechanism also interlink with the agreed risk allocation between the partners. One of the risks is that the volume of work done or services delivered differs from the assumed volume that the bid price was based on. For example, if a partner is responsible for administering a welfare benefit of some kind, an economic recession could result in an increase in the number of claimants of the benefit beyond what was anticipated when the contract was signed. The increased volume of claimants will cause the partner either to increase its expenditure, thus reducing its profit, to meet the higher demand or fail to administer claims as quickly and accurately as required in the contract. The issue would fall to the relevant public manager to resolve: essentially, they could agree to increase the payments to the partner or accept a lower level of performance.

Of course, it would be better if the original contract had recognized the risk of the volume of work materially increasing (or decreasing) and set out how the partners would deal with it if it happened. Sticking with this example, the PBE could have captured prices for the service at different volume levels and would know exactly how much it needed to pay when the volume increased. The advantage of this is that the variable prices are captured during the procurement process and, therefore, are subject to competitive pressure. If prices were not captured in this way at the outset, then the PBE and partner have to negotiate a new price when the volumes (materially) change—in a situation where the partner has no competitors and can name its price since the PBE has little alternative but to accept.

The payment mechanism might include the basis for making deductions from the fee in situations where the partner's performance fails to meet the contracted performance targets.

These types of arrangements are called 'price and performance mechanisms'. Often the mechanism allows the PBE to reduce the fee it pays the partner in response to the latter's failure to meet performance targets. However sometimes, instead of a fee deduction, service credits are accrued that entitle the client PBE to receive additional services or projects at no extra charge. Such mechanisms are useful for enabling the PBE to receive a financial benefit if the partner does not deliver on the promised level of performance without having to go through lengthy and expensive procedures of claiming damages and so on. The downside is that the supplier, if they are diligent, will have assessed the likelihood of their performance falling below the required standard and calculated the expected amount of fee that would be deducted (or service credits granted) over the lifetime of the partnership and factored it into their price. The PBE may pay a premium, therefore, in order to have the right to deduct the partner's fee if they under-perform, although, all other things being equal, the bidding organization that feels most confident about meeting the performance targets would add the smallest premium to their price and thus have an advantage over their competitors.

Procurement risks

The aim of procurement is to get the right quantity and quality of the product, at the right time, in the right place and at the right price. These are the **five rights of procurement**. There are lots of risks associated with procurement that can cause a PBE not to get everything it wants. Table 6.3 shows some of risks at each stage of the procurement process

Getting a procurement process wrong can have dire consequences for public services, whether it be procuring the wrong thing, selecting a supplier that is not good enough to deliver the requirements, or paying too much for the goods/services. This can happen in normal times, but at extreme times it can be worse. The coronavirus pandemic put pressure on the procurement processes of governments and PBEs and some were found wanting (Bandy and Metcalfe, 2021: 24–5). Rutter (2022) reports about the 'complete breakdown' of South Africa's public procurement systems during the pandemic. Over 60 per cent of the contracts awarded for personal protective equipment were awarded irregularly, with civil servants and politicians enriching themselves rather than serving the public interest.

Outsourcing critical functions

In general, outsourcing a service might offer the potential for improvement in efficiency and/or effectiveness but this will be at the cost of flexibility

Table 6.3 *Procurement risks*

Procurement stage	*Risks*	*Measures for mitigation*
Planning	Procuring wrong items or failure to procure on time or buying too much or too little than needed	Procurement strategy and plans need to be carefully prepared taking into account lead times, optimal ordering quantity, holding costs and so on.
Pre-qualification	Failure to exclude unsuitable bidders	Pre-qualification is partly used as a risk mitigation tool to prevent an unsuitable bidder winning the contract. The information submitted by potential bidders should be thoroughly assessed. Where possible the information should be corroborated with other available sources. Inconsistencies and other suspicious data should be investigated and resolved.
Bid receipt	Few (or no) bids received	The planning stage should include research into the marketplace so that the contract is packaged in a way that is attractive to bidders whilst being practically feasible to the client. Advertising widely in appropriate media can help. In some situations, it may be helpful to have an open event for interested suppliers to meet the client and discuss their thoughts and concerns about the project/ services.
Bid evaluation	An unsuitable bidder is selected Inappropriate bid evaluation criteria	Bid evaluation should be done against a well-defined set of criteria with distinct weightings assigned to each criterion. The criteria should cover both price and quality. If the 'wrong' criteria are selected, then the 'wrong' decision could follow. Therefore, getting the criteria right in the first place is important to mitigate this risk. If the criteria are used in a weighted evaluation model, then the weighting should be tested before the contract is advertised, so that the client is happy the weightings are robust and will identify the best value for money bid.
Contract award	Disgruntled unsuccessful bidders	Unsuccessful bidders should be swiftly notified of the decision with enough information that they understand why their bid was not selected. Having a clear process for complaints to be dealt with can also mitigate the risk of such grievances causing delays in the award of the contract to the preferred bidder.

(Continued)

Table 6.3 (Continued)

Procurement stage	*Risks*	*Measures for mitigation*
All stages	Fraud and corruption	Training staff in the proper procedures. Clear communication with potential bidders about what is acceptable and the consequences if they are found to be guilty of fraud or corruption. Electronic procurement systems can mitigate some of this risk if strong controls are programmed into them. They can, for example, ensure there is separation of duties and they can keep all submitted bids secret until the closing time for the submission of bids.

and control. Once a contract is entered into there are few levers available to the public manager to effect changes, especially if it is an outputs-specified contract. The organization also loses the skills and knowledge that the staff working in the activity take with them when they leave the PBE to work for the partner. Fundamentally, by outsourcing, an organization is placing its trust in a third party to perform an activity and this introduces the risk of poor performance or even non-performance. Not only that, if the outsourced provider is a specialist (which presumably it is) then it will have other client organizations demanding its time and attention to make sure that their contractual obligations are met.

All in all the lack of flexibility and extra risk might not be too much of a concern when a non-critical function is outsourced; it would be a cost worth paying in return for savings and efficiency improvements. But if it relates to an activity that is crucial to the overall objectives of a PBE it might be less acceptable.

Some functions are more critical to the successful achievement of objectives than others and management should prioritize their attention on ensuring that the more critical functions are operating efficiently and effectively. What an organization judges to be crucial will be unique to itself. If a manager believes that crucial functions are not as good as they should be then, rather than outsourcing, benchmarking would identify the potential for improvement and the manager can take on the challenge of achieving the best practice performance level.

Evaluation of bids

After potential suppliers have submitted their tenders, the task for the public manager is to decide which tender, if any, to accept.

Tender evaluation is a complicated process partly due to the fact that the tender process is high risk in terms of potential fraud and corruption; thus, ensuring it is a prescriptive and controlled process helps manage this risk. Some key components of the process include:

- upon receipt, tenders should not be opened but stored securely, unopened, until the published opening date;
- all tenders should be opened at the same time on the set date; and
- details of the tenders should be recorded immediately they are opened.

All of the above is made much easier and more secure where electronic procurement systems are used. This is one reason for e-procurement being recommended good practice for PBEs (Bandy and Metcalfe, 2021).

As part of the procurement process the bidders would be informed of the basis of the evaluation of their bid. There are basically two bases for awarding a contract:

- to the lowest price tender; and
- to the most economically advantageous tender.

Lowest price tender

> I felt exactly how you would feel if you were getting ready to launch and knew you were sitting on top of two million parts — all built by the lowest bidder on a government contract.
>
> Astronaut John Glenn, quoted by Cabbage, 1998

Awarding a contract to the lowest price tender is appropriate where the product or service to be supplied is clearly and unambiguously specified. In the case of a rocket ship and many, many public sector goods and services, such clarity and unambiguity might be difficult to achieve, and, in such cases, quality and other factors might be taken into account in the award decision.

However, awarding a contract to the lowest price tender is more likely to be adopted when goods are being purchased (for example, office furniture and fittings, machinery) than services. This is because it is easier to be sure that goods are the same from all suppliers. If several companies submitted bids, for example, for the supply and delivery of a thousand reams of 80gsm A4-size paper then the output is the same for every bid and the differences between the bidders are their prices.

Price-only evaluation is in two parts: first any tender that does not meet the specified requirements is eliminated and then the prices for each of the remaining tenders (the ones that are capable of acceptance) are compared and the lowest one selected as the winning tender.

Things can be more complicated when what is being bought is more than just goods. Often, for instance, a PBE is interested in after sales service (for example, for a piece of equipment) and this is an area where bidders might differentiate themselves in terms of quality separately from the prices they charge. If a PBE wants to evaluate bids on more criteria than price alone then it needs to use a different approach.

Most economically advantageous tender

For more complex procurement exercises, particularly ones where there has been a process of negotiation or dialogue which allows each bidder to fashion their own solution to the PBE's requirements, evaluating the financial aspect alone will not be enough. What is being sought in such circumstances is the tender that offers the best value for money; and this means the commercial and technical aspects of the bids should be evaluated as well as the financial aspects and, effectively, the organization is not obliged to accept the lowest priced tender.

In carrying out such an evaluation, the public manager would have to make a trade-off of price against quality. Only one of the tenders received will be the cheapest (have the lowest NPV), so the others would have to compete against it on quality grounds. To be fair to the interested bidders a PBE should inform all bidders about the evaluation criteria before their tenders are submitted. The criteria used will be specific to the PBE and the procurement but could include technical feasibility, sustainability, social value added, flexibility and risk allocation.

A common approach to evaluation is to construct an evaluation model that applies weightings against each evaluation criterion. Determining the weightings for the criteria is a matter of judgement. In some situations, price might be the most important consideration and weighted accordingly. This would be the case, for instance, where the principal reason for seeking a contract is to save money. In other circumstances the price might be less important and technical factors more important, such as seeking an ICT partner to bring their technical know-how and innovation to the PBE's services.

Having established the criteria and their weightings, it is relatively straightforward to create an arithmetic evaluation model that can take the scores for each element of each tender and calculate an aggregate score. This can be a useful tool but a public manager, but managers who use such a model should be aware of its limitations. Because scores for each criterion are inputted into it and a combined score emerges, the model may appear to be more scientific than it is. It is a subjective assessment appearing to be an objective one.

Unless the model has been tested for robustness before the tenders were received it may not always give the answer that is expected or it may be sensitive to small differences between tenders. As an illustration, a model that gives a high weighting to price and scores the lowest NPV bid at the maximum score for the criterion and awards the second-lowest bid 75 per cent of the maximum score, etc. means that a bid that is second lowest by only a tiny margin would score substantially less well in the evaluation model and will probably lose out. If two bids have practically the same NPV the evaluation model ought to award them very similar scores and the evaluation model should be tested to check that it does.

Even after testing the robustness of the proposed evaluation model, public managers should still be vigilant about the potential for bias. If the scores awarded to each bidder are subjective, then the combined score that results from them is a refined subjective opinion. There is a risk with such a model that some managers will realize how the weightings in the model operate and adjust their scoring of each bid in such a way as to ensure a preferred bid scores well and/or a disliked bid scores poorly.

Impact of a contract on the remainder of the PBE

If a part of a PBE is transferred to a PPP or contractor, then there may be financial consequences for the remainder of the PBE and they should be taken into account in the procurement decision.

In the first instance, the PBE has fixed costs and overheads that it could not transfer to the PPP. Some fixed costs, such as the public managers who directly manage the services included in the scope of the partnership, would transfer to the partnership but things like senior management costs, support services costs like ICT and the human resources team, and the cost of administrative buildings that are not going to be used by the PPP will remain with the PBE. At a stroke the PBE's balance between direct costs and overheads has changed for the worse and, potentially, the reallocation of the residual overheads to the remaining in-house services may affect their comparability with services delivered by other PBEs.

If the PBE outsources more services to a second and perhaps a third partnership, then the problem of overheads may become yet more challenging. Following this logic there would be a tipping point where the PBE has outsourced so much to suppliers that the residual part of the organization becomes unsustainable or uneconomic. A PBE in such a situation would have a cost structure where a high proportion of its costs are fixed, either as overheads or as contractually committed payments. If it is suddenly faced with making significant budget cuts, it could find itself in severe difficulty. It may have little to offer its partners to encourage them to reduce the committed costs of the partnerships and the remainder of the budget is made up of fixed costs that cannot be reduced, in the short term at least.

CONTRACT MANAGEMENT

After the commissioning and procurement processes are complete, the public manager's attention can turn to managing the contract. Arguably this is more important than the procurement process because it lasts for many years. However good the procurement process was, if it is followed by weak or poor (or non-existent) contract management, then the results will be bad.

Contract management is a continuous procurement process that ensures suppliers adhere to their agreed contractual obligations along with negotiating any future changes that need to take place. The objectives of contract management are:

- to ensures the supplier complies with the terms and conditions of the contract;
- to identify and resolve potential problems in a timely fashion;
- to identify ways of improving supplier performance;
- to monitor the payments to the supplier; and
- to ensure progress is made towards the contract's expected outputs/outcomes.

Contract management can be divided into three components:

- **contract administration**—which includes administering all the contract documentation, including changes and updates, and contract payments;
- **supplier relationship management**—because the public manager and supplier need to have constructive working relationships; and
- **supplier performance management**—monitoring the performance to ensure quality standards and so on are achieved, and taking action where performance is below standard.

Contract management requires skills different from those of a line manager of staff. Greve (2008: 85) suggests a number of competencies that a contract manager should have: political, strategic, controlling and street-level contracting competencies (2008: 88) supported by legal, human resource and consultancy competencies. He does not mention explicitly the requirement for contract managers to be competent in the financial management of contracts, yet, given the value of some public sector contracts and partnerships, it must be critically important that contract managers understand the financial arrangements of the contracts they are managing.

This section considers four finance-related aspects of contract management:

- budgeting and budgetary control;
- managing changes;
- continuous improvement and value for money; and
- dealing with things that go wrong.

Budgeting and budgetary control

Entering into a contract ought to be preceded by estimates of the income and expenditure (operating and capital) being included in the budget. Unless the new contract commences on the first day of the financial year, there would be part-year estimates in the first financial year and the full-year effects would be budgeted for in the subsequent year. In the first year the budget estimates would probably be based on what the PBE's spending would be, perhaps with a percentage reduction if the partnership is expected to make savings. This is because there would not be an agreed contract in place from which the prices could be lifted. For subsequent years, the budget estimates would be based on the prices in the contract/agreement adjusted for changes in volume and inflation as provided for in the agreement. This is assumed to be incremental budgeting (see Chapter 2) because once a contract is entered into there is little point doing zero-based budgeting. Only if the organization takes a strategic decision to end the contract or renegotiate its terms is its cost going to change.

If the partnership is an outsourcing or if for other reasons it involves the transfer of staff, equipment, etc. into the partnership organization, the subjective makeup of the budget would alter with estimates for salaries, premises, supplies, transport, etc. reducing and estimates for payments to the partnership being included as services instead. These changes might be exactly equal to each other but not necessarily.

The choice of payment mechanism in the contract agreement will have an impact on the budgeting process. If the payment mechanism is a fixed or firm price, then the estimate is straightforward to calculate. However, if the price is variable, then it means that the cost of the partnership will depend on the volume of work done and this means that the public manager needs to be able to estimate the volume of work in order to calculate the budget requirement. This is quite a different proposition from the conventional budgeting process where (regardless of budgeting process used) the budget is stated in terms of inputs: there will be a budget for an agreed level of staff, based, perhaps implicitly, on an understanding of the number of staff required to meet the expected workload. The impact of this will become clear when the public manager is carrying out their budgetary control work.

When a PBE's work is done internally, if the volume of work was higher than expected and thus beyond the level that the existing staff could meet, it would not show up in the budget control reports unless and until the public manager decided to increase expenditure to meet the extra workload. To do this, the manager would either need an approved increase to their budget or find savings elsewhere. If they did not do either of those and simply kept expenditure at the budgeted level, some of the work demand would not be met and a backlog would develop.

Under a contract that is output-based, the supplier would be obliged to meet the increase in workload and would be entitled to be paid for the extra work done, in line with the agreed prices in the contract. By the same token, if the demand were lower than expected, the partner would be entitled to a payment that is less than the budgeted amount, making savings for the public manager against their budget more quickly and easily than the public manager could have done if the staff were directly employed. What this type of contract arrangement means is that the change in volume is apparent in the budgetary control report as soon as the partner's invoices are processed into the financial system. But what should a public manager do if the workload differs from what was estimated?

In a situation like this a public manager might be tempted to ask the supplier simply to deal with the extra workload at no extra charge, in much the same way as they might have asked their staff to 'pull together' to deal with an increase in workload in the days before there was a contract. A public manager certainly can have such a conversation with the supplier and they may agree to do what is asked, but, unlike when dealing with a team of staff, the supplier may take a more commercial view and ask for something of value in return. They may agree, for instance, to deal with the extra workload at no extra cost provided that the performance target levels are relaxed a little, or the contract length is extended, or some other change that is in the partner's interest is implemented.

What the public manager should not do is wait until they have received the invoice from the supplier for the extra work they have done. By that stage, because the partner has done the extra work, the legal doctrine of *quantum meruit* means that the supplier is entitled to be paid for it. The public manager would be obliged to honour the payment of the invoice, but they would be free to discuss with the partner how they might deal with the change in volume in the future.

If the volume of work was lower than estimated, a public manager may prefer to ask the partner to do something that had not been budgeted for rather than crystallize the budget saving. As mentioned in Chapter 2, there is often pressure on public sector budget managers to spend their budgets in order to prevent them being cut the following year and a commercial-minded supplier is unlikely to turn down the additional turnover unless the extra work would be loss-making.

Managing changes

Events happen during the lifetime of a contract that could not be foreseen and planned for at the commissioning or procurement stage. It is important, therefore, to have in place a mechanism that allows the contract to flex in response to changes, whether they are changes being imposed from the external environment or internal changes required by one or other of the parties. Presuming that the contract is in writing, any changes should also be in writing and the mechanism for achieving this is the change control process. The name captures the most important feature—that any change is controlled.

The change control mechanism enables changes to be documented, but what is important in terms of financial management is that it sets out how changes should be priced. If this does not happen there would be an opportunity for the supplier to charge higher prices because they are no longer under any competitive pressure. Effectively, the public manager could find themselves in a take-it-or-leave-it situation. If the change control mechanism includes details of how prices will be determined for changes, then they can be evaluated as part of the original procurement process. This would help to prevent a bidder submitting a low price for the contract at day one coupled with high prices for changes so that the supplier could make higher profits later on from extra work that is not subject to competition.

The extra work that a supplier might receive through the change control process might add 10, 20 or even 50 per cent to the total turnover they earn from the contract. Given that it is crucial for the public manager to be confident that the extra work is commissioned at value for money prices. As was noted earlier, Krugman wrote, 'it's common for private contractors to bid low to get the business, then push their prices up' (Jensen and Stonecash, 2005: 775). In extreme cases a partner may take an ultra-commercial approach where they request lots and lots of low value changes that would substantially increase their total income. This might politely be called a 'claims-conscious approach' or, more colloquially, 'nickel-and-diming'.

Continuous improvement and value for money

The initial procurement of a contract will have resulted in a decision on the value for money of the alternative tenders that were received. Just because the winning proposals were value for money at that point in time does not mean that they will remain good value for money over the course of the contract. There will be developments in terms of processes, ICT, etc. that allow organizations to improve their performance and/or save money. What might be regarded as industry good practice at the time of the procurement could be out of date and relatively poor practice by the time the contract reaches its expiry date.

The supplier may be able to improve its performance but the issues for the public manager are (a) how to incentivize the partner to make improvements (which would ultimately be of benefit to the public) and (b) how to share in any financial gains. If the public manager can create a contractual relationship that does both of these things, then they can be confident about getting more output (i.e., value) for less cost (in real terms) during the contract's lifetime.

The initial commissioning process might be able to achieve this increasing value for lower cost by specifying service levels that increase and requesting bidders submit tenders to improve performance over the lifetime of the contract whilst also reducing their prices (in real terms). If such an arrangement were secured it would incentivize the supplier to identify and implement performance improvements if it is to avoid a fall in profitability. However, given the inherent riskiness for a supplier to sign-up to such an arrangement, they may be tempted to inflate their initial price as a hedge against being unable to identify sufficient improvements during the course of the contract.

Benchmarking

An alternative way of seeking an improvement in value for money during the contract is to use benchmarking. The approach here is to compare, from time to time, the supplier's performance and costs against agreed benchmarks, which might be specific, named organizations or might be relevant statistical indicators. If the benchmarking process identifies that the supplier's performance is lacking in some respect and/or its prices are too high, the supplier could be under a contractual obligation to improve its performance or reduce its prices to meet the benchmark.

This sounds straightforward enough but there are issues with using benchmarking, not least of which is that context affects performance so it is very difficult to find benchmarks that closely match the supplier's context. If such benchmarks are not used, the process will always be open to the criticism that it compares apples with bananas. Even if suitable benchmarks can be found, any improvement in the supplier's performance might require investment in new technology, systems and staff retraining and there may be redundancies, too. As the costs of all of these things is unknown at the commencement of the partnership, it would be difficult for the supplier to factor them into its tendered prices—if the public manager insisted on this approach then the partner would have to include a large risk premium and hope for the best. It might be more practical, then, for the benchmarking process to be used as guidance for the partners, who would subsequently discuss how the supplier could improve its performance and costs and, then, if the public manager wants to go ahead and there are sufficient funds, the change control process would be used to approve the required changes to the contract's service levels and prices.

When things go wrong

It is easy to think that when a contract says an output will be delivered, it will be delivered on time and without error. Sometimes outputs are not delivered despite the supplier's best efforts. Whilst any failure by the PBE or a partner is a breach of contract, it would be nonsense if the aggrieved party sued for damages for every small breach. However, it also would not be sensible for the parties to operate such that every breach is ignored, since what would be the point of having a partnership if the parties failed to deliver anything they promised?

In practice what tends to be put in place is a governance structure which gives the parties a series of escalating remedies with the aim being to resolve disputes without legal action if at all possible. The sorts of escalation process might be something like:

- the price and performance mechanism operates to deal with minor failures of performance but if there is a dispute about the fee deduction or anything else it would be referred to the relevant operational managers;
- if the operational managers cannot agree, it goes to the senior managers with overall responsibility for the partnership within their respective organizations;
- if the senior managers cannot agree, it goes to some sort of oversight board or committee (which is likely to include politicians/directors/governors as appropriate to the organizations);
- if the oversight board cannot agree, an independent expert could be called in to arbitrate; and
- if one of the parties refuses to be bound by the outcome of the arbitration, then they may pursue a legal remedy in the courts (and the relationship between the parties is, at the very least, wounded).

The escalation process of the sort described in the previous section would be appropriate for relatively minor breaches of contract. There would likely be a clause in the contract that permits each party to terminate the contract if the other party commits a 'material breach'. An example of a material breach is if the supplier became insolvent or bankrupt but each contract might include specific acts or omissions that would be construed as material breach. For example, in a contract for the implementation of a project that is time critical, failure to meet the agreed date for the final milestone could be a material breach of the contract.

EXITING A CONTRACT

Procuring a contract can be a time-consuming, expensive process and so might be the exit from it. There are three ways for a contract to come to an end:

1. it might expire naturally on delivery of the goods, at the end of the agreed term or on completion of the project;
2. it might be ended early, either by agreement of the parties or because of a breach by one of them; or
3. a force majeure event happens that makes one or more of the parties unable to continue its commitment to the partnership.

It is important that a contract includes the arrangements and processes to be followed for exiting the contract even though at the time a contract is being procured there is a tendency to concentrate on beginnings rather than endings. When the contract ends, either naturally reaching its expiry date or because it is terminated early, the contract manager will need to manage the process. Part of this will be paperwork, but most important will be ensuring that there is an orderly exit in line with the terms of the contract.

Expiry

Expiry is the way that a contract is expected to end when it was signed. It could be a specified date or it could be the completion of the final milestone of a project. The contract should specify what should happen regarding staff, assets, equipment, data and records, liabilities and so on to ensure the smooth run-down of the contract.

In a one-off contract like the construction of a building there will need to be confirmation that everything is complete and a process is in place for the contractor to return to remedy any problems ('snags') that are identified later.

Where a contract is delivering a service rather than a project the PBE may wish to run a new procurement exercise to find a new supplier (which might turn out to be a continuation for the existing supplier), they may decide to produce the service themselves, or they may take the opportunity to terminate the service, too.

There are three finance-related issues for a public manager to be aware of:

- agreeing on the final payment to the partner;
- agreeing on any settlement figure to be paid for any of the supplier's assets and equipment that will be transferring to the PBE or to the next supplier; and
- ensuring that the outgoing supplier cooperates with the procurement process, which might require them to provide information about employee costs and other financial data to bidders who are their competitors.

It is possible for a contract to include a provision that would allow its term to be extended, possibly more than once. Such a provision would have a procedure associated with it regarding how an extension would be priced and approved. Obviously if the initial period of the contract is extended, the exit provisions would be implemented at the end of the extended term.

Early termination

The early termination of a contract might be 'without cause', where the parties agree that the whole contract or a part of it should be terminated. Alternatively, early termination might be 'for cause' because a party is in breach of their obligations. Again, the partnership agreement may allow for the termination to apply to just a part of the contract's scope. This might be an important nuance in a contract. If a supplier performs well on most things but performs badly on a small, discrete element of the contract's scope, it is helpful to be able to terminate just the small part of the overall contract rather than either to terminate the whole thing or to live with the bad performance.

Termination for cause

It was mentioned earlier that a material breach may enable the termination of a contract. So too might a parties' persistent (minor) breaches of the contract, whether by repeating the same breach over and over or making numerous separate breaches.

The pursuit of termination is likely to be expensive and is not guaranteed to be successful. The party may not accept that their performance warrants the termination of the contract and they may defend themselves. Aside from the immediate loss of a contract and its income, the supplier has a reputation that it may wish to protect. If the action is defended, the supplier's case may prevail, leaving the PBE having spent a lot of time and money to end up with the prospect of continuing in a contract with a supplier that it had sued. In the worst case the PBE would have to pay costs and damages to the supplier as well.

All in all, seeking to terminate a contract against the will of the supplier has to be a last resort for a public manager. This is another reason for using contracts on things that are not critical to the PBE's objectives and mission.

Termination without cause

This is also called voluntary termination and it requires the agreement of the parties. Again, it could be for the whole contract or a part of it.

To obtain the agreement of a supplier to early termination will likely require the payment of compensation, probably based on the amount of the profit that the supplier would be foregoing over the remainder of the contract's expected duration. The exact terms of compensation should be incorporated in the contract documents.

There is little comfort for a public manager in terminating a contract early (whether for cause or without) because of the cost and time involved in managing the process of termination. Not only does the public manager have to deal with the financial matters such as claims for compensation from the supplier, but they also need the service or project to continue. Commissioning a replacement contract is one option but it would probably take a lot longer than the notice period given to the outgoing supplier, so the chances are that the public manager will have to step in and run the services or project for an interim period, or perhaps for good.

Force majeure

Force majeure (French for superior force) is a legal term used to cover the sorts of events that could disrupt the partnership's activities but for which no one is to blame. This includes fires, floods and lightning strikes; war; riot; and terrorist acts. A partnership agreement will usually have a clause that states that if a force majeure event occurs, the partners are freed from their obligations. This makes sense since it allows the partners to concentrate on dealing with the consequences of the force majeure event.

If the force majeure event has only a temporary effect, such as a flood might, then once the event has passed, the parties can return to their obligations to each other under the contract. If the force majeure event is such that the partners cannot get back to normal within an agreed period, the partnership would be terminated.

If force majeure causes the termination of a partnership, it is unlikely that the exit arrangements will run as smoothly as an exit at the expiry of the partnership. There is every chance that assets, equipment, data and records will be damaged or lost, rendering the continued running of the service or project very difficult.

There could be considerable costs connected with dealing with a force majeure event whether it is temporary or long enough to cause the termination of the partnership. The losses might be covered by insurance (if there were a policy in place); however, for many of the events each of the partners will have to bear their own costs.

CONCLUSION

Nearly one-third of public money is spent on acquiring goods, works and services from private sector suppliers. This ranges from small-scale purchases of commodity goods, such as stationery and personal computers, to massive public infrastructure projects, such as dams and highways, and major elements of public services like health care.

With so much money involved it is important that public managers do public procurement effectively. This means trying to achieve the five rights of procurement: obtaining the right quantity and quality of goods, works or services, at the right time, in the right place and at the right price.

The commissioning and procurement of contracts is only part of the story. Contracts need to be managed if they are to yield the right results. Contract management requires public managers to have competencies that are different from those needed to manage a service or project directly. There are differences, too, in the financial management arrangements and knowledge that are needed.

In the end, the private sector is used to contribute to, or even directly deliver, public services when they offer better value for money than an in-house arrangement. Measuring and managing value for money is the subject of the next chapter.

EXERCISES

1. In your country, whether at national, regional or local level, how effective and efficient were the public procurement arrangements during the coronavirus pandemic of 2020?
2. Many governments and PBEs achieve some or all of their outcomes via third parties. What is the difference between delivering public outcomes by giving grants and using contracts?
3. If you were conducting a commissioning project about the provision of public transport in a city that should be delivered over the next ten years what are some of the items of data you would require for the analysis stage?
4. What type of contract would you use for the provision of a maintenance contract for a PBE's fleet of vehicles?

REFERENCES

ACCA. (2020). *New Models of Public Procurement: A Tool for Sustainable Recovery*. London: ACCA. Available at: https://www.accaglobal.com/my/en/professional-insights/pro-accountants-the-future/New_models_public_procurement.html (Accessed: 24 June 2022).

Alford, J., & O'Flynn, J. (2012). *Rethinking Public Service Delivery: Managing With External Providers*. Basingstoke: Palgrave Macmillan.

Amirkhanyan, A. A., Kim, H. J., & Lambright, K. T. (2007). Putting the pieces together: A comprehensive framework for understanding the decision to contract out and contractor performance. *International Journal of Public Administration, 30*(6), 699–725.

Baker, C. R. (2003). Investigating Enron as a public private partnership. *Accounting, Auditing and Accountability Journal, 16*(3), 446–466.

Bandy, G. P. (2018) *How to Procure a Consultant in the Public Sector* [E-book]. Managing Public Money. Available at: https://www.amazon.co.uk/How-Hire-Consultant-Public-Sector-ebook/dp/B07G3H84PY/ (Accessed: 24 June 2022).

Bandy, G. P., & Metcalfe, A. (2021). *Rethinking Public Financial Management*. London: ACCA. Available at: https://www.accaglobal.com/gb/en/professional-insights/global-profession/rethinking-public-financial-management.html (Accessed: 25 April 2022).

Behn, R. D., & Kant, P. A. (1999). Strategies for avoiding the pitfalls of performance contracting. *Public Productivity and Management Review*, 470–489.

Bergmann, A. (2010). *Public Sector Financial Management*. Harlow: FT Prentice Hall.

Broadbent, J. and Laughlin, R. (2003). Public private partnerships: An introduction. *Accounting, Auditing and Accountability Journal, 16*(3), 332–341.

Cabbage, M. (1998). Rocket man. *Southern Illinoisan* (25 October), p. 33.

Greasley, K., Watson, P. J., & Patel, S. (2008). The formation of public-public partnerships: A case study examination of collaboration on a 'back to work' initiative. *International Journal of Public Sector Management, 21*(3), 305–313.

Greve, C. (2008). *Contracting for Public Services.* Abingdon: Routledge.

Grimsey, D., & Lewis, M. K. (2005). Are public private partnerships value for money? Evaluating alternative approaches and comparing academic and practitioner views. *Accounting Forum, 29*(4), 345–378.

Hood, C. (1991). A public management for all seasons? *Public Administration, 69*(1), 3–19.

Jensen, P. H., & Stonecash, R. E. (2005). Incentives and the efficiency of public sector-outsourcing contracts. *Journal of Economic Surveys, 19*(5), 767–787.

Kappeler, A., & Nemoz, M. (2010). *Public-Private Partnerships in Europe-Before and During the Recent Financial Crisis.* Luxembourg: European Investment Bank. Available at: http://bit.ly/1q6oib4 (Accessed: 4 May 2014).

Kettl, D. F. (1993). *Sharing Power: Public Governance and Private Markets.* Washington, DC: Brookings Institution Press.

Kundu, O., James, A. D., & Rigby, J. (2020). Public procurement and innovation: A systematic literature review. *Science and Public Policy, 47*(4), 490–502.

Open Contracting Partnership. *How Governments Spend: Opening Up the Value of Global Public Procurement.* Available at: https://www.open-contracting.org/wp-content/uploads/2020/08/OCP2020-Global-Public-Procurement-Spend.pdf (Accessed: 24 June 2022).

Romzek, B. S., & Johnston, J. M. (2002). Effective contract implementation and management: A preliminary model. *Journal of Public Administration Research and Theory, 12*(3), 423–453.

Rutter, C. (2022). *South African Investigators Criticise 'Complete Breakdown' of Procurement Systems During Pandemic.* Available at: https://www.publicfinancefocus.org/pfm-news/2022/01/south-african-investigators-criticise-complete-breakdown-procurement-systems-during (Accessed: 24 June 2022).

Sanchez, A. (2013). The role of procurement. In R. Allen, R. Hemming, & B. H. Potter (Eds.), *The International Handbook of Public Financial Management* (pp. 312–335). Basingstoke: Palgrave Macmillan.

Ury, R. F. W. (2020). *Getting to Yes in Challenging Times* [Video]. Available at: https://www.youtube.com/watch?v=-2lcXp-MiVQ (Accessed: 24 June 2022).

Ury, R. F. W., & Patton, B. (2020). *Getting to Yes*. Gramedia Pustaka Utama.

van Ham, H., & Koppenjan, J. (2001). Building public-private partnerships: Assessing and managing risks in port development. *Public Management Review, 3*(4), 593–616.

Verweij, S., & van Meerkerk, I. (2021) Do public–private partnerships achieve better time and cost performance than regular contracts? *Public Money & Management, 41*(4), 286–295. DOI: 10.1080/09540962.2020.1752011.

Wendling, C., Alonso, V., Saxena, S., Tang, V., & Verdugo, C. (2020). *Keeping the Receipts: Transparency, Accountability, and Legitimacy in Emergency Responses*. Special Series on Fiscal Policies to Respond to Covid-19. Washington DC: IMF Fiscal Affairs Department. Available at: https://www.imf.org/en/Publications/SPROLLs/covid19-special-notes (Accessed: 4 July 2022).

FURTHER READING (AND WATCHING)

Links to the following resources, and lots more, are available at www.managingpublicmoney.co.uk/extras.

Carston Greve's book in the Masters of Public Management series, *Contracting for Public Services* (2008), is a useful collation of issues in contract management, with case studies, coupled with a theoretical contract management model. Also, the chapter by Sanchez (2013) in *The International Handbook of Public Financial Management* is a good summary of general changes in public procurement since the mid-1990s. Third, there is *Rethinking Public Service Delivery: Managing with External Providers* by Alford and O'Flynn (2012).

There is a useful resource of reports and papers about the theory and politics of government outsourcing on the Institute for Government's website at www.instituteforgovernment.org.uk/our-work/policy-making/government-outsourcing. For a shortcut to some academic articles, there is a systematic literature review written by Kundu, James and Rigby (2020).

There are many places where you could find material about how to implement outsourcing. One option is the UK Government's sourcing and consulting playbooks (that is what they are called) at www.gov.uk/government/publications/the-sourcing-and-consultancy-playbooks.

The article by Behn and Kant (1999) mentioned in the chapter includes a really useful summary of pitfalls of performance contracting and how to avoid them. It includes some case studies to explain the issues.

For readers who are familiar with public procurement in general terms and wish to know more about the specifics of PPP procurement, the European PPP Expertise Centre (EPEC) publishes a *Guide to Guidance* and has a lot of information and reports on its website (www.eib.org/epec/index.htm). And for a different way of thinking about PPPs, try Baker's 2003 article, 'Investigating Enron as a public private partnership.'

More recently, in 2020 the ACCA published a report, *New Models of Public Procurement: A Tool for Sustainable Recovery.*

Bandy (2018) has written a short e-book, *How to Procure a Consultant in the Public Sector*, that includes some general tips on writing a specification of requirements and how to manage a service contract.

Negotiation is an important skill for public managers to have (and not just for procurement and contract management) and there is a good video lecture on it given by William Ury (2020) of Harvard's Program on Negotiation (PON). The PON also publishes a daily blog at www.pon.harvard.edu/blog, and Ury and Patton's (2020) book *Getting to Yes* is a seminal work that promotes a method of principled negotiation focused on the parties' interests rather than positions.

Chapter 7

Measuring performance and value for money

LEARNING OBJECTIVES

After reading this chapter you should:

- understand what is meant by the term 'value for money';
- have an appreciation of basic theory relating to performance measurement;
- have a framework for assessing the value for money of a public programme, project or service; and
- understand how non-financial costs and benefits can be monetized for inclusion in project evaluations and decision making.

KEY POINTS OF THIS CHAPTER

- The evaluation of value for money requires the assessment of economy, efficiency and effectiveness at the same time. Assessing economy and efficiency is relatively straightforward but assessing the effectiveness of a public service can be difficult, if not impossible.
- Equity and ethics may also be important dimensions in an assessment of value for money in the public sector.
- The prime reason for measuring performance is to improve performance but other reasons include control, budgeting, motivation, promotion, celebration and learning.

DOI: 10.4324/9781003250838-7

- There is no single measure of performance that can indicate how much public value a public benefit entity (PBE) creates. Instead, a range of measures is required, relating to multiple perspectives and, even then, the measures may be insufficient.
- Measuring performance can have unintended and undesirable effects on the behaviour of managers.
- Sometimes value has to be judged rather than measured (because public financial management is an art, not a science).

KEY TERMS

3Es—economy, efficiency and effectiveness.

Cost–benefit analysis—an analysis of a project or programme that takes into account, in monetary terms, the costs incurred and benefits received by the community as a whole, over the long term.

Monetization—the expression of something in money terms.

Performance indicator—an item of data that is collected by a performance management system for use by a manager.

Performance management system—the tools, technology and processes for ensuring objectives are met and for improving the performance of an organization and/or its people.

Revealed preference—a technique for estimating value which is based on the choices actually made by consumers.

Stated preference—a technique for estimating values which is based on statements consumers make about their preferences.

Value for money—when the benefits derived from a product or service are well worth the money spent on obtaining or producing the product or service.

The previous chapter was concerned with value for money in respect of the multitude of goods, works and services that PBEs acquire. The value for money of inputs is very important to enable PBEs to achieve their goals and missions efficiently and effectively. This chapter is concerned with assessing and managing the value for money of the outputs and outcomes created by PBEs rather than the value for money of inputs.

The three objectives of public financial management listed in Chapter 1 included 'to provide public goods and services efficiently'. The public, and politicians and public managers, want public services to be value for money: they do not want money wasted on extravagant services but nor do they want services that are not fit for purpose. The challenge for public managers is that there is not an objective, absolute definition of value for money. The public services they create have to meet the 'sweet spot' where they are good, but not too good, and not too expensive. They have to find the balancing point.

A public manager has to think about the whole system and how to improve the overall value for money for society rather than simply making marginal improvements to existing processes. If a service is not producing outputs of the right quality, making the process more efficient is not improving value for money: it is what Ackoff (2004) referred to as 'doing the wrong thing right'. He went on: 'almost every problem confronting our society is a result of the fact that our public-policy makers are doing the wrong things and are trying to do them righter.' He gives examples such as the United States having both a high crime rate and high levels of prison incarceration and the fact that much of the health care needs is created by the care that is given.

This chapter discusses issues relating to the measurement of performance, value and value for money in four sections. The first section contains a general discussion of performance measurement covering what can be measured and some of the undesirable side-effects that a performance management regime can have on managers' behaviour. The second section considers the particular issue of measuring public value. The third section is a discussion of what is meant by the term 'value for money' and how it can be measured. The fourth and final section revisits cost–benefit analysis (CBA) from Chapter 5 but in this chapter the focus is on how money values can be derived for non-financial costs and benefits.

MEASURING PERFORMANCE

Performance measurement is a key tenet of NPM (Hood, 1991: 4), and it is this that drives the process rather than the public value framework itself (Coats and Passmore, 2009: 46). As far as OECD countries go, 'performance tools have become an integral part of how governments do business' (Curristine and Flynn, 2013: 250). In fact, measuring and reporting on performance has become the way things are done for PBEs in low- and middle-income countries, too.

The measurement of performance dates back earlier than the late 1970s and the origins of NPM. Fryer, Antony and Ogden (2009: 479) cite Williams (2003) as having found evidence of performance management being used by the New York City Council is the early 1900s. Interestingly, such early performance measurement was focused on financial performance measures. Financial performance measures are still relevant to a modern public manager but they have been joined by a plethora of non-financial measures, all with the intention of quantifying the work of the public manager in some way.

Performance measurement is seen as fundamental to public services. The National Audit Office (2010: 7) stated that:

> measuring Government performance is vitally important for accountability and performance management. Such measurement can show the taxpayer what they are getting for their money. It also enables the Government to assess whether it is achieving its key objectives and to learn how to achieve them more effectively and at less cost.

On the other hand, Schick wrote, 'much more attention has been paid by governments to generating performance indicators than to using them' (2013: 53). Clearly, it is a waste of a PBE's limited resources to collect performance information for no reason.

Performance measurement in the private and public sectors might be broadly the same but there are two features of the public sector that tend to increase the complexity of a performance management system (Propper and Wilson, 2003: 253). First, public managers often have multiple principals to be accountable to (see Chapter 8 for more on accountability as a concept). Second, PBEs often have several ends to achieve rather than the single goal of increasing shareholder value.

There are many definitions of performance management (for example, Propper and Wilson, 2003; Radnor and McGuire, 2004). Fryer, Antony and Ogden have a relatively simple definition. Performance management is: 'monitoring that shows where change is required and which will in turn produce the desired behaviour that will produce improved performance' (2009: 479). This is a neat definition since it also gets to the heart of the purpose of measuring performance: improvement.

Reasons to measure performance

There are many reasons why a public manager would be interested in measuring their performance. Speklé and Verbeeten (2014) suggested three uses of performance measurement:

- **operational**—to monitor performance;
- **incentivizing**—to reward good performance; and
- **exploratory**—to align performance to the strategic goals of the organization.

Behn (2003) went further, identifying the eight purposes highlighted in Box 7.1. Within these purposes Behn recognized that there could be sub-purposes. However, he wrote that 'the only real purpose is to improve performance. The other seven purposes are simply means for achieving this ultimate purpose' (2003: 588).

BOX 7.1 EIGHT REASONS TO MEASURE PERFORMANCE

To evaluate—how well is the PBE performing?

To control—how can the public manager be sure their staff or partners are doing the right thing?

To budget—on what should the public manager spend public money?

To motivate—how can staff, partners, citizens and others be encouraged to do what it takes to improve performance?

To promote—how can the public manager persuade politicians and external stakeholders that the PBE is doing a good job?

To celebrate—what accomplishments are worthy of a celebration?

To learn—why is this working and that not working?

To improve—who should do what differently in order to improve performance?

Source: Behn, 2003: 588

There is another purpose: to comply with external obligations such as laws or regulations. A public manager may have no interest at all in some or all of the performance indicators they are asked to collect and report and yet will spend time and money doing just that. These are the kinds of performance indicators being referred to by Schick (2013).

In Chapter 2 there was a discussion of different approaches to budgeting, including performance budgeting. If a PBE uses it budgets to link resource allocations to performance, it is necessary for actual performance to be measured and reported.

A criticism of performance management regimes is that they themselves do improve performance, just as a pig does not get fatter by weighing it. It is not the act of measuring that makes any difference to an organization's performance; it is only if the manager takes some action (whether as a result of analysing the performance data or not) that anything changes. In taking action the manager (presumably) expects that performance will be improved but to know that they will need to review the performance information the next month or quarter or year. There is a continual cycle of plan, do, check, act:

- **plan**—how the service or product will be produced;
- **do**—implement the plan;
- **check**—collect performance information and assess whether the performance is in line with the plan; and

- **act**—if the performance information suggests that improvements should be made, identify the changes that are required and implement them.

This cycle of plan-do-check-act has obvious similarities with the PFM cycle that has been mentioned in earlier chapters and the commissioning cycle described in Chapter 6.

What to measure

Decisions about what to measure flow from an awareness of the purpose of measuring performance in the first place. If the purpose is to control a process, then the manager may require measures (performance indicators) of demand for the product, efficiency, error rates and costs. If the purpose is to motivate staff, then perhaps the manager wants measures of individual productivity and sales figures.

For any given service or project of programme a public manager could measure performance by collecting performance indicators about inputs, activities, outputs, outcomes or a combination of them. These four terms are described below.

Inputs

Inputs are the resources used in the production of goods or services. Typically, they include employees, equipment and supplies, raw materials and components, technology and money. For a production process that is reasonably organized and managed it should be relatively easy to measure the inputs. Indeed, the financial accounting system would capture inputs in terms of the costs that the organization incurs in obtaining them (the salaries and wages paid to employees, payments made to suppliers, and so on).

Activities

Activity measures quantify the processes that convert the inputs into outputs. A performance indicator might cover the whole of a process but equally it might relate only to a stage of the process. Activity measures tend to be easier to count than inputs, outputs and outcomes (Stevens, Stokes and O'Mahony, 2006: 83).

A process measure may show that people and/or machines are busy but being busy is not the same as being effective. Effective is measured by measuring outputs and/or outcomes.

Outputs

Outputs are the goods or services provided by the organization. Goods, being tangible products, ought to be easily countable by an organization from whatever system it uses to pack and deliver the goods. Measuring service outputs may be more difficult to measure because of the intangible nature of them. Some are easy to count, such as the number of visitors at a museum and the number of patients seen at a clinic. Other public services do not have direct users so the output has to be measured differently. For example, a street lighting service can be measured in terms of the total number of working streetlights or the total length of illuminated highway. In yet other public services, the desired output is the absence of something, such as the number of notifiable diseases in a given period.

Outcomes

The outcome of a programme, project or service is its external effect on the world, whether that be the effect on direct service users or citizens in general. For public sector goods and services, it can be argued that it is not the outputs that satisfies the users/society but the outcome(s) that the output(s) delivers. For instance, it is not how many children who have sat through the classes in a primary school but how many can read and write when they leave that is important.

Measuring outcomes, in financial or non-financial terms, can be a lot harder than measuring outputs for several reasons. Outcomes may be realized many, many years after the service was delivered. For example, the effect of education on an individual's career choices and earnings cannot be measured meaningfully at the point they leave the education system; realistically it might need to be measured five, ten or twenty years later.

Furthermore, the multiple beneficiaries of a public service might each value different characteristics of the service. Using the example of a public library: some library users might value the entertainment and pleasure they derive from the books they borrow; other users might value a library for being a safe, non-judgemental place to ask for advice; others for access to computers and the internet; and yet others might value the social contact they have at a book discussion group hosted by the library. Measuring these features of a library as outputs is easy enough: counting the book loans made, number of people asking for advice, and so on. What is hard is measuring the impact.

The notion of an outcome is complicated for some public services because they are consumed collectively (such as defence) and for others because the consumer of the service might not be the person who is intended to be satisfied by it (such as prisoners or others who are subject to regulation or enforcement by a PBE). In the case of a prison, the output might be measured as the number of prisoner-nights in custody, the number of prison break-outs and the number of prisoners gaining educational qualifications. The outcome, as far as society in general is concerned, might be a feeling of safety and reduced crime levels in the future. The latter might be assessed by measuring the recidivism rate of former prisoners but even then

Table 7.1 *Examples of input, activity, output and outcome measures*

	Public library	*Fire and rescue service*
Input measures	• Number of staff • Number of registered members • Number of books • Number of public PC terminals • Annual total budget • Annual spend on book stock	• Number of fire fighters • Number of fire appliances • Number of fire stations • Annual budget • Number of reported fires per 1,000 population per year
Activity measures	• Average waiting time for borrower's book request • Average time to check out a book • Average queueing time	• Average time to despatch a fire truck • Per cent of incidents reached by an appliance within n minutes
Output measures	• Number of books issued • Number of users of PCs • Per cent users satisfied with the service • Number of visitors to library	• Number of incidents attended • Per cent of incidents where fire contained to room of origin
Outcome measures	• Per cent of citizens satisfied with the service • Per cent of citizens accessing the internet • Percentage of population functionally literate	• Number of people saved per 1,000 population per year • Number of deaths per 1,000 fires • Per cent of citizens satisfied with the service

there are complications: if a former prisoner does not reoffend is that a result of the rehabilitation work of the prison or some other reason, perhaps because they are older and more responsible than they were when they offended or because they have learned how to avoid being caught?

Table 7.1 illustrates the above with examples of input, activity, output and outcome measures for a public library and a fire and rescue service.

Measuring public sector productivity

Input and output measures can often be linked together in a ratio. For example, from the library service measures shown in Table 7.1, it is possible to produce:

- book issues per registered member;
- book issues per 1,000 population; and
- cost per library visitor.

The first two ratios above are output/input ratios, whereas the third is an input/output ratio. Other examples of ratios relating to public services are pupil/teacher ratios, number of employees per 1,000 population and unit costs for any public service.

Whereas input measures can often easily be expressed in financial terms, outputs from PBEs are primarily expressed in non-financial terms (Jones and Pendlebury, 2010: 21). This is a distinction from private sector organizations that can (and do) measure outputs in financial terms by virtue of the selling price of the goods or services. This enables a calculation of productivity by dividing the value of output by the value of input. This calculation could be made for individual products, for divisions of a company or, at the macro level, for a whole industry.

The lack of a price for most of the output of PBEs causes problems for calculating an equivalent productivity measure for the public sector. Until 1998 the United Kingdom's Office of National Statistics (ONS) determined that the value of public sector outputs was equal to the cost of inputs. This approach nullified the notion of public sector productivity since it would always equal one; there was no way to ascertain whether productivity was improving or falling (Simpson, 2006: 10). Since 1998 the ONS has constructed measures of outputs, which were the subject of a review by Atkinson (2005) that affirmed that the approach that had been adopted by the ONS was the right one in principle but also made recommendations for major improvements. One particular recommendation was for output measures to take into account changes from year to year in the quality of goods and services produced.

Whilst the changes since 1998 mean that there are now data about public sector productivity at the national level (which could be referred to by a public manager as an 'industry benchmark'), such information should be interpreted cautiously:

> The statistic obtained by dividing outputs by inputs may no longer be equal to [one] by definition, but no single number, however carefully constructed, can fully capture the performance of complex public services with multiple objectives.
>
> (Atkinson, 2005: 183)

The United Kingdom's Office of National Statistics (ONS) has published data for public sector productivity from 1997 to 2019 (ONS, 2022). The data for 1997 to 2019 for the public sector as a whole show that over those 23 years inputs rose by 63.3 per cent and outputs rose by 69.3, meaning that the cumulative productivity increase was 3.7 per cent. (This is less than two tenths of a percentage point per year.)

There are data showing productivity calculations for different components of the public sector. The ONS still uses the outputs equals inputs convention for measuring the productivity for police and defence services, most social care services and non-NHS health services. See Table 7.2 for the cumulative changes for the service area.

Table 7.2 *UK public sector productivity 1997–2019*

Service area	*Non-quality-adjusted productivity change*	*Quality-adjusted productivity change*
Health care	+10.3	+19.6
Education	−18.3	+2.0
Adult social care	−13.9	−9.4
Children's social care	−16.9	−16.3
Social security administration	−15.5	−15.5
Courts, probation, prisons, fire service	−28.4	−28.1
Police	0.0	0.0
Defence	0.0	0.0
Other government services	0.0	0.0
Total	−3.4	+3.7

Source: ONS (2022).

Table 7.2 shows a much bigger productivity improvement in health care over the period compared with the other service areas. It perhaps reflects the government's budget priorities since 2010. Most government services faced real terms budget reductions as part of the austerity policy that was a response to the global financial crisis of 2008, but this was not the case for the budget of the National Health Service.

Measure what matters

As suggested above, measuring outcomes tends to be more difficult than measuring outputs and public managers might be tempted to focus on what is easier to do. As Bohte and Meier (2000: p174) put it: 'rather than measuring the final outcomes of bureaucratic activity, those who evaluate the performance of public bureaucracies often pay more attention to the outputs these agencies produce.'

Robinson (2021a) makes a similar point, reporting OECD studies showing 'that in half of member countries, available performance indicators are largely irrelevant for budgetary decision-making'. Instead, governments use performance indicators that happen to be available rather than indicators that genuinely indicate success or failure of policies. The chances are that these are measures of inputs, activities and outputs and not measures about outcomes and effectiveness.

It is very unlikely that a single measure or a collection of measures will capture everything that is important about an organization's performance in all circumstances (Kravchuk and Schack, cited by Behn, 2003: 593). This is true even in the private sector where the profit measure might be seen as the most important single indicator of success of failure, but it is not the only indicator collected by management. Profit is a measure of the residual amount left over for the owners of a business after all the payments have been made to the staff, suppliers and providers of capital and it is also a feedback signal, indicating 'clearly and quickly in which direction [managers] should move' (Farmer, 1965: 24). Even so, if a business had a profit margin of 5 per cent of turnover, is that a good or bad performance? Some businesses, such as supermarkets, have very low profit margins; they make large profits from their small margins because of the high volume of business that they do. Other businesses, such as jewellers, have large profit margins but smaller volumes of business.

Whilst one measure is unlikely to be sufficient, the public manager should be careful not to have too many. The point of measurement is to simplify matters, to reduce 'the complexities that we observe into simple objective components so that we can then deal with their essences with greater precision' (Jones and Pendlebury, 2010: 28). A public manager may seek to simplify matters so that the service they produce is evaluated using just one, or maybe two, indicators. They may feel that a smaller amount of data is more easily understandable by external stakeholders than reports with multiple measures.

Moore (2003: 15) takes the view that the temptation to reduce the volume of performance measures to a small number should be resisted: if the public manager is engaged in creating public value that has many effects on society, then it is likely that there needs to be many performance measures to capture the value being created. In this process of simplification through measurement, a public manager might bear in mind the quotation attributed to Einstein: 'Everything should be made as simple as possible, but no simpler' (Wikiquote, 2022).

It would be prudent for a public manager to have a range of performance measures relevant to their context; some of them measuring inputs, some measuring activities and processes and others measuring outputs and outcomes. This range of measures would, 'allow them to recognize value in what they are doing and find ways to improve their performance' (Moore, 2003: 15).

A public manager, therefore, might wish to monitor a combination of financial and non-financial input, activity, output and outcome measures. As far as financial performance is concerned, they are likely to receive some form of standard budgetary monitoring report from the finance department (as mentioned in Chapter 4). The public manager may wish to supplement this with customized reports that provide them with financial performance measures that are appropriate to their service context.

Brooks (2006: 306) provides an example of this by discussing the relative allocation of resources by charities between delivering the charitable objectives, on the one hand, and administration and fund-raising, on the other. He suggests that the expenditure on administration and fund-raising is worth incurring until the point of equimarginality is reached—the point where it will cost one pound or dollar to raise an additional pound or dollar. Beyond that point, the organization would lose more than it gained if it continued its fund-raising activity. If a charity wished to adopt this as a fund-raising strategy it would need to define a measure along the lines of 'marginal cost of fund-raising per pound raised' and monitor performance against it. Accurately defining such a performance measure and being able to collect it at a reasonable cost could be difficult. A proxy measure such as 'administration and fund-raising expenditure as a percentage of total income' would be operationally easier to collect.

Problems of performance management

It is often said that what gets measured gets attention. If that were true then management would be as easy as putting in a place measures for what needs to be done. Unfortunately, it is not so easy and, 'people—responding to the explicit or implicit incentives of the measurement—will do what [management] are measuring, not what [management] actually want done' (Behn, 2003: 599). This is one way that a performance management system might not give the public managers exactly what they are looking for. This sub-section discusses in more detail a number of challenges in using performance management systems.

SMART performance indicators

In Chapter 6 there was some emphasis on getting the specification of requirements right when procuring goods, works or services. Something similar applies to defining performance indicators. Clear definitions allow performance indicators to be meaningful, reliable and comparable.

Robinson (2021b) stresses the difference between performance indicators and performance targets. Indicators are the measurements that are made; targets are the objectives for the improvement of performance.

In respect of targets in the public sector, Robinson (2021b) recommends they should be SMART. The initialism SMART was first proposed by Doran (1981: 36), in respect of business objectives, meaning:

- **Specific**—target a specific area for improvement
- **Measurable**—quantify, or at least suggest an indicator of, progress
- **Assignable**—specify who will do it
- **Realistic**—state what results can realistically be achieved, given available resources
- **Time-related**—specify when the results can be achieved.

There are some differences in terms used by other people. Robinson (2021b) had achievable instead of assignable, relevant for realistic and time-bound rather than time-related. The essence is still the same and one important point is that only targets can be realistic/achievable because there are factors, such as organizational capacity and current performance, that need to be taken into account when assessing achievability of a target.

Measurement issues

Whilst there is a move towards performance-based budgeting (see Chapter 2), it would be very difficult, if at all possible, to manage a PBE only through the use of outcome performance indicators (and targets). Even if it were possible to find SMART measures of all the required outcomes, there is generally a time lag between the actions of the organization (and/or its suppliers and co-producers) that would prove problematic. It would not be possible to know what the current performance of the organization is, only how it performed months, years or even decades ago. It is like astronomy where it is not possible to know what a star looks like right now, but only what it looked like years ago (perhaps thousands of years ago). In fact, a star we can see from earth tonight might have ceased to exist many years ago just as it is possible that public value is being enjoyed today that was created by organizations that no longer exist.

The co-production of public services adds a further complication to the measurement of performance in producing public value. Simpson (2006: 13) gives an example related to education. If a parent helps their child who is attending a publicly funded school with their homework and pays for some additional tuition, then there are inputs to the child's education that are not recorded in the school's financial accounts. If the child performs well in examinations can the school claim all of the credit for it? Often the socio-economic makeup of a school population might mean that many pupils at one school would receive this sort of help and support from their parents/carers, whilst it would be relatively rare in another school in the same city. Comparing the performance of the two schools would then be problematic. What is required to compare the schools is a measure of the value added by each school. It is feasible that the school where parents are less engaged might add more educational value to its pupils despite their absolute achievement in terms of exam passes being lower than the other school and a value-added measure would demonstrate if that was the case.

Co-production could similarly affect outputs and outcomes as it does inputs (Simpson, 2006: 13). Indeed, if co-production did not have a positive effect on outputs and outcomes it would suggest that something is going wrong. That being the case, depending how the inputs and outputs/outcomes were measured there could be significantly different figures calculated for efficiency. An organization that receives a lot of 'free' inputs in the form of co-producers (such as a school where many of the parents are engaged in their children's education) may appear to be a lot more efficient than an organization that does not.

There could be implications of this for the measurement of public sector output at the national level, too. In a society where there are high levels of volunteering and other forms of civil participation then its public sector might be able to produce the same level of outputs and public value as another country that lacks the level of civil participation, from a lower input in the form of public spending.

Dysfunctional effects of performance management

Charles Goodhart was an economist and advisor to the Bank of England. In a speech in 1975 he stated his law as an aside: 'Any observed statistical regularity will tend to collapse once pressure is placed upon it for control purposes' (Chrystal and Mizen, 2003). What did he mean by this? Strathern (1997) restated the law more succinctly as: 'When a measure becomes a target, it ceases to be a good measure.' This simple notion is fundamental to understanding the problems of performance management. It suggests it is fine for information to be collected about actual performance, and such information could be used by a public manager to determine how to improve performance. Problems come, though, when the organization or senior management set the public manager a target to achieve.

There are many possible ways in which dysfunctional behaviour can manifest itself in a performance management regime. Smith identified and described seven categories of 'distorting and potentially dysfunctional effects' (1995: 141) and they are summarized in Table 7.3.

There are many examples in academic literature of the effects listed by Smith (1995). For example:

- Fitz-Gibbon (1997, cited by Van Thiel and Leeuw, 2002: 269) found that a sample of UK primary school head teachers were aware of problems relating to six out of the seven effects described by Smith (1995) (the missing one being ossification).
- Propper and Wilson (2003) report empirical evidence of gaming in education and health care.
- Bevan and Hood discuss the Soviet-style target-setting regime adopted by the Labour government in the United Kingdom in the late 1990s and include examples from health care, such as hospital trusts that had misreported or inappropriately adjusted information about waiting lists (2006: 532).

Gaming and misrepresentation occur even in law enforcement. O'Byrne wrote: 'Experience in policing powerfully shows that when robust performance management techniques come to the door, ethics tend to go out of the window' (2001). In 2014 the Public Administration Select Committee considered the

Table 7.3 *Distorting effects that can result from performance management regimes*

Effect	*Explanation*
Tunnel vision	By focusing attention on what is being measured, managers lose sight of the big picture and may not pay enough attention to other important aspects of their work. It is this sort of problem caused by a focus on profit and other financial measures that lays behind the concept of the balanced scorecard (Kaplan and Norton, 1996).
Sub-optimization	Just because an organization is achieving a certain level of performance against various performance measures does not mean that it is performing at its optimal level. Performance management systems can result in managers pursuing their narrow objectives rather than what is best for the organization as a whole.
Myopia	Performance targets may lead a manager to focus on how to achieve them in the short term and neglect the longer-term implications. They can do this, for example, by not investing in training or new equipment which might have a negative impact on performance in the short term but have a positive impact in the longer term.
Convergence	Rather than inspire or motivate managers to improve performance, performance management systems can result in managers seeking to perform at a similar level to other managers or organizations. The use of league tables to compare the performance of PBEs can result in this if managers are motivated to avoid being an outlier in terms of performance, rather than to deliver the best possible performance.
Ossification	This is connected with myopia and convergence. Performance targets can act as a disincentive for managers to take risks and innovate. If the organization is performing at a reasonable level, a manager may not wish to make changes to systems or processes since performance may reduce rather than improve (in the short term as the changes are made and possibly in the longer term, too).
Gaming	There may be managers who see the performance management regime as an elaborate game in which they might manipulate their targets and performance to get a strategic advantage. An example of this is meeting a target to answer a telephone within five rings by picking up the handset and replacing it without speaking to the caller at all. Another example is a manager performing at a comfortable level this year and using that as justification for the target not being increased the following year.
Misrepresentation	Managers may cheat the performance management system by submitting misleading or outright false performance data. A manager might do this if, for example, they are under pressure to meet a performance target or their remuneration is based on meeting the target and there is little or no auditing of the data.

Source: Smith (1995: 140–9).

findings of a report by Her Majesty's Inspector of Constabulary on the integrity of police crime recording statistics which suggested they were understated by 20 per cent. The committee was very critical of the target-chasing culture in many police forces. They wrote, 'we deprecate the use of targets in the strongest possible terms,' and they applauded the police and crime commissioners who had dropped all performance targets (Public Administration Select Committee, 2014: 3).

The dysfunctional effects of imposing performance targets in the police service has also made its way into television drama. In *The Wire* the fictional police department of Baltimore, MD, operate a system of performance management where senior police officers are charged with keeping crime figures in line with targets set by the mayor. In one scene the police commissioner and deputy commissioner instruct their senior officers to reduce the number of felonies by 5 per cent and that the total number of murders for the year must be fewer than 275. One of the majors replies that he and his colleagues understand how to manipulate the classifications of crimes to ensure the number of felonies falls but how could they make a murder victim's body disappear? The officers are told that they have to hit the targets come what may or they will be replaced by other officers who will meet the targets. And so a flawed system that discourages honest performance statistics would continue ('Time After Time,' 2004).

The past does not predict the future

A different problem related to performance measures is that they report past performance. In some cases, the time taken to gather and report the data might be very short. Some processes with high volumes of transactions, such as call centres, might produce daily or weekly performance reports. For other processes the frequency might be monthly, annually or even longer. This can often be the case for some of the outputs and outcomes that are produced by PBEs. High school examination results, for example, are published annually and yet they are the culmination of several years of schooling.

The purpose of performance measurement is to provide information to managers so that they can manage performance in the future (ideally to improve it but, as suggested above, possibly only to prevent unacceptable deterioration). There is a temptation to use the performance information that is collected to forecast future performance and this is a risky thing to do. It has been likened to driving forwards whilst looking in the rear-view mirror. There has to be a balance struck by a public manager between analysing past performance in order to learn lessons and being aware of changes in the environment that have to be managed.

If a public manager wishes to make predictions about future performance using the trend of past performance, there are mathematical techniques that can be used. Rolling averages, for example, smooth out the ups and downs in performance to give more cautious forecasts than simply extrapolating from the most recent performance information.

Composite performance indicators

A composite performance indicator is one that is derived from the combination of multiple indicators, possibly involving the relative weighting of the measures. Jacobs and Goddard (2007) describe the use of composite measures of performance and league tables. They showed that changing the weightings used in the Comprehensive Performance Assessment (CPA) of UK local authorities could have a significant effect on the resulting league table.

> The largest jump in position for an individual authority was 54 places, more than half the league table. On average, authorities changed between six and 13 places in the rankings, depending on the changes made to the weighting system.
>
> Jacobs and Goddard (2007: 107)

Stevens, Stokes and O'Mahony's work provides another warning about composite indicators. They showed that the star ratings awarded to hospital trusts as the result of external inspections—the star ratings were intended to allow citizens to compare easily their local hospitals with others—were 'almost entirely unrelated' to the hospitals' productivity (2006: 80). In short, composite indicators are best avoided. They are unsatisfactory 'because there is no convincing underlying rationale to the construction of such indicators. Rather the logic can be described as "any number is better than none"' (Watt, 2006: 16).

MEASURING PUBLIC VALUE

If the purpose of performance measurement is to improve performance and a public manager's purpose is to create public value, then should there be public value performance measures to improve the public manager's ultimate performance?

There are examples of PBEs adopting the public value concept to measure their performance and to guide their policymaking. These include the BBC (2004), the Scottish Government, police forces, local authorities, public sports and arts organizations (Talbot, 2008: 3). In the case of the BBC, it has published its guidelines on how the concept of public value should be applied as a test 'before a decision is taken to make any significant change to the BBC's UK Public Services' (BBC Trust, 2007: 3). The Public Value Test (PVT) is a lengthy process (taking about six months) and would be applied only to a small number of decisions. The PVT incorporates an 'assessment of the likely public value that will be created by the proposed change' (BBC, 2007: 12). This assessment includes consideration of the value for money of the proposed change.

The use of the concept of public value by the BBC is interesting and the BBC's global profile may have raised awareness of the concept. But the BBC is a unique organization and it is difficult for its interpretation of public value and the PVT to be translated to other public cultural organizations (Collins, 2006: 2), let alone to PBEs in general.

The public value scorecard

Moore himself has written his thoughts on performance measurement and public value (2003). The balanced scorecard (Kaplan and Norton, 1996) was conceived for private sector organizations to encourage their managements to broaden the focus of their attention beyond financial performance indicators (such as profitability and return on investment) to consider measures relating to the customer, internal business processes and learning and growth. The balanced scorecard has been adopted by PBEs—sometimes being adapted from its original form—in part because it seems to suggest that there is more to being a good performer than meeting financial objectives. Moore believes that the balanced scorecard as proposed by Kaplan and Norton is unsuitable for PBEs as its three non-financial dimensions are included because good performance in those dimensions would lead to sustained good financial performance. They are means to the private sector organization's main aim: profitability. The problem with financial performance measures is that they 'do not tell [public managers] how much public value they have produced through their efforts' Moore (2003: 7 8).

Moore proposed, instead, the public value scorecard, which has three perspectives—rather than the four in the balanced scorecard—aligning with the strategic triangle. Moore proposes generic headings for the performance measures that would fall within each of three perspectives, and he illustrated them with a schematic diagram (see Figure 7.1).

Moore (2003) does not prescribe what the precise performance indicators should be. Instead, he suggests the nature of the measures within each perspective and the public manager would determine the precise indicators based on their context. He also takes the view that if a public manager is expected to produce a lot of different outputs, then they would need lots of performance indicators.

It is important for a PBE to manage its finances well if it is to sustain itself to deliver its objectives (Moore, 2000: 195). At the very least it must maintain its spending within its income. Financial performance measures, therefore, make their way into the public value scorecard through the building operational capacity perspective.

Moore proposes that there would be measures of productivity and efficiency (2003: 21), a category that might include measures like unit costs, cost/benefit

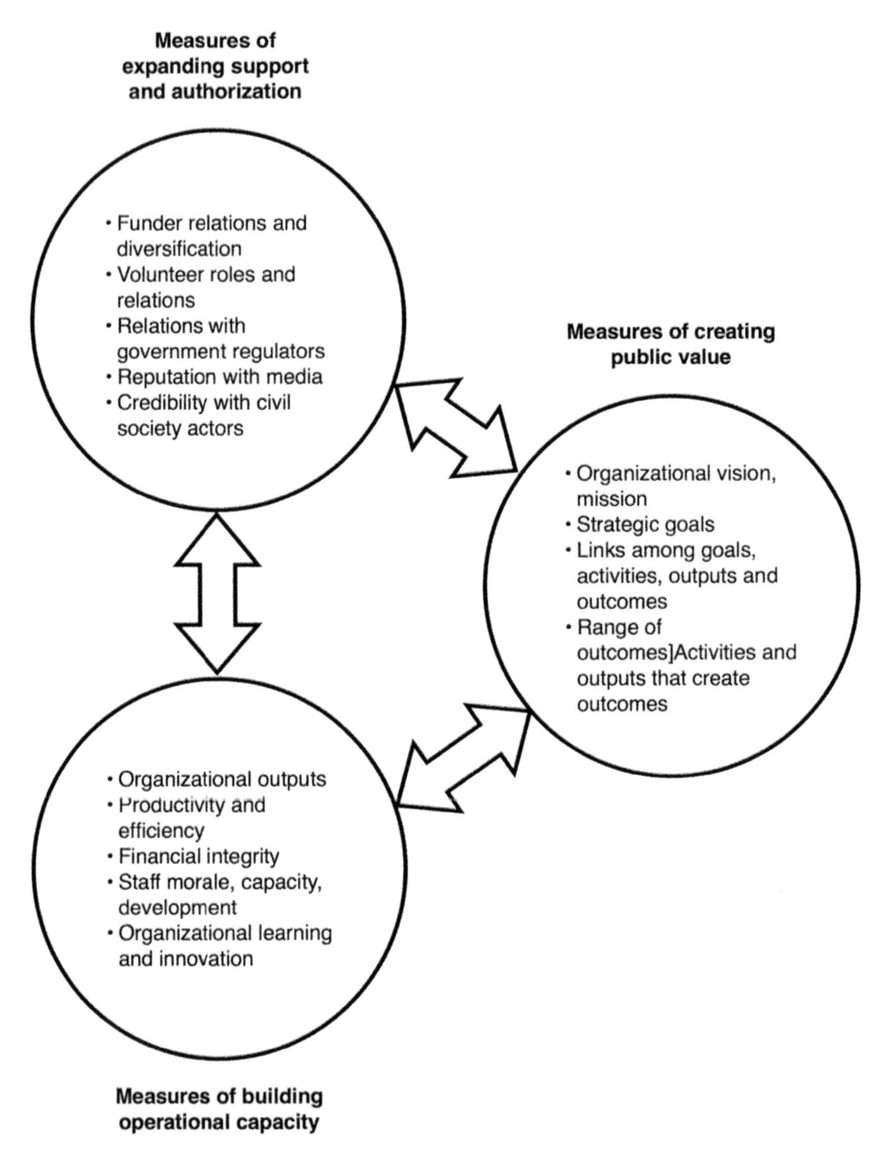

Figure 7.1 *Moore's public value framework for accountability and performance management.*

ratios, return on investment and the ratio of spending on administration and fund-raising suggested by Brooks (2006: 306) and discussed earlier in this chapter. Moore also proposes that there should be some measures of financial integrity (2003: 21), a proposal that recognizes the public's expectation that public money should not be wasted or lost to fraud.

MEASURING VALUE FOR MONEY

In creating public value through goods or services, a public manager also has to ensure that they obtain value for money from the use of resources. This section considers what is meant by the term 'value for money' and how it might be assessed.

Rational consumers carry out value for money assessments whenever they make a purchase of an item in a free market. It might be done intuitively but the consumer is making an assessment of whether the product they intend to buy is likely to deliver benefits that the consumer values more highly than the money in their pocket (they are exchange transactions as explained in Chapter 3). Sometimes a consumer gets a bargain because they would have been willing to pay more (perhaps lots more) than the market price; but other times the consumer makes a mistake and the product gives less benefit and was not worth the purchase price (for example, a shirt that looked good in the shop but only ever worn once or a train ticket for a trip not taken).

A public manager might manage their service using the same sort of intuitive approach to purchasing decisions. Similarly, a public service that operates in a competitive marketplace (such as a state-owned enterprise) can assess whether its products/services are value for money by the willingness of consumers to pay the fee. But most public services, even those that are not free of charge, are not delivered in a free market so we have to look for other ways of assessing whether they are value for money or not.

The *Oxford Dictionary of English* defines value for money as 'something that is well worth the money spent on it' (2010: 1,963) and the United Kingdom's National Audit Office (NAO) (2010) defines value for money as 'the optimal use of resources to achieve the intended outcomes'. Taken together these definitions sum up what a public manager has to do. They have to produce something that is regarded as important or useful, produce it in the best way possible and show that it is worth at least as much as it cost to produce.

The three Es

It is generally accepted that value for money in the public sector is characterized by the three Es: economy, efficiency and effectiveness. In short, these mean:

- minimizing the cost of inputs (economy);
- maximizing the ratio of outputs delivered from the inputs (efficiency); and
- achieving the intended results of the service/project (effectiveness).

Lapsley and Pong used an example of washing-up liquid to illustrate the three Es. The brand they refer to provides 'VFM because it exhibits the following characteristics: (a) economy (more clean plates per pound); (b) efficiency (more clean plates per squirt); (c) effectiveness (plates as clean as they should be)' (2000: 549). A public manager seeking to improve the value for money of their service could think along these lines. To improve value for money, they could seek to deliver more units of service per pound (or dollar or whatever), and/or deliver more units of service per member of staff, and/or improve the quality of the units of service.

The fourth and fifth E

The NAO (2022) suggest that there is a fourth E, equity, that might be appropriate in the assessment of value for money in some circumstances. This is the extent to which the public services are available to and reach all people that they are intended to reach.

Note that treating people equitably (that is, fairly) is not necessarily the same as treating people equally. For example, two people could have an identical need for a specific public service but perhaps they speak different languages or one of the people does not have internet access. To be equitable the PBE might need to make provision for these differences in its service delivery in order to make sure both people receive the service.

A value for money assessment could also involve a fifth E, ethics. This would be an assessment about the integrity, openness and transparency of the programme, project or service.

Now you have the notion that a public service is value for money if it is effective, economical, efficient, equitable and ethical. Alternatively, a public manager can think about their work like this: to achieve value for money they should:

- spend wisely;
- spend less;
- spend well;
- spend fairly; and
- spend properly.

When an auditor is conducting a value for money audit (see Chapter 8 for more about this aspect of audit work) they would be seeking to evaluate the extent to which the audit subject is economic, efficient and effective (and, possibly, equitable and/or ethical). All three (or four or five) have to be judged together, else an organization could be very efficiently doing the wrong thing (i.e., being efficient but not effective) or an organization could get great results by spending excessively (i.e., being effective but not economic).

Whilst the assessment of the three (or four or five) Es could be stated in absolute terms, often the assessment is a relative one, made by comparison with others (for example, a service is economic because it is below the average cost for its class of organization). This can lead to issues of comparability. A national study can identify the lowest cost and highest effectiveness achieved by the community of PBEs and it is tempting to calculate the potential saving if all the PBEs achieved the economy of the cheapest but what if the cheapest is relatively ineffective. If so, they would offer poor value for money and encouraging all others to be equally as cheap is likely to reduce the overall value for money across the country. It is important to understand, therefore, the extent to which the three (or four or five) Es are interrelated and not to treat them as independent of each other.

This approach to improving value for money over a period of time can avoid the question of whether the service is value for money in absolute terms. In the United Kingdom the government in the 2000s set targets for government departments, hospitals, police forces and local authorities to achieve annual efficiency savings. This approach sought year-on-year improvement in relative value for money. It may seem like a fair and reasonable approach but arguably it would be fairer to implement targets based on absolute value for money. This is because the latter would not penalize PBEs whose services are already the best value for money. The approach that was implemented required all PBEs to find a 3 per cent saving. The PBE with the best value for money would find much harder to find the savings compared with a PBE whose services are poor value for money. Indeed, if the latter's value for money was significantly poorer, then perhaps it is fairer to the PBEs, and better for local communities, if the poor performer had been asked to make a 5 per cent improvement and the good performer a 1 per cent improvement.

Let us say that a government does a national study of the value for money of breast cancer treatment amongst its major hospitals. It will identify the hospital with the lowest unit cost per patient and the hospital with highest effectiveness in terms of survival rates. It could then instruct all its hospitals to strive to achieve both the lowest unit cost and the best survival rates at the same time. However, it might be that the low-cost hospital has poor survival rates and the best survival rates come from a relatively expensive hospital. Not only that, but the hospital with the best survival rates has some patients from wealthy families who can and do pay for extra treatments, which means that they are subsidizing what is already an expensive hospital from their own pockets.

An alternative approach to improve value for money might be for the government to demand all hospital cut their costs by 5 per cent without reducing their performance. Would this be fair? The lowest cost hospital is likely to find it very hard to make savings whereas an expensive hospital might not.

In reality, the best value for money breast cancer treatment in the country might be in a hospital which has survival rates almost as good as the best, and a unit cost below the average. Could the government spot this optimal hospital from within its data? And if it could, how would it explain to taxpayers that it is aiming not for the best possible survival rates but for 'good enough' survival rates?

Affordability

Value for money is not the same as affordability, but affordability is critical to public managers since they have to deliver their programmes, projects and services within the constraint of the budget. Assessing value for money has to have some regard, therefore, to affordability. Private individuals do this: they have a budget for a car, say, and find the best value car in their price range. In the same way, there might be a very expensive drug treatment that offers great value for money in terms of the improvement in a patient's life expectancy and/or quality of life (and this will have been factored into the pricing decision by the drug company), but it could simply be too expensive for a government to approve for use. This happened, for example, in the late 1990s and early 2000s when anti-retroviral drugs that were effective in treating HIV/AIDS became available but were too expensive for developing countries to buy and the complexities of patent laws meant that countries like South Africa could not import the generic versions of the same drugs that were 95 per cent cheaper.

How to improve the VFM of a public service

How might a public manager go about improving value for money? One way is for the public manager to focus their improvement work on one or other of the five Es. By improving that without reducing the others would be an overall improvement.

Improving economy

Improving economy means spending less on the programme, project or service. While that might be the right thing to do for society, it is not necessarily in the public manager's interest. This is not to suggest that the public managers would be lining their pockets with public money, but their interests are not necessarily in line with those of the organization. For example, status and success might be measured in terms of budget size, giving a manager an incentive to increase their budget rather reduce it.

It is not just civil servants who want to see more spending rather than less. Often a politician will respond to a problem by promising extra money to be spent on it as if that would guarantee a better outcome. As mentioned in Chapter 2, politicians spend a lot of energy on the conflict that results in some items being in the budget and others not.

Just as more spending is not the same as more value, less spending does not necessarily mean less value, but it might do, and that is something a public manager should consider when thinking about improving the economy of something.

The amount of money spent on a public service is the product of

$$\text{Service standard} \times \text{Efficiency/Productivity} \times \text{Volume of activity}$$

To reduce spending, therefore, means doing one or more of the following:

- lowering the service standard;
- improving the processes used to deliver the results; and
- reducing the volume (the number of units delivered) of the service.

Lowering the service standard clearly reduces the value of the output as well as reducing the spending, so, depending on whether the reduction in value is greater or lesser than the reduction in spending, this could reduce or improve value for money. Either way, it is likely to provoke comment from citizens affected by the reduced standard.

There are three ways a public manager could reduce the volume of service:

- narrowing the scope of the service;
- increasing the qualifying threshold to restrict access to the service (so fewer people benefit from it); and
- reducing demand.

The first two of these reduce value as well as spending, just as reducing the service standard does. Reducing demand means making changes that mean fewer people want or need the service. For example, promoting healthier lifestyles reduces demand for health care services (which is the motivation for the soft drinks tax mentioned in Chapter 3). Another way that demand can be reduced is by working on the system in order to eliminate errors and waste, which generate what is called failure demand (that is, extra work has to be done as a direct result of the organization's failure to get things right first time).

Reducing demand is, potentially, a better solution to reducing spending without damaging the value of the project, programme or service. The big potential for increasing value for money comes from prevention being better than cure. The demand for treatment for type 2 diabetes is very high in the United Kingdom's NHS. Investment in programmes that reduce the number of obese people in the United Kingdom would, in time, reduce the cost of this treatment because fewer people would develop the illness.

Sometimes the value for money improvement in one programme can come from an investment in a quite different project or programme. Kenny (2012) describes a Mexican programme (*Piso Firma*, or firm floor) where families were given $150 worth of concrete to pave the floors of their houses. This protects, permanently, children from parasitic infections carried by hookworms that live in the soil, thus reducing their levels of sickness and improving their educational attainment because they did not miss so much schooling.

Improving efficiency?

An improvement in efficiency may happen as a corollary of improving economy or effectiveness. Sometimes, a public manager may focus on efficiency improvements in the first place. The reason for this could be that they have access to comparative benchmarks and recognize there is scope for improvement. Or it could be that the organization's budget process has requested an efficiency improvement of X per cent. Either way, the public manager might be interested in carrying out some business process reengineering to identify how to make improvements.

Improving effectiveness

This approach to improving value for money would mean trying to get more or better results from the current level of input. The process improvements mentioned above might result in exactly that. An alternative approach would be to review the outputs and outcomes and consider if there is a better way of meeting them.

Consider, for example, the change in demand for fire and rescue services. In the United Kingdom there are far fewer fires to extinguish than there were in the past (because fewer houses have open fires, and safety standards of electrical equipment are better), but there are some fires which need to be dealt with by experts.

If the outcome of the fire and rescue service is to save lives, it can achieve that, in part, by devoting more of its resources to fire prevention work, promoting the use of domestic smoke detectors and so on.

Improving equity or ethics

As mentioned above, the concept of value for money is broadening beyond the three Es. Public managers and other stakeholders may be happy with the level of inputs and processes being used to create the outputs from a particular public programme or service but there could perhaps be scope to review its fairness or its integrity. Before improvements can be made, the issues have to be identified and a public manager may or may not be able to do these alone. Assessing these aspects of programmes and services is something that internal auditors might be expected to do (see Chapter 8) or the organization may be able to commission a review by independent experts.

COST–BENEFIT ANALYSIS

Markets put prices on goods and services automatically, and the prices represent the value of the goods or services to the consumer. In the private sector, companies do not know the actual value they created for their consumers. They can, however, infer that the value is at least equal to the selling price (excluding taxes) and if the selling price is greater than the cost of producing the goods/service then the company can claim that it has created value.

A private sector organization's project appraisal process is likely to take into account just the costs and benefits that are (or would be) captured in economic transactions involving the organization. For example, an organization would include the cost of pollution only to the extent that it is required to pay for measures to prevent pollution or to pay environmental taxes. However, the value of benefits for non-customers, or costs imposed on them, would not be included because the organization makes profits only from customers who buy their products. A tobacco firm creates value for its customers but the cost of treating smoking-related illnesses is picked up by taxpayers, many of whom are not smokers. Indeed, some non-smokers pay the cost in terms of suffering from lung cancer themselves.

PBEs, such as state-owned enterprises, that can charge fees for some or all of their services/functions can use their fee levels as the basis of approximating the value of the services provided. But for most public programmes and services, by definition, there is not a market and no prices are paid. What can you do then to put a financial figure on the value of the programme or service?

The most thorough method of assessing value for money is to conduct a cost–benefit analysis (CBA). A CBA assesses costs and benefits from the perspective of the community as a whole rather than simply one organization's perspective. The assessment will include placing a financial value on any intangible costs and benefits associated with the project. Intangible costs might include the pollution from a new road, the blocking out of a scenic view, and the reduced levels of physical activity caused by the use of lifts and automatic doors in buildings. Intangible benefits might be time savings from using a new road and the increase in quality of life from a new drug treatment. As an example, Box 7.2 summarizes costs and benefits related to the introduction of a law to make the wearing of a helmet compulsory when cycling.

BOX 7.2 COSTS AND BENEFITS OF A CYCLE HELMET LAW

A country is considering the introduction of a law requiring adults and children to wear a crash helmet when cycling.

Costs	*Benefits*
For the cyclist Purchase of helmet Reduced pleasure of cycling Bad hair when the helmet is removed	**For the cyclist** Reduced risk of head injury in a crash Reduced risk of death from a crash
For society Enforcement of the law	**For society** Reduced health care costs (although this may be mitigated if the law results in cyclists riding more aggressively when wearing helmets) Increased pollution (if some cyclists switch to driving as a result of the law)

Source: Adapted from Boardman et al. (2018).

A CBA is akin to the investment/project appraisal described in Chapter 5. The result of a CBA can be a net present value calculation that takes account of the timing of the costs and benefits as well as their magnitudes. If this is a positive number it would indicate the present value of benefits outweighs the present value of the costs.

An alternative metric is the benefit:cost ratio (BCR), where anything greater than 1 shows benefits exceeding costs. A BCR can be used as decision benchmarks. For example, the Department for Transport (DfT) uses the following categories to assess the value for money of potential capital schemes (Department for Transport, 2015: 25):

- poor value for money if its BCR is less than 1;
- low value for money if its BCR is between 1 and 1.5;
- medium value for money if its BCR is between 1.5 and 2;
- high value for money if its BCR is between 2 and 4; and
- very high value for money if its BCR is over 4.

The Copenhagen Consensus Center (2015) has analysed the 169 Sustainable Development Goals (SDGs) (United Nations, 2015) in terms of benefits and costs and calculated BCRs for them. They have published their findings to show which SDGs offer the biggest bang for the buck. They identify the following eight SDGs as 'quick wins' where investment of US$30 billion a year would result in benefits of US$1,200 billion a year (that is, the eight SDGs therefore have an average BCR of 40):

- lower chronic child malnutrition by 40 per cent;
- halve malaria infections;
- avoid 1.1 m HIV infections through circumcision;
- increase immunization to reduce child deaths by 25 per cent;
- make family planning available to everyone;
- cut indoor air pollution by 20 per cent;
- boost agricultural yield growth by 40 per cent; and
- achieve universal primary education in sub-Saharan Africa.

The Copenhagen Consensus Center also identifies seven medium-term targets with an average BCR of 22 and four long-term goals with an average BCR of 128! spending US$140 billion a year on these targets would yield over $10 trillion of annual benefits. Essentially, CCC's argument is that the global results would be better from focusing on just 19 SDGs with such high BCRs because trying to do 169 at one time would dilute resources and likely achieve less overall.

Taking a CBA approach to assessing value for money is not always appropriate or necessary. There are lots of decisions where an assessment of the NPV of direct, tangible cash inflows and outflows is sufficient, such as a decision about whether to lease or buy new vehicles for a PBE's fleet. There are other decisions where political manifestos means that certain projects will go ahead and others will not. In such a situation an option appraisal is irrelevant although one may be done 'for political purposes to advance a case or protect an organization from outside interference, rather than for purely evaluative reasons' (McAlister, 1990: 49). However, where a CBA is done there will need to be some thought given to how financial values will be assigned to intangible costs and benefits.

Monetizing intangible costs and benefits

CBA is a useful technique for assessing VFM but it requires monetary values to be assigned to the costs and benefits associated with the project or service. Money 'provides a common measure of all transactions between for-profit organizations and all other organizations and individuals, however intrinsically different the goods and services provided may be' (Jones and Pendlebury, 2010: 20). Many (sometimes all) of the costs associated with a project or service are incurred as exchange transactions (see Chapter 3) and would therefore have a monetary value captured in the accounting system. Similarly, benefits in the form of income or future savings in expenditure are (relatively) easy to estimate in money terms to include in a CBA. This leaves the problem of assigning money values to (monetizing) the intangible costs and benefits of the programme, project or service. Below are some examples from published reports:

- The UK Government uses the value of £13,000 as the value of a 1 point improvement in wellbeing (on a scale of one to 10) (HM Treasury, 2022).
- Fields in Trust (2018) estimated that parks and green spaces in the United Kingdom creates £34 billion a year in wellbeing and saves over £100 million a year in health care costs.
- On a less positive note, the economic and social costs of domestic abuse include harm to victims of £47 billion a year and lost economic output (because of time off from work) of £14 billion (Home Office, 2019).

There are a number of techniques for monetizing costs and benefits, broadly falling into the categories of revealed preference and stated preference methods.

Revealed preference methods

The revealed preference approach infers monetary values for the effect that the programme, project or service will have on people or assets by observing how people act in real life, such as observing what people actually spend their money on and how much they spend. Several possibilities are outlined below, to illustrate the approach.

First, it might be possible to compare the output of the project with the price of private sector outputs. For instance, the benefit of building new social housing as part of a city regeneration scheme might be estimated from private sector housing rents in the same neighbourhood for similar properties. Or the value of education might be inferred from the fees paid to private sector schools (if there is a market for fee-paying schools), although there may need to be some adjustment in terms of the quality of education. For example, a fee-paying school may have smaller classes or lower pupil:teacher ratios that should be adjusted for.

A second method to monetizing intangible outputs (benefits) might be to value the outcomes produced by the project or service. Sticking with education, if average earnings levels are higher for people who have attained higher levels of education, then the value of, for example, obtaining a first degree can be inferred from this information. Walker and Zhu's study in 2013 estimated the difference in net lifetime earnings from having a degree as 28 per cent for men (equivalent to £168,000) and 53 per cent for women (equivalent to £252,000) (Walker and Zhu, 2013: 5).

A third technique is to consider the impact that the project or service has on asset values. Public schools that have good performance records can, for example, affect the value of houses in their catchment area because they increase the demand for them. Given that parents pay for the houses (whether they buy them or rent them), they are revealing something about the value they place on education. The difference in the capital value of houses can indicate the value parents place on education at the local school. Collinson (2014) reported on a study that demonstrated the effect in England was, on average, a premium on the value of 8.5 per cent (equivalent to £21,000 at the time).

This technique could also be used where there is a negative impact on asset values. For example, if a project is expected to have a detrimental effect on a scenic view, the value of the view might be approximated by comparing house prices and rents in places that have good views with prices and rents in places that do not.

A fourth revealed preference technique is measuring travel costs. This is particularly pertinent to visitor attractions that do not charge entry fees. Given that people are willing to travel to visit parks, museums and so on then by identifying how long and how much visitors spend to reach the attraction indicates the value that they place on it. This method should be used cautiously since the location, accessibility and capacity of an attraction can affect the number of visitors. As Watt puts it:

> If a museum is sited a long way from any conurbation, it may be that many relatively wealthy people come and visit it but fewer of the poor are able to. If a million people in London every year travel two miles to a museum, is it more or less valuable than one [to] which 10,000 people travel 200 miles?
>
> (Watt, 2006: 9)

A monetary value for a negative output (an intangible cost) could be estimated by identifying how much the community would pay to avoid the negative output or to defend themselves from it. The value of a clean water supply, for example, could be inferred from the cost of using bottled water or the cost of installing suitable water filters in every home. One has to be careful with this, though. Bottled water is sold at a premium price because it is for drinking, something that people are willing to pay more for than for bathing or washing their car.

Stated preference methods

Rather than assessing what people do, stated preference methods assess what people ***say*** they would do. Put simply, the value of an output would be ascertained by asking a person how much would they pay to receive the output or how much money would they accept in return for giving up the output? There is an inherent weakness in stated preference methods because there is, by definition, no evidence of the subjects actually doing what they say. Such studies have to consider this and seek to mitigate it through the design of the survey.

An example of using stated preferences was a study of terminally ill people in Singapore (Finkelstein et al., 2015). The study found that people were prepared to pay an average of US$20,000 extra on treatment that would mean they could be at home to die (rather than dying in hospital) and US$43,000 on treatment that would mean they were not in pain. In comparison, they were prepared to pay only USS$11,000 to be able to survive for an extra 12 months. Studies like this can inform policy decisions about end-of-life care. This one raises a question about whether to spend more resources on palliative care that enables people to be home with their families rather than spending money on life extending drugs and technology.

The price of a life

One of the necessities for many cost–benefit analyses is putting a value on life itself, not just an aspect of it like wellbeing. For example, cost–benefit assessment of implementing safety features that are intended to reduce fatalities (perhaps for a road project) needs an estimate of how many lives would be saved and a financial value placed on those lives. Box 7.3 explains a number of approaches that can be taken.

BOX 7.3 PUTTING A PRICE ON A LIFE

The value of a statistical life (VSL) is an estimate of how much a society would pay to save one human life (an anonymous, average person, not a specific person). Social Value UK (2016) set our several different ways that this could be estimated. The human capital method estimates the future earnings that would be lost as a result of death. Labour market data can also be used to estimate the value people place on the risk of death by comparing wage levels for riskier jobs against safer jobs. A similar method looks at the extra costs a consumer will pay for a safer product (such as the extra cost a consumer would pay for airbags in a car). The Social Value UK has a table comparing the VSLs derived in different ways (2016: 7) and suggests the acceptable range is US$7 million to US$12 million, and this compared well against the US$9.2 million value recommended by the US Department of Transport for its analyses.

In the United Kingdom the measure used is the 'value of a prevented fatality' or VPF. In 2020 HM Treasury's VPF was £2 million (Dolan and Jenkins, 2020). It was originally calculated in a study in 1999 and the original estimate of £1 million has been increased annually by the increase in GDP.

Displacement and drop-off

In estimating the benefits that a programme, project or service might yield, a public manager should consider the concepts of displacement and drop-off. Displacement relates to the situation where the benefit is an avoided cost for the group under consideration but some or all of that cost is passed on to others. For example, if a project improves the security of houses in a neighbourhood one benefit is a reduction in crime for the residents of those houses. However, if the burglars simply carry out their burglaries in another neighbourhood there is no overall benefit to society.

The public manager should also consider whether over time there will be drop-off of benefits resulting from the project or programme. For example, a new road may reduce average journey times by X minutes on the day the road is opened. However, the expected growth in population and vehicle usage over time may cause congestion on the new road, thus reducing the journey time savings. By making an allowance for drop-off the public manager will obtain a more realistic and conservative assessment of benefits.

Social return on investment

The social return on investment (SROI) methodology (Lawlor et al, 2009) is similar to CBA. The methodology differs from CBA by putting an emphasis on consultation with and involvement of stakeholders in the identification of the impact of the project or programme and the valuation of costs and benefits. This makes it a more participative technique than CBA (and perhaps is complementary to the participatory budgeting approach mentioned in Chapter 2).

The stages of the SROI process are:

- establish the scope of the project or programme and identify the stakeholders;
- map the outcomes;
- gather evidence of the outcomes and give them a value;
- establish the impact;
- calculate the SROI; and
- report to stakeholders.

SROI results are stated as a ratio of the present value of the outputs divided by the inputs, just like the BCR mentioned earlier in this chapter, but expressed as a percentage return on the initial investment. Sport England (2020), for example, concluded there is a return of 391 per cent (£391 for every £100 spent) on community sport and activity.

Another example is *Valuing the Impact of Adult Learning* by Daniel Fujiwara (2012). Fujiwara found that for adults, participating in two part-time courses during a single year will lead to:

- improvements in health, which has a value of £148 to the individual;
- a greater likelihood of finding a job and/or staying in a job, which has a value of £224 to the individual;
- better social relationships, which has a value of £658 to the individual; and
- a greater likelihood that people volunteer on a regular basis, which has a value of £130 to the individual.

Cost-effectiveness analysis

Rather than trying to conduct a full CBA, with all its complications of monetizing intangible costs and benefits, an alternative strategy is to avoid putting values on the intangible costs and benefits and to carry out a cost-effectiveness analysis instead. Cost-effectiveness analysis requires a focus on a single effect (i.e., output) so that the cost of producing the effect can be calculated for each option.

A cost-effectiveness approach would be appropriate, therefore, where the options under consideration are all expected to have the same impact on the community in terms of benefits. In such a scenario the benefits are common in each option and can therefore be ignored. (To borrow from Chapter 5, because these costs and benefits do not change under the alternative options, they are not relevant costs and benefits.) For example, if a new primary school is to be built to serve an expanding town and there are two possible locations it would be reasonable to assert that the value of education delivered by the school is not dependent on the location and therefore it does not need to be valued. If the possible locations are close to each other, it would also be possible to assert that the total time taken by parents to take their children to and from school are equivalent for both locations and can also be ignored. However, if the schools would be of different sizes allowing a different number of pupils to attend, a cost-effectiveness analysis could produce a figure for the cost per pupil place for each of the two schools.

CONCLUSION

The evaluation of value for money requires the measurement of performance as well as cost. The latter is a staple of the accounting profession, but we have seen in earlier chapters that the question 'what is the cost of X?' does not always have a single or easy answer. There are issues, too, about how performance is measured and what effect the act of measurement and target-setting has on performance.

Despite all of these issues, a public manager is expected to provide services and projects that are value for money. Techniques like cost-effectiveness studies, cost–benefit analysis and social return on investment can help to demonstrate the value that they produce when they are asked to give an account of what they have done with public money.

EXERCISES

1. For a public service that you are interested in, what are its principal inputs, activities, outputs and outcomes?
2. How might you estimate monetary values for the outcomes you identified in exercise 1?
3. Think of some suitable performance measures for a police service.

REFERENCES

Ackoff, R. L. (2004). Transforming the systems movement. *The Systems Thinker, 15*(8), 2–5. Available at: https://thesystemsthinker.com/wp-content/uploads/pdfs/150801pk.pdf (Accessed: 7 July 2022).

Atkinson, A. B. (2005). *Atkinson Review: Final Report: Measurement of Government Output and Productivity for the National Accounts.* Basingstoke: Palgrave Macmillan.

BBC. (2004). *Building Public Value: Renewing the BBC for a Digital World.* London: BBC.

BBC Trust. (2007). Public Value Test (PVT): Guidance on the Conduct of the PVT. Available at: https://downloads.bbc.co.uk/bbctrust/assets/files/pdf/about/how_we_govern/pvt/pvt_guidance.pdf (Accessed: 8 July 2022).

Behn, R. D. (2003). Why measure performance? Different purposes require different measures. *Public Administration Review, 63*(5), 586–606.

Behn, R. D. (2007). *What All Mayors Would Like to Know About Baltimore's CitiStat Performance Strategy.* Washington, DC: IBM Center for the Business of Government. Available at: https://www.businessofgovernment.org/report/what-all-mayors-would-know-about-baltimore's-citistat-performance-strategy (Accessed: 6 July 2022).

Bevan, G. & Hood, C. (2006). What's Measured Is What Matters: Targets and Gaming in the English Public Health Care System. *Public Administration, 84*(3), 517–38.

Boardman, A. E., Greenberg, D. H., Vining, A. R., & Weimer, D. L. (2018). *Cost-Benefit Analysis: Concepts and Practice* (5th ed.). Boston, MA: Pearson Education.

Boardman, A. E., Laurin, C., Moore, M. A. and Vining, A. R. (2009). A Cost-Benefit Analysis of the Privatization of Canadian National Railway. *Canadian Public Policy, 35*(1), 59–83.

Bohte, J., & Meier, K. J. (2000). Goal displacement: Assessing the motivation for organizational cheating. *Public Administration Review, 60*(2), 173–182.

Brooks, A. C. (2006). Efficient nonprofits? *Policy Studies Journal, 34*(3), 303–312.

Chrystal, A., & Mizen, P. (2003). Goodhart's law: Its origins, meaning and implications for monetary policy. *Central Banking, Monetary Theory and Practice: Essays in Honour of Charles Goodhart*, 221.

Cities X. (2018). *CompStat in New York, Boston and Chicago* [Video]. Available at: https://www.youtube.com/watch?v=c6Q9qHAnY_E (Accessed: 11 July 2022).

Coats, D., & Passmore, E. (2009). *Public Value: The Next Steps in Public Service Reform*. London: The Work Foundation.

Collins, R. (2006). *The BBC and Public Value* [CRESC Working Paper No. 19] (CRESC Working Paper No. 19). Milton Keynes: Open University.

Collinson, P. (2014). Good schools add £21,000 to local property prices. *The Guardian*, 26 August. Available at: https://www.theguardian.com/money/2014/aug/26/good-schools-add-21000-pounds-property-prices (Accessed: 11 July 2022).

Copenhagen Consensus Center. (2015). *Post-2015 Consensus* [Webpage]. Available at: https://www.copenhagenconsensus.com/post-2015-consensus (Accessed: 10 July 2022).

Curristine, T., & Flynn, S. (2013). In search of results: strengthening public sector performance. In M. Cangiano, T. Curristine, & M. Lazare (Eds.), *Public Financial Management and Its Emerging Architecture* (pp. 225–258). Washington, DC: International Monetary Fund.

Department for Transport (2015). *Value for Money Framework*. London: Department for Transport. Available at: https://www.gov.uk/government/publications/dft-value-for-money-framework (Accessed: 6 July 2022).

Dolan, P., & Jenkins, P. (2020). *Estimating the Monetary Value of the Deaths Prevented From the UK Covid-19 Lockdown When It Was Decided Upon – And the Value of "Flattening the Curve"*. London School of Economics. Available at: https://www.lse.ac.uk/PBS/assets/documents/Estimating-the-monetary-value-of-the-deaths-prevented-from-the-UK-Covid-19-lockdown-when-it-was-decided-upon-and-the-value-of-flattening-the-curve-June-2020.pdf (Accessed: 7 July 2022).

Doran, G. T. (1981). There's a S.M.A.R.T. way to write management's goals and objectives. *Management Review, 70*(11), 35–36.

Farmer, R. N. (1965). Two kinds of profit. *California Management Review, 8*(2), 21–28.

Fields in Trust. (2018). *Revaluing Parks and Green Spaces: Measuring Their Economic and Wellbeing Value to Individuals*. Available at: https://www.fieldsintrust.org/Upload/file/research/Revaluing-Parks-and-Green-Spaces-Report.pdf (Accessed: 11 July 2022).

Finkelstein, E. A., Bilger, M., Flynn, T. N., & Malhotra, C. (2015). Preferences for end-of-life care among community-dwelling older adults and patients with advanced cancer: A discrete choice experiment. *Health Policy, 119*(11), 482–489. https://doi.org/10.1016/j.healthpol.2015.09.001.

Fryer, K., Antony, J., & Ogden, S. (2009). Performance management in the public sector. *International Journal of Public Sector Management, 22*(6), 478–498.

Fujiwara, D. (2012). *Valuing the Impact of Adult Learning: An Analysis of the Effect of Adult Learning on Different Domains in Life.* Leicester: National Institute of Adult Continuing Education. Available at: https://learningandwork.org.uk/resources/research-and-reports/valuing-the-impact-of-adult-learning/ (Accessed: 6 July 2022).

HM Treasury. (2022). *The Green Book 2022.* London: TSO. Available at: https://www.gov.uk/government/publications/the-green-book-appraisal-and-evaluation-in-central-governent/the-green-book-2020 (Accessed: 22 June 2022).

Home Office. (2019). *The Economic and Social Costs of Domestic Abuse.* Available at: https://www.gov.uk/government/publications/the-economic-and-social-costs-of-domestic-abuse (Accessed: 11 July 2022).

Hood, C. (1991). A public management for all seasons? *Public Administration, 69*(1), 3–19.

Jacobs, R., & Goddard, M. (2007). How do performance indicators add up? An examination of composite indicators in public services. *Public Money and Management, 27*(2), 103–110.

Jones, R., & Pendlebury, M. (2010). *Public Sector Accounting* (6th ed.). Harlow: Pearson Education.

Kaplan, R. S., & Norton, D. P. (1996). Using the balanced scorecard as a strategic management system. *Harvard Business Review, 74*(1).

Karnon, J., Afzali, H. H. J., & Edney, L. C. (2015). *New Cancer Drugs Are Very Expensive—Here's How We Work Out Value for Our Money* [Online Article]. Available at: https://theconversation.com/new-cancer-drugs-are-very-expensive-heres-how-we-work-out-value-for-our-money-44014 (Accessed: 6 July 2022).

Kenny, C. (2012). Paving paradise. *Foreign Policy, 191*(January/February), 31–32.

Lapsley, I., & Pong, C. K. M. (2000). Modernization versus problematization: Value-for-money audit in public services. *European Accounting Review, 9*(4), 541–567.

Lawlor, E., Neitzert, E., Nicholls, J., & Goodspeed, T. (2009). *A Guide to Social Return on Investment.* London: The Cabinet Office. Available at: https://neweconomics.org/2009/05/guide-social-return-investment (Accessed: 11 July 2022).

McAlister, D. (1990). Option appraisal: Turning an art into a science? *Public Money and Management, 10*(4), 43–50. https://doi.org/10.1080/09540969009387627.

Moore, M. H. (2000). Managing for Value: Organizational Strategy in For-Profit, Nonprofit, and Governmental Organizations. *Nonprofit and Voluntary Sector Quarterly, 29*(1) (Supplement), 183–204.

Moore, M. H. (2003). *The Public Value Scorecard: A Rejoinder and an Alternative to 'Strategic Performance Measurement and Management in Non-Profit Organizations' by Robert Kaplan.* Cambridge, MA: The Hauser Center for Nonprofit Organizations.

National Audit Office. (2010). *Taking the Measure of Government Performance.* London: The Stationery Office. Available at: https://www.nao.org.uk/report/taking-the-measure-of-government-performance/ (Accessed: 6 July 2022).

National Audit Office. (2022). *Assessing Value for Money* [Web page]. Available at: https://www.nao.org.uk/successful-commissioning/general-principles/value-for-money/assessing-value-for-money/ (Accessed: 8 July 2022).

O'Byrne, M. (2001). *Changing Policing: Revolution not Evolution.* Lyme Regis, Dorset: Russell House.

Office of National Statistics. (2022). *Public Service Productivity Estimates: Total Public Service.* London: ONS. Available at: https://www.ons.gov.uk/economy/economicoutputandproductivity/publicservicesproductivity/datasets/publicserviceproductivityestimatestotalpublicservice (Accessed: 8 July 2022).

Propper, C., & Wilson, D. (2003). The use and usefulness of performance measures in the public sector. *Oxford Review of Economic Policy, 19*(2), 250.

Public Administration Select Committee. (2014). *Caught Red-Handed: Why We Can't Count on Police Recorded Crime Statistics.* London: The Stationery Office. Available at: http://bit.ly/1iUWfBC.

Radnor, Z. J., & McGuire, M. (2004). Performance management in the public sector: Fact or fiction? *International Journal of Productivity and Performance Management, 53*(3), 245–260.

Robinson, M. (2021a). *Non-Performing Performance Indicators* [Blog]. Available at: https://blog.pfmresults.com/choosing-the-right-performance-indicators/ (Accessed: 8 July 2022).

Robinson, M. (2021b). *Don't Confuse Indicators and Targets* [Blog]. Available at: https://blog.pfmresults.com/dont-confuse-indicators-and-targets/ (Accessed: 8 July 2022).

Schick, A. (2013). Reflections on two decades of public financial management reforms. In M. Cangiano, T. Curristine, & M. Lazare (Eds.), *Public Financial Management and Its Emerging Architecture* (pp. 21–77). Washington, DC: International Monetary Fund.

Simpson, H. (2006). *Productivity in Public Services.* Bristol: Centre for Market and Public Organisation. CMPO Working Paper Series 07/164.

Smith, P. (1995). On the unintended consequences of publishing performance data in the public sector. *International Journal of Public Administration, 18*(2), 277–310.

Social Value UK. (2016). *Valuation of a Life.* Available at: https://socialvalueuk.org/wp-content/uploads/2017/08/Valuation-of-a-life-1.pdf (Accessed: 7 July 2022).

Speklé, R. F., & Verbeeten, F. H. (2014). The use of performance measurement systems in the public sector: Effects on performance. *Management Accounting Research,* 25(2), 131–146. https://doi.org/10.1016/j.mar.2013.07.004.

Sport England. (2020). Available at: https://www.sportengland.org/how-we-can-help/measuring-impact?section=social_and_economic_value_of_community_sport (Accessed: 6 July 2022).

Stevens, P. A., Stokes, L., & O'Mahony, M. (2006). Metrics, targets and performance. *National Institute Economic Review, 197*(1), 80–92.

Strathern, M. (1997). Improving ratings: Audit in the British university system. *European Review, 5*(3), 305–321.

Talbot, C. (2008). *Measuring Public Value.* London: The Work Foundation.

TED. (2010). *Take Turns* [Video] Available at: https://www.ted.com/talks/gary_lauder_take_turns (Accessed: 7 July 2022).

'Time after Time' (2004). *The Wire,* Season 3 episode 1. Directed by Ed Bianchi. Written by David Simon and Ed Burns. First broadcast 19 September 2004 [DVD] London: Warner Home Video.

United Nations. (2015). *Sustainable Development Goals* [Webpage]. Available at: https://www.un.org/en/sustainable-development-goals (Accessed: 10 July 2022).

van Dooren, W., Bouckaert, G., & Halligan, J. (2015). *Performance Management in the Public Sector* (2nd ed.). London: Routledge.

van Thiel, S., & Leeuw, F. L. (2002). The performance paradox in the public sector. *Public Performance and Management Review, 25*(3), 267–281.

Walker, I., & Zhu, Y. (2013). *The Impact of University Degrees on the Lifecycle of Earnings: Some Further Analysis.* London: Department for Business, Innovation and Skills. BIS Research Paper 112. Available at: http://bit.ly/Q6z7Jt.

Watt, P. A. (2006). *Measuring Efficiency Gains in Local Government That Derive From Improved Service Quality.* Birmingham: Institute of Local Government Studies.

Wikiquote. (2022). *Albert Einstein* [Webpage]. Available at: https://en.wikiquote.org/wiki/Albert_Einstein (Accessed: 7 July 2022).

FURTHER READING (AND WATCHING)

Links to the following resources, and lots more, are available at www.managingpublicmoney.co.uk/extras.

There is a book on performance management in the Masters of Public Management series by van Dooren, Bouckaert and Halligan, *Performance Management in the Public Sector* (2015) that would give the reader a more thorough understanding of the theory and practice of performance management.

If you want to find out something about how the Baltimore mayor really managed performance, then read Behn's *What All Mayors Would Like to Know about Baltimore's CitiStat Performance Strategy* (2007). There is also a short video from Harvard's CitiesX (2018), *CompStat in New York, Boston and Chicago*, that briefly explains the promise and pitfalls of using crime statistics to manage policing.

Cost-Benefit Analysis: Concepts and Practice by Boardman et al. (2010) is a good book for readers who would like to know more about the theory and practice of conducting CBAs. Two of the authors were also amongst the authors of an article describing a CBA of the privatization of the Canadian National Railway (Boardman et al., 2009). In this case, the CBA technique is used for evaluation of something that has happened rather than as part of the decision-making process regarding a potential project.

There is a light-hearted, short presentation by Gary Lauder called *Take Turns* (TED, 2010) where he does a cost-benefit analysis of replacing a stop sign in his neighbourhood with a roundabout. He suggests benefits of US$2 million from just one roundabout.

One important use of cost–benefit analysis by governments is making decisions about the value for money of new health care treatments. Karnon, Afzali and Edney (2015) explain in a short article how the concept of the quality-adjusted life year (QALY) is used in such assessments.

Chapter 8

Accountability and financial reporting

LEARNING OBJECTIVES

After reading this chapter you should:

- understand the importance of accountability in public financial management;
- recognize the difference between managerial accountability and political accountability;
- understand the characteristics of public sector accounting and how it differs from the private sector; and
- recognize the components of a set of financial statements.

KEY POINTS OF THIS CHAPTER

- The public have high expectations about the management of public money and the conduct of public managers and there are many types of accountability in place.
- The online publishing of financial data so that citizens can analyse it how they wish may impact in the future on the accountability of PBEs and public managers.
- Accounting is an important function in all organizations and it enables complete and accurate external financial reports.
- Cash-based accounting is based on facts but is limited in its usefulness. Accrual-based accounting enables better decision making because it is more complete, but it requires a lot of subjective judgements.

DOI: 10.4324/9781003250838-8

- The International Public Sector Accounting Standards Board (IPSASB) develops and publishes accounting standards (called IPSASs) specifically for use by governments and PBEs.
- The global move to harmonize the accounting standards tends to be focused on the needs of private sector organizations and their stakeholders. The adoption of such standards by PBEs can result in misleading financial statements so there is an argument that PBEs should have different accounting standards.

KEY TERMS

Accounting—the recording, analysing and summarizing of the transactions that occur as a result of an organization's activities.

Accrual accounting—the basis of accounting where transactions are recognized in the accounting period where the transaction occurred (regardless of when any related payments are made or received).

Balance sheet—a statement of the assets, liabilities and reserves of an organization at a particular point in time.

Capital expenditure—expenditure on substantial items (such as land and buildings, fixtures and fittings) which will have a benefit for the organization beyond the current year.

Cash-based accounting—the basis of accounting where transactions are recognized in the accounting period where the payment is made or received.

GAAP (generally accepted accounting principles)—the framework of standards and guidelines that are expected to be applied in general purpose financial reports in a given jurisdiction, for example, UK GAAP and US GAAP.

Managerial accountability—the accountability of an agent to a principal in respect of the responsibility that has been delegated to the agent.

Operating expenditure—the items of expenditure which are not capital expenditure (including salaries, wages, training, utilities, travel, fuel, rents, repair and maintenance of premises and equipment, stationery, interest on loans).

Political accountability—the accountability of politicians (or other representatives) to the people they represent (the principals) for the authority given to them.

High expectations about the accountability and the public scrutiny of accounting information that should accompany the spending of public money stretch back at least as far as Aristotle in the fourth century BCE:

> To prevent the exchequer from being defrauded, let all public money be delivered out openly in the face of the whole city and let copies of the accounts be deposited in the different wards, tribes and divisions.
>
> (Aristotle, no date, Book V, Chapter VIII)

In the public sector in modern times there are many accountability mechanisms. Chapter 9 will concentrate on one of them, auditing, as a follow-up to this chapter on accountability as a concept and financial reporting as a mechanism for accountability. This chapter begins with a discussion about the concepts of accountability and transparency and makes a link with the ethical standards expected of a public manager. The second part of this chapter focuses on financial reporting. Specifically, it will cover:

- what is accounting;
- characteristics of public sector accounting;
- public sector financial reporting;
- accounting standards; and
- whole of government accounts.

ACCOUNTABILITY AND TRANSPARENCY

What is meant by the term 'accountability'? The terms 'authority', 'responsibility' and 'accountability' are closely related to each other and might be used interchangeably in everyday speech. In respect of a project, for instance, a public manager might say, 'I'm responsible for it,' or, 'I have authority to deliver it,' or, 'I'm accountable for it.' As rough definitions:

- **authority** means the power or right to give orders and directions and to make decisions;
- **responsibility** means having control over something or someone; and
- **accountability** means the expectation to justify actions and decisions.

Barton (2006: 257) employs principal-agent theory to explain accountability:

> Accountability involves an obligation to answer for one's decisions and actions when authority to act on behalf of one party (the principal) is transferred to another (the agent).

This suggests that the principal can demand explanations and reasons from the agent and the agent will provide them. Barton (2006: 259) explains the reasons for accountability being important in the public sector arise from the nature and role of democratic governments. Citizens want accountability in return for delegating the power to make collective decisions (about political and judicial issues as well as economic ones) to the people they elect.

In the public sector there is a chain of accountability (Barton, 2006: 258) where an agent in one level becomes the principal for the next level down. Government is accountable to its citizens for good governance; ministers are accountable to parliament; a permanent secretary or chief of staff is accountable to their minister; and so on down through the tiers of the organization's hierarchy until the staff working on frontline delivery of services are reached. This model works, in broad terms, for sub-national government and other PBEs, too. Elected or appointed officials (such as mayors, councillors, trustees, and so on) are accountable to the (local) citizens; the chief executive to the officials; senior managers to the chief executive; and so on.

Multiple accountabilities can occur along the chain of accountability, too, especially given the growing interest in public-public partnerships and shared services. Since the late 2000s there are many instances in the United Kingdom where two local authorities have decided to share a single chief executive. The authorities remain distinct in all other respects but the chief executive obviously has to be accountable to both sets of councillors. There have also been examples of multi-agency partnerships where several PBEs collaborate in a partnership to tackle a difficult social problem, such as crime and disorder or youth offending. In such arrangements, the public managers are accountable to the partnership's governance body but they retain accountability to their 'home' organization as well. In terms of financial management, the maxim who pays the piper calls the tune is apposite. In the event of a conflict in accountability, the organization that pays a public manager's salary is likely to receive their prime accountability.

Kluvers and Tippett (2010: 46) believe that the adoption of NPM has resulted in 'a private-sector version of accountability [being] imported into the public sector, resulting in a more managerial-style accountability'. This means that there is a greater emphasis on the agent's compliance with the principal's expectations and less emphasis on being accountable for the stewardship of resources to the principal and to other interested parties.

However, a case can be made that the politicians are under pressure to do more to improve performance. Citizens are becoming better educated and informed about what it possible and this leads to higher expectations about the quality of public services they receive. Furthermore, 'politicians have felt compelled to produce visible results and to demonstrate to the public that they are accountable' (Curristine and Flynn, 2013: 225). There are an increasing number of countries with freedom on information laws and there are more and more civil society institutions with a focus on government transparency and accountability. At the international level these include Transparency International, the International Budget Partnership and the Open Contracting Partnership.

The Sustainable Development Goals (United Nations, 2015) also include two targets directly relating to this, namely:

- target 16.6 is to develop effective, accountable and transparent institutions; and
- target 16.10 is to ensure public access to information and protect fundamental freedoms, in accordance with national legislation and international agreements.

Even with the emphasis on improving accountability of governments there is plenty of room for improvement. Take, for example, the response to the coronavirus pandemic in 2020 and 2021. Bandy and Metcalfe's (2021) research highlighted a gap between the public's expectations and the actual level of transparency provided to them.

Types of accountability

There are different types of accountability operating in the public sector. Financial accountability is central to public financial management, but there are others which are also outlined below.

Financial accountability involves preparing financial statements that can be validated by an independent person, usually a professional external auditor. Financial accountability may also be achieved or enhanced by public sector organizations publishing additional information (such as strategic plans and medium-term budgets) and making them available for public scrutiny. The organization may also publish financial performance information that enables the public to assess whether the organization has achieved targets (especially if performance-based budgeting is being used).

Legislative accountability is a series of procedures by which the relevant body is able to carry out checks on public expenditure to ensure that it is in accordance with the purposes approved by the legislature (such as a Parliament or a Council).

Although not all public bodies are funded through taxation directly or entirely, they are nevertheless ultimately dependant on a legislature for their authority to carry out their role. The legislature is therefore entitled to demand information, including financial information, on the activities of each public sector organization to assure itself that the money is properly spent.

Political accountability is different from legislative accountability. It applies 'particularly to governments who are accountable to their electors for the *authority* granted to them' (Broadbent and Laughlin, 2003: 24, emphasis in the original). With political accountability the electorate has the right of accountability from government but no direct control of it. 'Increased pressure [by the electorate] on governments can increase the extent of the detail that is provided to meet the accountability demands in their political/public form' but this is not giving the electorate any control or giving the decision-making power back to the electorate.

Managerial accountability 'applies to managers being made accountable for the *responsibilities* delegated to them' (Broadbent and Laughlin, 2003: 24, emphasis in the original). Managerial accountability gives the principal (the manager) control over the actions of the agent (the worker). Perhaps this control is not exercised day to day but whenever the agent gives an account of what they have done (a weekly or monthly report, say) the principal can give new instructions or, if they wish, rescind or amend the delegated authority and responsibility. If the principal places more pressure on the agent by requiring more frequent and/or more detailed reports they will have greater control over what is done.

Legal accountability is simply the requirement to demonstrate that the organization's activities have been within the law and it has not engaged in any activities that go beyond its legal powers.

Accountability mechanisms

There are lots of external accountability mechanisms operated by governments and other PBEs (the internal mechanisms are part of the internal control system explained in Chapter 4). A key external financial accountability mechanism is the publication of audited statements of accounts (which are the subject of the second part of this chapter). Other accountability mechanisms include:

- holding official meetings in public;
- publication of budgets and other key strategies and policies;
- publication of details of financial transactions;
- permitting individuals to inspect financial records and ask questions directly to the auditor;
- parliamentary select committees where members can call ministers, civil servants and others to give evidence; and
- holding public enquiries.

In the public sector, but not the private sector, budgets have an accountability role. Publishing budgets give taxpayers (and others) information about why they are being asked to pay taxes and what they can expect from their governments and PBEs in terms of services and performance.

Transparency

There are increasing demands for transparency about public money, not just for transparency by PBEs about their income and expenditure, but also for transparency about the tax affairs of multinational companies and elected representatives.

The demands for transparency are being met in some countries by PBEs publishing details of their spending in the form of databases and spreadsheets. The UK Government, for example, requires government departments (i.e., ministries), local councils and hospitals to publish details of all payments made in excess of £500.

Finding the data you want is not as easy as it might be. In the United Kingdom there is a central hub website at https://data.gov.uk for central government data of all kinds, not just spending data. However, each of the 1,000 or so local councils and National Health Services bodies publish their own data on their own website. If you have a specific target in mind this can be a great resource, but it is not easy to aggregate data.

The importance of transparency in budgeting as well as spending is reflected as principle 4 in the OECD's principles of budgetary governance (see Chapter 2): Ensure that budget documents and data are open, transparent and accessible.

On the assumption that governments and PBE use budgets to allocate their resources to their priorities, it follows that it should be possible to analyse published budgets to ascertain whether they actually reflect the government's (or other public body's) stated priorities.

There is a global lobbying organization, the International Budget Partnership (IBP) that believes that, when citizens have access to their government's budget, there are improvements in governance and a reduction in poverty.

The IBP produces its Open Budget Index from a survey of the national budget process in 120 countries. Each country's budget transparency score assesses the public's access to timely and comprehensive budget information. A transparency score of 61 (out of 100) or higher indicates a country is publishing sufficient information to support informed public debate. In the 2021 results, 35 of the 120 countries achieve this benchmark level. The most open (transparent) national budgets are Georgia (87), South Africa (86), New Zealand and Sweden (both 85) (International Budget Partnership, 2022).

The Open Budget Survey also measures the extent to which governments include the public in budget decision making and monitoring, as well as the role and effectiveness of the legislature and the supreme audit institution in the budget process.

When it comes to inclusion of the public no country reaches the benchmark of 61. South Korea is highest at 59. And the most open countries are not necessarily near the top of the rankings for public inclusion. Sweden, for example, has a score of only 15 for public inclusion and South Africa's score is 19.

Regarding oversight, Germany is the top-ranked with 91, with Norway and South Korea with 87. At the other end of the rankings, Sudan, Yemen and Qatar have scores of 6 out of 100.

Ethics and ethical decision making

Ethics are the moral values and beliefs about right and wrong an individual has that guide behaviour. These values and beliefs can be about things like:

- honesty;
- management or leadership style;
- having a public service ethos;
- respect, for self and for others;
- risk-taking; and
- being a good citizen.

When it comes to public financial management it is important that decisions and actions are ethical, although they can be real or principle based. Rule-based ethics concerns judging whether an action is right or wrong based on its adherence to a set of rules. Principle-based ethics judge actions based on their adherence to wider principles.

Gardner (2007: 54–5) recognizes that an individual leader's ethics are tested when they or their organization is under pressure. In terms of public sector financial management, this might be when a public manager is tempted to 'bend the rules' to claim some extra income from a grant giver or to report an expense in the wrong accounting period or renege on a contract commitment in order to save money. Gardner's advice is: 'if you are a leader, the best way for you to retain an ethical compass is to believe doing so is essential for the good of your organization.' Or, as Dr Martin Luther King Jr (1964) put it:

> The time is always right to do the right thing.

Unfortunately, too many public managers and politicians fall short of this standard. Doig (2006: 17–18) wrote that there is a tendency for government to assume that the ethical framework is robust even though the evidence suggests otherwise.

> There are cases of schools finding ways to improve SATs and other exam results, of police massaging clear-up figures, of hospitals rigging waiting lists, of public appointments made for personal and political ends and, most

> recently, of GPs using surgery appointment timetabling to meet the financial and performance targets of waiting times set by the government.
>
> Doig (2006: 19)

The statistics about the level of fraud committed within and against the public sector in the United Kingdom reported in Chapter 4 also suggest that the ethical framework is not robust enough.

The seven principles of public life

A British parliamentary scandal in the United Kingdom in the early 1990s about MPs' unethical conduct (such as allegations of receiving money in return for laying down parliamentary questions and instances of members of Parliament taking up posts after they left government with businesses they had dealt with as ministers) resulted in the creation by John Major of the Committee on Standards in Public Life. The Committee was chaired by Lord Nolan from 1994 to 1997 and its first report, *Standards in Public Life* (1995), included a statement of the seven principles of public life that should be adhered to by all who are involved with public service. The Committee on Standards in Public Life reviewed the principles in 2013. They did not change the principles but they amended the descriptions that accompany them. The principles, with amended descriptions, are listed in Box 8.1.

BOX 8.1 THE SEVEN PRINCIPLES OF PUBLIC LIFE

Selflessness

Holders of public office should take decisions solely in terms of the public interest.

Integrity

Holders of public office must avoid placing themselves under any obligation to people or organizations that might try inappropriately to influence them in their work. They should not act or take decisions in order to gain financial or other material benefits for themselves, their family or their friends. They must declare and resolve any interests and relationships.

Objectivity

Holders of public office must act and take decisions impartially, fairly and on merit, using the best evidence and without discrimination or bias.

Accountability

Holders of public office are accountable to the public for their decisions and actions and must submit themselves to the scrutiny necessary to ensure this.

Openness

Holders of public office should act and take decisions in an open and transparent manner. Information should not be withheld from the public unless there are clear and lawful reasons for so doing.

Honesty

Holders of public office should be truthful.

Leadership

Holders of public office should exhibit these principles in their own behaviour. They should actively promote and robustly support the principles and be willing to challenge poor behaviour wherever it occurs.

Source: Committee on Standards in Public Life, 2013

Having a set of principles or values for public officials to adhere to is not new. In the Palazzo Pubblico (town hall) in Siena, built in the fourteenth century, there are three frescoes by Ambrogio Lorenzetti collectively known as the *Allegory and Effects of Good and Bad Government*. They are located in the room where the city's governors, the Council of Nine, deliberated. The *Effects of Good Government* shows a prosperous city with fields ready for harvest, whilst the *Effects of Bad Government* shows diseased citizens, crumbling buildings and drought-ridden fields. The message to the Council of Nine about their responsibility to the city was clear: whenever they met, govern well and the city will prosper, govern badly and the city will wither and die.

The Committee on Standards in Public Life stated that the seven principles should be adhered to by 'all who serve the public in any way' (1995: 14), whether they are paid or unpaid, elected or appointed. This means that politicians, civil servants, every employee of public bodies, members of boards, trustees and volunteers are all expected to meet these very high standards at all times. They must, therefore, be adhered to in respect of the management of public money, whether by qualified accountants (who are also subject to professional ethics) employed as the chief finance officers of massive organizations or volunteers who find themselves handling cash for a small charity.

The principles of accountability and honesty are perhaps the two principles most closely related to the public manager's role in terms of handling money. Other principles are relevant, too. There is an expectation that public managers will always make decisions in the 'public interest', whatever that is. (Emerson [2006: 47] distinguishes the idealized, Platonic vision of public good, which is typical in European countries, from the American notion, which holds that the public interest at any time is what the public say it is.) If public managers made financial decisions that were subjective and in their self-interest, they would make the wrong decision whenever there was a conflict between their self-interest and the public interest.

Threats to ethical behaviour

An individual's integrity and compliance with ethics can be threatened in numerous ways. Recall the description of the fraud triangle in Chapter 4 for some insight into this.

More substantively, there are six classes of threat outlined below. The first five threats above are relevant in the private or the public sectors. This sixth threat, about political bias, is specific to the public sector, where there are elected politicians controlling the organizations.

- **Self-interest**—the threat that a financial or other interest will inappropriately influence an individual's judgement or behaviour. Public managers and politicians should therefore avoid having interests that would conflict with their work.
- **Self-review**—the threat that a previous judgement or piece of work will not be appropriately evaluated because the individual or a colleague did the original work.
- **Advocacy**—the risk that an individual's objectivity will be compromised because they are promoting a client's or an employing organization's position.
- **Familiarity**—the threat that a long and/or close relationship with a client or employing organization will affect objectivity or independence.
- **Intimidation**—the threat that an individual will be deterred from acting ethically because of actual or perceived pressures, including attempts to exercise undue influence over the individual.
- **Political bias**—the threat that there could be pressure to espouse a particular political viewpoint rather than give objective, neutral advice.

Given all these possible threats to an accountant's compliance with the ethical standards expected of them, the primary safeguard is for the accountant to be vigilant, always considering whether what they are doing is ethical.

One tool that can help with this is the SELF test. In making decisions, the accountant, and anyone else in a public sector organization for that matter, should ensure that it meets the following:

- **Scrutiny**—will your decision withstand public scrutiny by the community, and oversight bodies?
- **Ethical**—is your decision ethical and in compliance with our policies, practices or procedures? Does your decision comply with our Code of Ethics and our professional and ethical standards?
- **Lawful**—is your decision lawful having regard to the law, regulations and instructions?
- **Fair**—is your decision fair with respect to the community, your colleagues, your family, yourself and others?

WHAT IS ACCOUNTING?

Accounting is a system of recording, analysing and summarizing the transactions that occur as a result of an organization's activities. Every transaction needs to be recorded for future use and for reference. As you will see later, recording a transaction requires rules for recognition (in what period is the transaction recorded) and measurement (what is the money value to be used for the transaction).

Analysing transactions requires categorizing into accounts and ledgers, so that similar/related items are collected together. The categorization of transactions allows information to be analysed in different ways, such as analysing spending by its nature (salaries, transport, equipment, etc.) or by its objective (programme A, service B, etc.).

Large PBEs may have thousands (even millions) of transactions every day, so they have to be summarized in order to be useful to decision-makers and others.

Accounting information is important to PBEs. Whilst they do not make profits (except perhaps state-owned enterprises) they need to know whether they are spending more than they are receiving and they need to keep track of who owes them money and who they owe money to. And, as explained earlier in this chapter, as well as using accounting information for internal management decisions, PBEs are expected to be accountable for what they have done with public money.

Double-entry bookkeeping

The earliest accounting records date back 7,000 years and were discovered in what was ancient Mesopotamia (Ezzamel and Hoskin, 2002). Single-entry bookkeeping is a system that is simply a list of entries in a journal or ledger. There may be separate pages or columns for receipts and payments and/or for transactions relating to different periods or types of transaction, nut each transaction is recorded once only. These are books of account that look something like a bank statement.

Double-entry bookkeeping was first described in a school textbook by Luca Pacioli published in 1494. The book was titled *Summa de Arithmetica, Geometria, Proportioni et Proportionalità* (meaning 'Everything about Arithmetic, Geometry and Proportion'), and the description of the accounting practices of merchants in Venice was just one of the many topics it covered. The distinction, and major advantage, of double-entry bookkeeping is that every transaction has two entries, a debit and a credit, that balance each other out.

The origin of the words 'debit' and 'credit', like the double-entry system itself, is in Italy. Debit derives from *debito*, meaning 'he owes me', and credit derives from *credito*, meaning 'he trusts me' to pay him. In mediaeval times a person running a business might not need to keep complicated accounts but they would need to keep a list of debts owed to them and the debts they owed to other people. What Pacioli (and presumably other merchants and bankers) noticed was that when financial transactions were made, two things happened. For example, when some supplies are bought by a shop using cash, the cash balance goes down and the value of stock (or inventory) increases by the same amount; when the same supplies is bought on credit the amount owed to creditors goes up and so does stock; when the debt to the supplier is settled (paid off) the creditors balance falls and so does the cash balance.

The system of double-entry bookkeeping means that at all times the total value of the debits must equal the total value of the credits. This helps an organization keep control of their finances because if the totals do not agree then there is one or more transactions that have not been entered completely and accurately. This is a fundamental control within a double-entry accounting system and computerized systems are designed so that it is not possible to make an entry which does not balance. The same control is required for manual ledger-based accounting systems but there is greater potential for arithmetic errors occurring than with a computerized system.

In one's personal life all manner of systems might be used to keep track of one's finances—or no system at all. In the case of organizations, all but the smallest of them would use a system based on double-entry bookkeeping. Similarly, all but the smallest would use a computerized system although the level of functionality might be considerably different. Regardless of the bookkeeping system, though, there are two main bases for accounting: cash and accruals.

Cash-basis accounting

Accounting requires rules for the recognition and measurement of transactions. The easiest way to maintain accounts (whether using double-entry or single-entry bookkeeping) is to recognize a transaction only when money is paid out or received (as the case may be). If a supplier delivered some goods but you did not pay for them until a month later, the transaction would show up in your accounts only after the payment was made. Similarly, if you sell something on credit the sale is entered in the accounts only when the creditor settles their debt. Accounts drawn up in this way are said to be on the 'cash basis' or the 'receipts and payments basis'.

One advantage of cash-based accounting is that it is based in fact. Transactions are recorded only when cash changes hands, and this is something that either has happened or not. There will be (or should be) receipts and other documentation to support and justify every transaction.

Whilst relatively straightforward to do, and being based on facts, cash-based accounts do not necessarily give the full picture of an organization's finances at any point in time. Cash-based accounts do not show if an organization has sold a lot of goods and is awaiting payment from its debtors, nor does it show if goods have been acquired on credit and the organization has debts to settle.

Cash-based accounts show whether the organization has a positive or negative cash balance at any point in time (i.e., whether there is cash in hand or an overdraft), but they do not show whether a profit or loss has been made. (Or in the case of a public or third-sector body, whether a surplus or deficit has been made.) This might be critically important to a user of the accounts. For instance, a bank or other lender would want to know the extent of other debts owed by the organization before agreeing to loan any money.

The traditional approach to financial reporting by PBEs used cash based accounting (Hodges and Mellett, 2003: 102). To get a fuller picture of an organization's financial position, though, it is necessary to draw up the accounts on what is called the 'accruals basis' or 'income and expenditure basis'.

Accrual accounting

Accrual accounting is based on the principle of matching income and expenditure to the time period when a transaction occurs rather than when payments are made or received. This means that a transaction is recognized at the point the goods or services are received by an organization rather than at some future time(s) when the associated payment(s) is/are made. The measurement of transactions can often be the amount of the cash payment(s) just like cash-basis accounting, but not always. If there are long delays between the economic incidence of a transaction and actual payments or receipts, there might need to be an adjustment to the nominal value of the transaction to reflect the time value of money. Because of situations like this, therefore, transactions are measured at fair value or open market value.

The matching of expenditure to time periods also requires the concept of depreciation to be employed to spread the expense of investing in fixed assets (see 'capital expenditure' later in this chapter) over the period of time that the assets will be used by the organization. Where the asset was bought using a loan that is repaid in annual instalments the accounting entries would be broadly similar under cash accounting and accrual accounting. However, if the fixed asset were bought from the organization's existing cash balance the entries would be markedly different: cash accounting would incur the full charge in the year the asset is bought whereas accrual accounting would spread the charge to the income and expenditure account over the number of years that the fixed asset is expected to be used by the organization.

Another feature of accruals-based accounting is the balance sheet (more formally called the statement of financial position). Cash-based accounting does not have a balance sheet because the only balance that exists is the cash balance. Accrual accounting makes time-based adjustments in the income and expenditure account, both relating to the past and the future, and the balance sheet holds the amounts that are yet to be charged to the income and expenditure account.

This can be illustrated with the example of a fixed asset, such as a vehicle. Under accrual accounting the expense of the vehicle has to be charged to the income and expenditure account to match the vehicle's useful life. If the vehicle costs $50,000 to buy and has, say, five years of useful life, and at the end of five years the vehicle will have zero value, then the simplest thing is to charge $10,000 each year for five years.

When the vehicle is acquired for $50,000, the cash balance falls by $50,000. Under cash accounting there would be a balancing item of $50,000 as an expense in the current year's income and expenditure account. Under accrual accounting this cannot be done and instead a fixed asset is created with the value of $50,000. Then each year $10,000 is charged as an expense in the income and expenditure account and the fixed asset value falls by $10,000. The balance sheet, therefore, holds the uncharged element of the fixed asset until it is charged to the income and expenditure account.

Similar transaction processes are used for all assets and liabilities and at any point in time the balance sheet holds all the organization's assets and liabilities, and also the reserves (or equity) that are a special kind of liability. The following formula always holds:

$$\text{Assets} - \text{Liabilities} = \text{Equity}$$

Accrual accounting has the advantage of showing a fuller picture of the financial affairs of an organization. Rowles (2004: 65) said: 'possession of accrual accounting information ... provides a comparative advantage to entities that possess and employ it.' In business, apart from anything else, accrual accounting allows profits and losses to be identified and measured, thus enabling the trading of shares and all kinds of financial deal-making.

The accrual basis also fits with all three objectives of PFM. It provides a fuller picture of a PBE's financial position because it includes liabilities that will be paid in future years. It improves the allocation of resources because programmes or departments are charged with the cost of resources they consume, regardless of the account from which payment is made. And it improves financial accountability because citizens have a fuller picture of the cost of their public services and projects.

Unlike cash-basis accounting, accrual accounting requires opinion and not just facts. There are lots and lots of judgements made by an organization's managers and accountants whilst preparing financial statements. The depreciation charges mentioned above require estimates of the current value of assets and their useful lifetimes. Judgements also have to be made about the likelihood of debtors paying their debts in full, the usefulness or obsolescence of inventory items and many more items.

All of these judgements makes the creation and use of accounting standards (rules for where and how judgements should be made) and auditing (review that accounting standards have been complied with) critically important. Users of accounts need assurance about the judgements that have been made before they can rely on the information in statements of account.

The overall benefits of accrual-based accounting means more governments and their PBEs are adopting it for their financial reporting. IFAC and CIPFA's (2021) report identifies that 49 jurisdictions had adopted accrual accounting by 2020. They also report that a further 34 plan to adopt the accruals basis by 2025 and 120 by 2030 (which would be over 70 per cent of the jurisdictions included in the study).

This move towards accrual accounting is positive and will perhaps reveal a substantial store of government-owned net assets that could be used for service delivery (or sold if they are surplus to requirement). Harris, Senhadji and Tieman (2019) note that, on average, advanced economies have more assets but lower net worth than emerging economies because they tend to have larger liabilities for things like pensions and welfare benefits. Adopting accrual accounting might therefore be particularly beneficial to emerging economies because it could reveal to decision-makers (and citizens) a hidden store of value.

Providing a fuller picture about a PBE's financial position may, also, prove uncomfortable for those in charge. Accrual accounting requires the disclosure not just of liabilities that are certain, but also 'contingent liabilities', being estimates of the amounts an organization is liable to pay but there is some uncertainty about the value and/or the timing. The nature of public services means that PBEs often find themselves taking on such liabilities, and perhaps not always realizing it.

> Governments in all advanced economies indemnify households against unemployment, disability, illness, and other income losses or expenses;

> many indemnify firms against assorted risks such as changes in prices, interest rates, and exchange rates, and natural or environmental disasters. [PBEs] also accumulate contingent liabilities by guaranteeing personal and business loans and various other transactions.
>
> (Schick, 2013: 48)

In practice, many governments and PBEs that have adopted accrual accounting do not include on their balance sheets the full extent of their contingent liabilities and this is explained later.

Another issue for politicians to address is the difference between the income and expenditure recognized in the accounts differs, perhaps very significantly, from the cash flow of receipts and payments. This difference can lead to governments using the cash basis for budgeting, since it allows them to set tax yields based on the cash flow. This causes issues of a difference between the budget and the financial reports that has to be reconciled and explained. It also means that when politicians are engaged in budget preparation and approval, they are basing their decisions on the cash basis and not the accruals basis. This is why Bandy and Metcalfe (2021: 9) called for governments to adopt accruals-based budgeting as well as accounting.

It is costly and time consuming to make the change from cash-based accounting to accrual accounting. It would be a major change programme and this would need:

- trained staff (to implement the programme and, subsequently, to operate the system);
- IT systems;
- collection of masses of data about assets and liabilities;
- commitment from politicians and senior managers to the programme;
- funding (for multiple years);
- training of politicians and other public managers to be able to make proper use of the improved and fuller financial information; and
- explanation and understanding of the impact that the new accounting basis will have on reported finances.

The move from cash-based accounting to accrual accounting by the United Kingdom's central government bodies took place under a programme called Resource Accounting, which began in 1994. The UK Government produced the first accounts using accruals in 2001. It was ten more years, though, before it could produce whole of government accounts (WGA) that consolidated the (accrual-based) accounts of over 1,500 public bodies (see later in this chapter for more about WGA).

Institutions like IFAC and the World Bank are encouraging governments to adopt accrual accounting in order to improve the quality of information to support policy and decision making, but legitimate questions could be asked about whether it is worth the investment.

> No complete cost-benefit analysis of accrual reporting has been done, probably because of the difficulty of placing a financial value on the hoped-for benefits, such as transparency and accountability.
>
> (Blondy et al., 2013: 267)

Whilst there may not be any complete cost-benefit analyses, Blondy et al. report that the cost of implementing an accrual reporting regime in the central government of the Netherlands was estimated at €129 million initially and at least €13 million a year thereafter (2013: 267).

Modified cash accounting

Accounting systems are not binary. It is possible for organizations to adopt a hybrid form, whether that is modification of the cash basis or accrual basis. The IFAC and CIPFA (2021), in reporting about the status of adoption of accrual accounting, identified 66 of the 165 jurisdictions (40 per cent) as using a partial version of accrual accounting.

Modified cash accounting (sometimes referred to as modified accrual accounting) is a system that uses the cash basis (recognizing transactions at the point when cash changes hands) for income and expenses, including short-term assets and liabilities. This means debtors, inventory and creditors are accounted for on the cash basis, and therefore do not appear on the balance sheet. Long-term assets and liabilities are accounted for using accruals and therefore are included on the balance sheet and depreciation has to be used to amortize the value of fixed assets into the income and expenditure account.

The modified cash (or accrual) basis of accounting seeks an acceptable balance between improving on the shortcomings of cash-based accounting without requiring the full implementation of accruals-based accounting. There are no official global accounting standards for these bases of accounting; they will be context-specific to the countries using them.

Assets and liabilities still exist whether a government uses accrual accounting, cash-based accounting or some modified version that is unique to itself. Metcalfe and Taylor (2020) proposed that PBEs without full accrual-based accounting could still take a 'balance sheet approach' to decision making. This means taking into account the impact of decisions on an organization's assets and liabilities, both at the time of the decision and in the future. For example, if a government decides to recruit additional civil servants in order to deliver a new programme, then it should recognize that the financial cost is not only the salary payments, but also future pension rights. Thinking in this way may cause the government to consider alternative ways of achieving its desired outcomes.

CHARACTERISTICS OF PUBLIC SECTOR ACCOUNTING

Public sector accounting is broadly the same as private sector accounting but there are some conceptual and practical differences.

Capital and operating expenditure

A critical distinction in accounting is between capital and operating expenses. In simple terms, capital expenditure is expenditure on assets that provide long-term benefit to the organization (that is, for more than one year). This would be, for example, the purchase of land and buildings, construction projects, major computer application projects and, in the case of public bodies, the giving of grants to third parties for them to incur capital expenditure of their own.

Private sector businesses have distinguished capital and operating expenses, too. Both the private and the public sectors use capital expenditure as a term. In the private sector capital expenditure results in the creation of an asset that is expected to generate sales revenue over a number of years (such as the purchase of a new machine to manufacture widgets, or a whole factory, or a fleet of delivery vehicles, or a computer system or even buying another company). The asset is called a fixed asset (or non-current asset) and its value would be spread over its useful life (as a depreciation charge) in order to match the use of the asset with the revenue (income) it generates.

Aside from state-owned enterprises, public sector capital expenditure is not intended to lead to cash inflows in the future. In fact, it will do the opposite because the public sector capital expenditure might result in a fixed asset that will bring benefits over a number of years (although rarely will the benefits be in the form of sales income), but it also might result in something that will bring only liabilities over future years. For example, the acquisition of land to use as a park or as a non-toll road will cause the organization to have to pay for the maintenance and repair of the park or road for many years without receiving any income. The capital expenditure thus produces some public value when people use the park or drive along the road but at an ongoing cost to the organization.

PBEs can also incur capital expenditure when they give a grant to another organization for the latter to use to finance its own capital expenditure on acquiring land, construction or whatever. In such a case the PBE has incurred expenditure and has nothing to show for it, in terms of legal title. This is a problem in accounting terms because the organization cannot show in its accounts that it has a fixed asset in return for incurring the capital expenditure. In such cases the PBE shows the grant as an operating expense and matches it with the relevant source of funding for the grant. This has a net zero impact on the overall level of operating expenditure so it does not disadvantage the taxpayer. However, the gross expenditure for the accounting period is increased and this can cause problems of comparison if the giving of grants occurs in some periods and not others.

It is possible to have capital income, too. These are referred to as capital receipts and they occur when a PBE disposes of its land or buildings or other fixed assets.

Operating expenditure

In short, operating expenditure and income is everything that is not capital expenditure or income. It covers items that are consumed in the short term (that is, within a year). It includes expenditure on:

- staff wages, salaries and pensions;
- supplies and services;
- running costs of vehicles and other transport expenses;
- repair and maintenance of premises, equipment and vehicles;
- rent of premises;
- lease rentals;
- interest payments; and
- depreciation charges.

Operating income includes:

- taxes, duties and levies;
- fees and charges;
- non-capital grants and donations;
- interest received; and
- income from investments.

In the public sector operating expenditure is sometimes referred to as revenue expenditure and this can be confusing. In private sector accounting, revenue is a noun and it means 'income'. A private sector accountant or manager might talk about, 'sales revenue' or 'revenue for the year to date'. In the public sector revenue is sometimes used as an adjective, meaning 'non-capital' and so a public sector accountant or manager might talk about 'revenue expenditure' or 'the revenue cost of implementing project X'.

Fund accounting

A fund is an amount of money whose use has been limited by the donor, grant giver or other individuals or organizations or by law. National and local governments and other PBEs tend to use fund accounting in order to capture the transactions separately according to which fund they relate to.

The source of funds and how they are applied can often matter very much in PBEs. For example, if a government operates a social insurance fund for citizens, then it matters that all the deductions from citizen's incomes are credited to the fund, and the payment of benefits debited to it.

Charities and other non-profit organizations can often be obliged to operate separate funds because some of the resources it receives are restricted for use on a specified purpose. For example, a donor to a cancer charity may request their donation is spent on cancer research rather than on hospices or palliative care and this money would have to be accounted for as part of a restricted fund. For each fund a set of financial statements can be produced and therefore the organization's overall financial statements would be a consolidation of its funds' financial statements.

This kind of accounting could be done by a business but it is unlikely to be so important to them. Sales income is unlikely to be received with some kinds of limitation or restriction on it. Therefore, whilst a business might design its accounting system in a way that would allow the business to analyse sales income and expenses by product line or by geographic region (say), this is not the same as fund accounting.

Often there will be a fund for transactions that are not restricted by the donor or grant giver. This might be called the General Fund or Consolidated Fund or some similar term.

If a PBE has two or more funds, then each fund requires a separate income and expenditure account and balance sheet. To do this requires the PBE to set up its accounting system in a way that it captures, for each and every transaction, which fund it relates to. It can then produce accounting statements for each fund separately and also a consolidated statement covering all the PBE's funds. This could be done by having separate bank accounts for each fund but this is not necessary if the bookkeeping within the accounting system records the fund information for each transaction.

The use of fund accounting puts more of an emphasis on accountability because it requires the PBE to demonstrate what money it received for various purposes and what it did with it. Funds are used by governments and PBEs because people who give money to them, whether as taxpayers, aid donors or lenders, are much more likely to be interested to know how that money was spent than a customer who buys a product from a business.

Accrual accounting in the public sector

There has been a trend for PBEs to move from cash accounting to accruals accounting as one aspect of NPM (new public management) and this was discussed in Chapter 1. 'In the past, [accrual-based accounting] information was "good to have," now it is "must have"' (Schick, 2013: 56).

Accruals-based accounts give the reader more information about an organization's financial affairs because it matches accounting transactions to the relevant accounting period. As explained in Chapter 1, accruals-based accounting supports the major objectives of PFM. An important factor for PBEs, particularly governments, is that accrual accounts make clear the extent of their assets and liabilities. 'Contemporary governments are holders of an enormous range of risks for society, some explicitly recognized in guarantees and insurance schemes, some based only on the expectation that government will provide assistance if certain contingencies [floods, for example] occur' (Schick, 2013: 35). Accrual accounting puts a value on these risks and places them on the balance sheet—or at least it should.

> Although nondisclosure of fiscal risks has traditionally been the norm, the trend to greater disclosure among countries at all levels of development is increasing. In general, more developed economies have higher levels of disclosure.
>
> Budina and Petrie (2013: 190)

Even so, as will be explained later, not all of the guarantees and public expectations are recognized in government accounts.

One issue that stems from the move to accrual accounting by PBEs is how non-exchange transactions should be accounted for. Non-exchange transactions generally do not apply to the private sector so this issue does not arise for them. As mentioned in Chapter 3, tax collection and the awarding of grants and donations do not have equal, or approximately equal, exchanges in return. In cash-accounting terms, this would not be a problem: the transaction would be recorded in the accounting period when the payment or receipt was made. It can be difficult to identify the correct value and accounting period for tax transactions and it is difficult to have an accounting system that can reliably record transactions in the correct accounting period at a reasonable cost (Jones and Pendlebury, 2010: 123).

It is difficult to account for taxes on the accrual basis for two main reasons:

- It is difficult to identify the correct accounting period for when tax transactions occur.
- It is difficult to have an accounting system that can reliably record transactions in the correct accounting period at a reasonable cost (Jones and Pendlebury, 2010: 123).

For many taxes the government has to wait until a return is completed, possibly many months after the period to which it relates, to have an indication of the tax income due. On top of this it would still have to estimate the extent of tax that ought to have been declared by taxpayers but has not been if the accounts are to show the true, gross amount of tax income due in a particular period. There may also be a longer period (it is six years in the United Kingdom) during which tax returns can be amended (up or down). Even with tax that is collected through a PAYE system, at the point of a salary being paid the information is the employer's, not the government's, so it is not straightforward for the government to enter into its accounts the income due. All in all, it could take a government several years after the end of a financial year before it could close its accounts. In practice, these problems mean that the receipts and payments basis of accounting for tax is likely to remain in use for many governments even when the remainder of the financial statements are accruals-based (Jones and Pendlebury, 2010: 123).

Organizations (private as well as public) should include liabilities in their accounts (i.e., on their balance sheets) when they have little or no discretion to avoid the payment in the future. This is clear enough in connection with supplies: if an order has been placed and goods received by the organization then it is obliged to pay the invoice. But governments and public bodies might have made pledges and other commitments that are not legally binding but which third parties have an expectation to receive. How much of a commitment has to be made before the liability is included on the balance sheet? There is little guidance on this but public bodies tend to include the liability on their balance sheet only when an amount is due and payable or the eligibility criteria for a payment has been met. This would also apply when recognizing assets, such as the amount of tax income due.

Public pensions is an interesting example to consider in this light. Many countries have a national, public pension scheme to provide for retirement, disability and death pensions on the basis of defined benefits. These schemes are rarely funded in the way a company would have a pension fund; instead, they are financed on a pay-as-you-go basis. What this means is that the taxes being paid by current taxpayers is being used to pay out pensions to current pensioners. As populations are ageing and the proportion of workers to pensioners changes it is easy to imagine that there is an imbalance; that the government has got into a position where its future liabilities for pensions have outgrown its future contributions. Indeed, given the figures mentioned above for the net liabilities in the pension schemes of the United States and the United Kingdom that are just for public employees, the liabilities for the wider population must be enormous.

It could be argued that the value of this difference is in effect a public debt and should be included on the government's balance sheet. Actually, current accounting practice in the public sector does not include this debt (although some governments do include the equivalent debt [liability] for the occupational pension schemes they operate for civil servants and military personnel). The argument for not including this debt is that a citizen has an entitlement to benefits only when they have met the criteria of, for example, meeting the retirement age and having made contributions for a sufficient number of years). There is also the possibility that a government could pass legislation to change the scheme and the future pension entitlements of citizens.

Irwin (2019) poses a different, interesting question about the valuation for long-term government borrowing by issuing bonds. There are three common methods for such valuations:

- face value, where the nominal amount of the bond is used for the whole term;
- market value, where the value will fluctuate during the term of the debt to reflect the market price of bonds; and
- amortized cost, where initially the debt is valued as the principal amount plus a premium that reflects the perceived creditworthiness the government and during the term the premium amount is amortized.

There are problems with all of these methods, with the potential for two governments issuing the same amount of bonds but report quite different amounts of indebtedness. Irwin's proposal is that, instead of the above, governments should use the 'policy value, which is the cost to the government of carrying out its policies.' This means that if, for example, the government's policy is to honour its debt, then it would use the present value of its payments of interest and the redemption of the principal, using the risk-free interest rate as the discount rate.

The award of grants can also lead to accounting difficulties under accruals-based accounting. If a grant is awarded to a PBE on condition of attaining a certain performance and being repayable if the performance is too poor, then it is akin to an exchange transaction and the recipient organization could account for it as income in each relevant accounting period by reference to its achievement (or not) of the performance target. However, if the donor organization is a PBE, too, it would account for the grant on a similar basis, provided it gets details of performance to know if and how much of the grant is repayable. But what about unconditional grants for capital projects? The principle of matching might say the grant income should be spread over the useful lifetime of the capital asset but the donor would want to show the donation as a one-off expenditure item.

The application of other accounting principles designed with for-profit organizations in mind can also cause problems. The move to accrual accounting has often been accompanied by another NPM innovation: a split of the democratic, service-commissioning aspect of government away from the operational, service delivery aspects. In the United Kingdom this started in the 1980s with the creation of 'Next Steps' agencies and today there are hundreds of NDPBs (even after the cull in 2010), each producing their own accounts.

The split of government into commissioner and provider elements suggests that business accounting principles could be applied but there can be problems.

Barton (2004) describes how in 2000/1 the Australian Department of Defence was the country's most profitable organization. The Department had a turnover of AUS$17.1 billion from the sale of defence services to the government, reported a surplus of AUS$6.4 billion and paid a dividend back to the government of AUS$5.0 billion (2004: 281). This arose because the government was both the owner (equivalent to shareholder) of the provider organization and its sole customer. The government therefore provided capital funding to the Department and expected a return on its investment; and to generate the return on investment the Department had to sell its services to the government at a profit.

Issues with fair value accounting

Accounting systems are very good at capturing payments and receipts and, therefore, the easiest way to compile accounts is to value each transaction using the amount of money that was paid/received. Accounts that are compiled using this approach are said to be on a 'historic cost basis' because all the amounts are captured with their value at that point in time. However, the value of items varies over time (usually, but not always, rising). This is especially the case for fixed assets like land and buildings. Historic cost accounting does not reflect such changes. To address this, the production of accounts on the basis of 'fair value' has become favoured and enshrined in accrual-based accounting standards.

Fair value is the amount for which an asset could be exchanged, or a liability settled, between knowledgeable, willing parties in an arm's length transaction (IPSASB, 2022: 232). For a private sector company, showing its assets at their fair value is more helpful to potential investors than their historic cost—if nothing else they indicate (although only roughly) how much the assets might be sold for if the company were liquidated.

To maintain accounts on this basis requires regular revaluation of assets and liabilities to reflect the prevailing fair value rather than how much was paid to acquire the asset in the first place (something that is recorded once and never has to be reviewed). The difference between the fair value of an asset or liability and its historic cost is either an accounting gain or accounting loss and these amounts have to be recorded in the accounts, too. However, if an asset is sold, the sale is recorded at the actual sale value and the accounting gain or loss will be replaced by the actual gain or loss that was realized when the sale was made.

Carnegie and West (2003: 84) explain why this is a relevant practice for private sector accounting: 'within entities that have primarily commercial objectives everything is ultimately for sale if the pursuit of those objectives or other circumstances require it.' It may be the case that there are PBEs where everything is sellable, too, but more often that would not be the case. As Ellwood and Newbury put it, 'The balance sheet focus does not fit well with a public service perspective. The matching principle is valuable in determining comparable performance data, but wealth creation has little relevance in the context of [PBEs]' (Ellwood and Newbury, 2006: 31).

Carnegie and West (2003: 86) go further, stating they are not against accrual accounting by PBEs but that the adoption of a one-size-fits-all approach to accounting standards is not appropriate. 'Non-financial resources are not financial assets and have no legitimate place in the statements of financial position of public sector organisations which pursue social objectives.' Indeed, there are two classes of assets where the fair value accounting approach is problematic, if not inappropriate, for a PBE. These are heritage assets and infrastructure assets.

Heritage assets

Heritage assets are 'land and buildings of historical importance, artefacts and artworks, often in museum collections' (Jones and Pendlebury, 2010: 121). Where a PBE holds such assets—possibly held in trust rather than owned—they are not held for the purpose of deriving economic benefits (Carnegie and West, 2003: 84). Such assets are likely to be held for the public good, quite possibly not even for public display.

The definition of fair value invokes the concept of a willing exchange between knowledgeable parties, but there is often no market for heritage assets making the assignment of a fair value difficult. Nevertheless, accounting standards require such values to be ascertained and used in financial statements. It is a waste of time and effort, say Carnegie and West, to assign financial values to items that will never be for sale and could never be replaced. Such values are 'accounting fictions' (2003: 85).

Carnegie and West's article (2005) gives several examples of the meaninglessness of the valuation of heritage assets. The Australia Museum's '2001 annual report disclosed in a note that its collection had been valued at $4,083 million, but added that "the [collection] valuation exercise ... was not considered to be reliable"' and so the collection was not classified as an asset in the statement of financial position (2005: 911). The following year the museum declined to include a value in the notes to its accounts. Meanwhile, Museum Victoria, which has a similar-sized collection, reported its value as AUS$218 million and AUS$227 million in 2001 and 2002, respectively (2005: 911).

Carnegie and West also give examples of library collections being valued in financial terms and commenting that the 'essential "value" of a library collection resides in its capacity to meet the needs and interests of its users and serve as a repository for documents and other artefacts of historical significance and cultural value' (2005: 912).

Perhaps the key issue in valuing heritage assets is captured in Carnegie and West's story about the Eureka Flag, which is the symbol of an 1850s uprising by goldminers that has acquired iconic status within Australia. The city of Ballarat holds the Eureka Flag and valued it at $10 million, apparently because the mounted hide of Phar Lap, another Australian icon, had been valued at AUS$10 million. The mayor of the city of Ballarat is reported as saying 'the true value of the flag could never be recorded in dollars' and that it was 'priceless' (Danaher, 2000 cited by Carnegie and West, 2005: 913).

Infrastructure assets

The issue with infrastructure assets (such as roads, tunnels, bridges, streetlights, water supply, sewerage and drainage systems and other networks) is slightly different from the issue in respect of heritage assets, but it is connected with the notion that the assets are not, realistically, sellable to anyone. Accounting standards require PBEs that are responsible for roads to value them with respect to the value of the land that lies underneath them. If the road were a toll road the land could be valued based on the expected level of future income or profits from toll fees.

There are technical problems, though, with ascertaining the current, fair value for a very long, very thin strip of land from which no income can be earned but on which (significant) expenditure will have to be incurred to maintain its usability. The PBE might have some historic information about the price paid to acquire the land but values vary over time. One possible method would be to value the road based on the values of land adjacent to it. If this could be done there would remain a question mark over it because if the road land were sold and no longer used as a road then the value of the adjacent land would fall, because it had lost its access from the road.

There is a second issue relating to infrastructure assets and that is whether they should be depreciated or not. The standard accounting treatment of long-term fixed assets is that their value is depreciated to reflect the 'wearing out' or 'using up' of the asset over its lifetime. The argument in relation to infrastructure assets is that they have very long useful lives and there is a requirement for frequent repair and maintenance (such as the resurfacing of roads). Instead of depreciating such assets in the usual way, an 'engineer's preference' for depreciation (Jones and Pendlebury, 2010: 122) is to include the cost of maintaining the infrastructure assets in the statement of financial performance (i.e., the operating income and expenditure account). The UK Government and US state and local governments use this engineers' approach to accounting for infrastructure assets (Jones and Pendlebury, 2010: 123).

ACCOUNTING STANDARDS

There's a (bad) joke: if you ask an accountant "What is two plus two?" They will reply: "What do you want it to be?" Users of accounts do not want to guess about how they have been compiled. They want to be able to compare the statements of two organizations, or even the same organization over a number of years. This is the basic reason why accounting standards exist.

The need for accounting standards

Accounts drawn up on the cash basis of accounting are objective because each accounting record is accounted for on the date the cash changed hands and its value is the value of the cash involved. There is no need for any estimates or judgements to be made. Accrual accounting, on the other hand, involves lots and lots of estimates and judgements. Accountants have to judge which period or periods a transaction relates to, and how to value transactions for things like depreciation, impairment of debts and the value of inventories.

Where subjective judgement is involved, it is possible for many different results to emerge from the same set of underlying transactions, but it is important for users of accounts (auditors, investors, suppliers, customers, employees, etc.) to be able to trust the consistency of the accounts—consistency between organizations and consistency of an organization's accounts over time. To achieve this consistency requires accounts to be prepared in accordance with a prescribed set of accounting standards.

The rise of globalization and multinational corporations led to a drive to standardize accounting practices around the world. This led first to the International Federation of Accountants (IFAC) creating a set of International Accounting Standards (IASs). Some of the IASs are still in force but most have been replaced by International Financial Reporting Standards (IFRSs). IFRSs are intended primarily for use by profit-seeking entities and they have been adopted by many countries, but the exceptions include China, India and the United States.

In 2022, 98 out of 175 jurisdictions, including 31 within the European Union/ European Economic Area, require the use of IFRSs for stock-market listed companies (IASPlus, 2022a).

The purpose of accounting standards

In general terms, any set of accounting standards is intended to reduce the differences in financial statements, in particular in relation to:

- the form of statements;
- the definition of the components of statements (i.e., assets, liabilities, incomes, expenses);
- the criteria for recognition of items; and
- the scope and disclosure of financial statements.

The overall purpose of accounting standards is to identify proper accounting practices for the preparation of financial statements. Accounting standards create a common understanding between users and preparers on how particular items are treated.

Should public sector accounting differ from private sector?

Blondy et al. (2013: 259) refer to Jeremy Bentham, an eighteenth-century social reformer who 'hated the idea that the British government might adopt commercial accounting, because he believed that its terminology would make public finances obscure.' A move has been underway in the private sector in recent times to harmonize the accounting standards that apply across different territories and between public and private sectors. Laughlin reports that 'the assumption over many years is that private sector financial reporting and accompanying domestic and international accounting standards, taking aside, for the moment, the narrative reporting requirements, will satisfy some of the accountability needs of PBEs' (Laughlin, 2008: 251).

In the United States the Government Accounting Standards Board takes the view that 'separate accounting and financial reporting standards are essential because the needs of users of financial reports of governments and business enterprises differ' (Laughlin, 2008: 250). This is also the view taken by Ellwood and Newbury because 'business firms do not levy taxes or provide goods freely to customers. The accounting rules for public service organisations and their reporting model should be different from those of commercial firms' (2006: 19).

Whilst there are advantages about being able to compare the financial affairs of organizations across territories, the argument for it is perhaps less strong when it comes to comparing public organizations. The users of private sector accounts include investors and other creditors. They would react to the deterioration in the balance sheet of companies they were interested in but would something similar happen in relation to a public sector balance sheet? Perhaps the answer is yes for those PBEs that could become bankrupt (such as charities and local government in some territories) because their balance sheets could be interpreted in the same way as for a business. For governments, though, the balance sheet could not be interpreted in the same was a private sector one.

Essentially, a private sector balance sheet identifies the organization's wealth: a bigger balance sheet means a wealthier organization. That does not translate to a government; a bigger government balance sheet means a bigger government and, as was mentioned in Chapter 1, there is no consensus about how big a government should be. Also, the examples of whole of government accounts at the end of this chapter show that when the accounts are consolidated, governments often have a considerable negative net worth (and if their full contingent liabilities and guarantees were included on the balance sheet, they would be worth even less). If governments were businesses, they would be bankrupt, but the normal rules of business do not apply to them, even if the accounting techniques are applied to them.

No one can buy and sell shares in a government or PBE in the way that they can for a company so there is not the same driver for consistency between the organizations' financial statements. Nevertheless, there are people who want or need to compare PBEs or make assessments about their financial standing (for example, credit rating agencies) and they would appreciate consistency in PBEs' accounting practices. Having said that, the development of accounting standards, and the expectation that members of professional accounting institutes comply with them, means that PBEs' financial reports have adopted the same accounting standards as used by the private sector, as far as they are able. In the United Kingdom, for example, PBEs were required to adopt the IFRSs with effect from April 2010. The change in accounting practice meant significant changes, in particular to the way that fixed assets were valued and accounted for.

International Public Sector Accounting Standards

The International Public Sector Accounting Standards Board (IPSASB) develops and publishes International Public Sector Accounting Standards (IPSASs) specifically for use by governments and other PBEs. These are secondary accounting standards, which means that they are supplementary to whatever accounting standards are mandated for use in a given jurisdiction (for example, the use of IFRS is mandated for the whole of the EU). IPSASs provide standards for items that are not covered in the accounting standards for the private sector (such as how to account for tax collection) and guidance on how to adapt private sector standards to the public sector context.

IPSASs are based on IFRS and, indeed, they use the same wording as far as possible. There are some IPSASs, however, that do not have an equivalent IAS or IFRS. IPSAS 23, for example, is about the revenue from non-exchange transactions, which is vitally important to any organization that levies taxes but irrelevant to a business. Similarly, IPSAS 42 Social Benefits sets out how governments should account for their liabilities to pay benefits like pensions to people who were not government employees and again this is not something that a company would ever do.

The process of developing IPSASs is thorough and time consuming with consultation on proposals—based on documents called 'exposure drafts'—before any pronouncement is made by the IPSASB. Major changes to IPSASs, or the introduction of a whole new standard, occurs from time to time but there are frequent minor improvements made and there is an annual publication of the complete set of IPSASs (IPSASB, 2022).

Developing IPSASs from existing IASs and IFRSs has a common-sense appeal to it: why go to the trouble and expense of creating a set of accounting standards that are completely new and unique? The problem is that IPSAS can be seen as an afterthought. Laughlin (2008: 250) wrote: 'The implication [...] is that differences between the sectors are so small that the consideration of [PBEs] can be left until all the other major issues have been resolved.'

The differences are not, in fact, small or trivial, and there are issues that arise from use by PBEs of accounting standards that were developed for use by the private sector. This chapter has already outlined some of the issues—the use of accrual accounting and the concept of fair value valuations of things where there is no market.

Carnegie and West (2003) also wrote about the self-interest of accountants. The consultation on exposure drafts, for instance, tends to be responded to by accountants, whether as individuals, accountancy institutes, accounting firms, academics and so on, because the technical nature of the documents makes them accessible only to those with a grounding in accounting. The problem Carnegie and West saw was that private sector accountants were imposing accounting standards on the public sector without necessarily understanding what is different about the sector.

> As Corbett (1996, p. 138) observes, the self-interest of the accounting profession was an important influence on the standard setting agenda: 'there is a large measure of self-serving self-interest in what the accounting profession's senior bodies are trying to do. If they can impose a common set of standards on the public sector, their members, whose experience is mainly in the private sector, will suddenly become experts in what public sector accounts should contain and will thus become eligible to serve as consultant experts and contract auditors.'
>
> (Carnegie and West, 2005: 918)

Heiling (2020) goes a bit further in his article. He observed that 'there is hardly any public university that is not offering courses in IFRS in business studies' and argued that there should be dedicated education and training programmes for public sector accounting.

Other accounting standards

Two of the world's biggest economies do not use IFRS for companies (or IPSAS for public sector organizations). In the United States any company registered with the Securities and Exchange Commission (SEC) is not permitted to use IFRS and must instead comply with the USA's own generally accepted accounting practices (referred to as US GAAP). The SEC published a roadmap in 2008 that indicated there could be a decision about the adoption of IFRS in 2011. That decision was not made and the final staff report (SEC, 2012) did not include any recommendations or an action plan for the convergence of US GAAP with IFRS.

In China, companies are required to use Chinese Accounting Standards for Business Enterprises (CAS), which are largely converged with IFRS. There is a roadmap for the Ministry of Finance to continue its work on converging CAS with IFRS.

Sticking with the public sector there are many countries, including Indonesia, Malaysia, Tanzania, Colombia and Barbados, that use or are in the process of adopting IPSAS. There are others that have adapted IPSAS to their own situation. For example, New Zealand uses Public Benefit Entity International Public Sector Accounting Standards (External Reporting Board, 2022). These were developed by reviewing the application of IPSAS to New Zealand's context. Two of the IPSASs were deemed irrelevant (IPSAS 18, *Segment Reporting*, and IPSAS 24, *Presentation of Budget Information in Financial Statements*) and the others modified, although only a small number of substantive modifications were made.

In Europe a project is underway to adapt IPSAS into harmonized European Public Sector Accounting Standards for the whole European Union (see https://ec.europa.eu/eurostat/web/epsas).

IFR4NPO is an initiative to develop internationally applicable financial reporting guidance for non-profit organizations. See www.ifr4npo.org for more information.

PUBLIC SECTOR FINANCIAL REPORTING

In the private sector, the owners of the business, the shareholders and potential investors are seen by the International Accounting Standards Board (IASB) as the main users of financial statements. The accounting standards issued by the IASB are designed to ensure that these users receive useful and relevant financial information.

In the public sector, it is harder to define who the main users of financial information are. They could include taxpayers, users of services, government bodies, funding providers, international institutions and more. Each of these potential or actual users may have different interests and therefore have different needs for financial information.

The Aristotelian expectation of public money being managed in full sight of the citizens has its modern equivalent in the online publication of financial data by government organizations. This kind of publishing of data is proactive, giving citizens the opportunity to investigate the data however they choose. It is quite different from the reactive nature of access to information legislation that many countries now have.

Fiscal Transparency Code covers the full cycle of PFM, including transparency about budgets. The principles of the Code are shown in Box 8.2. The Code itself sets out more detail about each of the line items in Box 8.2.

BOX 8.2 THE FISCAL TRANSPARENCY CODE

The Code is structured into the following dimensions grouped into four principles.

Fiscal reporting

Fiscal reports should provide a comprehensive, relevant, timely and reliable overview of the government's financial position and performance.

- Coverage: Fiscal reports cover all entities engaged in public activity according to international standards.
- Frequency and timeliness: Fiscal reports should be published in a frequent, regular and timely manner.
- Quality: Information in fiscal reports should be relevant, internationally comparable, and internally and historically consistent.
- Integrity: Fiscal statistics and financial statements should be reliable, subject to external scrutiny, and facilitate accountability.

Fiscal forecasting and budgeting

Budgets and their underlying fiscal forecasts should provide a clear statement of the government's budgetary objectives and policy intentions, and comprehensive, timely and credible projections of the evolution of the public finances.

- Comprehensiveness: Fiscal forecasts and budgets should provide a comprehensive overview of fiscal prospects.
- Orderliness: The powers and responsibilities of the executive and legislative branches of government in the budget process should be defined in law, and the budget should be presented, debated and approved in a timely manner.
- Policy orientation: Fiscal forecasts and budgets should be presented in a way that facilitates policy analysis and accountability.
- Credibility: Economic and fiscal forecasts and budgets should be credible.

Fiscal risk analysis and management

Governments should disclose, analyse and manage risks to the public finances and ensure effective coordination of fiscal decision making across the public sector.

- Risk analysis and disclosure: Governments should publish regular summary reports on risks to their fiscal prospects.
- Risk management: Specific risks to the public finances should be regularly monitored, disclosed and managed.
- Fiscal coordination: Fiscal relations and performance across the public sector should be analysed, disclosed and coordinated.

Resource revenue management

Pillar IV has been designed to cover the full spectrum of natural resource fiscal transparency issues.

- Resource ownership and rights: There should be a sound legal framework and disclosure practices for resource exploration and extraction.
- Resource revenue mobilization: The design, implementation and administration of the fiscal regime consisting of tax and non-tax instruments is critical for collecting government revenue.
- Resource revenue utilization: a more in-depth focus on resource rev enue forecasting and integration into the budget framework, and the management of natural resource funds.
- Resource activity disclosure: emphasizes clear and comprehensive reporting on natural resource activity.

Source: IMF (2019)

The increased transparency about payments may be welcomed by many, but as Funnell states: 'information, while the essential ingredient of accountability, alone does not ensure accountability' (2003: 111). This sentiment is echoed by Tippett and Kluvers (2010: 22). Raw data are meaningless unless the analyst understands them. Within a PBE, raw financial information is interpreted by staff who are trained and knowledgeable about the database. Without such knowledge there must be scope for non-specialist readers to misunderstand the data.

There are limitations to the data that are provided by UK public bodies. Low value payments are omitted (by definition) and details of salary payments (except for the most senior postholders) and welfare benefit payments are excluded because of the personal nature of the data. This means that the details about, typically, 70 to 80 per cent of an organization's expenditures are unavailable to the public. Similarly, commercially sensitive payments are excluded and the extent of payments redacted in this way would be unknown to someone analysing the published data. Such non-disclosure of financial information is consistent with the approach that is taken in access to information legislation: information that is personal data about an individual; commercially sensitive in terms of the business affairs of a person or a non-public organization; could be prejudicial to national security or law enforcement activity; could endanger the health or safety of someone; or is covered by legal privilege does not have to be disclosed to enquirers. All of this means that the spending of a significant proportion of public money is not transparent.

For the payments that are included in the published financial datasets, there is only a limited amount of data for each one (such as date, department making the payment, payee and amount), so it is not possible to infer the reason for the payments (such as which service or project it relates to or if it is the full amount or a part payment).

Herbert (2010) states that these limitations means that few conclusions can be drawn from the published data. The data may enable a citizen to challenge the size of a payment but it would be difficult to make any assessment of the overall value for money of an organization as a whole, or of any of its services. As Herbert (2010) puts it, 'the public can look at transactions, but this does not allow judgement of processes and controls or outcomes.'

General purpose financial reports

Providing raw financial data about payments for the public to interrogate and analyse is one mechanism for accountability, but another, that has a longer history, is the publication of financial statements, typically on an annual basis.

Financial statements are a means of ensuring accountability. They provide information to demonstrate that public funds have been spend for the purposes for they were intended, and that resources have not been wasted. Taxpayers are not usually able to opt out of paying taxes, unlike the customers of private sector businesses who can choose not to buy certain products or services. This increases the need for transparency in the public sector's finances and for organizations to demonstrate that they have used tax-funded resources effectively.

A PBE may produce all kinds of reports for internal use, such as the budgetary control reports mentioned in Chapter 4, but there are two classes of financial statements reports produced for external audiences: special purpose reports and general purpose reports.

Special purpose financial reports (SPFRs) are reports tailored to meet a specific user's needs and are therefore, in general, the response to a request (or command) for the report. For example, the due diligence information prepared for a potential buyer of an organization is an SPFR. Public sector examples include statistical returns to government (for their completion of whole of government accounts perhaps) or a progress report requested by a donor or grant giver. They may be subject to an external audit if required by the party requesting the report.

General purpose financial reports (GPFRs) are reports that are provided to meet the needs of users who are not able or empowered to demand specific financial reports to meet their needs (IPSASB [International Public Sector Accounting Standards Board], 2022: 14). The users of GPFRs are:

- resource providers whether they are involuntary providers (such as taxpayers) or voluntary providers (such as lenders, creditors, employees or donors);
- service recipients, including taxpayers and other members of the community that benefit from services provided by the organization; and
- others, such as special interest groups, auditors, regulators, governments, the media and voters.

The IPSASB's *Conceptual Framework for General Purpose Financial Reporting by Public Sector Entities* (IPSASB 2014) sets out some specific areas that the main users are likely to be interested in, either for accountability or decision making. Resource providers are likely to be interested in information that helps to assess other aspects of the PBE's financial performance, such as whether the PBE:

- is achieving the objectives established as the justification for the resources raised during the period;
- has funded the current operations from funds raised in the current period from taxpayers or from borrowings or other sources; and
- is likely to need additional (or fewer) resources in the future, and the likely sources of those resources.

Service recipients, on the other hand, are likely to be interested in assessing whether:

- the PBE is using resources economically, efficiently, effectively and as intended, and whether such use is in their interests;
- the range, volume and cost of services provided during the period, and the amounts and sources of their cost recoveries, are appropriate; and
- the current levels of taxes and other charges are sufficient to maintain the volume and quality of services currently provided.

The external users of financial statements use them to make many decisions, including:

- buying, holding or selling equity investments;
- assessing stewardship and accountability;

- assessing the organization's ability to pay employees;
- assessing the security of loans;
- determining taxation policies;
- determining distributable profits and dividends;
- incorporating in governmental statistics; and
- regulating corporate activities.

Components of financial statements

GPFRs comprise the general purpose financial statements plus financial information about potential or actual future events and non-financial information about the organization's performance in meeting its objectives. GPFRs, unlike internal reports, are subject to review by independent auditors whose opinion on the fairness and accuracy of the reports will be included within them.

International Public Sector Accounting Standard 1 (IPSAS 1), *Presentation of Financial Statements* (IPSASB, 2022: 111), states that a complete set of general purpose financial statements comprises:

(a) a statement of financial position;
(b) a statement of financial performance;
(c) a statement of changes in net assets/equity;
(d) a cash flow statement;
(e) when the PBE makes publicly available its approved budget, a comparison of budget and actual amounts either as a separate additional financial statement or as a budget column in the financial statements;
(f) notes, comprising a summary of significant accounting policies and other explanatory notes; and
(g) comparative information in respect of the preceding period as specified in [...] IPSAS 1.

IPSAS 1 was developed from (private sector) International Accounting Standard 1 (IAS 1) and the contents of private sector financial statements would be the same except for item (b) being a statement of profiteer loss and there would not be item (e). And the accounting standards used by PBEs in territories that do not use IAS 1 or IPSAS 1 would be similar, if not identical to IPSAS 1.

Statement of financial position

A statement of financial position is what would commonly be referred to as a balance sheet (see Box 8.3). It is a snapshot of the financial affairs of an organization and is a feature of accrual accounting. A balance sheet does not exist in single-entry bookkeeping and is meaningless in a cash accounting system since the only balance would be the balance in the cash/bank account.

In the financial statements the balance sheet would be prepared as at the final day of the year (with comparator figures for the equivalent day the previous year) but a balance sheet may be produced on any date. In the private sector, they may be prepared at least monthly for review by the board of directors but might be produced weekly, or even daily, if appropriate. Stock Exchange listed companies have to publish their balance sheets at least twice a year. Public organizations in the United Kingdom, on the other hand, are less likely to be concerned about their balance sheets because they are not reliant on the markets for financing.

A balance sheet is produced by assembling the balances on every account and the aggregate of debit balances will naturally equal the aggregate of credit balances. A simplified balance sheet (statement of financial position), set out in the conventional groupings, is illustrated in Box 8.3.

BOX 8.3 SIMPLIFIED STATEMENT OF FINANCIAL POSITION

Fixed assets	(e.g., the book value of land and buildings)
plus	
Current assets	(investments, cash in hand and in bank accounts, debts owed to the organization, prepayments, stocks)
gives	
Total assets	
less	
Current liabilities	(debts owed by the organization to others that fall due within one year, bank overdrafts)
less	
Long-term liabilities	(debts owed by the organization to others that fall after one year, pension scheme liabilities)
equals	
Total assets less liabilities	
Represented by	
Reserves and balances[a]	(the accumulated surplus or deficit earned up to the date of the balance sheet and other amounts that have been set aside)
equals	
Total net worth	

[a]In the private sector this would be Shareholders' Funds—comprised of issued share capital, the retained profit or loss and other reserves.

The balance sheet is very important in the private sector, possibly more important than the profit and loss account. Banks, for example, are judged on the 'strength' of their balance sheets. For a private sector entity, total assets minus total liabilities gives the balance of the owners' funds (profits that have not been paid out in dividends and other reserves) and accounting standards have been developed with a focus on preparing a statement of financial position that reflects fairly what the entity is worth to its owners. In practice, the balance sheet would often be the starting point for the analysis of a company's financial health because it indicates the ability of the company to meet its commitments and liabilities.

On the face of it, a balance sheet tells the reader:

- what an organization controls (usually through ownership but not always);
- what an organization owes to others; and
- where the organization obtained its financial resources.

An organization's net worth is its total assets minus total liabilities. If net worth is negative, it is insolvent since this means that, in total, there are fewer assets than liabilities. In practice, in the private sector such an organization could keep going but would have to take some action to bring the net worth back to positive. One way to do this would be to seek additional investment from shareholders (which is how businesses like Amazon and Uber can operate for many years without making profits).

PBEs with negative net worth can continue to operate because either they are the government or they are guaranteed by the government, and there is the potential of future tax receipts to finance the negative net worth.

A balance sheet could also show the reader whether the organization has a lot of tangible assets that, if it were in financial difficulty, could be liquidated to generate cash to pay staff and suppliers.

However, not everything owned by a PBE will be in its balance sheet. For example, intellectual property may not be included as an asset. The foreword of HM Treasury (2018) *Getting Smart About Intellectual Property and Other Intangibles in the Public Sector* includes

> The world's five most valuable companies are worth £3.5 trillion together but their balance sheets report just £172 billions of tangible assets. 95% of their value is in the form of intangible assets, including intellectual property, data and other knowledge assets.

Conversely, not all liabilities will necessarily be included. For example, the future cost of meeting the challenges of sustainability and climate change are not identified in financial terms as liabilities. This may soon change. In 2022 the IPSASB published a consultation paper, *Advancing Public Sector Sustainability Reporting*, proposing that it take on the role of setting global standards and guidance for PBEs to publish sustainability-related information and climate-related disclosures.

A balance sheet is backward looking. It tells you the financial position on a given date, which could be recent but could be many months ago. It does not tell you how things are today, or what may happen in the coming months and years.

Statement of financial performance

A statement of financial performance (see Box 8.4 for the layout) is an income and expenditure statement and is the public sector equivalent of a profit and loss account. It illustrates whether or not an organization is economically viable.

PBEs generally are focused on expenditure rather than income, whereas a private sector organization would focus on its income (revenue). As a result, the public sector format for a statement of financial performance is to state expenditure at the top, then income, giving a net expenditure to be funded from taxes. If the income from taxes is greater than the net expenditure there is a surplus for the year; if the taxes are lower than net expenditure there is a deficit; and these are the equivalents of profit and loss. The private sector format for accounts would place income (revenue) at the top followed by expenditure with the difference being the profit or loss for the period.

BOX 8.4 SIMPLIFIED STATEMENT OF FINANCIAL PERFORMANCE

Total revenue (or income)	(Income from taxes, user charges, transfers from other PBEs, etc.)
minus	
Total expenses by function	(The analysis of functions would be specific to the kind of organization)
equals	
Surplus/deficit for the period	
plus	
Net gains/losses for the period	(Changes in the net worth of the PBE's assets or liabilities
plus	
Net assets at beginning of the period[a]	
equals	
Net assets at end of the period[a]	

[a]The net assets figures provide a link between the statement of financial performance and the corresponding statements of financial position (balance sheets).

There are many things a statement of financial performance does not and cannot tell the reader. Like the statement of financial position, it is, by definition, a backward-looking statement and may be published many months after the end of the period. It may therefore tell the reader nothing about how the business is operating right now, let alone in the future.

It also does not assess whether the organization is sustainable. A profitable business can become bankrupt, often very quickly, if it does not collect it debts from customers or something changes in its trading environment. Similar problems could befall a PBE. Would the 2019 statements of financial performance for PBEs give readers any idea of how sustainable the PBEs would be in the face of the coronavirus in 2020?

Statement of movement of net assets/equity

The statement of movement of net assets or equity reflects the balance sheet focus of the accounting standards and it gives users of the GPFRs more information about the additions to and deductions from the organization's reserves from the statement of financial position at the start of the year and the statement of financial position at the end of the year.

It captures (for businesses as well as PBEs) whether the organization made gains and losses from things that were not the usually operating activities whose financial aspects are captured in the statement of financial performance. For example, if a PBE has a pension fund for its employees pensions that is invested in bonds and stocks and shares, then any increase or decrease in the value of those investments would be accounted for as movements of net assets (up or down, respectively).

As the statement is essentially a reconciliation it tells you little that could not be discovered from the three main statements and the notes, but it is included for completeness and transparency.

Statement of cash flows

A cash flow statement is another analysis of changes between the financial position at the start and at the end of the financial year, this time focusing on the reasons for changes in the level of the organization's cash and bank balances and other liquid assets.

Table 8.1 shows the main inflows and outflows of cash for a PBE.

For the private sector this shows the user of the accounts how much cash is generated (or lost) from operations, how much from investments and how much from financing of the organization. Box 8.5 shows a simplified statement of cash flows.

Table 8.1 *Cash inflows and outflows for a PBE*

Cash is generated from	*Cash is used for*
• Receipt of taxes, fees, charges and donations	• Purchase of supplies, etc.
	• Payments to employees
• Sale of non-current assets	• Purchase of non-current assets
• Decrease in inventory	• Increase in inventory
• Decrease in receivables	• Increase in receivables
• Loans received	• Loans repaid
• Increase in payables	• Decrease in payables

BOX 8.5 SIMPLIFIED STATEMENT OF CASH FLOWS

Net cash flows from operating activities	(Receipts from taxes, fees, sales, grants, etc. minus payments to employees, suppliers, interest on loans, etc.)
plus	
Net cash flows from investing activities	(Receipts from sale of assets and investments minus payments on capital items and purchase of investments)
plus	
Net cash flows from financing activities	(Receipts of cash borrowed from third parties minus repayments of borrowings)
gives	
Net increase/decrease in cash and cash equivalents[a]	
plus	
Cash and cash equivalents[a] at beginning of the period	(as shown on the corresponding balance sheet)
equals	
Cash and cash equivalents[a] at beginning of the period	(as shown on the corresponding balance sheet)

[a]Cash equivalents are investments that can be readily converted to cash, such as deposit accounts and investments in bonds, etc. that mature within three months.

Cash flow statements are important because a profitable organization can become bankrupt if it fails to collect its debts. In the same way, a government could provide services efficiently, financed by the taxes it levies, but if it fails to collect the taxes the government could have both an accrued surplus in its statement of financial performance and a cash deficit.

When reviewing a business's financial statements, it is important to evaluate whether it is generating cash from its operating activities (basically collecting more money from customers than it spends on staff and suppliers) or from financing activities (getting money from investors or lenders).

A cash flow statement, when analysis in combination with other financial statements, provides information for users about things like the organization's financial structure.

Cash transactions are more objective and less subject to manipulation so a cash flow statement makes it easier to compare the reported performance of different organizations (private or public sector) because it eliminates the effects of using the organizations using different accounting treatments. For example, two state-owned enterprises could have very similar profit and loss accounts in terms of turnover and profit but if one makes almost all its sales as cash sales and the other has 80 per cent credit sales and only 20 per cent cash sales, then the former will have a much stronger cash position. The other enterprise is, in effect, loaning money to its credit sale customers and will need to collect this money, or borrow some from a bank, before it can pay its suppliers and pay out any dividends to its owners, the government).

As with statements of financial positions and financial performance, a statement of cash flows is a backward-looking statement and it cannot tell you anything about the present or future financial situation of the organization.

Comparison of budget and actual spending

As implied by IPSAS 1, many but not all PBEs publish details of their budget. There are some jurisdictions that have standardized the form and content of published budgets for PBEs as the United Kingdom does for local government by prescribing how the budget should be summarized on council tax demands (i.e., bills)—but it is probably more likely for individual PBEs to determine their format. Some might choose to reflect their organizational structure; others might reflect their services or programmes; and the level of detail may differ, too (Jones and Pendlebury, 2010: 111).

Where a budget is published before the commencement of the financial period (or sometimes for practical reasons a little later than that), it is reasonable for the public to receive a report at the end of the financial year that compares the actual levels of income and expenditure with what was budgeted. This practice is a fundamental difference from the private sector. In the latter, the budget is a private matter, although the companies listed on the stock exchange are required to disclose some information in terms of forecasts. There is, therefore, no requirement in the private sector accounting standards regarding the presentation of budget information.

The public sector, on the other hand, has IPSAS 24, *Presentation of Budget Information in Financial Statements*, (IPSASB, 2022: 543-61), which not only requires a comparison of actual income and expenditure against the original budget, but also against the final budget ('revised budget') and giving an explanation of material variances. If the budget is prepared on a different basis from the financial statements—and it could be because there are no accounting standards applicable to budgeting—the PBE should compare its actual expenditure and income with the budget on the same basis as the budget and then provide a reconciliation between the actual expenditure and income on the budget basis with the figures in the Statement of Financial Performance.

Explanatory notes

Explanatory notes are needed, in part, to confirm the accounting policies that have been used and, in part, to amplify the usefulness of the financial statements by providing additional details about the numbers that are on the face of the financial statements. Anyone who has looked at a GFPR for a private or public organization will have noticed that the notes to the accounting statements is the longest section. For larger organizations the notes could easily run to 100 or more pages. The aim of the notes is to help the reader understand what is included or not in the various statements—but the sight of the notes can be enough to put off many readers.

There are questions to be asked about the understandability of financial statements, especially for financial statements by PBEs where the target audience includes the general public. Whilst a user of financial statements might be expected to have a reasonable education, they should not be expected to be experts to be able to understand the documents. The readability and usefulness of financial statements would be improved if PBEs cleared some of the clutter. As Scott (2014) observed, 'Too often, organizations play safe by including every disclosure required by standards, in case an omission is questioned. And too often, auditors question the omission of non-material disclosures, encouraging this behaviour.'

The standard financial statements that PBEs are required to publish might enable consistency between the bodies but they have three weaknesses (Chan and Xu, 2013: 776). They look different from the monthly or quarterly budget monitoring reports that public managers and politicians would base their financial management on; some very significant liabilities are omitted (as discussed earlier); and they are voluminous and difficult to understand. There is often a difference between the bottom line surplus or deficit on an accrual basis and on the cash basis which has to be reconciled and explained.

WHOLE OF GOVERNMENT ACCOUNTS

Each organization or entity is required to produce financial statements that report the transactions to which it is directly involved. In the private sector groups of companies can be economically interrelated (such as one company owning the shares of another company), and, in such cases, a consolidated set of financial statements has to be produced for the group as if it were a single entity. This can be quite a complicated exercise because it requires the reporting of the group's dealings with the outside world only and therefore any intra-group transactions (such as one group company selling its product to another group company) have to be ignored. In practice, for the production of whole of consolidated accounts, there would be too many small transactions amongst the tens, or perhaps hundreds, of organizations for them all to be excluded, so only material intra-group transactions would be excluded.

The concept of consolidation applies to PBEs, too. In the public sector the definition of a group is also based on the control relationship between the reporting organization (the parent of the group) and the other organizations in the group, but control might not be exercised by owning shares in the subsidiary organizations. National governments control their ministerial departments and local governments through regulations and financing.

The production of consolidated accounts is not a simple addition of the figures in each organization's financial statements. Consolidation requires the financial transactions that occur between the organizations being consolidated are excluded so that the resulting financial statements show the financial transactions with the 'outside world' only.

The consolidation of financial statements can continue with larger and larger groups of PBEs until the national government is reached. At this top level the financial statements are called whole of government accounts (WGA) and they would be a set of consolidated financial statements—an income and expenditure account, a balance sheet and a cash flow statement—on an accruals basis, covering the whole public sector.

Relatively few countries have been able to produce complete, government-wide audited financial statements (i.e., an income statement, a cash flow statement and a balance sheet in which financial and non-financial assets are recognized.) on an accrual basis. New Zealand was the first in 1992, and it was joined by Sweden in 1995 and Australia in 1998. The others include the United States, which has produced them since 2002 and the United Kingdom since 2011 (Blondy et al., 2013: 264).

The United States has produced what it calls the government-wide financial statements (Jones and Pendlebury, 2010: 119) for a number of years. The *FY21 Financial Report of the US Government* consolidates the finances of 162 organizations (Department of the Treasury, 2022: 218). These are federal government organizations; the report does not consolidate, for example, state and local government finances. For the year ended 30 September 2021 the US federal government spent $7.4 trillion, down $62 billion on 2020. Tax and other revenues were $4.3 trillion, giving a net cost of $3.1 trillion.

The balance sheet on 30 September 2021 showed assets of $4.9 trillion and liabilities of $34.8 trillion (including federal debts of about $22.3 trillion and pension liabilities for federal employees and armed forces personnel of $10.2 trillion). As of 30 September 2021, the US federal government, therefore, had a negative net worth of $29.9 trillion. (Or, if you take the modern monetary theory view of public finances, at 30 September 2021 the US federal government has an investment into the US economy of $29.9 trillion. Whichever view you take, at some point in the future the federal government will have to collect this money in the form of taxes.)

Note, however, that the Government Accountability Office, which audits the consolidated financial statements, stated they were unable to express an opinion on the 2021 financial statements because of 'material weaknesses in internal control over financial reporting and other limitations on the scope of our work,' and this has been the case every year since 1997 (Department of the Treasury, 2022: 228).

For the United Kingdom, the WGA were published for the first time for the year ended 31 March 2010. The United Kingdom consolidates the financial affairs of some 1,500 bodies from central government, local government, the health service and public corporations. The United Kingdom typically publishes its WGA reports 15 months after the year end, whereas the US federal reports are published within five months.

The WGA for the United Kingdom for the year ended 31 March 2020 (therefore with very little coronavirus pandemic impact). They report the operating expenditure for the year as £919 billion and income of £813 billion. This means there was a net cost (or deficit) of £106 billion (just about £2 billion every week).

The assets on 31 March 2020 as £2.1 trillion. This includes £1.3 trillion of physical assets like property and equipment and £0.5 trillion in financial assets (which are things like cash, loans to third parties including students and government investments).

The liabilities on that date were £5.0 (including £1.4 trillion billion of government borrowings and £2.2 trillion of pension liabilities for public employees) giving a negative net worth of £2.9 trillion. The accounts described this difference as 'total liabilities to be funded by future revenues,' (HM Treasury, 2022: 96).

These consolidated accounts have been given a qualified audit opinion (for the 11th year in a row). The grounds for the qualification include:

- the accounts for NatWest Group plc, a bank that the government owns, are not included in the consolidation;
- train operating companies were effectively nationalized as part of the COVID-19 response and should have been included in the accounts;

- a number of the bodies' financial statements that are consolidated into the WGA were themselves qualified by their auditors;
- there are other bodies' financial statements included even though their audits have not been completed; and
- some of the financial statements consolidated into the WGA have year-end reference dates that are more than three months different from the 31 March date.

These two examples show governments with massive net liabilities as a result of the financial policies they have pursued. New Zealand offers a contrast. The New Zealand Treasury publishes financial statements for the Government of New Zealand to its website very quickly. The accounts for the year ended 30 June 2021 were published on 12 October 2021 (New Zealand Treasury 2021). (Interim part-year financial statements are published even more quickly.) The Government of New Zealand financial statements consolidate the financial statements of the 'core crown segment' (the government ministries), state-owned enterprises and 'crown entities' that are controlled by the government (New Zealand Treasury, 2021: 54–6). Local councils are not included.

These financial statements cover the prime period of the coronavirus pandemic and there was an operating deficit of NZ$4.6 billion (expenses of NZ$133.7 billion and revenues of NZ$129.3 billion). This is not a major issue, though, because the New Zealand government had a substantial positive net worth at the start of the period. On 30 June 2021 the net worth was still NZ$157.2 billion.

The Controller and Auditor-General's opinion on this set of financial statements is unqualified, although there are some 'key audit matters' that are explained for the benefit of the readers.

CONCLUSION

The public demand for those who control public money to be accountable for it is not an NPM innovation; it goes back to ancient times. Modern technology, however, enables PBEs to use new ways of publishing information and data cheaply and efficiently, enhancing their accountability to the public.

Financial reporting is an important accountability mechanism for PBEs. A set of financial statements for a PBE looks on the face of it substantially the same as the financial statements of a private business. The move to harmonize accounting around the world is attractive, but there are some difficulties in applying private sector accounting practices to PBEs. Care should be taken by the users of financial statements to ensure they understand what the statements say, and what they do not, and cannot, say.

The next chapter looks at another important accountability mechanism: auditing.

EXERCISES

1. In terms of your own organization, whether public or private, what are the accountability mechanisms that are operated? How effective do you think they are?
2. How would you go about placing a financial value on the treasures owned by your local museum?

REFERENCES

Aggestam-Pontoppidan, C., & Andernack, I. (2016). *Interpretation and Application of IPSAS*. West Sussex: John Wiley & Sons.

Aristotle. (no date). *Politics: A Treatise on Government*. Translated by William Ellis. Available at: https://en.wikisource.org/wiki/Politics_(Ellis)/Book_5 (Accessed: 11 July 2022).

Bandy, G. P., & Metcalfe, A. (2021). *Rethinking Public Financial Management*. London: ACCA. Available at: https://www.accaglobal.com/gb/en/professional-insights/global-profession/rethinking-public-financial-management.html (Accessed: 25 April 2022).

Barton, A. D. (2004). How to profit from defence: A study in the misapplication of business accounting to the public sector in Australia. *Financial Accountability and Management, 20*(3), 281–304.

Barton, A. D. (2006). Public sector accountability and commercial-in-confidence outsourcing contracts. *Accounting, Auditing and Accountability Journal, 19*(2), 256–271.

Blondy, G., Cooper, J., Irwin, T., Kauffmann, K., & Khan, A. (2013). The role of fiscal reporting in public financial management. In M. Cangiano, T. Curristine, & M. Lazare (Eds.), *Public Financial Management and Its Emerging Architecture* (pp. 259–282). Washington, DC: International Monetary Fund.

Broadbent, J., & Laughlin, R. (2003). Control and legitimation in government accountability processes: The private finance initiative in the UK. *Critical Perspectives on Accounting, 14*(1–2), 23–48.

Budina, N., & Petrie, M. (2013). Managing and controlling fiscal risks. In M. Cangiano, T. Curristine, & M. Lazare (Eds.), *Public Financial Management and Its Emerging Architecture* (pp. 175–205). Washington, DC: International Monetary Fund.

Carnegie, G. D., & West, B. P. (2003). How well does accrual accounting fit the public sector? *Australian Journal of Public Administration, 62*(2), 83–86.

Carnegie, G. D., & West, B. P. (2005). Making accounting accountable in the public sector. *Critical Perspectives on Accounting, 16*(7), 905–28.

Cavanagh, J., Flynn, S., & Moretti, D. (2016). *Implementing Accrual Accounting in the Public Sector*. Washington, DC: International Monetary Fund.

Chan, J. L., & Xu, Y. (2013). Government financial reporting standards and practices. In R. Allen, R. Hemming, & B. H. Potter (Eds.), *The International Handbook of Public Financial Management* (pp. 767–796). Basingstoke: Palgrave Macmillan.

Committee on Standards in Public Life. (1995). *Standards in Public Life: First Report of the Committee on Standards in Public Life*. London: HMSO (Cm 2850-1).

Committee on Standards in Public Life. (2013).*Standards Matter: A Review of Best Practice in Promoting Good Behaviour in Public Life*. London: The Stationery Office.

Consultative Committee of Accounting Bodies. (2022). *Ethical Dilemmas Case Studies* [Webpage]. Available at: https://www.ccab.org.uk/ethical-dilemmas-case-studies-2022/ (Accessed: 15 July 2022).

Coombs, H. M. and Jenkins, D. E. (2002). *Public Sector Financial Management* (3rd ed.). London: Thomson Learning.

Curristine, T., & Flynn, S. (2013).In Search of Results: Strengthening Public Sector Performance. In M. Cangiano, T. Curristine, & M. Lazare (Eds.), *Public Financial Management and Its Emerging Architecture* (pp. 225–58). Washington, DC: International Monetary Fund.

Department of the Treasury. (2022). *Financial Report of the United States Government* [Webpage]. Available at: https://fiscal.treasury.gov/reports-statements/financial-report/ (Accessed: 17 July 2022).

Doig, A. (2006). Half-Full or Half-Empty? The Past, Present and Future of British Public Sector Ethics. *Public Money and Management, 26*(1), 15–22.

Ellwood, S., & Newbury, S. (2006). A bridge too far: A common conceptual framework for commercial and public benefit entities. *Accounting and Business Research, 36*(1), 19.

Emerson, S. (2006). The public, politics and ethics of public officials: Corporate scandals of 2002. *Public Money and Management, 26*(1), 47–54.

External Reporting Board. (2022). *Tier 1 and 2 Public Sector Standards* [Webpage]. Available at: https://www.xrb.govt.nz/standards/accounting-standards/public-sector-standards/tier-1-and-2/ (Accessed: 18 July 2022).

Ezzamel, M. & Hoskin, K. (2002). Retheorizing Accounting, Writing and Money With Evidence From Mesopotamia and Ancient Egypt. *Critical Perspectives on Accounting, 13*(3), 333–67.

Gardner, H. (2007). The ethical mind: A conversation with psychologist Howard Gardner. Interview by B Fryer for *Harvard Business Review, 85*(3), 51–56.

Harris, J., Senhadji, A., & Tieman, A. F. (2019). *A Global Picture of Public Wealth* [Online Article]. Available at: https://blogs.imf.org/2019/06/18/a-global-picture-of-public-wealth/ (Accessed: 16 July 2022).

Heiling, J. (2020). *Public Sector Accounting—A Discipline in Its Own Right* [Online Article]. Available at: https://www.ifac.org/knowledge-gateway/contributing-global-economy/discussion/public-sector-accounting-discipline-its-own-right (Accessed: 18 July 2022).

Herbert, D. (2010). You and Whose Army? *Public Finance,* 16 September. Retrieved from http://bit.ly/RldZAn (Accessed 6 May 2014).

HM Treasury. (2018). *Getting Smart About Intellectual Property and Other Intangibles in the Public Sector.* Available at: https://www.gov.uk/government/publications/getting-smart-about-intellectual-property-and-intangible-assets (Accessed: 18 July 2022).

HM Treasury. (2022). *Whole of Government Accounts, 2019–20.* Available at: https://www.gov.uk/government/publications/whole-of-government-accounts-2019-20 (Accessed: 18 July 2022).

Hodges, R. & Mellett, H. (2003). Reporting Public Sector Financial Results. *Public Management Review, 5*(1), 99–113.

IASPlus. (2022a). *Use of IFRS By Jurisdiction* [Webpage]. Available at: http://www.iasplus.com/country/useias.htm (Accessed: 18 July 2022).

IASPlus. (2022b). *IPSAS in Your Pocket — 2022 Edition.* Available at: https://www.iasplus.com/en/publications/public-sector/ipsas-in-your-pocket-2022 (Accessed: 13 July 2022).

IFAC. (2015). *Why Every Citizen Should Care About Government Spending* [Video]. Available at: https://www.youtube.com/watch?v=UtCDCT-vJfo (Accessed: 18 July 2022).

IFAC & CIPFA. (2021). *International Public Sector Financial Accountability Index: 2021 Status Report.* Available at: https://www.ifac.org/publications/international-public-sector-financial-accountability-index-2021-status-report (Accessed: 16 July 2022).

IMF. (2019). *The Fiscal Transparency Code.* Washington, DC: IMF. Available at: https://www.imf.org/en/Topics/fiscal-policies/fiscal-transparency (Accessed: 12 July 2022).

Institute for Government. (2018). *Accountability in Modern Government: What Are the Issues?* Available at: https://www.instituteforgovernment.org.uk/publications/accountability-modern-government-issues (Accessed: 18 July 2022).

International Budget Partnership. (2022). Open Budget Survey 2021. Available at: https://internationalbudget.org/wp-content/uploads/Open-budget-survey-2021-1.pdf (Accessed: 14 July 2022).

IPSASB. (2014). *Conceptual Framework for General Purpose Financial Reporting by Public Sector Entities.* Available at: https://www.ipsasb.org

/publications/conceptual-framework-general-purpose-financial-reporting-public-sector-entities-3 (Accessed: 18 July 2022).

IPSASB. (2022). *2022 Handbook of International Public Sector Accounting Pronouncements*. New York: International Federation of Accountants. Available at: https://www.ipsasb.org/publications/2022-handbook-international-public-sector-accounting-pronouncements (Accessed: 13 July 2022).

Irwin, T. C. (2019). Not taking debt at face value, or market value or amortized cost: Policy value as a measure of the burden of public debt. *Financial Accountability & Management, 35*(3), 275–289. https://doi.org/10.1111/faam.12196.

Jones, R., & Pendlebury, M. (2010). *Public Sector Accounting* (6th ed.). Harlow: Pearson Education.

King, M. L., Jr. (1964). *The Future of Integration* [Speech]. Finney Chapel at Oberlin College, Oberlin, Ohio, 22 October.

Kluvers, R., & Tippett, J. (2010). Mechanisms of accountability in local government: An exploratory study. *International Journal of Business and Management, 5*(7), 46–53.

Laughlin, R. (2008). A conceptual framework for accounting for public-benefit entities. *Public Money and Management, 28*(4), 247–254.

McCallum, J. (2016). *Seven Times Accounting Changed History* [Online Article]. Available at: https://intheblack.cpaaustralia.com.au/accounting/7-times-accounting-changed-history (Accessed: 11 July 2022).

McPhail, K., & Walters, D. (2009). *Accounting and Business Ethics: An Introduction*. Abingdon: Routledge.

Metcalfe, A., & Taylor M. (2020). *Sustainable Public Finances Through COVID-19*. London: ACCA. Available at: https://www.accaglobal.com/uk/en/ professional-insights/global-profession/Sustainable_public_finances_Covid-19.html (Accessed: 16 July 2022).

National Audit Office. (2014). *Understanding Central Government's Accounts*. London: NAO. Available at: https://www.nao.org.uk/report/understanding-central-governments-accounts-introductory-guide-oversight-role/ (Accessed: 18 July 2022).

National Audit Office. (2022). *Good Practice in Annual Reporting*. Available at: https://www.nao.org.uk/report/good-practice-in-annual-reports/ (Accessed: 18 July 2022).

New Zealand Treasury. (2021). *Financial Statements of the Government of New Zealand for the Year Ended 30 June 2021*. Available at: https://www.treasury.govt.nz/publications/year-end/financial-statements-2021 (Accessed: 18 July 2022).

Rowles, T. (2004). Accrual accounting in the public sector: Its usefulness in economic decision-making. *Journal of Finance and Management in Public Services, 3*(2), 63–77.

Schick, A. (2013). Reflections on two decades of public financial management reforms. In M. Cangiano, T. Curristine, & M. Lazare (Eds.), *Public Financial Management and Its Emerging Architecture* (pp. 21–77). Washington, DC: International Monetary Fund.

Schmidthuber, L., Hilgers, D., & Hofmann, S. (2022). International Public Sector Accounting Standards (IPSASs): A systematic literature review and future research agenda. *Financial Accountability & Management, 38*(1), 119–142.

Scott. (2014). Clear out the clutter. *Public Finance*, April, p. 42.

SEC. (2012). *Work Plan for the Consideration of Incorporating International Financial Reporting Standards into the Financial Reporting System for U.S. Issuers: Final Staff Report.* Washington, DC: SEC. Available at: https://www.sec.gov/spotlight/globalaccountingstandards/ifrs-work-plan-final-report.pdf (Accessed: 18 July 2022).

Securities and Exchange Commission. (2008). *SEC Proposes Roadmap Toward Global Accounting Standards to Help Investors Compare Financial Information More Easily.* Washington, DC: SEC. Available at: https://www.sec.gov/news/press/2008/2008-184.htm (Accessed: 18 July 2022).

United Nations. (2015). *Sustainable Development Goals* [Webpage]. Available at: https://www.un.org/en/sustainable-development-goals (Accessed: 10 July 2022).

van Helden, G. J., & Hodges, R. (2015). *Public Sector Accounting and Budgeting for Non-Specialists.* New York, NY: Palgrave Macmillan.

FURTHER READING (AND WATCHING)

Links to the following resources, and lots more, are available at www.managingpublicmoney.co.uk/extras.

Accounting and Business Ethics: An Introduction by McPhail and Walters (2009) is a source for more depth about ethical issues.

The Consultative Committee of Accounting Bodies (2022) has developed five sets of case studies to illustrate how the codes of ethics can be applied in five different work contexts, including working in the public sector and in not-for-profit organizations. These case studies are written from the perspective of professional accountants but they are helpful for non-accountants, too.

The Institute for Government (2018) published a discussion paper titled *Accountability in Modern Government: What Are the Issues?*

There are many books on accounting but relatively few that focus on accounting in the public sector. Coombs and Jenkins *Public Sector Financial Management 3rd Edition* (2002) and Jones and Pendlebury *Public Sector Accounting Sixth Edition* (2010) offer a good introduction to the subject. More recently, van Helden and Hodges wrote *Public Sector Accounting and Budgeting for Non-Specialists* (2015).

The National Audit Office published an introductory guide in 2014 titled *Understanding Central Government's Accounts.* Whilst it is written specifically about the UK Government, it explains what each of the main financial statements contains and what it is aiming to tell the reader, which are of broader interest.

IFAC promotes the adoption of accrual accounting by PBEs with its *Accountability Now* programme. This include a video on YouTube (IFAC, 2015): *Why Every Citizen Should Care About Government Spending.* More substantial is the IMF's Fiscal Affairs Department's handbook for implementing accrual accounting in the public sector (Cavanagh, Flynn and Moretti, 2016).

For more information about the IASB, and the IFRS in particular, explore the material on the website at www.ifrs.org/.

There is a lot of material available for IPSAS. You can find the full text of all the IPSASs in the annually published handbook of pronouncements at the IPSASB's website (www.ipsasb.org). Much briefer is the *IPSAS In Your Pocket* guide from the IASplus (2022b). There is also *Interpretation and Application of IPSAS* by Aggestam-Pontoppidan and Andernack (2016). Schmidthuber, Hilgers, and Hofmann (2022) have produced a literature review about the adoption of IPSAS and the implementation of accrual accounting based on IPSAS. Lastly, the United Nations provides a free online IPSAS training programme at www.un.int/pm/ipsas-line-training.

If you are involved in the preparation and publication of financial statements you might want to check out the National Audit Office's *Good Practice in Annual Reporting* (2022). This is an interactive guide that sets out good practice principles for annual reporting with examples from British public sector organizations.

Finally, there is a fun article by McCallum (2016): *Seven Times Accounting Changed History.*

Chapter 9

Audit

LEARNING OBJECTIVES

After reading this chapter you should:

- understand how the audit risk model affects an auditor's plans;
- recognize the types of audit tests that can be used by auditors to gather evidence;
- understand the different purposes of external and internal auditing;
- be able to explain the meaning of the opinions available to an external auditor; and
- know the difference between regularity auditing and performance (value for money) auditing.

KEY POINTS OF THIS CHAPTER

- Auditors provide independent assurance to principals about the activities of their agents.
- There are international standards for the conduct of external audits in the public sector, covering the planning and scope of audit work, gathering evidence, analysis and sampling, independence of the auditor and audit reporting.
- Auditors of PBEs have a wider set of concerns than whether the financial statements present fairly the financial affairs of the PBE. They are likely to have more regard to issues of fraud, waste and extravagance and to give an opinion on value for money.

DOI: 10.4324/9781003250838-9

- The development of performance (or value for money) auditing was pioneered in the United States where it was led by the private sector, whereas the later development in other English-speaking countries was led by the public sector.
- Auditors may detect frauds and irregularities during their work, but the prime responsibility for preventing and detecting fraud lies with an organization's governors and managers.

KEY TERMS

Audit risk—the possibility that the auditor expresses an inappropriate audit opinion

External audit—the process of review of an organization's financial statements, and possibly its management arrangements, by an independent person with a view to providing assurance to the organization's stakeholders

Internal audit—an audit function set up within an organization to provide an independent, objective assurance and consulting activity to managers. It is intended to add value and improve the organization's operations.

Performance audit—an audit that is carried out to review some aspect of an organization's activities to reach a conclusion about the economy, efficiency and effectiveness of the activity. Performance audits are also known as operational audits, management audits and value for money audits.

Regularity audit—an audit that is carried out to provide an opinion on financial statements

Supreme audit institution—a national-level organization that conducts independent audits of government activities

The fourth stage in the public financial management cycle is budget oversight. Auditing fits into that element of the cycle.

Auditing is an accountability mechanism that dates back many centuries. The term has its roots in the Latin verb *audire*, which means 'to hear'. Back then, the procedure would have involved an oral account rather than a review of documentary evidence because most people could not read or write.

The first record of an audit in Britain dating to around 1430. Having appointed the sheriffs the king also appointed barons to oversee them (the barons eventually evolving into justices of the peace) (Coombs and Edwards, 1990). It was also the case that, in the United Kingdom, the requirement for public money to be audited is much older than for business's financial statements to be audited. The latter was first enacted in the Companies Act, 1900. (Even then, companies were not statutorily compelled to comply with accepted accounting principles in drawing up their profit and loss accounts and balance sheets for a further half-century, when the Companies Act, 1948 came into force.)

This chapter begins with an outline of what an auditor does in general terms, followed by sections that describe external and internal audit, respectively. The next section about auditors' responsibilities relating to fraud and corruption and the final section briefly covers some issues exposed by the auditing of government responses to the coronavirus pandemic.

WHAT DOES AN AUDITOR DO?

Audit fits into the principal-agent theory (mentioned in Chapter 8) as the third corner of the accountability triangle (see Figure 9.1). In a small organization the owner/principal can supervise and control the manager as closely as they wish. However, in larger and more complex organizations this would not be possible. The principal can put in place accountability mechanisms, such as regular reporting from the agent (manager) to the principal (owner), but how would the principal know that they are receive complete, accurate and truthful reports? The principal would look for assurance about the manager's performance and reports, and hiring an independent auditor achieves this (subject to the auditor being competent and professional).

Fundamentally, an auditor's role is about giving an independent opinion, whether on financial statements or on systems or other information, to an organization's owners, managers, creditors, finance providers, customers or the general public. In the public sector, in particular, there can be some overlap between internal and external auditors' responsibilities (Bergmann, 2009 11), although the general objective of an auditor is to provide assurance, which Bergmann defines as, 'any measure undertaken by independent and mandated professionals to increase the confidence of the user in the information provided' (2009: 11).

The auditor needs to be independent of both the principal and the agent. This means the auditor should not have any connection with either the principal or the agent beyond the actual engagement as the auditor. They should also be free from outside control and not dependant on the principal for their livelihood. This means

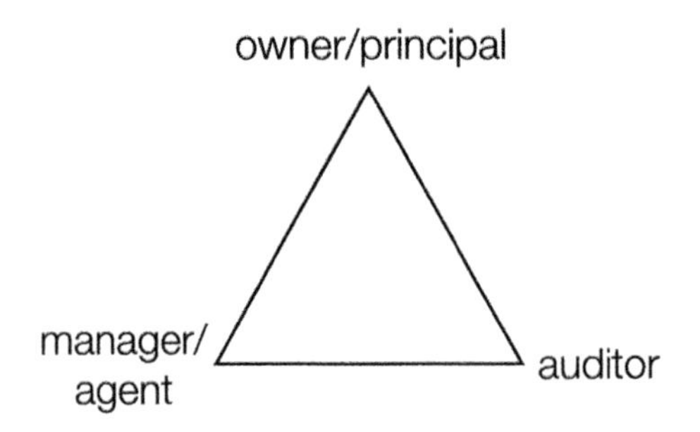

Figure 9.1 *The accountability triangle.*

the auditor should have sufficient income from other clients that their judgement is not influenced by the fact it is paid to carry out the audit. Independence also means the auditor being capable of thinking objectively and being able to use their own judgement to evaluate audit evidence and reach an opinion.

Often auditors are qualified or trainee accountants because much of the work relates to financial statements and financial information systems. There are aspects of audit work, however, where a different background could be more appropriate, such as auditing computer systems or environmental controls, so not all auditors are accountants. Performance auditing, in particular, demands more than accounting knowledge because it is, 'not grounded in the accounting profession, as is financial auditing, or in the legal profession, as are some aspects of financial and compliance auditing' (Shand, 2013: 825). (Performance auditing is explained later in this chapter.)

The basic process of carrying out an audit involves planning the audit, using tests to gather audit evidence, evaluating the evidence and reporting the auditor's conclusions and opinion. These stages are explained in the following sub-sections.

Types of audit

External and internal auditors can each be involved in regularity, performance and compliance audits. These three terms are explained below.

Regularity auditing

Regularity auditing is what is seen as the traditional focus of auditing. A regularity audit is focused on financial statements or processes and the purpose is to reach an opinion about whether the statements or processes are 'regular' in the sense that they conform with appropriate standards and conventions. Regularity auditing is sometimes referred to as financial auditing because of its focus on financial statements, or as statutory auditing, because it is the type of audit that public and private sector organizations are legally required to have in respect of their published financial statements. The potential scope of a regularity audit is shown in Box 9.1.

BOX 9.1 THE SCOPE OF A FINANCIAL AUDIT

The financial management audits of PBEs might cover the following aspects:

- budget preparation in accordance with instructions of the executive;
- acceptable estimates;
- budget structure in compliance with the law;

- budget process in compliance with the law;
- architecture of budget accounting system;
- accounting systems and internal control;
- safety, continuity, and verifiability of the budget system;
- safety, continuity, and verifiability of systems in general;
- efficiency of the budget system;
- efficiency of systems in general;
- effective budget control;
- supervision structure;
- feedback systems;
- timely updating of budgets;
- accurate and complete collection of taxes;
- feasibility and verifiability of new laws and regulations;
- acceptability of commitments;
- acceptability of contracts;
- structure of the accounting system;
- timeliness of accounting transactions;
- registration of performance information;
- materials management;
- inventories;
- efficient risk management; and
- frequent screening of risk indicators.

Source: Bac, 2007: 240

Regularity audit is linked to the concept of stewardship. Arguably any person who is charged with using public money for some purpose (i.e., any public manager) has a responsibility to take care of it (to steward the money), but it would particularly be seen as the responsibility of the chief finance officer or treasurer of a PBE. The latter is required to produce a set of financial statements that demonstrate, inter alia, the stewardship of public money and those financial statements are subject to audit, to provide assurance to third parties that the financial statements are complete and accurate.

Regularity auditing is clearly relevant to external auditors as described earlier but internal auditors can carry out regularity audits. For example, an internal auditor might carry out an audit of the accounts payable computer system with the emphasis to ensure that all the payments made are correct and valid and the subsequent accounting entries are complete and accurate. In fact, internal audit may undertake just this sort of regularity audit work in a coordinated programme with the external auditors so that the two auditors' resources are used most efficiently (i.e., effort is not duplicated) and there is less disruption to the organization's finance staff and managers.

Performance auditing

A performance audit is 'a systematic, non-financial evaluation of an entity's operations, and an organized search for ways to improve managerial efficiency and effectiveness' (Flesher and Zarzeski, 2002: 93). This definition mentions efficiency and effectiveness, two of the 3Es that are often seen as the definition of value for money (which was discussed in more depth in Chapter 7). This is why performance auditing is sometimes referred to as value for money auditing, comprehensive auditing, management auditing or operational auditing. (Operational auditing is the term used in much of the literature but performance auditing is preferred in this chapter because it is clearer about the purpose of the audit and it chimes with performance budgeting in Chapter 2 and performance management in Chapter 7.)

Performance auditing developed in the United States in the 1950s and 1960s, in both the private and the public sectors (Flesher and Zarzeski, 2002). Canada was the next English-speaking nation to develop performance auditing, apparently separately from the United States because it did not use the principles that had been developed there. In Canada the development was in the public sector, with credit being given for popularizing it to J. J. Macdonell, who, before being appointed as Auditor-General of Canada in 1972, had a private sector background (Parker, cited by Flesher and Zarzeski, 2002: 100).

Outside of the United States the development of performance auditing has been led by the public sector. The United Kingdom developed its approach to performance auditing in the 1970s and 1980s based on the Canadian experience, as did Australia and New Zealand. In fact, in the United Kingdom there is little evidence of performance auditing in the private sector, 'although in 1969 a Companies Bill was introduced into the House of Commons that would have given shareholders the power to require directors of a company to allow a management audit' (Flesher and Zarzeski, 2002: 100). Clearly, private companies in the United Kingdom identify improvements in economy and efficiency otherwise they would be uncompetitive, but they do not routinely identify such improvements through their external or internal auditors.

However, the United Kingdom's public sector auditors' remits have explicitly included giving an opinion on the arrangements in place for achieving value for money for more than 30 years. There are legislative requirements for this. First, in 1981 there was legislation relating to the Monopolies and Mergers Commission conducting annual efficiency audits of the United Kingdom's nationalized (i.e., state-owned) industries (Gamer, cited by Flesher and Zarzeski, 2002: 100). It was followed by legislation requiring value for money studies of local government in the form of the Audit Commission, which was created under the Local

Government Finance Act 1982. Finally the National Audit Act 1983 created the National Audit Office (NAO) and extended the legislative requirement for value for money studies to central government bodies. Following the abolition of the Audit Commission the codes of audit practice still require auditors to give an opinion on value for money, and the NAO will have a remit of oversight.

Performance auditing by external auditors covers either or both of reviews of the economy, efficiency and effectiveness of projects, programmes or organizations and reviews of published performance information (Shand, 2013: 824).

These legislative requirements focus the auditor's attention on the systems operated by a PBE rather than specific transactions. It is both more practical for the auditor and more meaningful to the PBE and anyone else who reads the auditor's report for the auditor to give an opinion on the PBE's management arrangements for achieving value for money than to give an opinion on whether a small number of individual transactions were themselves value for money.

Compliance auditing

A compliance audit is about reviewing and checking whether an organization is carrying out a particular activity or function in line with the relevant laws or regulations.

Different approaches to compliance audit can be taken depending on the organization and focus of the audit. In most cases, a specially trained auditor is assigned to work through a checklist, thus ensuring that all requirements are met, and nothing falls short of the relevant regulations.

Compliance auditing is very important in some sectors, particularly where regulations are complex and changing, such as financial services like banking and insurance. Compliance auditing is also particularly relevant where an organization needs to be accredited to carry out certain activities, such as forensic science laboratories. In these organizations the compliance audit provides assurance that they can be accredited and can continue in that activity or business.

Audit planning

Audit assignments (whichever type of audit) need to be carefully planned. Planning an audit assignment, like planning any project, contributes to successfully meeting the objectives. The complexity of the plan will typically depend on the size of and complexity of the organization being audited.

Audit plans can be recognized at two levels. First, there is an overall audit strategy which sets the scope, timing and direction of the audit. The strategy then informs the development of the detailed audit plan, which sets out more specifically how the audit will be conducted, including the procedures for obtaining audit evidence.

Let us use the audit of a public hospital's financial statements as an example. The audit strategy might state that the approach to be taken in the audit is to get as much evidence as possible from testing the controls operating on a hospital's main financial systems (payroll, accounts payable, general ledger and so on) in order to reduce the volume and extent of detailed testing of transactions. The audit plan would then develop the detail testing plans needed to get enough evidence about the operating of the controls that auditors working on the audit would be assigned to complete.

Planning an audit is not a single, discrete activity undertaken before the assignment begins. Instead, it needs to be a continuing, iterative process where the plan is updated to reflect changes in the auditor's knowledge about the organization being audited. As the auditor becomes aware of new information, their assessment of audit risk (see next sub-section) may change with consequential changes being required to detailed plans of audit work to be carried out. Often, therefore, the planning process will begin shortly after the completion of the previous audit and continues until the completion of the current audit engagement.

Audit risk

Audit risk is the possibility that the auditor expresses an inappropriate audit opinion. In practice, this is the possibility that the auditor gives a positive opinion when, in fact, the financial statements are materially misstated. This means the risk is a combination of the risk of material misstatement in a set of accounts and the risk that the auditor does not detect the misstatement.

The risk of material misstatement can be further separated into inherent risk and control risk. Inherent risk is the susceptibility of elements in the financial statements to be misstated before taking into consideration any related controls. These can be thought of as the risks of misstatement that stem from the nature of the organization, its activities or transactions. For example, a high volume of cash transactions is riskier than electronic transactions; transactions based on judgements, such as market values of assets and depreciation charges; and external factors, such as technological changes that could affect inventory valuations.

Control risk is the risk that a misstatement, possibly material, could occur because the organization's internal controls did not prevent it, or detect and correct it. As explained in Chapter 4, it is the responsibility of management to implement internal controls that, amongst other things, ensure that there are complete and accurate records of financial transactions.

The auditor cannot affect the strength of management control (at least not in the short term) but must assess its strength. The auditor's assessment of control risk could be affected by factors, such as the quality and quantity of management and staff and the nature and extent of the internal control system. If, for example, the auditor believes staff are inadequately skilled, or basic controls such as segregation of duties are not effectively operated, they would assess the control risk to be relatively high.

The possibility that the work done by the auditor will not detect a misstatement that is material, whether individually or when aggregated with other misstatements, is called detection risk. This could be because of ineffective planning of audit procedures by the auditor; failure to target audit procedures to high-risk areas; and/or the lack of appropriately skilled audit staff.

Although it is a management responsibility to manage inherent and control risk, detection risk is the responsibility of the auditor. Auditors first assess the levels of inherent and control risk, then they must decide on an audit strategy that will reduce detection risk to a level such that the consequent audit risk is acceptably low. The more audit testing the auditor conducts the lower detection risk will be and, as consequence, the lower audit risk will be.

Audit risk is therefore a combination of inherent, control and detection risks.

$$\text{Audit Risk} = \text{Inherent Risk} \times \text{Control Risk} \times \text{Detection Risk}$$

Audit risk can never be wholly eliminated, but it is the responsibility of the auditor to bring it to an acceptably low level by obtaining sufficient, appropriate audit evidence using audit tests.

Inherent risk and control risk are management's responsibility. To reduce audit risk to an acceptably low level, the auditor must thus focus on reducing detection risk. The higher the inherent risk and control risk are assessed to be, the lower the detect risk has to be in order to bring audit risk to an acceptable level. To lower the detection risk, the auditor will have to do more audit testing.

Audit testing

Power described audit as 'an *inferential* practice which seeks to draw conclusions from a limited inspection of documents, such as budgets and written representations, in addition to reliance on oral testimony and direct observation' (2000: 111, italics in original). Auditors base their opinions on the results of the audit tests they carry out (although in some circumstances they may choose to rely on the work carried out by other auditors or inspectors, but only if they have satisfied themselves that the other auditors' work meets appropriate standards). The tests to be carried out would be detailed in the audit plan that was prepared prior to undertaking the audit.

There are seven methods of testing that an auditor might use to gather audit evidence. They are:

- **inspection**—examining records and documents whether on paper or digital media;

- **observation**—watching the performance of a process or procedure;
- **enquiry**—seeking information in writing or verbally, from relevant people, who could be internal or external to the organization;
- **external confirmation**—seeking confirmation of facts from a third party;
- **recalculation**—checking the mathematical accuracy of documents or transactions;
- **re-performance**—where the auditor carries out a process or control that the organization has originally performed; and
- **analytical procedures**—checking information for plausibility and consistency.

Each type of test has strengths and weaknesses (described below) that affect when they are used.

Inspection

Inspection of documents can be effective, but it depends on what is being inspected. Inspection of a purchase invoice gives better quality evidence than inspection of a sales invoice because a purchase invoice is created by a third party.

Inspection of tangible assets that are recorded in the accounting records confirms their existence, but it does not confirm rights and obligations or valuation. Seeing a vehicle in a depot does not prove who owns it or what it is worth on the open market. Another weakness is that an auditor cannot inspect something they are unaware of, so if, for example, an organization excludes assets from the financial statements how would the auditor know they should inspect them?

Observation

Observation is a relatively weak test. It only confirms that the procedure is performed correctly when the auditor is watching. It is most suited, therefore, to things that are directly included in the financial statements, such as observing the stocktake on the final day of the accounting period.

Enquiry

The effectiveness of enquiry tests will depend on who the enquiry is being made about. A member of the organization's staff could misrepresent matters to the auditor if they misunderstood the nature of the question or they are seeking to conceal a misstatement.

External confirmation

External confirmation can be a very strong test resulting in good evidence from a third party. For example, asking a debtor to confirm the amount of debt owed to the organization, or a lender to confirm the details of loans. Nevertheless, there may be instances where the third party is motivated to misrepresent the situation so the auditor should be vigilant about this risk.

Recalculation

Recalculation is a relatively strong test as it is carried out by the auditor. The limits on an auditor's time means that recalculation can be used only sparingly and therefore should be targeted to test areas where it will bring the most benefit to the audit (that is, where it will give the most assurance).

Re-performance

Re-performance is also a strong test and provides good evidence because it is carried out by the auditor.

Analytical procedures

Analytical procedures consist of evaluations of financial information through analysis of plausible relationships among both financial and non-financial data. The strength of this procedure is limited by the strength or weakness of the underlying data. It can be strong if comparison is made to items that do not rely on the same accounting system or that the auditor can corroborate using information from outside the organization or the organization's financial information system.

Evaluation and reporting

The auditor's opinion is an objective and professional opinion based on a significant body of evidence, gathered and considered in a systematic way. It should not be personal in the sense of reflecting individual bias.

The evidence obtained by an auditor needs to be sufficient to base an opinion on. To assess sufficiency, auditors consider the persuasiveness of the evidence, the risks involved and the importance or materiality of the matter in question. If an auditor is evaluating a critical matter, then they should look for corroborating evidence rather than rely on only one source.

External and internal audit assignments result in reports. The International Auditing Standards (ISA) 700 *Forming an Opinion and Reporting on Financial Statements* includes specific and detailed requirements for the format of the external auditor's report on the financial statements (IAASB, 2016). The auditor's report must be in writing and must provide a clear expression of the auditor's opinion and there should be a section directly after the opinion that explains the basis for the opinion.

The *International Standards for the Professional Practice of Internal Auditing* states that 'internal auditors must communicate the results of engagements' (Institute of Internal Auditors, 2016: 17). Internal audit engagements (or assignments) are more varied in nature than external audit assignments so it would not be practical for the Institute of Internal Auditors (IIA) to prescribe the form and content of all internal audit reports. There could, though, be a standard template developed and used by an internal audit team for its particular internal audit assignments.

A question arises about the extent to which an auditor's opinion can be relied upon. In other words, what is the level of assurance that they provide?

There are two levels of assurance that can be given by an auditor. Reasonable assurance is provided where the auditor gathers sufficient and appropriate evidence to be able to give a positive conclusion. A positive conclusion is something like, 'In my opinion, the financial standards comply with all relevant accounting standards.'

Limited assurance, on the other hand, is where the auditor gathers a limited amount of evidence that is sufficient and appropriate to be able to give a negative conclusion. Unlike a positive conclusion where the opinion is that something is all right, a negative conclusion is one where the auditor says they have no evidence that something is not all right. A limited assurance opinion is along the lines of, 'In the course of reviewing the financial statements, nothing has come to my notice to indicate they do not comply with all relevant accounting standards.'

Whether an auditor gives reasonable to limited assurance depends on the terms of their engagement to do the work. A user of an organization's financial statements, or any other place where there is an auditor's certificate, should therefore take notice of whether the auditor's opinion is giving reasonable or limited assurance and make their inferences and conclusions about the statements appropriately.

EXTERNAL AUDITING

External audit is the independent review of an organization's financial statements in order to provide assurance to the stakeholders about them. This means giving an opinion on whether the financial statements accord, in all material respects, with the relevant financial reporting framework (accounting standards and other regulations and guidance).

The International Standard on Auditing (ISA) 200 gives the objectives of an external auditor as:

(a) To obtain reasonable assurance about whether the financial statements as a whole are free from material misstatement, whether due to fraud or error, thereby enabling the auditor to express an opinion on whether the financial statements are prepared, in all material respects, in accordance with an applicable financial reporting framework; and
(b) To report on the financial statements, and communicate as required by the ISAs, in accordance with the auditor's findings.

(IAASB, 2020: 83)

An external auditor's opinion amounts to reasonable assurance about the accuracy and completeness of the financial statements and is not a guarantee that they are error free. Auditors are not able to check every transaction and they rely on the organization's managers and staff to provide the correct information and answers to questions. And, as explained in Chapter 8, if the accounts are accruals-based (or modified cash-based) there will be many judgements made in preparing the financial statements. Auditors can assess judgements on their reasonableness but there may be many possible reasonable judgements that could be made that would be accepted by the auditor.

External audit applies equally to PBEs as it does to private sector organizations. In the private sector, the external auditor is appointed by the shareholders, perhaps by a vote at the annual general meeting of the shareholders based on the board of directors' recommendation. For PBEs the appointment of the external auditor might be made in a number of ways. For government bodies the country's supreme audit institution (SAI) might be appointed by virtue of the constitution or legislation. Other PBEs may be free to appoint their external auditors in much the same way as a private sector company but where there are no shareholders the appointment is likely to fall to the organization's governing body (rather than to its executive management team).

As many stakeholders would not be in a position to know what the reporting framework is and how it should be applied, they require the external auditor to be professionally qualified in order to carry out the work on their behalf and report an opinion to them.

Auditing standards

Chapter 8 explained the importance of accounting standards for the preparation of financial statements. It is perhaps no surprise that there are also auditing standards, both for external and internal auditing.

The main international auditing standards used for external auditing in the private sector are the International Standards on Auditing (ISAs). A couple of the ISAs have been mentioned already and there is a full list in Box 9.2.

BOX 9.2 THE INTERNATIONAL STANDARDS ON AUDITING

There are professional standards for the conduct of audits just like there are accounting standards. The International Standards on Auditing (ISAs) are set by the International Assurance and Auditing Standards Board (IAASB), which is part of the International Federation of Accountants (IFAC). There are 36 International Standards on Auditing (ISAs) and International Standard on Quality Control (ISQC) 1 included in the latest publication, the *Handbook of International Quality Control, Auditing, Review, Other Assurance, and Related Services Pronouncements* (IAASB, 2020). The standards are listed below (and the full handbook runs to more than 2,000 pages across three volumes).

ISA 200 Overall objectives of the independent auditor and the conduct of an audit in accordance with international standards on auditing
ISA 210 Agreeing the terms of audit engagements
ISA 220 Quality control for an audit of financial statements
ISA 230 Audit documentation
ISA 240 The auditor's responsibilities relating to fraud in an audit of financial statements
ISA 250 (Revised) Consideration of laws and regulations in an audit of financial statements
ISA 260 (Revised) Communication with those charged with governance
ISA 265 Communicating deficiencies in internal control to those charged with governance and management
ISA 300 Planning an audit of financial statements
ISA 315 (Revised) Identifying and assessing the risks of material misstatement through understanding the entity and its environment
ISA 320 Materiality in planning and performing an audit
ISA 330 The auditor's responses to assessed risks
ISA 402 Audit considerations relating to an entity using a service organization
ISA 450 Evaluation of misstatements identified during the audit
ISA 500 Audit evidence
ISA 501 Audit evidence-specific considerations for selected items
ISA 505 External confirmations
ISA 510 Initial audit engagements-opening balances
ISA 520 Analytical procedures
ISA 530 Audit sampling

ISA 540 (Revised) Auditing accounting estimates including fair value accounting estimates and related disclosures
ISA 550 Related parties
ISA 560 Subsequent events
ISA 570 (Revised) Going concern
ISA 580 Written representations
ISA 600 Special considerations—audits of group financial statements (including the work of component auditors)
ISA 610 (Revised) Using the work of internal auditors
ISA 620 Using the work of an auditor's expert
ISA 700 (Revised) Forming an opinion and reporting on financial statements
ISA 701 Communicating key audit matters in the independent auditor's report
ISA 705 (Revised) Modifications to the opinion in the independent auditor's report
ISA 706 (Revised) Emphasis of matter paragraphs and other matter paragraphs in the independent auditor's report
ISA 710 Comparative information—corresponding figures and comparative financial statements
ISA 720 (Revised) The auditor's responsibilities relating to other information in documents containing audited financial statements
ISA 800 (Revised) Special considerations audits of financial statements prepared in accordance with special purpose frameworks
ISA 805 (Revised) Special considerations—audits of single financial statements and specific elements accounts or items of a financial statement
ISA 810 (Revised) Engagements to report on summary financial statements
International Standard on Quality Control (ISQC) 1 Quality controls for firms that perform audits and reviews of financial statements and other assurance and related services engagements.

Source: IAASB (2020)

ISAs are issued by the International Auditing and Assurance Standards Board (IAASB), which operates within the International Federation of Accountants (IFAC) just as the IPSASB does (Chapter 8). These standards are designed so that an audit opinion presented in one country is comparable with that presented in other countries. This is clearly important for businesses that operate in multiple countries. From time to time the IAASB publishes a handbook, in three volumes, that includes the text of all of the ISAs. The latest version was published in 2020 (IAASB, 2020).

The financial statements of national governments (and sometimes other PBEs) are audited by their SAI. Chapter 8 explained how public financial statements differ in some respects from private sector financial statements. There are therefore some differences in the work of the external auditors. The International Organization of Supreme Audit Institutions (INTOSAI) therefore issues International Standards of Supreme Audit Institutions (ISSAIs).

The INTOSAI standards framework consists of four levels:

1. founding principles;
2. prerequisites for the functioning of SAIs;
3. fundamental auditing principles; and
4. auditing guidelines.

The founding principles are contained in ISSAI 1 *The Lima Declaration*. The chief aim of the declaration is to call for independent government auditing. The rule of law and democracy are essential premises for really independent government auditing and are the pillars on which the Declaration of Lima is founded. An SAI that is not independent does not come up to standard.

There are a number of countries where the SAI's independence is limited. A World Bank report (2021) assessed the independence of the SAI in 118 countries—not North America, Europe, Australia, New Zealand, Japan and Korea—and only South Africa and Seychelles had SAIs that met all ten criteria for independence. Unfortunately, 29 had score of 5.5 or less, meaning that they had low levels of independence, and 39 had scores between 6 and 7.5, which was assessed as moderate independence.

The ten factors that were assessed were:

1. constitutional and legal framework;
2. transparency in the process for appointing the SAI head;
3. financial autonomy;
4. types of audits (whether the SAI completed regularity, performance and compliance audits);
5. operational autonomy;
6. staffing autonomy;
7. audit mandate;
8. audit scope autonomy;
9. access to records and information; and
10. right and obligation on audit reporting.

The other sections of the Lima Declaration make clear, in very few sentences, the principles for government auditing in terms of the relationships with the legislature and government; the powers of SAIs; audit methods; and reporting to the legislature and the general public.

Audit opinions

External auditors are required to give an opinion on the financial statements they have audited. An auditor's opinion can be either unmodified or modified. An unmodified opinion means 'the auditor concludes that the financial statements are prepared, in all material respects, in accordance with the applicable financial reporting framework is often referred to as a clean audit opinion' (IAASB, 2020: 728–9).

The external auditor's objective relates to the absence of material errors or mistakes so the level of materiality is crucial to the auditor's opinion. The level of materiality affects both the amount of work that the auditor has to undertake to be confident about their opinion and the usefulness of the financial statements to the user. If, let us say, the auditor determined that a material error was equivalent to 10 per cent of the organization's turnover, then the auditor might not have to do much work to be satisfied that the figure in the accounts for the turnover is correct to within a tolerance of plus or minus 5 per cent. The user of the accounts might expect the accounts to be much more accurate than that. An amount of 5 per cent of the turnover of a large organization could run into hundreds of millions or billions of currency units. If, on the other hand, the auditor had to be assured that the accounts were accurate to within 1,000 currency units, the task may be very onerous (and thus time consuming as well as expensive for the auditee organization). A balance has to be struck such that the audit can be completed in a reasonable time (allowing the financial statements to be published whilst they are still relevant) and accurate enough for the users to be able to rely on them.

International Auditing Standard 320 *Materiality in Planning and Performing an Audit* is concerned with the determination of materiality by an external auditor. It does not prescribe a hard and fast rule for the materiality that should be used in the planning of an audit. Instead, it states:

> The auditor's determination of materiality is a matter of professional judgment, and is affected by the auditor's perception of the financial information needs of users of the financial statements.
>
> (IAASB, 2020: 332)

That said, often an auditor will determine materiality by applying a percentage to a benchmark value, which might be the organization's turnover or the value of its assets or some other value. ISA 320 suggests that for PBEs the

> total cost or net cost (expenses less revenues or expenditure less receipts) may be appropriate benchmarks for program activities. Where a public sector entity has custody of public assets, assets may be an appropriate benchmark.
>
> (IAASB, 2020: 338)

Just as a guide, the level of materiality for a PBE might be set in the range 0.25 to 1 per cent of the total cost. The level of materiality might be set at a much smaller value for classes of transactions that are more sensitive (as provided for by paragraph 10 of ISA 320 [IAASB, 2020: 334]). By way of example, a local council's overall financial statements might be audited with a materiality of 1 per cent of the annual total expenditure, but the audit of expenses paid to the elected councillors might be audited with a materiality level set at zero, or very close to it, in recognition of the public attention given to such payments.

The exact wording of opinions differ across countries. ISA 700 allows the opinion either to be whether the financial statements present fairly or give a true and fair view of the organization's finances. In this context:

- **true** means that information is factual and conforms with reality, conforms with required standards and law and the financial statements are based on data that has been correctly extracted from the financial systems; and
- **fair** means that information is free from discrimination and bias and reflects the substance of the organization's underlying transactions.

A modified opinion means that the auditor cannot affirm that the financial statements are true and fair. This can be because the auditor concludes that the financial statements are not free from material misstatement or because the auditor was unable to obtain sufficient appropriate audit evidence to conclude that they are free from material misstatement.

There are three types of modified audit opinions according to ISA 705 *Modification to the Opinion in the Independent Auditor's Report* (IAASB, 804):

- qualified (either on the basis of misstatement or on the basis of an inability to obtain sufficient, appropriate audit evidence);
- adverse; and
- disclaimer.

A qualified opinion is given when the auditor concludes that the financial statements are materially misstated. This could be because they conclude the level of monetary error in a balance was material or that the organization had failed to apply an accounting standard correctly.

Where the auditor is unable to obtain sufficient appropriate audit evidence on which to base their opinion, but the auditor concludes that the possible effects on the financial statements of undetected misstatements, if any, could be material but not pervasive, then they would issue a qualified opinion. In this situation the auditor would explain the circumstances of the limitation on the scope of their audit in the basis of their opinion.

An adverse opinion is given when the auditor has obtained and evaluated sufficient audit evidence and 'concludes that misstatements, individually or in the aggregate, are both material and pervasive to the financial statements' (IAASB, 2020: 806). Once again, the auditor is required to explain the nature of the disagreement and to attempt to quantify, if possible, the effect it has had on the financial statements.

The auditor shall disclaim an opinion when they are unable to obtain sufficient appropriate audit evidence on which to base an opinion and concludes that the possible effects on the financial statements of undetected misstatements, if any, could be both material and pervasive. This audit opinion might not be expected but it could happen if, for example, an organization had a lot of its financial records and systems destroyed in a disaster such as a fire or flood (although, of course, management should have in place internal controls that prevent such catastrophic losses from happening). A disclaimer opinion would also be appropriate for an organization that is so chaotically managed that the auditor is unable to gather audit evidence with any confidence.

Emphasis of matter

Occasionally auditors will identify an aspect of the financial statements that is adequately measured and disclosed within the financial statements but which they feel is so fundamental to a proper understanding of the financial statements that users should have their attention drawn to it. In these circumstances, they would include 'emphasis of matter' paragraphs into their report. Such paragraphs do not modify or qualify the auditor's opinion.

External audit of public sector organizations

The external audit of a PBE might differ from the audit of a private sector organization in a number of ways. For a PBE the auditor may:

- be required to give an opinion about lawfulness of expenditure (and may have the power to declare items of expenditure as unlawful);
- place a greater emphasis on fraud and corruption (such as by carrying-out data-matching to detect frauds);
- place a greater emphasis on the value for money achieved by the organization;

- carry out audit checks on grants, on behalf of the grant givers;
- conduct special investigations; and
- may be obliged to answer questions and consider objections from members of the public about the financial statements being audited.

It is crucial that the users of accounts can rely on the opinions that auditors give and this requires the auditor to be independent of the organization that they are auditing. One particular instance where independence is critical is the audit of government itself. In that situation the auditor needs to have independence from the politicians and government that they are charged with auditing. The importance of this is the basis for the Lima Declaration by INTOSAI, which stated that independence should be guaranteed in the country's constitution (INTOSAI, 2022). SAIs should also have financial independence, which means they have sufficient financial resources to accomplish their work.

There are two institutional models for Supreme Audit Institutions (Shand, 2013: 822). The francophone system includes a court of accounts that passes a judgement on the legality and correctness of the accounts. If/when the court is satisfied with the report and accounts it acquits the officials and their accounts. The government then passes a law based on the court's report.

The other main model is the use of an auditor-general, based on the Westminster system enacted in the 1860s. Here the auditor-general is independent of government and reports to the legislature, often through a public accounts committee. Often the auditor-general is a single person, but, in some countries, there is a collegial body or board to carry out the role.

There is a practical limit to the independence an SAI can achieve, even if it were written in a constitution. A sovereign government is not likely to yield some of its sovereignty to its supreme audit institution (Jones and Pendlebury, 2010: 129). The auditor can be granted independence from the executive arm of government, which at a national level is the auditee, but it is difficult for the auditor to be independent of the legislature. There is not an issue for the auditor of a private company being independent of the company's management but not independent of the shareholders since it is the shareholders who appoint the auditor. However, at a national government level the equivalent of the shareholders, the legislature, is a political organization. The government auditor is potentially caught in the position of being expected to give opinions about government that are frank, honest and free of political interference; however, they are appointed by a legislature that is by its nature political (Jones and Pendlebury, 2010: 129). In fact, as Jones and Pendlebury point out in some jurisdictions the call for auditors to be independent is:

> outweighed by the demand for government officials to be directly accountable to voters, whereby the auditors are headed by a politician

> whose mandate is subject to a specific popular election-a common practice in the USA (2010: 128).

Having said that, some countries, including Australia, have arrangements for independently reviewing their supreme audit institution (SAI) whilst INTOSAI has established arrangements for peer review, which can give governments some independent assurance about the work of its SAI.

INTERNAL AUDITING

The Institute of Internal Auditors (IIA) defines internal auditing as:

> an independent, objective assurance and consulting activity designed to add value and improve an organization's operations. It helps an organization accomplish its objectives by bringing a systematic, disciplined approach to evaluate and improve the effectiveness of risk management, control, and governance processes.
>
> (Institute of Internal Auditors, 2022)

Internal audits were carried out in the Middle Ages although what would be recognized as an internal audit tends to be dated to the mid-nineteenth century when limited liability companies were created and the gap between the owners of a business and its managers widened (Bac, 2007: 228). When private organizations are small the owner can closely supervise their employees and assets without needing to involve anyone else. As organizations grow this is not feasible and owners want assurance that everything is in order. An early example of internal auditing relates to the railway companies where it was seen as a form of insurance to protect the company's assets by 'discovering problems sooner than the external auditor would' (Flesher and Zarzeski, 2002: 94).

Modern internal audit is dated from the 1940s. The IIA itself was formed in 1941 (Flesher and Zarzeski, 2002: 95). Flesher and Zarzeski (2002) describe how the role of the internal auditor has changed over the next 50 years becoming more involved in performance auditing (see later in this chapter) and the management of risks in general rather than just financial risks.

The traditional perception of internal audit was as a kind of internal police force with a focus on financial transactions and compliance with systems and procedures (Baltaci and Yilmaz, 2007: 207). Traditional internal audit work was reactive and sought to protect and secure the organization's tangible assets. Internal audits would focus on financial systems. Internal auditors would do things like randomly visit staff who handled cash and count the money in the till; check staff travel expenses claims to receipts; review contract amendments; and carry out stock checks. The modern role perceives internal auditors as partners in the organization. Their focus is now on governance and they seek to carry out work proactively based on risk assessment. The broader role stretches beyond financial transactions, and internal auditors may review the controls that are in place to protect organization's intangible assets (such as knowledge and reputation) as well as its tangible assets.

The definition of internal audit at the top of this section is a general one, applicable to the private and public sectors. Whilst internal auditing may have begun as a process of checking financial systems and transactions, the IIA definition does not mention finance or money or resources at all. Modern internal audit is a broader aid to management than just financial, giving an opinion about the system of internal control (see Chapter 4) and the extent of compliance with it.

Internal audit might be carried out by employees of the organization or it might be outsourced to a specialist provider. The latter is particularly attractive to small organizations whose requirements for internal audit do not justify the employment of full-time staff.

The overall head or manager of the internal audit team is referred to in internal auditing standards as the 'chief audit executive'. If the internal audit is provided by direct employees, the chief audit executive could be appointed by shareholders (or the governing body of a PBE) or by an audit committee or by management. Generally, it would not be practical for the shareholders and audit committees to be involved in the appointment of the other staff in the internal audit team: this is more suitable for the chief audit executive to do.

If the organization outsources its internal audit work, then the award of the contract could still be made by management, but if there is an audit committee, they are likely to be involved in the appointment, if not wholly responsible for it.

Internal auditors cannot, by definition, be wholly independent of the organization that is employing them (although outsourced internal auditors are much more independent if they have many other clients). Nevertheless, what is crucial is that internal auditors are not part of the organization's day-to-day systems and procedures because that would compromise their ability to give an opinion on at least a part of the overall system of internal control.

International Standards for the Professional Practice of Internal Auditing

The IIA issues International Standards for the Professional Practice of Internal Auditing. The latest version came into effect in January 2017.

The underlying principles in internal auditing are generally similar to those for external auditing. Internal auditors should act diligently, professionally and with integrity at all times. Internal auditors should protect their actual and perceived objectivity and independence and take steps to avoid or remove any actual or perceived conflicts of interest.

The main elements of the IIA's standards are:

- the purpose, authority and responsibility of internal audit to be set out in an internal audit charter;
- internal audit to be independent of management and internal auditors must be objective in their work;
- the chief audit executive should be able to report directly to a level within the organization that allows internal audit to be effective;
- internal auditors should carry out their work proficiently and with due professional care;
- the chief audit executive must operate a system of quality assurance and improvement covering all aspects of internal audit work;
- there should be an independent, professional external assessment of internal audit at least once every five years;
- internal audit needs to be managed effectively, to add value to the organization;
- the chief audit executive must have a risk-based plan to determine internal audit's priorities;
- the chief audit executive should report periodically to senior management and the board on internal audit's activity and performance against the overall plan;
- internal audit activity must evaluate and contribute to the improvement of the organization's governance, risk management, and control processes using a systematic, disciplined, and risk-based approach;
- internal auditors must develop and document a plan for each engagement, including the engagement's objectives, scope, timing, and resource allocations;
- internal auditors need to identify, analyse, evaluate and document sufficient information about each audit engagement;
- the results of each engagement must be communicated to management in an objective, concise and timely manner; and
- the results of audit engagements, including the follow-up of management's actions resulting from previous internal audit reports, must be monitored.

An individual organization may customize the IIA's standards to its circumstances. For example, CIPFA, HM Treasury, and several other internal audit standard setters produced *Public Sector Internal Audit Standards* which apply the IIA's international standards to the United Kingdom's public sector (CIPFA et al, 2017).

Internal audit code of ethics

Whichever sector they are working in, internal auditors are expected to comply with a code of ethics. The four principles of the code are shown in Box 9.3, and there is some read over between them and the seven principles of public life described in Chapter 8.

BOX 9.3 THE FOUR PRINCIPLES OF THE IIA CODE OF ETHICS

Integrity

The integrity of internal auditors establishes trust and thus provides the basis for reliance on their judgement.

Objectivity

Internal auditors exhibit the highest level of professional objectivity in gathering, evaluating and communicating information about the activity or process being examined. Internal auditors make a balanced assessment of all the relevant circumstances and are not unduly influenced by their own interests or by others in forming judgements

Confidentiality

Internal auditors respect the value and ownership of information they receive and do not disclose information without appropriate authority unless there is a legal or professional obligation to do so.

Competency

Internal auditors apply the knowledge, skills and experience needed in the performance of internal audit services.

Source: Institute of Internal Auditors (2021)

AUDITORS AND FRAUD AND CORRUPTION

There was a discussion of fraud and corruption in Chapter 4 that made clear that the primary responsibility for preventing and detecting it rests with the public manager. Lord Justice Topes summarized this in a judgement in 1896 (re Kingston Cotton Mill Company (No. 2), 1896) when he said: 'The auditor [...] is a watchdog, but not a bloodhound.' An auditor should be vigilant in their work but it is not their responsibility to uncover every instance of fraud and other wrongdoing.

Auditors can, though, help with both prevention and detection of fraud. Their work on reviewing the internal control system can identify gaps in the system where frauds or errors could happen and where additional controls are needed. They can assess whether controls that should prevent errors and fraud are (a) being operated properly and (b) are effective.

An auditor is not expected to detect all frauds, but the results of their audit testing may identify fraud. If an auditor uncovers an anomaly in one of their tests, then they are obliged to undertake further tests until they can reach a firm conclusion about the subject under test. Therefore, if an auditor's test results raised their suspicions about a fraud, then they would be expected to carry out further audit work until their suspicions are either confirmed or allayed. They might then advise the relevant manager of their findings in a report and expect the manager to take appropriate action to deal with the fraud and to prevent any recurrence. Auditors would adopt this approach because they are supposed to remain independent of the organization's management systems.

If a fraud were perpetrated on an organization of such a magnitude that it affected the organization's financial statements by a sum equal to or greater than the auditor's level of materiality, then the auditor's tests should detect it (since they are giving an opinion that the accounts do not include material errors). Sometimes the level of fraud is so high that the external auditor is unable to reach a conclusion about financial statements and will either issue a qualified audit opinion or not issue an opinion at all.

A rather dramatic example of this relates to the United Kingdom's Department for Work and Pensions (DWP), which is responsible for administering a wide range of pensions and benefits. In 2010/1 the level of benefits overpaid because of fraud and error was estimated at 2.1 per cent of expenditure on benefits. This stayed around 2 per cent of expenditure each year unto and including 2018/9. In 2019/20 (the first financial year affected by the coronavirus pandemic) the rate was 2.4 per cent. In 2020/1 it rose to 3.9 per cent and in 2021/2 it was 4.0 per cent, which amounts to £8.6 billion of public money (Department of Work and Pensions, 2022).

These levels of fraud means that every year since 1988 that the external auditor has issued a qualified audit opinion on the DWP's financial statements. Given the nature of the DWP's work and the likelihood of fraud against it, one wonders if there is a realistic prospect of it ever reducing the level of fraud low enough for the auditors to give an unqualified opinion on its accounts.

AUDIT OF COVID-19 RESPONSES

As mentioned in Chapter 1 and elsewhere in this book, the responses by governments and other PBEs to the coronavirus pandemic in 2020 and 2021 tested the resilience and the effectiveness of public financial management systems. At first thought the pandemic put pressure on government's ability to deliver public services, such as health care, and at the same time tested them to maintain their economies during lockdowns. These challenges to the budget execution phase had to be enabled by governments revisiting their budget preparation and approval stages, legislating supplementary budgets, changing the plans for tax receipts and government borrowing.

But what about the budget oversight stage of the public financial management cycle? The need for accountability, transparency and audit did not go away because there was a crisis; indeed, perhaps the need for it at that time was greater and more urgent. The reality is, though, that people would die and businesses would be bankrupt if governments did not use their financial systems to buy vaccines and personal protective equipment and pay benefits to people who were unable to work. No one would die as a direct result of not completing the audit of financial statements: the audit could be done later. This sentiment is well illustrated by the International Monetary Fund's statement (2020): 'do whatever it takes, but keep the receipts.'

Whilst understandable as a strategy, it was perhaps not the best way of protecting public money. Even before the pandemic, PEFA (2021) had written that 'internal audit, management of fiscal risks, external audit and scrutiny by Supreme Audit Institutions and the legislature remain the weakest areas of PFM.'

The International Budget Partnership and INTOSAI Development Initiative (2021: 5) put it like this:

> When putting in place fiscal policy responses to the pandemic, governments are taking a series of measures out of a sense of urgency—such as bypassing legislation, relaxing procurement procedures and not seeking citizens input—that undermine accountability.

During a crisis such as the coronavirus pandemic, an effective, independent SAI can be an asset to government as well as the general public and other stakeholders. They can give stakeholders assurance about whether public financial management systems and controls are being complied with and provide some transparency and accountability for the government's financial management.

In the United Kingdom, for example, the National Audit Office created and published an online tracker of government spending on the pandemic. The Comptroller and Auditor-General (who is the head of the National Audit Office) also wrote a blog post about auditing the government's pandemic response. In it he summarized a number of shortcomings in the government's response. He noted, 'the speedy response has come at a cost—higher levels of fraud and error than government would have otherwise expected' (Davies, 2021). He also illustrated the risk of financial loss with the example of the Bounce Back Loan scheme. By March 2021, 1.5 million loans amounting to £47 billion had been given by banks based on a 100 per cent guarantee from the government, but the credit checks were weak (or non-existent) and it was estimated that between 35 and 60 per cent of the loans would not be repaid by lenders. This is £16 billion to £28 billion.

Bandy and Metcalfe (2021: 24–5) accepted that governments had to make changes to the normal PFM processes in order to deal with the pandemic. They suggested that the changes did not have to be only the budget preparation, approval and execution stages of the PFM cycle. They said: 'Governments could have put in place some extraordinary oversight arrangements as part of their PFM changes.' An example they gave to illustrate this related to the emergency award of contracts for the supply of personal protective equipment and vaccines. If governments decided to implement fast-track procurement processes that reduce or completely eliminate competitive tendering, they could have made changes to the oversight arrangements by creating a panel of independent experts to review procurement decisions and give assurance that the prices and terms and conditions were reasonable and the contracts were value for money. They could also have enhanced transparency by insisting with the suppliers that, in return for being awarded a contract without competition, the contract would be published without redactions; thus, there was some pressure for the supplier not to overcharge for the goods or services.

Audit is usually seen as a retrospective activity, looking back as what has been done or not done, but there is a growing use of 'real time audits', which are audits conducted while (public) money is being spent. In the case of the pandemic this would mean auditors reviewing systems and spending during the crisis rather than waiting to conduct reviews of financial statements after the crisis has abated. A real-time audit uses live data and information from the organization being audited and applies algorithms and monitoring by auditors to identify problems and issues as they arise. The major potential benefit from this is preventing things going wrong (public money being wasted, lost or stolen) rather than pointing it out afterwards.

Such real time auditing is challenging to do. It requires commitment from leaders, including politicians, and it requires SAIs having staff who are capable and empowered to do the work (Willcox, 2021). Perhaps the biggest challenge for public sector auditors was summarized by Smithson, quoted by Willcox (2021): 'Complex organizations are difficult to understand, and if you do not understand them, you cannot effectively audit them.'

CONCLUSION

Auditing is an accountability mechanism with a long heritage; even internal auditing dates back more than 150 years. Traditionally auditing was perceived as a kind of policing activity, but in modern times auditors, external and internal, are coming to be seen more and more as advisors to managers, adding value to organization overall.

For PBEs in particular, auditors are integral to the assessment of whether the organization is getting value for money from its use of public money. The difficult part of this assessment is evaluating a PBE's effectiveness, which was the subject of Chapter 7.

EXERCISES

1. The external auditor of a PBE is auditing the income for the year. The level of materiality is set at €1 million. The total income is €50 million. Within this total, there was €47.5 million of government grants. All those grant claims and receipts have been checked and verified. Does the auditor need more evidence to be assured of the income figure?
2. When carrying out an audit, what are some warning signs that may cause an external auditor to suspect there could be fraud or irregularities in the financial statements?
3. The internal audit code of ethics mentioned in the chapter has principles rather than rules. Why do you think this approach is adopted?
4. If you were carrying out a performance audit of a service or project you are familiar with, what would be the main areas that you would examine? How easy or difficult would it be to measure the effectiveness of the service or project?

REFERENCES

Bac, A. (2007). External auditing and performance evaluation, with special emphasis on detecting corruption. In A. Shah (Ed.), *Local Public Financial Management* (pp. 227–254). Washington, DC: World Bank.

Baltaci, M. and Yilmaz, S. (2007). Internal Control and Audit at Local Levels. In A. Shah (Ed.), *Local Public Financial Management*. (pp. 193–225). Washington, DC: World Bank.

Bandy, G. P., & Metcalfe, A. (2021). *Rethinking Public Financial Management*. London: ACCA. Available at: https://www.accaglobal.com/gb/en/professional-insights/global-profession/rethinking-public-financial-management.html (Accessed: 25 April 2022).

Bergmann, A. (2009). *Public Sector Financial Management*. Harlow: FT Prentice Hall.

Bonollo, E. (2019). Measuring supreme audit institutions' outcomes: Current literature and future insights. *Public Money & Management, 39*(7), 468–477.

Bringselius, L. (2018). Efficiency, economy and effectiveness—But what about ethics? Supreme audit institutions at a critical juncture. *Public Money & Management, 38*(2), 105–110.

CIPFA, Department of Health, HM Treasury, Scottish Government, Welsh Government, Northern Ireland Department of Finance and Personnel, & IIA. (2017). *Public Sector Internal Audit Standards*. London: HM Treasury. Available at: https://www.gov.uk/government/publications/public-sector-internal-audit-standards (Accessed: 21 July 2022).

Coombs, H. M., & Edwards, J. R. (1990). The evolution of the district audit. *Financial Accountability and Management*, *6*(3), 153–176.

Davies, G (2021). *Auditing Government's Pandemic Response* [Blog]. Available at: https://www.nao.org.uk/naoblog/auditing-governments-pandemic-response/ (Accessed: 21 July 2022).

Department of Work and Pensions. (2022). *DWP Annual Report and Accounts 2021 to 2022*. London: The Stationery Office. Available at: https://www.gov.uk/government/publications/dwp-annual-report-and-accounts-2021-to-2022 (Accessed: 21 July 2022).

Flesher, D. L., & Zarzeski, M. T. (2002). The roots of operational (value-for-money) auditing in English-speaking nations. *Accounting and Business Research*, *32*(2), 93–104.

IAASB. (2016). *International Standard on Auditing 700 (Revised) Forming an Opinion and Reporting on Financial Statements*. New York: IFAC. Available at: https://www.ifac.org/system/files/publications/files/ISA-700-Revised_8.pdf (Accessed: 21 July 2022).

IAASB. (2020). *Handbook of International Quality Control, Auditing, Review, Other Assurance, and Related Services Pronouncements (2020 Edition)*. New York, NY: IFAC. Available at: https://www.iaasb.org/publications/2020-handbook-international-quality-control-auditing-review-other-assurance-and-related-services (Accessed: 19 July 2022).

Institute of Internal Auditors. (2016). *International Standards for the Professional Practice of Internal Auditing (2016 Edition)*. London: IIA. Available at: https://www.theiia.org/globalassets/documents/standards/standards-2017/ippf-standards-2017-english.pdf (Accessed: 20 July 2022).

Institute of Internal Auditors. (2021). *Code of Ethics* [Webpage]. Available at: https://www.theiia.org/en/content/guidance/mandatory/standards/international-standards-for-the-professional-practice-of-internal-auditing/ (Accessed: 19 July 2022).

Institute of Internal Auditors. (2022). *Definition of Internal Audit* [Webpage]. Available at: https://www.theiia.org/en/about-us/about-internal-audit/ (Accessed: 21 July 2022).

International Budget Partnership and INTOSAI Development Initiative. (2021). *All Hands on Deck: Harnessing Accountability through External Public Audits*. Available at: https://internationalbudget.org/publications/all-hands-on-deck-harnessing-accountability-through-external-public-audits/ (Accessed: 21 July 2022).

International Monetary Fund. (2020). *Fiscal Monitor April 2020*. Available at: https://www.imf.org/en/Publications/FM/Issues/2020/04/06/fiscal-monitor-april-2020 (Accessed: 21 July 2022).

INTOSAI. (2022). *Independence* [Webpage]. Available at: https://www.intosai.org/focus-areas/independence (Accessed: 21 July 2022).
Jones, R. & Pendlebury, M. (2010). *Public Sector Accounting* (6th edition). Harlow: Pearson Education.
Kingston Cotton Mill Company (No. 2) [1896] Court of Appeal. 2 Ch. 279.
Nerantzidis, M., Pazarskis, M., Drogalas, G., & Galanis, S. (2022). Internal auditing in the public sector: A systematic literature review and future research agenda. *Journal of Public Budgeting, Accounting & Financial Management, 34*(2), 189–209.
PEFA. (2021). *2020 Global Report on Public Financial Management.* Washington, DC: PEFA. Available at: https://www.pefa.org/global-report-2020/ (Accessed: 25 April 2022).
Power, M. (2000). The audit society - Second thoughts. *International Journal of Auditing, 4*(1), 111–119.
Rana, T., Steccolini, I., Bracci, E., & Mihret, D. G. (2021). Performance auditing in the public sector: A systematic literature review and future research avenues. *Financial Accountability & Management* (December).
Shand, D. (2013). External audit. In R. Allen, R. Hemming, & B. H. Potter (Eds.), *The International Handbook of Public Financial Management* (pp. 817–836). Basingstoke: Palgrave Macmillan.
Willcox, R. (2021). *Running in Parallel: The Challenges of Implementing Real-Time Auditing* [Online Article]. Available at: https://www.publicfinancefocus.org/depth/2021/10/running-parallel-challenges-implementing-real-time-auditing (Accessed: 21 July 2022).
World Bank. (2021). *Supreme Audit Institutions Independence Index.* Available at: https://documents.worldbank.org/en/publication/documents-reports/documentdetail/885041626769025475/supreme-audit-institutions-independence-index-2021-global-synthesis-report (Accessed: 21 July 2022).

FURTHER READING (AND WATCHING)

Links to the following resources, and lots more, are available at www.managingpublicmoney.co.uk/extras.

For more information about international auditing standards, a starting point would be the International Auditing And Assurance Standards Board's website at www.ifac.org/IAASB/.

The INTOSAI website has a lot of useful material for those interested in auditing by Supreme Audit Institutions, including the International Standards for Supreme Audit Institutions (ISSAIs) (www.intosai.org/documents/open

-access). INTOSAI also publishes the *International Journal of Government Auditing,* which can be found at http://intosaijournal.org.

The IIA's website (www.theiia.org) is a starting point for resources on internal auditing. Many of the resources are freely available, but others are for members of the IIA only. There are also a number of video resources covering things like fraud and ethics, governance, risk and the internal audit function at its YouTube channel, www.youtube.com/c/IIAGlobalHQTheInstituteofInternalAuditors.

Rana et al. (2021) have produced a literature review on public sector performance auditing, and Nerantzidis et al. (2022) have a literature review on internal auditing in the public sector.

Appendix A

Budgeting in public enterprise: the State Social Security Fund of Sri Lanka

Chathurani Rathnayaka

THE CONTEXT

Sri Lanka finds itself financially strapped, politically unstable and encumbered with both commercial and development loans. Consequently, this will hinder further social and development activities of the country whilst maintaining the status quo. Sri Lanka has a well-defined legal framework in controlling public financial management but its implementation is at stake due to the prevailing socio-political environment.

Sri Lanka has two distinctive mechanisms within the state with respect to state budgeting: the General Budget and the Self-Funding Budget. General Budgets are used to allocate funds in various activities of the state constituents which fully depend upon government funding. In contrast, Self-Funding Budgets are used by state enterprises, which have their own income and funding flows. Although, state enterprises are formulated as a separate entity within the state under a special act of Parliament, they are governed by a state (line) ministry.

TWO DISTINCT APPROACHES

The key differences between the General Budget and the Self-Funding Budget can be attributed to the source of funding, control over budget and the reporting and governance mechanism. The General Treasury of Sri Lanka issues its 'budget call' for a specific financial year to each line ministry and department of the central government. The budget call specifies guidelines to be followed in the preparation of each organization's budget requirement. This cascades further down to relevant constituents through each line ministry or department.

The general budget approach follows a centralized bottom-up approach in budget formulation, control and reporting, whereas self-funding budgets are unique for specific state actor or an institution in which institutional specific framework and relevant state controls are applied in controlling and reporting.

THE CASE OF THE STATE SOCIAL SECURITY FUND (SSF)

State Social Security Fund—context

This fund was established in a Special Act of Parliament on 1 March 1981, and it is administered by the Corporate Board functioning under the Ministry of National Policies and Economic Affairs. The provisions of the Act shall apply to every state and non-state sector undertaking belonging to any class or category of state or non-state as is specified in an order made by the relevant minister and published in the *Gazette*. Self-employed and migrant workers also could contribute to the SSF on their own and obtain membership. To decentralize the SSF operations and to provide a better service to its members, a branched network was introduced in 1995.

The budget of the SSF reflects the Corporate Plan

Respective line ministries advise the SSF to prepare the corporate plan for four to five years. In line with that, management studies the environment in which it operates in order to identify strategic choices available for the SSF. Through this the SSF:

1. identifies internal and external forces that may influence the organization's performance and choice of strategies; and
2. assesses the organization's current and future strengths, weaknesses, opportunities and threats.

Following the above, they identify strategic results that the SSF expects to achieve during the period for each division of the fund. Each result is further broken down into objectives, outcomes, performance indicators and outputs as shown in Figure A1.

The above process is followed for each result expected by the fund. The next is the development of an action plan for each year as per results, objectives, outcomes, performance indicators and output.

An action plan is developed for each result (and its respective objectives, outcomes and outputs). The action plans specify outcomes, activities for each

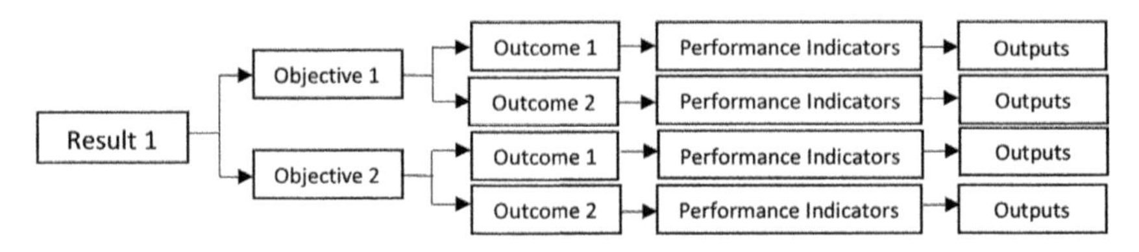

Figure A1 *SSF corporate plan.*

outcome, responsible individual or division, key performance indicators, baseline value/quantity and planned performance.

Implementation and achievement of the corporate plan

The budget is prepared according to the action plan by each division and amalgamated at corporate level. The responsibility for achievement and implementation of the corporate plan is assigned to a Management Committee of SSF, which comprises the Chairman/CEO, Working Director, General Manager, Additional General Manager, Deputy General Manager and Assistant General Manager.

Controlling and monitoring

The Deputy General Manager (Finance) and the Finance Manager (Strategic Planning and Monitoring) are responsible for coordinating, monitoring and reporting the performance of the Action Plan Implementation, which is, in turn, the implementation, control and reporting of the budget. The management committee reviews the performance of the action plans on a quarterly basis.

Issues in implementation

The SSF is a semi-governmental organization. Thus, it has been subjected to two governance structures: line ministry and Management Committee. This twofold organizational governance structure poses issues, particularly in corporate plan and budget implementation such as obtaining approvals, making policy decisions, obtaining certification and so on.

REVIEW QUESTION

How do you evaluate the effectiveness of corporate plan-driven budgets compared to a traditional public sector budgeting systems?

Suggested answers for exercises

CHAPTER 1

1 **Is a fact-finding service a public or a merit good?**

To be a public good it would have to be non-excludable and non-rivalrous. Such a service is excludable because it could feasibly be provided only to those who pay for it and therefore it is not a public good.

Fact-checking is not rivalrous as far as access to its publications might be concerned. It is rivalrous in respect of answering specific requests. Given a finite amount of staff to check the facts, there will be a limit on the questions from the public (or those who subscribe to the service) that can be answered. A government could see this as a merit good if it believes that there are positive externalities that mean a free market would under-produce the service.

If left to a free market, there could be less use made of such a service than if it were freely available because it is funded from taxation. There could be positive externalities from such a service since it could perhaps reduce misinformation in the community and thus improve cohesion and reduce negatives, such as conflicts. These are arguments a government could use in a decision to treat fact-checking as a merit service.

Having said that, if fact-checking were government funded, it may cause people to doubt its independence and objectivity in checking government policies and pronouncements, thus not achieving the government's aims.

2 **Are public goods provided only by governments?**

The definition of a public good means that a free market would under-produce it, if it produced it all. This is because of the problem of free riders. Citizens may want such public goods to be delivered to them, but who would pay for them? This means that there would have to be some coercion placed on payment and this needs the government's power to impose taxes.

When it comes to the actual delivery of the service the government does not have to do it directly: it could use its money to fund the delivery of the service by a private sector or non-profit organization.

3 **What do you think is the optimum level of public expenditure as a proportion of a country's GDP?**

There is not a universal formula for the optimum level because it would depend on so many factors, including the public's expectations for the standard of living and willingness to pay taxes. It is perhaps like the definition of the size of a dram of whisky. It is the amount that offends neither the giver nor the receiver.

The coronavirus pandemic and the post-pandemic period give some insight into how the balance of government spending, taxation levels and GDP can vary in a short period of time. One challenge for some governments in the post-pandemic period will be finding a sustainable level of spending given the way that the pandemic changed expectations about what the government could and should do with public money.

CHAPTER 2

1 **Budget assumptions**

It is not possible to give a standard answer to this question. If the organization you have in mind approves the budget in a public meeting and/or publishes its budgets, then you may be able to get a copy of the budget report or budget speech and it may contain information and commentary on the most important assumptions. There may also be clues about whether the budget has been prepared using incremental, zero-based, performance-based or some other approach.

2 **What are the reasons for and the aims of preparing a capital budget that are separate from an organization's operating budget?**

Reasons could include:

- separate governance and authorization processes exist for capital and operating budgets
- ensuring the capital programme balances the needs of all departments or divisions in the organization
- grouping all possible capital projects in one document can help with prioritizing them
- providing estimates of the impact on the operating budgets, including the impact of depreciation and financing costs as well as the running costs of the completed project
- identifying the cash flow requirements of projects

- matching capital expenditure requirements to available funding and therefore avoiding overcommitment
- feeding into project and resource plans within the organization

CHAPTER 3

1 **Evaluate two or three taxes in your country**

It is not possible to give a suggested answer to this question.

2 **If a government collects a toll from people who cross a bridge, is that a tax?**

No, because a toll is an exchange transaction and, therefore, a fee rather than a tax, even if it is the government that is demanding it be paid.

3 **Why do governments impose fees or charges on some of the services they provide?**

The reasons could include:

- the services are relevant only to a small number of citizens and it would be unfair to taxpayers in general to pay for these services
- they are services which are used only rarely by an individual
- they are services which are used by tourists and visitors who do not pay taxes in the country
- they are services where there are equivalents in the market and the government does not (or should not) compete unfairly
- they are services where there is a limited supply (such as space on public buses and trains) and the government needs to ration their use
- they are services where it would be appropriate for the users to pay because they get the direct benefit from them

4 **Is it fair for a government to use borrowed money to cover a deficit because future generations of taxpayers will have to repay the loans?**

Questions of fairness always need to consider fairness in terms of fairness to whom? On one hand, borrowing money for 25 or more years to finance the construction of infrastructure like railways and public assets like schools can be argued to be fair to future generations because it will be these generations (more than the current generation) who will use the infrastructure and assets and their taxes will repay the loans.

At the other extreme, taking out long-term loans to finance the budget gap between tax receipts and operating expenses is putting the burden of a current budget problem onto future generations.

There is no single right answer to such questions of intergenerational equity. The fair treatment of different generations is a topic for public finance managers and policymakers to keep in mind as they do their work.

5 **What would be the benefits and costs of implementing a minimum alcohol price?**

Assuming the consumption of alcohol falls then the benefits might include:

- lower incidence of alcohol-related disease and a reduction in health care spending
- fewer anti-social incidents for the police and other public services to deal with, which could allow their budgets to be reduced
- the government will have some extra income from the alcohol tax that it could use to finance spending in areas unrelated to health.

The costs of this policy might include:

- spending money to promote the change in policy and persuade the public of its benefits
- investment in setting up a system to impose and collect the tax
- costs of enforcement if it became apparent that the tax is being avoided
- the yield from the tax could fall if the policy is very successful, causing a gap in the government's budget

CHAPTER 4

1 **Identify some prevent and detect controls**

It is not possible to give a suggested answer to this question.

2 **What are some of the actions a government could take to mitigate the risk of non-compliance with rules and regulations?**

Possible mitigations include:

- clear communication of the rules and regulations
- implementing controls in computer systems that prevent non-compliance
- training of all staff in the procedures when they take up their posts and at frequent intervals thereafter
- clear and visible sanctions on individuals for not following the rules and procedures
- effective supervision
- random and/or routine checks of compliance by inspectors and/or auditors

3 **As a budget-holder in a PBE should you underspend your budget?**

It is not possible to give a definitive answer because context matters. However, some of the issues you might consider in reaching an answer for your particular context include:

- what do the financial rules and procedures say about over- and under-spending a budget? They may be clear that budgets should not be over-spent but be silent about underspending

- it is unlikely that a budget-holder can spend their budget exactly so organizations are likely to operate a tolerance for over and underspending, even if this is not explicitly stated anywhere
- if there are opportunities to deliver projects or services more efficiently that would lead to a budget underspend, then this may be expected to be achieved by the budget-holder
- underspending a budget by reducing the quality and/or volume of the service or project is (probably) undesirable
- some politicians may take the view that, having imposed the taxes on people, the public services that were promised to them (explicitly or implicitly) should be delivered and the money spent
- budget-holders may be tempted to avoid underspending their budget out of fear that their budget the following year will be reduced accordingly

4 **What are some reasons for a government to include the treasury function within its Ministry of Finance rather than transferring it to an independent agency?**

- better communication between stakeholders since they are within one organization
- better coordination of the treasury's activities with the other elements of budgeting and budget execution
- avoids spreading skills and experience between the Ministry of Finance and the agency, which could be important if there are limited people with the necessary skills
- lower costs since there would be economies of scale for management and overheads
- clearer lines of accountability if the minister of finance is responsible for the treasury activities as well as the other budget execution functions.

CHAPTER 5

1 **Cost classification in an organization you are familiar with**

It is not possible to give a suggested answer to this question.

2 **In what circumstances would it not be necessary to use net present value technique to appraise a project?**

By definition the net present value technique has to consider the present value of future cash flows (and monetized flows for non-cash costs and benefits) so there would be no point using the technique for projects where there is no future cash flow. It is unlikely that this is literally the case (that is, all cash flows out and in take place on one day), but an organization can, for example, have a policy that, if cash flows all happen within one year, then they are treated as current and not future cash flows.

Another circumstance is where a project has limited financial implications and the basis of the decision to implement it or not will be based on non-financial factors.

Similarly, an organization could have a financial threshold where projects below the threshold are not appraised using net present value.

An organization could have a policy that it always uses payback or accounting rate of return for its project appraisals.

3 **What other non-financial factors might be relevant to a public project you are familiar with?**

It is not possible to know what factors would be relevant in your example but below are some ideas:

- public opinion, which could be divided between different groups of the public such those who will use/benefit from the project and those who would not
- relationships with other organizations, whether other PBEs or private sector organizations. For example, the project could have an impact on the market for goods and services that has a financial impact on local businesses
- impact on the organization's risk management and resilience
- sustainability considerations
- legacy from previous projects
- time (how long has the organization got to achieve the project?)

CHAPTER 6

1 **How effective and efficient were the public procurement arrangements during the coronavirus pandemic of 2020?**

It is not possible to give a suggested answer to this question.

2 **What is the difference between delivering public outcomes by giving grants and using contracts?**

A contract is an agreement between two (or more) parties to do something. It sets out what will be done and the terms and conditions include the financial compensation to the supplier. All of this is (ideally) in writing and intended both to ensure clarity between the parties and to allow arbitrators or courts to rule on disputes. All of this gives a high level of protection to the parties but takes time and money to create.

Governments and PBEs can attach conditions to the grants they give (perhaps restricting how money should be spent and requiring grants to be refunded if not used), but there are not the same remedies available for breach of a grant as there are for a contract.

This means that sometimes a PBE may prefer to undertake a procurement process that results in a contract with a supplier whilst in other situations they may prefer the flexibility of using grant payments.

3 **Data needed for the analysis stage in commissioning public transport**

The data might include the following:

- **Data about whose needs should be met**—population and demographic data analysed by location in the city, age
- **Data about extent of need**—data on current usage of each mode of transport, including popular and unpopular routes/services, current spending/subsidy on the services, income from fares and other sources
- **Data about what contributes to need**—data on employment status, income, access to private transport, survey data on both existing users of transport and people who choose not to use the transport
- **Data about likely future demand**—population trends from census data especially the demographic groups who most use public transport, plans for development of the city for residential, commercial and industrial uses.

4 **What type of contract would you use for the provision of a maintenance contract for a PBE's fleet of vehicles?**

A significant proportion of maintenance work is planned or predictable so a fixed price contract would be suitable, giving the client organization certainty about the cost of the service. An experienced provider of vehicle maintenance ought to be able to identify the cost of providing the service using data about the number, age and usage of the vehicles in the fleet. This type of contract then gives the provider an incentive to be efficient in their work if they are to make a profit.

If the contract runs for a few years there could be an arrangement for indexation of the contract price to cover the risk of rising prices for vehicle parts and labour.

One area of uncertainty would be the costs of repairing vehicles that have been in collisions. This could mean a lot of extra, unplanned work and spare parts. This alone is not a reason to base the whole service on a time and materials contract since such a contract would put the financial risk wholly on the client. Instead, either the client organization could award a separate contract for collision damage (which could be sensible if the fleet is large and there are lots of collisions) or the main fixed price contract could include a provision that extra work on collision damage would be paid at an agreed hourly or daily rate plus materials costs.

CHAPTER 7

1 **For a public service that you are interested in, what are its principal inputs, activities, outputs and outcomes?**

It is not possible to give a suggested answer to this question.

2 **How might you estimate monetary values for the outcomes you identified in exercise 1?**

It is not possible to give a suggested answer to this question. However, you could look to adapt the revealed and stated preference methods explained in the chapter to your example.

3 **Possible performance measures for a police service.**

Here are some suggested measures. In practice they might be further analysed into different types of crime.

Inputs	Number of crimes reported Crime rate per 1,000 population Number of police officers Size of annual budget Cost of service per citizen
Activities	Per cent of emergency calls answered in 15 seconds Per cent of calls requiring a police response Average time to attend to an emergency call Average time to complete a crime report Per cent of incidents attended within target times Per cent of police officer time on active duty
Outputs	Per cent of crimes resolved (there is a result achieved for the victim) Number of incidents attended Number of arrests made Number of public events attended
Outcomes	Per cent of citizens who feel safe Per cent of citizens satisfied with the police service Number of people killed or seriously injured in road traffic collisions

CHAPTER 8

1 **Accountability mechanisms in your own organization**

It is not possible to give a suggested answer to this question.

2 **How would you go about placing a financial value on the treasures owned by your local museum?**

There are three main ways that an organization could value an asset such as a building for inclusion on its balance sheet. One way is the market value: looking at recent data for the sales of similar buildings in similar places and/or asking for valuations by expert estate agents.

The second way is to estimate how much it would cost to create the building if it did not exist. Unless the building is very new this has to include an element of depreciation to reflect the fact that a replacement building would need to be 'aged' to match the existing building.

The third way is to consider the future earning potential of the building and commute that into a capital sum. This would mean estimating the future rental income and using an interest rate to calculate the capital value.

Perhaps there are some treasures in the museum where one or other of these three methods could be applied. For example, the museum could have artworks or jewellery where there is an active market and an estimated value could be inferred. There may be some treasures where the replacement cost approach could be used and perhaps the museum itself is housed in an old building that could be valued using the future earnings method.

Chances are there will be some treasures where none of these methods is satisfactory. For those, perhaps the insurance value could be used. This involves a third party, the insurer, so there is some independence but there will also be a constraint imposed by the insurer in terms of the maximum exposure it will accept in return for a premium that is affordable to the museum.

Another way would be to use the amount paid by the museum to acquire the treasure but, of course, this cannot be used for treasures that were gifted or bequeathed to the museum.

CHAPTER 9

1 **Is more audit evidence needed to be assured of the income for the year?**

The auditor has verified 95 per cent of the €50 million income. This is good but there is no evidence of the remaining €2.5 million of income that is from other sources and there is potential for that to be materially mis-stated (that is, be wrong by €1 million or more). Some extra evidence should be sought to confirm the total income is €50 million.

2 **When carrying out an audit, what are some warning signs that may cause an external auditor to suspect there could be fraud or irregularities in the financial statements?**

There are many indicators that could raise an auditor's suspicions but none of them are proof that fraud is taking place. The auditor would have to conduct suitable tests to find evidence that either confirms or negates their suspicions.

The signals could include:

- lack of records
- weak or non-existent internal controls
- poor or non-existent segregation of duties
- auditor has difficulty obtaining source documentation (because this could indicate such records have been destroyed or concealed)
- unsatisfactory explanations given to queries raised

- defensive attitude by staff, such as being unwilling to answer reasonable questions
- unusual payments in terms of amounts, frequency or nature, being made
- staff with lifestyles beyond the level commensurate with salary
- fragile accounting systems
- problems with the organization's bankers, solicitors and previous auditors
- staff who work long hours and never take a holiday because this might suggest they are worried others will discover discrepancies

3 **Why is the internal audit code of ethics based on principles rather than rules?**

The advantage of principles over rules is the flexibility. All internal audit teams, whether in the public or in the private sector, can adopt processes and practices that comply with the principles whilst also fitting their context. Principles can also be written concisely because they do not have to be explicit about all the possible variations in circumstances. A rules-based approach would have the problem of either having simple rules, which do not fit every circumstance, or having very long and complicated rules, which cover (almost) every circumstance.

Principles-based codes usually operate on the basis of 'comply or explain'. Generally, an internal auditor is expected to comply with the principles but perhaps there are occasions where they choose not to comply because that would be in the best interests of stakeholders (not the internal auditor). In such situations the internal auditor could write down their reasons for non-compliance with the code.

The disadvantage of principles-based codes is that the subjective nature of principles may make it harder to judge when an internal auditor is in breach of them.

4 **Carrying out a performance audit in your context**

It is not possible to give a standard answer to this question.

Glossary of terms

accounts payable the amounts owed to creditors. Sometimes used to refer to the team that processes such payments and/or the computer system they use

accounting principles general instructions for accounting to ensure that the accounts produced are complete, accurate and consistent with other organizations

accounts receivable the amounts owed to the organization by debtors. Sometimes used to refer to the team that collects such payments and/or the computer system they use

accrual-basis accounting the basis of accounting where transactions are recognized in the accounting period where the transaction occurred, regardless of when any related payments are made or received

accruals the adjustments made at the end of each accounting period to convert receipts into income and payments into expenditure

acid-test ratio an alternative to the liquidity ratio, calculated as: {current assets excluding stocks & prepayments} ÷ {current liabilities}

activities work undertaken to produce and deliver outputs

activity-based costing a method for allocating overheads to products/services by identifying the activities which cause the costs to be incurred

asset money, goods and property that an organization owns and can obtain benefit from

audit an independent process of checking the accuracy, completeness and integrity of financial records and the effectiveness of internal controls. See also internal audit and external audit

bad debt a debt which is unlikely to be paid by the debtor. Such debts have to be written off, effectively removing the income from the income and expenditure account in the current year

balance sheet a statement of the assets, liabilities and reserves of an organization at a particular point in time, usually prepared at the last day of the month or year

base rate the rate of interest at which the central bank of a jurisdiction will lend money to other banks

benchmarking a process of comparing an organization's processes and results with best practice within the same industry, or best practice in other industries

benefits in kind a payment received in something other than money, for the supply of goods or services

bond a form of savings account available to save in for a fixed period of time. They can be issued by banks, governments or companies.

budget the expression of an organization's plans in financial terms (i.e., the planned income and expenditure for a specific period of time)

budget approval the step in the public financial management cycle where the legislature/board/governors consider, amend and enact the budget

budget cycle the annual cycle of budget formulation, approval, execution and oversight

budget execution the step in the public financial management cycle where the executive collects the taxes and income and spends the money according to the allocations in the approved budget

budget formulation the step in the public financial management cycle where estimates of income and expenditure are prepared based on the organization's plans and policies

budget-holder a manager who is given responsibility for controlling the expenditure for one or more business units or projects

budget oversight the step in the public financial management cycle where accounts are audited and published, along with a report by the legislature/board/governors

budgetary control report a regular (typically monthly) report provided to a budget-holder showing the actual and budgeted income and expenditure for the latest period and, usually, the actual and budgeted income and expenditure for the financial year so far

capital expenditure or capex expenditure on substantial items (usually in the form of projects) which will have a benefit for the organization beyond the current year. Includes:

- purchase of land and buildings
- construction projects (including fees paid to architects, project managers, etc. and fitting out with fixtures and equipment)
- purchase and/or development of major computer systems and their implementation
- refurbishment of buildings where it extends the useful life of the building

capital programme the collection of all the capital expenditure projects which have been approved for implementation. Often expressed as a three- or five-year programme

cash-basis accounting the basis of accounting where transactions are recognized in the accounting period where the associated payment is made or received

cash flow the total amount of money paid out and received

CIPFA the Chartered Institute of Public Finance and Accountancy

commitment accounting where the financial information system recognizes transactions as soon as a purchase order (or similar) is issued. This allows a budget-holder to know how much budget is still available

concession the right to use an asset for a specific purpose granted by the owner (in return for a fee)

Consultative Committee of Accounting Bodies (CCAB) the group of six accounting bodies that represent the accounting profession in the United Kingdom

contingent liability a liability that is not included in the balance sheet because there is uncertainty about either its amount or its timing (often because the liability will crystallize as a result of external factors beyond the organization's control). Whilst not included in the balance sheet, an explanation of the contingent liability is included in the notes to the balance sheet

co-production a form of governance where users and providers of (public) services collaborate and cooperate in the delivery of the services

cost (*noun*) the amount spent to buy or produce a good or service

cost–benefit analysis or **CBA** an analysis of a project or service that takes into account, in monetary terms, the costs incurred and benefits received by the community as a whole, over the long term

cost-effectiveness analysis an analysis of a project or programme that takes into account the costs incurred in the achievement of a specified output (i.e., the effect that results from the expenditure)

cost-plus pricing a method of pricing where the sale price is the cost of buying/producing the goods/service plus a margin (either in absolute terms or as a percentage of the cost)

credit in double entry bookkeeping a credit is an item of income or an increase in a liability

creditor a person or organization to whom you owe money (because they have provided goods or service to you)

current asset cash, money in bank accounts and other assets that can be (or are expected to be) converted into cash within one year

current cost basis see historic cost basis

current liability creditors, loans and lease payments which are expected to be settled within one year

debit in double-entry bookkeeping a debit is an item of expenditure or an increase in an asset

debtor a person or organization who owes money to you

deficit where more resources have been used than received in a given period

defray (verb) to provide money to pay for a cost or expense

depreciation the charge made annually to the income and expenditure account to represent the use made of fixed assets. The value of the fixed asset in the balance sheet is reduced by an equal amount

direct costs costs that can be easily traced to a product or service. It includes cost of labour in producing the product/service and the components used

discount rate the rate used in the calculation of present value for a future cash inflow or outflow

discounted cash flow a model where the expected cash flow for a project over a period of time is converted to present value using a discount rate. See net present value

double-entry bookkeeping a system where each transaction is entered as a debit and a credit thus keeping the total system balanced to zero. For example, when a grant is received it is entered as an item of income and also as an increase in an asset (the bank balance)

due diligence a process of investigating and checking facts prior to the signing of a legal agreement

economic taxpayer the person who bears the cost of a tax

effectiveness achieving the intended results of a service or project

efficiency the ratio of outputs to inputs. Efficiency is improved when the same level of output is produced using fewer inputs

estimate (*noun*) the value of an item of income or expenditure included in a budget

exchange transaction a transaction where the two parties exchange things (such as goods and money) that are equal or approximately equal in value

expenditure the use of financial resources to acquire or produce goods and services

external audit the process of review of an organization's financial statements and, possibly its management arrangements, by an independent person with a view of providing assurance to the organization's stakeholders

externality a concept from economics meaning a cost or benefit incurred by a party that did not agree to the action causing the cost or benefit

fiat currency a currency declared by a government to be legal tender for use in its jurisdiction even though it has no asset backing

financial accounting the aspects of accounting that focus on bookkeeping, control of systems and producing statements of accounts for external users. Often carried out by a central team on behalf of the whole organization. Contrast this with management accounting

financial procedure rules or financial regulations the internal document that sets out the approved procedures for controlling financial transactions. It includes, for example, authorization limits for placing of orders

financial year the period that is covered by financial statements. In the public sector it will generally match the year used by the government for its budgeting and accounts. In the private sector, companies may choose any period to be their financial year, although they often choose January to December for convenience

fisc an old word for treasury, derived from the word for the public treasury of Rome

fiscal of or related to government income, especially taxes

fiscal policy the process by which a government determines its spending and income (from taxation and other sources) with the intention of delivering a surplus or deficit

fiscal rule a constraint on a government's fiscal policy set as a numerical target (for example, a limit on the ratio of net debt to GDP)

fiscal year the tax year which, for example, runs from 6 April to 5 April in the United Kingdom and from 1 October to 30 September in the United States. Sometimes the term is used interchangeably with financial year

fixed asset an asset that is bought/constructed for long term use (i.e., for more than a year). See capital expenditure

fixed cost costs that remain constant in the short term regardless of the volume of production, such as the rent of premises and the salaries of head office staff

force majeure a legal term for circumstances (such as floods) that prevent someone from fulfilling their contractual obligations (the literal translation from French is 'superior strength')

GAAP generally accepted accounting principles

general grant a grant received by an organization that can be applied to any of its activities or functions

general purpose financial report (GPFR) financial reports which are published to meet the needs of all users. They include the general purpose financial statements plus additional financial information about prospective events and non-financial information about the meeting of the organization's objectives. See also special purpose financial reports

general-purpose financial statements (GPFS) for a public sector entity a complete set of financial statements comprises:

- a statement of financial position (i.e., a balance sheet)
- a statement of financial performance (i.e., an income and expenditure account)
- a statement of changes in net assets/equity
- a statement of cash flows
- when the entity makes publicly available its approved budget, a comparison of budget and actual amounts either as a separate additional financial statement or as a budget column in the financial statements

- notes, comprising a summary of significant accounting policies and other explanatory notes

grant (*noun*) sum of money given to an organization for a purpose

historic cost basis a system of accounting where the actual prices paid and income received are used in the financial statements. In times of very high inflation current cost accounting may be implemented. In such a system the prices that were actually paid earlier in the year are inflated to current prices, which is very complicated

hypothecate (*verb*) to pledge money for a specific purpose

hypothecated tax a tax which is dedicated for a specified purpose, such as the television licence in the United Kingdom where the proceeds fund public broadcasting, or the gasoline tax in the United States, which is used to fund transport infrastructure

income the resources receivable by an organization from sales, grants, gifts and investments

income and expenditure statement comprehensive statement of income and expenditure, a summary of the financial transactions in a given period

incremental budgeting an approach to budgeting where next year's budget is based on this year's budget adjusted for pay and price inflation and changes in policies

indexation automatically linking the value of something to changes in an index

indirect costs costs that cannot be easily traced to a product or service. Often referred to as overheads

inflation the increase in prices paid by consumers (and consequently a fall in the purchasing power of money)

inputs resources (such as labour, equipment, raw materials, premises) used to carry out activities to produce outputs

internal audit an audit function set up within an organization to provide an independent, objective assurance and consulting activity designed to add value and improve an organization's operations

internal control system procedures, methods and measures designed to optimize the effectiveness of the organization, to ensure the reliability of the accounting system and financial information, to protect assets from loss or waste, and to ensure compliance with laws, directives and guidelines

International Accounting Standards Board (IASB) an independent standard-setting board which aims to 'provide the world's integrating capital markets with a common language for financial reporting by setting accounting and financial reporting standards.' It is responsible for issuing International Financial Reporting Standards (IFRS) and updating the International Accounting Standards (IAS), which preceded the IFRS

International Financial Reporting Standards (IFRS) a set of accounting standards that strive to harmonise accounting practices across the world.

International Public Sector Accounting Standards (IPSAS) accounting standards for use by PBEs. IPSASs are secondary standards for many jurisdictions where other accounting standards are mandated for use (for example, EU countries must use IFRS). This means that the IPSASs are turned to where they cover issues that are not covered by the primary accounting standards (such as tax collection) or where they provide extra guidance on adaption of the primary accounting standards to the public sector context

International Public Sector Accounting Standards Board (IPSASB) an independent standard-setting board within the International Federation of Accountants (IFAC) focusing on the accounting and financial reporting needs of national, regional and local governments and related governmental agencies. It issues International Public Sector Accounting Standards (IPSASs)

invest to put money into something such as property, stocks, or a business in order to earn interest or make a profit

legal taxpayer the person who is liable to pay a tax

liability amount owed to others for purchases, loans, bank overdrafts

line item an entry that appears on a separate line within a ledger or budget document

liquidity the availability of liquid assets (namely cash and other assets that can be easily and quickly converted into cash)

liquidity ratio the ratio of current assets to current liabilities. See also working capital

loan (*noun*) a sum of money that is borrowed and is expected to be paid back (usually with interest)

long-term liability an amount owed to a third party that is not expected to be repaid within one year

management accounting the aspects of accounting that focus on supporting the organization's managers in their day-to-day decision making. In large organizations this work will tend to be done by teams who specialise in specific service areas, and often it will be decentralized. Contrast this with financial accounting

marginal cost the extra cost incurred when the volume of production is increased by one unit

market value the amount for which something may be sold in an open market

medium-term financial strategy an outline of the revenue and capital budgets for a three- to five-year period

merit goods commodities that are excludable but which for reasons of equity governments decide to provide to all citizens

monetary policy managing the base rate as a way of influencing the behaviour of the economy

monetize express in the form of money

money a promise to pay denominated in the fiat currency of the country issuing it

net present value the excess of the present value of future cash inflows over the present value of cash outflows

nickel-and-diming charging a client for many small, low-value changes to a contract

nominal discount rate a discount rate that includes the effect of inflation

nominal interest rate an interest rate that includes the effect of inflation

non-exchange transaction a transaction (such as payment of taxes) where the two parties do not exchange things that are equal or approximately equal in value

operating expenditure or **opex** the ongoing costs for running an organization. See also revenue expenditure

opportunity cost the potential benefits (i.e., gains or avoided costs) that have been foregone when one option is chosen from a range of alternatives

outcomes changes to individuals or society brought about by outputs. For example, a hospital's output is a completed surgical procedure, its outcome is the improvement in the patient's health

output budgeting see performance budgeting

outputs goods or services provided by an organization or person to or for a third party

outturn the actual amount of an item of income or expenditure as opposed to the budgeted amount

overhead allocation the method used to allocate overheads (indirect costs) to products or services

overheads another term for indirect costs

Pareto principle the principle that roughly 80 per cent of the effects of something come from 20 per cent of the causes. It is also known as the '80: 20 rule' and 'the law of the vital few'

participatory budgeting a democratic process allowing citizens to take part in the allocation of a public budget, usually involving extensive consultation with citizens to develop and agree on the spending proposals to be voted on

payments in kind payment for goods or services in something other than money

penetration pricing a pricing strategy where the initial price of a good or service is low and then later increased. Sometimes referred to as loss-leader pricing

performance budgeting a budgeting systems which uses performance information to link funding allocations to results (outputs and/or outcomes)

performance indicator an item of data that is collected by a performance management system for use by a manager

Pigouvian tax (or Pigovian tax) a tax which is levied on a market activity where there are negative externalities, thereby making the consumer take into account the cost of the externalities. Named for the British economist Arthur Pigou

planning, programming budgeting system (PPBS) a performance budgeting system based on multi-year rolling plans comprised of multiple programmes

poll tax a tax on a person

present value the value of a future cash flow expressed in today's money, based on a discount rate

price discrimination a pricing strategy where the vendor sets different prices for different classes or groups of customers

price-skimming a pricing strategy where the price of a good/service is initially high and over time is reduced. Often used for high-technology products because it allows the research and development costs to be recouped more quickly

profile (of expenditure) the spread of expenditure across the periods making up a financial year

profit the surplus of income over expenditure

programme budgeting an approach to budgeting where multi-year programmes of activities are developed for meeting the PBE's objectives and budgets are prepared for each activity

provision an amount set aside in the accounts of an organization for a known liability, such as a bad debt or the diminution in value of an asset

public goods commodities that are non-rivalrous and non-excludable

public–private partnership (PPP) a long-term arrangement where private sector organizations take on risk and responsibility for the delivery of a public project, usually involving the creation or enhancement of a fixed asset

public–public partnership two or more PBEs who collaborate to achieve a joint objective

QALY (quality-adjusted life year) a measure of the state of health of a person or group in which the benefits, in terms of length of life, are adjusted to reflect the quality of life. One QALY is equal to 1 year of life in perfect health

quantum meruit Latin phrase used in contract law which means 'as much as he deserved.' Basically, if a person has done some work for another they are entitled to be paid for the value of the work even if it is an implied contract

quick ratio an alternative name for the acid-test ratio

rate of return the ratio of the profit made from an investment and the total amount invested

real discount rate a discount rate that excludes the effect of inflation

real interest rate an interest rate that excludes the effect of inflation

receipts and payments accounting see cash-basis accounting

relevant cost in option appraisal, the future costs that have not yet been committed

reserves the surpluses made in previous financial years that have not been utilized (i.e., spent)

return on capital employed the ratio of the profit made in a financial year and the total amount of capital invested by the organization's owners

revenue expenditure the items of expenditure which are not capital expenditure. Includes salaries, wages, training, utilities, travel, fuel, rents, purchase of small items of equipment, repair and maintenance of premises and equipment, subsistence and hospitality, stationery, interest paid on loans

running costs another term for revenue expenditure or operating expenditure

salami slicing an approach to budget cutbacks where all business units' budgets are cut by the same proportion (as opposed to an approach where different levels of reduction are made reflecting relative priorities)

self-insurance an approach to mitigating the financial impact of specific perils by making annual contributions to a fund (the equivalent of insurance premiums) which can then be used in the event of fire, theft, flood, etc.

semi-fixed cost cost items that are fixed for a given volume of production but at some critical level they increase to a new level. For example, the number of teachers needed as pupil numbers increase. Sometimes called step costs. See also fixed cost

semi-variable cost cost items that include a fixed component and a component that varies with the volume of production. For example, photocopiers where there is a fixed rental and a usage charge. See also variable cost

sequestration withdrawal or withholding of budget appropriations by the Ministry of Finance (or central finance department)

special purpose financial reports financial reports produced by an organization which are intended to meet the needs of only a specific user or group of users. For example, a progress report commissioned from a PBE by a grantor or donor

specific grant a grant received by an organization that can be applied only for a specified service or project, in accordance with the grantor's conditions

spurious accuracy the claiming of a greater level of accuracy in calculations than is justified by the inputs to the calculations

standstill budget the estimated cost of doing next year exactly what is being done this year

statement of cash flows a statement analysing the changes in the level of the organization's cash and bank balances between two dates

statement of financial performance a statement of the operating income and expenditure for an organization for a specified period (usually a year)

statement of financial position a statement of what an organization owns and owes on a given date (sometimes referred to as the balance sheet)

Statement of Recommended Practice (SORP) guidance issued by government as a supplement to accounting standards

statement on internal control a published statement made by 'those charged with governance' of an organization which sets out their opinion about the effectiveness of the organization's system of internal control and details proposals for addressing any weaknesses

step cost see semi-fixed cost

sunk cost a cost that has already been incurred or committed. Sunk costs are not affected by any current or future decision and should therefore be ignored when making decisions on future investments

surplus excess of income over expenditure in a given period

tax base the value of assets, property or transactions that are subject to a particular tax

tax buoyancy a measure of how quickly the yield from a tax rises or falls as the tax base rises or falls

tax elasticity a measure of the change in total revenue from a tax as a proportion of the change in GDP. Governments like to have taxes with elasticity of more than one so that the income from the tax rises at least as fast as GDP does

tax farming a system of tax collection where the right of collection is transferred from the state to private individuals (tax farmers) in exchange for a fee

tax haven a jurisdiction that has arranged its tax policy to be attractive to individuals and organizations who are engaged in tax avoidance

tax rate the amount that is applied to the tax base to determine the amount of tax that is payable for a given period

treasury management the function of managing an organization's cash position by making short- and long-term loans and investments

treasury single account (TSA) a bank account or a set of linked bank accounts through which all government payments and receipts are made enabling the consolidation and optimum use of government cash

unit cost the cost of producing a single unit of a good or service. It is usually calculated as an average

value-added tax a tax which is levied on the value added at each stage of the manufacture and supply of goods and services

value for money (VFM) the optimum combination of benefits derived by the user of goods and services from the available level of resources

variable costs cost items that vary in proportion to the volume of production, such as the components used on a production line

variance the difference between the estimated and the actual amount for an item of income or expenditure

vire to transfer an amount from one budget line to another

virement the amount of money that is vired

zero-based budgeting an approach to budgeting where each item is estimated anew each year, rather than by reference to its value in the previous budget

Index

Taylor & Francis eBooks

www.taylorfrancis.com

A single destination for eBooks from Taylor & Francis with increased functionality and an improved user experience to meet the needs of our customers.

90,000+ eBooks of award-winning academic content in Humanities, Social Science, Science, Technology, Engineering, and Medical written by a global network of editors and authors.

TAYLOR & FRANCIS EBOOKS OFFERS:

A streamlined experience for our library customers

A single point of discovery for all of our eBook content

Improved search and discovery of content at both book and chapter level

REQUEST A FREE TRIAL

support@taylorfrancis.com